EXPLORING THE POLICE
A Book of Readings

John Hill

Second Edition

Custom Publishing

New York   Boston   San Francisco
London   Toronto   Sydney   Tokyo   Singapore   Madrid
Mexico City   Munich   Paris   Cape Town   Hong Kong   Montreal

Cover Art: Courtesy of Photodisc/Getty Images

Printed in the United States of America

10   9   8   7   6   5   4   3   2   1

2008340065

CM/LD

**Pearson
Custom Publishing**
is a division of

www.pearsonhighered.com

ISBN 10: 0-555-02953-0
ISBN 13: 978-0-555-02953-4

Contents

Part One: Who Are the Police?

Part Two: What Are the Police Doing?

Part Three: What Should the Police Be Doing?

Dedicated to my Father, Police Detective John T. Hill,
and to my Grandfather, Police Detective Francis A. Hill,
whom both served proudly with
the City of Newark, NJ, Police Department,
one of the finest police agencies in this nation.

————————

And, to Erin, Brianne, & John,
the next generation.

Foreword

by John Hill

"All we were doing was chasing 911 calls"

—William J. Bratton
Describing conditions at the
Boston Police, circa 1973.
(Bratton & Knobler, 1998, p. 110)

The purpose of presenting the ensuing twenty-four chapters that you are about to read is to gain an understanding of *who* are the police, what *have* they been doing, and what *should* they be doing? Hopefully, you will come away with a better understanding of the characteristics of American police officers and the intricacies of the job they are called upon to perform daily. Additionally, it is trusted that you will better comprehend the traditional duties, tactics, and services they have been called upon to perform and provide. Some of these have worked quite well, and others have not and yet are continually embraced because of tradition and an inherent resistance to change among police organizations.

Part One: Who Are the Police seeks to delineate just what type of person the police officers are, and how much of that is shaped by the stressful, demanding and thankless task that they perform every hour of every day. Professor George L. Kirkham, in *A Professor's Street Lessons*, left his college classroom and climbed into a patrol car. Policing in crime-infested South Florida neighborhoods, he vividly demonstrates to us that the changes in a person called upon to serve as a police officer—the metamorphosis—can and will happen to anyone.

Cherokee Paul McDonald, in *Blue Truth,* graphically and candidly details the emotional toll taken by the ups and downs of policing, from the mundane to the horrific. As a police officers career develops, this usually builds to a crescendo in which the police officer starts to make the distinction between *us* (the police) and *them* (everyone who is not the police), and ends up seeing the public as enemy. This is graphically illustrated in Chuck Milland's *Why Cops Hate You.*

The police are among the most *misunderstood* entities in the criminal justice system. Television and the movies are the two principal reasons why the police are so misunderstood. The exploits of Officer Norm Nelson, the LAPD's *Real-life Dirty Harry* show us that whatever policing is, it sure as hell *is not* like what is portrayed in the entertainment industry.

Scholars Lawrence Sherman in *Learning Police Ethics* and Jerome Skolnick in *The Police Officer's "Working Personality"* help us to understand the socialization and solidarity that is the foundation of "thin blue line" that is America's police force. Once inside this thin blue line, we go out on patrol with an evaluative academic perspective in Professor Albert J. Reiss' *The Police and the Public*, in order to begin to understand how the police operate in *Part Two: What Are the Police Doing?* Successive chapters on the *Kansas City Preventive Patrol Experiment and The LAPD is Treated to a Business Analysis and it Comes up Short* reveal what traditional police functions have not been conducive to effective police services. Appearing just as policing seems to bog down in operational despair, Jack Maple takes a hold of policing and, in *The Crimefighter,* provides much-needed direction toward a whole new era.

In *Part Three: What Should the Police be Doing?* James Q. Wilson and George L. Kelling's *Broken Windows* theory, although published in 1982, comes to realization in the 1990's as the New York City Police Department, and subsequently the Philadelphia Police Department, change the very 180-year-old face of police work with service-driven proactive policing and Compstat. Any police agency that has not taken notice of the lessons learned in New York City and Philadelphia will be operating blindfolded in this especially challenging era of policing in America. Any police officer who does not take notice of what his or her predecessors have done is, as history states, bound to repeat it, and there are too many factors working against these officers already.

For this revised edition of *Exploring the Police: A Book of Readings,* the author sought to respond directly to students and law enforcement colleagues who strenuously requested expanded subject matter on the intricacies of police work. This resulted in a significantly-expanded *Part One: Who Are the Police.* In many ways, the six newly-added chapters therein also present such positive policing examples, that they wonderfully augment *Part Three: What Should the Police be Doing?* Similarly, the six newly-added chapters should also considerably enhance the reader's comprehension of *Part Two: What Are the Police Doing?*

Preface

In 1829, Sir Robert Peel, who later became prime minister of England, formed what many have hailed as the world's first modern police force. Passage of the Metropolitan Police Act that same year allocated the resources for Peel's force of 1,000 uniformed, handpicked men. The London Metropolitan Police Force was instituted as an efficient police system that would be free of the taint of repressive political behavior, but at the same time an effective force to prevent and prosecute crime (Johnson & Wolfe, 2003, p. 215). The police force soon became a model for police forces around the world (Schmalleger, 2003, p. 186). Fifteen years later in America, New York's separate day and night police forces were combined into the New York City Police Department (p. 187), considered to be the first professional police department in the nation.

In 180 years since the establishment of policing as we know it, the entity has evolved considerably into a professional public safety organization. Still, as a group, they're among the most *reluctant to change* (Bailey, 1996). Moreover, they are among the most *misunderstood* institutions in contemporary times.

The author here in *Exploring the Police: A Book of Readings,* draws upon his career as a street cop, and then as an academician, to help readers fully understand and comprehend this new phenomenon (after all, mankind is a million years old, so 180 years of policing is but the blink of any eye in history) known as the *police.*

This is accomplished by asking just three questions:

1. Who are the police?
2. What are the police doing?
   and,
3. What should the police be doing?

Let's start turning pages and find out . . .

Acknowledgements

The author would like to profusely thank my Editors, Carie M. Jones, and Courtney Mullen of Pearson Publishing, for all their assistance in helping me in getting this revised edition to come to fruition. Additionally, for their efforts in the previous edition, Katherine Ashley Bell and Danielle L. Meier of Allyn Bacon Longman/Pearson Publishing for their advocacy and professionalism. Also, Supporting police, primarily by order of highest agency rank first; Miami Police Chief John F. Timoney (a Retired New York City Police Deputy Commissioner, and Philadelphia Police Commissioner), Lieutenant Susan Slawson and Corporal Jim Pauley of the Publics Affairs Office of the Philadelphia Police Department.

From the Middletown Township (NJ) Police Department; Retired Police Chief Joseph M. McCarthy, Deputy Chief Fred Henry, Deputy Chief Gene Hannafey, Deputy Chief Joseph Braun, Captain Joseph Shaffery, the late Captain James Kerrigan, Lieutenant William F. Brunt, Sr., Lieutenant William F. Brunt, Jr., Lieutenant Neal Hansen, Lieutenant George Freibott, Sr., Lieutenant Edward A. Kryscnski, the late Lieutenant Timothy H. Lake, Lieutenant William Best, Lieutenant John Lenge, Sergeant Dennis J. Vaspory, the late Sergeant James Keogh, the late Sergeant Mike Pinto, Sergeant John E. Kaiser, Jr., Sergeant Michael Shaffery, Sergeant Ernie Volkland, Sergeant Stephen Dollinger, Sergeant Charles Terefenko, Sergeant Richard Deickmann, Sr., Sergeant Richard Deickmann, Jr., Sergeant Fred Deickmann, Sergeant William Straniero, Detective Adam Finck, Detective Barry Grimm, Detective Arthur Schreppel (my former street patrol partner), Detective Wayne "Chuck" Bradshaw, Detective Kimberly Best, Detective Peter White, Detective Jeffrey Barner, Detective Richard W. Heidel, Detective John Urbine, Detective Irvin B. Beaver, Detective John E. Kaiser Sr., the late Detective John T. Estock, the late Corporal Herman A. Grillon, Corporal Patrick McConnell, Corporal Robert W. Johnston, Corporal James J. Rooney, Corporal James J. Murphy, Corporal Jack Bauers, Corporal Anthony Gonzalez, Corporal James J. Griffin, Corporal Ronald Chesek, Corporal Daniel Murdoch, Corporal Keith McDonald, Officer James Prosinski, Officer Joseph Glynn, Officer John J. Marinan, Officer William D. Kennelly, Officer Thomas Meckier, Officer Darrin Simon, Officer James Roese, Officer Joseph Ahlemeyer, Officer Lisa Ahlemeyer, Officer Bernard Chenoweth, Jr., Special Officer Bernard Chenoweth, Sr., Officer Frank Holden, Officer Jamie McCarron, Officer Adam Heck, Officer George Freibott, Jr., Officer Steve Keller, Officer Michael Nolan, Officer Richard Raike, Officer Lawrence Seymour, Officer William Strohkirch, Officer Felipe Bennedit, Officer Robert Shannon, and Computer Specialist John Gilligan.

From the Monmouth County Sheriff's Office; Officer Joseph Tuohy, Officer Edward P. Kelly, Sergeant Mark Brawley, and Lieutenant John Kolodziej.

From the New Jersey State Police; Sergeant Patrick O'Dwyer, Sergeant John Mulvey, Trooper Daniel Murphy, and Trooper Thomas Chambers.

From the Newark (NJ) Police; Deputy Chief Kevin Snyder, Officer Glenn O'Neill, Officer Edward "Doc" Frable, and Retired Police Chief Thomas C. O'Reilly.

From the Red Bank (NJ) Police; Officer Kenneth Smith, Officer James D. Erving, Officer Dave Hicks, Officer Dennis Kerr, Officer William Anderson, and Sergeant Daniel Bannon.

From my Metro New Jersey-New York "support unit"; Special Agent William R. Snow, DHS, Bloomfield Police Sergeant Dave Reilly, Steven J. Kossup, Esq., Larry S. Loigman, Esq., Arthur S. Wiener PhD, John A. Young, Esq., Robert G. Jarmon, MD, Steven Field, MD, Hal Mitnick, MD, Kenneth Eng, MD, William Orsini, MD, David J. Foley, Esq., Investigator Bill Nicholl, Ret. DEA Special Agent Dennis McCarthy, Deputy U.S. Marshal John Cuff, Union City (NJ) Police Lieutenant Leonel Ortega, FBI Special Agent Kevin C. Donovan, Jersey City Police Officer Leon Tucker, Greenburgh (NY) Police Sergeant Frank Farina, South Kingston (RI) Police Sergeant James Tierney, Laurence Reilly, PhD, Colts Neck Police Officer Kevin Walsh, Manasquan Police Detective Brian Gillespie, Thomas J. Smith III, Esq., the late Thomas Smith Jr., Esq., Mr. Ed Donley, Mr. James P. Erving, Miss Gina Sidney, the Men and Women of the N.J. Police Honor Legion, and the Men and Women of the Police Emerald Societies of Essex County, NJ and the NYPD.

From the New York City Police (NYPD); Captain "Jack" Donohue, Retired Sergeant Steve Adams, Retired Detective John R. Wales, Retired Detective Al Sheppard, Retired Officer Gary Gorman, Sea Gate Police Deputy Chief Dave Gold, Esq./Police Counsel, and "Joey" Fugel.

From the Utah law enforcement community; Officer Eric Jensen of the South Salt Lake Police Department, Officer Steve Jensen of the West Valley City Police, Detective Jason Hauer of the West Valley City Police, Sergeant Chad Evans of the West Valley City Police, Sergeant Mike Cupello of the Salt Lake Sheriff's Office, Detective Lex Bell of the Salt Lake Sheriff's Office, Special Agent Keith Jensen, Officer Joseph Selph of the Draper City Police, Judge Frederic Oddone of the Utah State Superior Court, Judge Michael Kwan of the Taylorsville City Utah Court, Officer Bart Woolley of the Utah Courts, Sergeant Greg Butler of the West Jordan Police Department, Deputy Chief Gary Jeffs of the West Jordan Police Department, James Hoffman of the SLCC Institute of Public Safety, Larry Barlage of the SLCC Institute of Public Safety, Director Pete Nelson of the Utah Department of Corrections, SLCC Adjunct Professor Bonnie Sims, Investigator Kelly Madsen, Mrs. Colleen Thistle, and Sarah M. Muir-Dehaan, MS, of the University of Phoenix, Utah Campus.

From the Port Authority Police of NY-NJ; Officer Thomas Johnson, Officer Paul Hadinger, Officer George Santiago, and Police Bagpiper John E. Ward. And, among those tragically killed-on-duty, on September 11, 2001, at the World Trade Center; Officer Richard Rodriguez, and Officer Kenneth F. Tietjen—two of the most courageous street cops that I've known.

From the Pennsylvania law enforcement community; Sergeant Vince Pacifico, and Officer Michael Barrett of the Phoenixville Police, Retired Muhlenberg (PA) Detective Dean Patton, now serving as a Pennsylvania District Justice, Lieutenant Douglas J. Burig of the Pennsylvania State Police, Detective Lieutenant Ron Camacho, Jr., and Captain David Arnold of the York City Police.

From my Utah "support unit"; The Republican crew consisting of Jason, David, Damien, Kory, Tay and Becca. The Puck crew consisting of Anne, James, Star, Andy, John, Brian, Rachael, Monica, Lisa, Jason, Stew, and Gordon.

From Jim Thorpe Borough (PA); Darren Behan, Mark Behan, Paul Behan, and Noel & Bernadette Behan.

From Nova Southeastern University (FLA.); Dr. Jerry Ryan, Dr. Gail Johnson, Dr. Richard Conrath, and Dr. Stan Hanna.

From Salt Lake Community College (UT); Sociology Professor Spencer Blake, Psychology Professor Katerina Calderone, and Sergeant Phil Leiker, College Police (Retired LAPD).

A hearty thanks to my trusty Proofreader, Journalism/Communications graduate from Westminster College (Utah), Joshua Stasinos, BA.

And, a very special thanks to—and heartfelt appreciation of—my peaceful and prosperous *Amish* neighbors, especially those who suffered so terribly on October 2, 2006.

1

A Professor's Street Lessons

by George L. Kirkham

"I cannot help but wonder how many times they (the police) have clenched their teeth and wished they could expose their critics to only a few of the harsh realities which their job involves."

—George L. Kirkham,
A Professor's Street Lessons
(1974)

As policemen have come under increasing criticism by various individuals and groups in our society in recent years, I cannot help but wonder how many times they have clenched their teeth and wished they could expose their critics to only a few of the harsh realities which their job involves.

Persons such as myself, members of the academic community, have traditionally been quick to find fault with the police. From isolated incidents reported in the various news media, we have fashioned for ourselves a stereotyped image of the police officer which conveniently conforms to our notions of what he is. We see the brutal cop, the racist cop, the grafting cop, the discourteous cop. What we do not see, however, is the image of thousands of dedicated men and women struggling against almost impossible odds to preserve our society and everything in it which we cherish.

For some years, first as a student and later as a professor of criminology, I found myself troubled by the fact that most of us who write books and articles on the police have never been policemen ourselves. I began to be bothered increasingly by many of my students who were former policemen. Time and again, they would respond to my frequently critical lectures on the police with the argument that I could not possibly understand what a police officer has to endure in modern society until I had been one myself. Under the weight of this frustration, and

From "A Professor's 'Street Lessons'" *FBI Law Enforcement Bulletin*, March (1974): pp. 14–22.

my personal conviction that knowledge has an applied as well as a theoretical dimension, I decided to take up this challenge: I would become a policeman myself as a means of establishing once and for all the accuracy of what I and other criminologists had been saying about the police for so long.

FROM PROFESSOR TO COP

Suffice it to say that my announced intention to become a uniformed patrolman was at first met with fairly widespread disbelief on the part of family, friends, and colleagues alike. At 31, with a family and an established career as a criminologist, I was surely an unlikely candidate for the position of police recruit. The very idea, it was suggested to me, was outrageous and absurd. I was told that no police administrator in his right mind would allow a representative of the academic world to enter his organization. It had never been done and could not be done.

Fortunately, many of my students, who either had been policemen or were at the time, sounded a far more optimistic and enthusiastic note. Police administrators and officers alike, they said, would welcome the opportunity to expose members of the academic community to the problems of their occupation. If one of us were really willing to see and feel the policeman's world from behind a badge and blue uniform, instead of from the safe and comfortable vantage point of a classroom or university office, police officers themselves would do everything in their power to make the opportunity available. Despite these assurances from my policemen-students, I remained skeptical over my chances of being allowed to do such an unorthodox thing.

This skepticism was, however, soon to be overcome. One of my better criminology students at the time was a young police officer on educational leave from the Jacksonville, Fla., Sheriff's Office. Upon learning of my desire to become a police officer in order to better understand the problems of policemen, he urged me to contact Sheriff Dale Carson and Undersheriff D.K. Brown of his department with my proposal. I had earlier heard other police officers describe the consolidated 800-man force of Jacksonville Duval County as one of the most progressive departments in the country. I learned that Sheriff Carson and Undersheriff Brown, two former FBI Agents, had won considerable respect in the law enforcement profession as enlightened and innovative administrators.

The size and composition of Jacksonville, as well as its nearness to my university and home, made it appear to be an ideal location for what I wished to do. Numbering just over one-half million residents, Jacksonville impressed me as being the kind of large and rapidly growing American city which inevitably experiences the major social problems of our time: crime and delinquency, racial unrest, poverty, and mental illness. A seaport and industrial center, Jacksonville offered a diversity of urban, suburban, and even rural populations in its vast land area. I took particular note of the fact that it contained a fairly typical inner-city slum section and black ghetto, both of which were in the process of being transformed through a massive program of urban redevelopment. This latter feature was especially important to me insofar as I wanted to personally experience the stresses and strains of today's city policeman. It was, after all, he who had traditionally been the subject of such intense interest and criticism on the part of social scientists such as myself.

Much to my surprise, both Sheriff Carson and Undersheriff Brown were not only supportive but enthusiastic as well over my proposal to become a city patrolman. I made it clear to them at the outset that I did not wish to function as an observer or reserve officer, but rather wanted to become a fully sworn and full-time member of their department for a period of between 4 and 6 months. I further stated that I hoped to spend most of this period working as a uniformed patrolman in those inner city beats most characterized by violence, poverty, social unrest, and high crime rates. They agreed to this, with the understanding that I would first have to meet the same requirements as any other police candidate. I would, for example, have to submit to a thorough character investigation, a physical examination, and would have to meet the same training standards applied to all other Florida police officers. Since I was to be unpaid, I would be exempted from departmental civil service requirements.

RESTYLING AN IMAGE

Both Carson and Brown set about overcoming various administrative and insurance problems which had to be dealt with in advance of my becoming a police officer. Suppose, for example, I should be injured or killed in the line of duty, or should injure or kill someone else. What of the department and city's liability? These and other issues were gradually resolved with considerable effort on their part. The only stipulation set forth by both administrators was one with which I strongly agreed: for the sake of morale and confidence in the department, every officer must know in advance exactly who I was and what I was doing. Other than being in the unusual position of a "patrolman-professor," I would be indistinguishable from other officers in every respect, from the standard issue .38 Smith and Wesson revolver I would carry to the badge and uniform I would wear.

The biggest and final obstacle which I faced was the necessity that I comply fully with a 1967 Florida Police Standards law, which requires that every police officer and deputy sheriff in the state complete a minimum of 280 hours of law enforcement training prior to being sworn in and assigned to regular duty. Since I had a full-time university job nearly 200 miles from Jacksonville, this meant that I would be unable to attend the regular sheriff's academy. I would have to attend a certified academy in my own area, something which I arranged to do with Sheriff Carson's sponsorship.

For 4 months, 4 hours each evening and 5 nights a week, I attended the Tallahassee area police academy, along with 35 younger classmates. As a balding intellectual, I at first stood out as an oddity in the class of young men destined to become local law enforcement officers. With the passage of time, however, they came to accept me and I them. We joked, drank coffee, and struggled through various examinations and lessons together. At first known only as "the professor," the men later nicknamed me "Doc" over my good-natured protests.

As the days stretched into weeks and the weeks into months, I took lengthy notes on the interviewing of witnesses at crime scenes, investigated imaginary traffic accidents, and lifted fingerprints. Some nights I went home after hours of physical defense training with my uniformly younger and stronger peers with tired muscles, bruises, and the feeling that I should have my head examined for undertaking such a rugged project.

As someone who had never fired a handgun, I quickly grew accustomed to the noise of 35 revolvers firing at the cardboard silhouettes which our minds transformed into real assailants at the sound of the range whistle. I learned how to properly make car stops, approach a front door or darkened building, question suspects, and a thousand other things that every modern police officer must know. After what seemed an eternity, graduation from the academy finally came, and with it what was to become the most difficult but rewarding educational experience of my life: I became a policeman.

THE SCHOOL OF HARD KNOCKS

I will never forget standing in front of the Jacksonville police station on that first day. I felt incredibly awkward and conspicuous in the new blue uniform and creaking leather. Whatever confidence in my ability to "do the job" I had gained during the academy seemed to evaporate as I stood there watching other blue figures hurrying in the evening rain toward assembly. After some minutes, I summoned the courage to walk into the station and into my new career as a core city patrolman.

That first day seems long ago now. As I write this, I have completed over 100 tours of duty as a patrolman. Although still a rookie officer, so much has happened in the short space of 6 months that I will never again be either the same man or the same scientist who stood in front of the station on that first day. While it is hard to even begin to describe within a brief article the many changes which have occurred within me during this time, I would like to share with fellow policemen and colleagues in the academic community a few of what I regard as the more important of what I will call my "street lessons."

I had always personally been of the opinion that police officers greatly exaggerate the amount of verbal disrespect and physical abuse to which they are subjected in the line of duty. During my first few hours as a street officer, I lived blissfully in a magic bubble which was soon to burst. As a college professor, I had grown accustomed to being treated with uniform respect and deference by those I encountered. I somehow naively assumed that this same quality of respect would carry over into my new role as a policeman. I was, after all, a representative of the law, identifiable to all by the badge and uniform I wore as someone dedicated to the protection of society. Surely that fact would entitle me to a measure of respect and cooperation— or so I thought. I quickly found that my badge and uniform, rather than serving to shield me from such things as disrespect and violence, only acted as a magnet which drew me toward many individuals who hated what I represented.

I had discounted on my first evening the warning of a veteran sergeant who, after hearing that I was about to begin work as a patrolman, shook his head and cautioned, "You'd better watch yourself out there, Professor! It gets pretty rough sometimes!" I was soon to find out what he meant.

Several hours into my first evening on the streets, my partner and I were dispatched to a bar in the downtown area to handle a disturbance complaint. Inside, we encountered a large and boisterous drunk who was arguing with the bartender and loudly refusing to leave. As someone with considerable experience as a correctional counselor and mental health worker, I hastened to take charge of the situation. "Excuse me, Sir," I smiled pleasantly at the drunk, "but I wonder if I could ask you to step outside and talk with me for just a minute?" The man stared at me through bloodshot eyes in disbelief for a second, raising one hand to scratch the stubble of several days' growth of beard. Then suddenly, without warning, it happened. He swung at me, luckily missing my face and striking me on the right shoulder. I couldn't believe it. What on earth had I done to provoke such a reaction? Before I could recover from my startled condition, he swung again—this time tearing my whistle chain from a shoulder epaulet. After a brief struggle, we had the still shouting, cursing man locked in the back of our cruiser. I stood there, breathing heavily with my hair in my eyes as I surveyed the damage to my new uniform and looked in bewilderment at my partner, who only smiled and clapped me affectionately on the back.

THEORY vs. PRACTICE

"Something is very wrong," I remember thinking to myself in the front seat as we headed for the jail. I had used the same kind of gentle, rapport-building approach with countless offenders in prison and probation settings. It had always worked so well there. What was so different about being a policeman? In the days and weeks which followed, I was to learn the answer to this question the hard way. As a university professor, I had always sought to convey to students the idea that it is a mistake to exercise authority, to make decisions for other people, or rely upon orders and commands to accomplish something. As a police officer myself, I was forced time and again to do just that. For the first time in my life, I encountered individuals who interpreted kindness as weakness, as an invitation to disrespect or violence. I encountered men, women, and children who, in fear, desperation, or excitement, looked to the person behind my blue uniform and shield for guidance, control, and direction. As someone who had always condemned the exercise of authority, the acceptance of myself as an unavoidable symbol of authority came as a bitter lesson.

I found that there was a world of difference between encountering individuals, as I had, in mental health or correctional settings and facing them as the patrolman must: when they are violent, hysterical, desperate. When I put the uniform of a police officer on, I lost the luxury of sitting in an air-conditioned office with my pipe and books, calmly discussing with a rapist or armed robber the past problems which had led him into trouble with the law. Such offenders had seemed so innocent, so harmless in the sterile setting of prison. The often terrible crimes which they had committed were long since past, reduced like their victims to so many printed words on a page.

Now, as a police officer, I began to encounter the offender for the first time as a very real menace to my personal safety and the security of our society. The felon was no longer a harmless figure sitting in blue denims across my prison desk, a "victim" of society to be treated with compassion and leniency. He became an armed robber fleeing from the scene of a crime, a crazed maniac threatening his family with a gun, someone who might become my killer crouched behind the wheel of a car on a dark street.

LESSON IN FEAR

Like crime itself, fear quickly ceased to be an impersonal and abstract thing. It became something which I regularly experienced. It was a tightness in my stomach as I approached a warehouse where something had tripped a silent alarm. I could taste it as a dryness in my mouth as we raced with blue lights and siren toward the site of a "Signal Zero" (armed and dangerous) call. For the first time in my life, I came to know—as every policeman knows—the true meaning of fear. Through shift after shift it stalked me, making my palms cold and sweaty, and pushing the adrenaline through my veins.

I recall particularly a dramatic lesson in the meaning of fear which took place shortly after I joined the force. My partner and I were on routine patrol one Saturday evening in a deteriorated area of cheap bars and pool halls when we observed a young male double-parked in the middle of the street. I pulled alongside and asked him in a civil manner to either park or drive on, whereupon he began loudly cursing us and shouting that we couldn't make him go anywhere. An angry crowd began to gather as we got out of our patrol car and approached the man, who by this time was shouting that we were harassing him and calling to bystanders for assistance. As a criminology professor, some months earlier I would have urged that the police officer who was now myself simply leave the car double-parked and move on rather than risk an incident. As a policeman, however, I had come to realize that an officer can never back down from his responsibility to enforce the law. Whatever the risk to himself, every police officer understands that his ability to back up the lawful authority which he represents is the only thing which stands between civilization and the jungle of lawlessness.

The man continued to curse us and adamantly refused to move his car. As we placed him under arrest and attempted to move him to our cruiser, an unidentified male and female rushed from the crowd which was steadily enlarging and sought to free him. In the ensuing struggle, a hysterical female unsnapped and tried to grab my service revolver, and the now angry mob began to converge on us. Suddenly, I was no longer an "ivory-tower" scholar watching typical police "overreaction" to a street incident—but I was part of it and fighting to remain alive and uninjured. I remember the sickening sensation of cold terror which filled my insides as I struggled to reach our car radio. I simultaneously put out a distress call and pressed the hidden electric release button on our shotgun rack as my partner sought to maintain his grip on the prisoner and hold the crowd at bay with his revolver.

How harshly I would have judged the officer who now grabbed the shotgun only a few months before. I rounded the rear of our cruiser with the weapon and shouted at the mob to move back. The memory flashed through my mind that I had always argued that policemen should not be allowed to carry shotguns because of the "offensive" character and the potential damage to community relations as a result of their display. How readily as a criminology professor I would have condemned the officer who was now myself, trembling with fear and anxiety and menacing an "unarmed" assembly with an "offensive" weapon. But if circumstances had dramatically changed my perspective, for now it was my life and safety that were in danger, *my* wife and child who might be mourning. Not "a policeman" or Patrolman Smith—but *me*, George Kirkham! I felt accordingly bitter when I saw the individual who had provoked this near riot back on the streets the next night, laughing as though our charge of "resisting arrest with violence" was a big joke. Like my partner, I found myself feeling angry and frustrated shortly afterward when this same individual was allowed to plead guilty to a reduced charge of "breach of peace."

LOUD DEFENDANTS AND SILENT VICTIMS

As someone who had always been greatly concerned about the rights of offenders, I now began to consider for the first time the rights of police officers. As a police officer, I felt that my efforts to protect society and maintain my personal safety were menaced by many of the very court decisions and lenient parole board actions I had always been eager to defend. An educated man, I could not answer the questions of my fellow officers as to why those who kill and maim policemen, men who are involved in no less honorable an activity than holding our society together, should so often be subjected to minor penalties. I grew weary of carefully following difficult legal restrictions, while thugs and hoodlums consistently twisted the law to their own advantage. I remember standing in the street one evening and reading a heroin "pusher" his rights, only to have him convulse with laughter halfway through and finish reciting them, word for word, from memory. He had been given his "rights" under the law, but what about the rights of those who were the victims of people like himself? For the first time, questions such as these began to bother me.

As a corrections worker and someone raised in a comfortable middle class home, I had always been insulated from the kind of human misery and tragedy which became part of the policeman's everyday life. Now, the often terrible sights, sounds, and smells of my job began to haunt me hours after I had taken the blue uniform and badge off. Some nights I would lie in bed unable to sleep, trying desperately to forget the things I had seen during a particular tour of duty: the rat-infested shacks that served as homes to those far less fortunate than I, a teenage boy dying in my arms after being struck by a car, small children clad in rags with stomachs bloated from hunger playing in a urine-spattered hall, the victim of a robbery senselessly beaten and murdered.

In my new role as a police officer, I found that the victims of crime ceased to be impersonal statistics. As a corrections worker and criminology professor, I had never given much thought to those who are victimized by criminals in our society. Now the sight of so many lives ruthlessly damaged and destroyed by the perpetrators of crime left me preoccupied with the question of society's responsibility to protect the men, women, and children who are victimized daily.

For all the tragic victims of crime I have seen during the past 6 months, one case stands out above all. There was an elderly man who lived with his dog in my apartment building downtown. He was a retired bus driver and his wife was long deceased. As time went by, I became friends with the old man and his dog. I could usually count on finding both of them standing at the corner on my way to work. I would engage in casual conversation with the old man, and sometimes he and his dog would walk several blocks toward the station with me. They were both as predictable as a clock: each evening around 7, the old man would walk to the same small restaurant several blocks away, where he would eat his evening meal while the dog waited dutifully outside.

One evening my partner and I received a call to a street shooting near my apartment building. My heart sank as we pulled up and I saw the old man's mutt in a crowd of people gathered on the sidewalk. The old man was lying on his back, in a large pool of blood, half trying to brace himself on an elbow. He clutched a bullet wound in his chest and gasped to me that three young men had stopped him and demanded his money. After taking his wallet and seeing how little he had, they shot him and left him on the street. As a police officer, I was enraged time and again at the cruelty and senselessness of acts such as this, at the arrogance of brazen thugs who prey with impunity on innocent citizens.

A DIFFERENT PERSPECTIVE

The same kinds of daily stresses which affected my fellow officers soon began to take their toll on me. I became sick and tired of being reviled and attacked by criminals who could usually find a most sympathetic audience in judges and jurors eager to understand their side of things and provide them with "another chance." I grew tired of living under the ax of news media and community pressure groups, eager to seize upon the slightest mistake made by myself or a fellow police officer.

As a criminology professor, I had always enjoyed the luxury of having great amounts of time in which to make difficult decisions. As a police officer, however, I found myself forced to make the most critical choices in a time frame of seconds, rather than days: to shoot or not to shoot, to arrest or not to arrest, to give chase or let go—always with the nagging certainty that others, those with great amounts of time in which to analyze and think, stood ready to judge and condemn me for whatever action I might take or fail to take. I found myself not only forced to live a life consisting of seconds and adrenaline, but also forced to deal with human problems which were infinitely more difficult than anything I had ever confronted in a correctional or mental health setting. Family fights, mental illness, potentially explosive crowd situations, dangerous individuals—I found myself progressively awed by the complexity of tasks faced by men whose work I once thought was fairly simple and straightforward.

Indeed, I would like to take the average clinical psychologist or psychiatrist and invite him to function for just a day in the world of the policeman, to confront people whose problems are both serious and in need of immediate solution. I would invite him to walk, as I have, into a smoke-filled pool room where five or six angry men are swinging cues at one another. I would like the prison counselor and parole officer to see their client Jones—not calm and composed in an office setting, but as the street cop sees him—beating his small child with a heavy belt buckle, or kicking his pregnant wife. I wish that they, and every judge and juror in our country, could see the ravages of crime as the cop on the beat must: innocent people cut, shot, beaten, raped, robbed, and murdered. It would, I feel certain, give them a different perspective on crime and criminals, just as it has me.

HUMANENESS IN UNIFORM

For all the human misery and suffering which police officers must witness in their work, I found myself amazed at the incredible humanity and compassion which seems to characterize most of them. My own stereotypes of the brutal, sadistic cop were time and again shattered by the sight of humanitarian kindness on the part of the thin blue line: a young patrolman giving mouth to mouth resuscitation to a filthy derelict; a grizzled old veteran embarrassed when I discovered the bags of jelly beans which he carried in the trunk of his car for impoverished ghetto kids—to whom he was the closest thing to an Easter Bunny they would ever know; an officer giving money out of his own pocket to a hungry and stranded family he would probably never see again; and another patrolman taking the trouble to drop by on his own time in order to give worried parents information about their problem son or daughter.

As a police officer, I found myself repeatedly surprised at the ability of my fellow patrolmen to withstand the often enormous daily pressures of their work. Long hours, frustration, danger, and anxiety—all seemed to be taken in stride as just part of the reality of being a cop. I went eventually through the humbling discovery that I, like the men in blue with whom I worked, was simply a human being with definite limits to the amount of stress I could endure in a given period of time.

I recall in particular one evening when this point was dramatized to me. It had been a long, hard shift—one which ended with a high-speed chase of a stolen car in which we narrowly escaped serious injury when another vehicle pulled in front of our patrol car. As we checked off duty, I was vaguely aware of feeling tired and tense. My partner and I were headed for a restaurant and a bite of breakfast when we both heard the unmistakable sound of breaking glass coming from a church and spotted two long-haired teenage boys running from the area. We confronted them and I asked one for identification, displaying my own police identification. He sneered at me, cursed, and turned to walk away. The next think I knew I had grabbed the youth by his shirt and spun him around, shouting, "I'm talking to you, punk!" I felt my partner's arm on my shoulder and heard his reassuring voice behind me, "Take it easy, Doc!" I released my grip on the adolescent and stood silently for several seconds, unable to accept the inescapable reality that I had "lost my cool." My mind flashed back to a lecture during which I had told my students, "Any man who is not able to maintain absolute control of his emotions at all times has no business being a police officer." I was at the time of this incident director of a human relations project designed to teach policemen "emotional control" skills. Now here I was, an "emotional control" expert, being told to calm down by a patrolman!

A COMPLEX CHALLENGE

As someone who had always regarded policemen as a "paranoid" lot, I discovered in the daily round of violence which became part of my life that chronic suspiciousness is something that a good cop cultivates in the interest of going home to his family each evening. Like so many other officers, my daily exposure to street crime soon had me carrying an off-duty weapon virtually everywhere I went. I began to become watchful of who and what was around me, as things began to acquire a new meaning: an open door, someone loitering on a dark corner, a rear license plate covered with dirt. My personality began to change slowly according to my family, friends, and colleagues as my career as a policeman progressed. Once quick to drop critical barbs about policemen to intellectual friends, I now became extremely sensitive about such remarks—and several times became engaged in heated arguments over them.

As a police officer myself, I found that society demands too much of its policemen: not only are they expected to enforce the law, but to be curbside psychiatrists, marriage counselors, social workers, and even ministers, and doctors. I found that a good street officer combines in his daily work splinters of each of these complex professions and many more. Certainly it is unreasonable for us to ask so much of the men in blue; yet we must, for there is simply no one else to whom we can turn for help in the kind of crises and problems policemen deal with. No one else wants to counsel a family with problems at 3 a.m. on Sunday; no one else wants to enter a darkened building after a burglary; no one else wants to confront a robber or madman with a gun. No one else wants to stare poverty, mental illness, and human tragedy in the face day after day, to pick up the pieces of shattered lives.

As a policeman myself, I have often asked myself the questions: "Why does a man become a cop?" "What makes him stay with it?" Surely it's not the disrespect, the legal restrictions which make the job increasingly rough, the long hours and low pay, or the risk of being killed or injured trying to protect people who often don't seem to care.

The only answer to this question I have been able to arrive at is one based on my own limited experience as a policeman. Night after night, I came home and took off the badge and blue uniform with a sense of satisfaction and contribution to society that I have never known in any other job. Somehow that feeling seemed to make everything—the disrespect, the danger, the boredom—worthwhile.

AN INVALUABLE EDUCATION

For too long now, we in America's colleges and universities have conveyed to young men and women the subtle message that there is somehow something wrong with "being a cop." It's time for that to stop. This point was forcibly brought home to me one evening not long ago. I had just completed a day shift and had to rush back to the university with no chance to change out of uniform for a late afternoon class. As I rushed into my office to pick up my lecture notes, my secretary's jaw dropped at the sight of the uniform. "Why, Dr. Kirkham, you're not going to go to class looking like *that*, are you?" I felt momentarily embarrassed, and then struck by the realization that I would not feel the need to apologize if I appeared before my students with long hair or a beard. Free love advocates and hate-monger revolutionaries do not apologize for their group memberships, so why should someone whose appearance symbolizes a commitment to serve and protect society? "Why not," I replied with a slight smile, "I'm proud to be a cop!" I picked up my notes and went to class.

Let me conclude this article by saying that I would hope that other educators might take the trouble to observe firsthand some of the policeman's problems before being so quick to condemn and pass judgment on the thin blue line. We are all familiar with the old expression which urges us to refrain from judging the worth of another man's actions until we have walked at least a mile in his shoes. To be sure, I have not walked that mile as a rookie patrolman with barely 6 months' experience. But I have at least tried the shoes on and taken a few difficult steps in them. Those few steps have given me a profoundly new understanding and appreciation of our police, and have left me with the humbling realization that possession of a Ph.D. does not give a man a corner on knowledge, or place him in the lofty position where he cannot take lessons from those less educated than himself.

2

Blue Truth

by Cherokee Paul McDonald

*"I never abandoned the truth of the law. Its spirit remains pure, even as its imple-
mentation is perverted by egotistical opportunists and sanctimonious hypocritical
overseers."*

—Cherokee Paul McDonald,
Blue Truth,
(1991)

It was a hard-metal trinity: the badge, the gun and the handcuffs. Each was cold and heavy
with inherent power and responsibility; each was forged with precise purpose.

I wore that hard-metal trinity as part of my Fort Lauderdale police uniform the day I stood
at proud attention and graduated with the 33rd Police Academy class in Broward County. The
virginal handcuffs lay coiled in their leather pouch, still unaware of the taste of angry sweat or
the pull of resisting tendons. The gun rode in its holster, waiting, confident, a passive judge in
condescending repose. And on my chest, stroked by the rhythmic beating of my heart, lay the
badge. It was pinned to the fabric of my uniform shirt, and it summed up with a singular clar-
ity everything I worked for, stood for and represented. It was my identity, my reason, my pass-
port to the truth.

And what of the flesh and blood that was me?

I was a young soldier come home from Vietnam, curiously aged by a war I did not yet know
I had lost. Battle had triggered something in me. I was fueled by the sure knowledge that I had
fought for the right, the good. I liked soldiering against evil, I liked taking up arms and pitting
myself against an enemy who would do bad things to good people. I came home to the only

---

Sergeant Cherokee Paul McDonald resigned from the Fort Lauderdale police force in 1980, after ten years of service.

war in town, the only battle I could soldier in—the field of struggle where the good side needed me, where an identifiable enemy could be met in physical combat and defeated.

I came home to the street.

Here we go, out of the car and feet sliding in the gravel of the alley. There *you* are, roundin' the Dumpster, one crushed-down sneaker comin' off while your feet grab for traction. I see you look over your shoulder, eyes wide, mouth open. You tryin' to be cool and run from me at the same time, asshole?

"Freeze, motherfucker, or I'll blow your face off!"

So you look over your shoulder again and turn right between the buildings, heading for the open field and the green apartments on the other side. You and I both know that when you get to those apartments, you gonna disappear like a rat in a hole, huh? Well, guess again, asshole, 'cause there's my partner in the cruiser, waitin' for you.

"I said *stop*, asshole—I swear I'll blow you away!"

But you keep on runnin', turnin' again to get back into the alleys. Did you run this fast when you grabbed that old lady's purse? Did you have to knock her down and break her hip, dirtbag?

Now! Now you slip right in front of me, don't you? Now you roll and fall, and you look up at me with those big eyes. What you coverin' your head for, boy? 'Cause you know I'm comin' *down*, huh? *Yeah.* You so bad when you be takin' that old woman's purse, so bad when you be knockin' her down and runnin' off like the wind. If you so bad, how come a little Paddy motherfucker honkie cop like me done got you down in this alley? Huh? Why you be lookin' so helpless now? *Why, motherfucker?*

I stand over him, breathing hard. He's lookin' up at me with those big, wide eyes. His mouth is open, and when his shuddering breaths come out, his lips quiver and the spit falls on his chin. And he stinks—he stinks 'cause he's scared. I watch his mouth as he looks up to say, "Why you crackin' on me, man? I din' do nuthin', man. Why you crackin' on me?"

And my fist hits his face so hard it makes me want to shout. I *do* shout, "Yeah, motherfucker, let's see how bad you really are!"

And I come down with the other fist. I'm gettin' good leverage 'cause I'm standin' on the balls of my feet, puttin' everything into it, left and right, my fists crunch into his face.

He screams, "*No*, man!" as his nose shatters and the blood goes everywhere. "I ain't bad, man! Oh, *please*, mister, I ain't bad."

But you were so bad back there on the sidewalk, weren't you? You *so* bad, and *so* cocky. Yeah, knock that old woman down—old woman lives only a couple of blocks from you, shithead. Knock her down and run off with her sorry little Social Security check. Such a *bad* little motherfucker.

I lose my grip on him and he falls to the gravel, bleedin' real good all over.

So here comes the sergeant and my partner, both sweating from running. I straighten up, clip my radio back on and tuck my shirt back into my pants, dusting myself off.

Sarge says, "What happened?"

Partner says, "You OK?"

I say, "Motherfucker fought with me, tried to take my gun, went for my throat, so I beat his ass."

Sarge looks down at the spitball, who is slowly trying to sit up. Sarge says, "*Guilty*," and we stuff him into the back seat and drive out of the alley.

The people look. They say, "They hurt that boy."

Yeah. We did. *I* did.

"Alpha two-three, make it code three, baby choking, not breathing. E.M.S. also en route."

I'm on Commercial Boulevard, just west of 18th Avenue, when it comes down—only a short distance away. I stuff the accelerator through the floor, make a wild, sliding turn north through the intersection, and with my siren and lights blazing, I head for the address. Nothing gets a police officer going like a report of a child in trouble. All you want to do is get there and fix the problem. Now.

From several blocks away, I can see a man standing in the middle of the avenue, waving his arms. He moves out of the way as I roar up and slide into the parking lot. I pop the trunk, jump out, grab the oxygen and run toward the apartment. The door is standing open, and inside, a young woman is crying on a sofa, her face buried in her hands. The man in the street is behind me. He looks terrified and points excitedly toward one of the back rooms.

Baby's room. Winnie the Pooh and Garfield the cat. Blue sailboats and yellow kites. Tiny T-shirts and miniature jogging shoes. Hopes and dreams and Ferris wheels.

I run into the room and look into the crib. There's the baby, about one year old, lying on his back in a little blue jumper. The muscles in his neck are stretched tight and his face is bright purple. I throw down the oxygen, sensing I don't have time to fool with it, and grab the baby out of the crib, letting his little head fall back against my hand.

His skin feels cool but not dead cool.

I open my mouth, cover his nose and mouth with it and blow carefully. I do it again, and then again. Each time I do, I watch the tiny chest rise and fall. Snoopy the dog and Mickey Mouse. Both parents are standing in the doorway behind me now, the father with a stricken look on his face and the mother with tears in her eyes, wringing her hands. A furry monkey from Grandma and a mobile made of little airplanes. Prayers and wishes and baseball caps.

I bend down and blow once more into the baby's nose and mouth. He hiccups, struggles, gags, turns pink, and then starts crying like you wouldn't believe—his small chest heaving as he takes big shuddering gulps of air. He spits up on my shirt and grabs my collar with his tiny hands. He is *breathing*. And crying. And breathing.

I stand there with the E.M.S. guys, watching as the parents drive off with the baby to the hospital. Then I drive a few blocks away and sit on a park bench in the shade, drinking a lemonade. It tastes great, and as I bring it to my lips, I notice that my hand is shaking pretty good. I think about Dad standing in the street waving his arms around, and Mom sitting on the sofa crying her eyes out while the hopes and dreams and wishes and prayers lay there turning purple. I shake my head.

After that baby started breathing again, I should have put him back in his crib, turned around and kicked his parents' asses.

"Why are you turning the car around? What did you see back there? We have dinner reservations for eight. We don't have time—"

"Wait a minute, honey, something didn't look right back there at that convenience store."

"Something didn't look right? So you have to turn around and go back, while we're supposed to be on our way to dinner? You already did a shift today. You're *off duty* now!"

"Yeah, but somethin' just didn't look right. One dude by the side of the building and the other one hangin' by the phone."

"So who are you, John Wayne? Can't you just leave it alone?"

"Well, damn it, they're gone now, anyway. Must've just been looking the place over. Gee, honey, don't get upset. I just had to take a look, that's all."

"But what if they'd still been there? You would have done . . . *what*?"

"I don't know, watched them for a moment, that's all. They're gone, let's forget it, OK?"

"You're supposed to leave the job at the station when you get off duty."

"Uh-huh."

"I don't want to play cops and robbers when we go out to dinner."

"All right."

"I want my husband to be a person all of the time and a cop only some of the time. I feel like I don't even know you when you're a cop."

Silence.

Three bad guys in a blue Torino. I'm right on their ass as they skid across a big parking lot and run off the pavement into a ditch.

I'm screaming into the radio as I jump out. The doors fly open and the driver and two passengers try to flee. I scream, "*Freeze!*" and concentrate on the driver, who runs toward the front of the car and falls down. I run to the edge of the ditch and yell "*Freeze!*" again and he looks up at me with big eyes and turns to run. My gun's in my hand, but, hell, the rules of the game say I can't shoot him, and I guess he knows that. So as he starts to move, I hurl myself at him and land beside him with my right arm around his neck, trying to pull him down. At the same time, I'm screaming, "*Hold it, asshole!*" and we both fall into the heavy underbrush. Then I realize that this dude is no midget—probably 6'3", 230 pounds, big, round and strong.

We struggle on the ground and neither one of us can get to our feet. He's trying to pull away from me, we swap a couple of punches and I realize right away that he's gonna knock the shit out of me if I let him. So I stick my revolver right in his face and I scream, "*I'll fuckin' blow your head off!*"

"Nooo!" he yells, and grabs me in a bear hug and we roll down into the scrub again. I climb to my knees, but then he grabs my gun with both hands. I've got the gun solid by the grips, but I can feel him beginning to pull it away from me, so I grab it with both hands.

There we are, on our knees, face to face, chest to chest, with the gun between us. There is no screaming now, just heavy breathing and grunting. I think he can smell my fear, because he's getting stronger and starting to grin, and I can feel his hands, like steel, slowly pulling mine apart. I can see how it's gonna look and feel when this motherfucker gets my gun away from me and starts pumping .38 bullets into my chest with my own gun.

I know he's going to kill me, so, fuck it, I'm gonna pull the trigger anyway and let the bullet blow away whichever one of us it hits. So I grab as tight as I can around the grips and get ready to jerk my head back hard before I pull the trigger. I start to squeeze that motherfucker when suddenly I see this shiny black shoe hit the side of the guy's head. His face jerks sideways and his eyes open wide, but he still hangs on to the gun with his big hands. I'm trying to pull back when the shiny black shoe gets him again, just above the left ear, and I hear a voice screaming, "*Die, you motherfucker!*" His grip loosens and I fall back and see three guys jump into the ditch all over the guy and start beatin' the piss out of him. They're all screaming, "*Die! Die, motherfucker!*" and punching and kicking the crap out of him. I can hear him screaming and moaning as I lie looking up into the sky, breathing hard.

All the guys start grouping around me now. They're shouting and yelling, happy as shit because all three suspects are *in custody*. The two other guys had run across a field and into another compound, where they tried to hide in some trucks, but the K-9 sniffed 'em out and the dogs are on both of 'em and it's fucking beautiful.

I'm pulling my act together, dusting myself off, when one of the officers comes over and stands in front of me. There's blood all over his right shoe and pants leg. He just smiles and says, "You owe me one, Cherokee."

Walter has no way of knowing how hungry Alvin is. He has no way of knowing that Alvin and three other scumbags want to put together a cocaine deal so bad that they will do anything to make it work. It isn't a big coke deal by today's standards, but Alvin and his partners take it very seriously.

The only things Walter takes seriously are the love for his wife and his undying belief that life is about having a good time. He's a prankster, a guy with a quick wit and a sharp tongue. In briefing, he always has a gag going or harasses some new guy or a lieutenant, to everyone's delight. On the street, with the public, he is neat, courteous, professional and efficient. He just doesn't take it seriously, that's all.

Walter has no way of knowing that it's Alvin and his partners who have prompted the manager at the seafood restaurant to set off the silent robbery alarm. The dispatcher advises the north-end units about the alarm, and Walter drives his cruiser that way. Silent alarms go off all over town, every day, and most of the time, there is a malfunction or some clerk has hit the button unknowingly. This is ten A.M. on a beautiful Sunday, and Walter still has parts of the morning newspaper scattered all over the front seat of his car.

Walter has no way of knowing, as he approaches the restaurant, that Alvin's partners have seen him coming and have driven off, leaving only Alvin inside. Walter parks his cruiser on the north side of the building and grabs his clipboard so he can record the pertinent information for his false-alarm report. He walks easily into the restaurant through the kitchen door and meets Alvin in a small hallway leading out to the parking lot. There he stands, a pen in one hand and his clipboard in the other; and there is Alvin, with a cut-down .22-caliber rifle—a small gun that shoots a small bullet, and, as a high-noon weapon, is pretty hard to take seriously.

Alvin shoots Walter three times with the .22, and as Walter goes down, Alvin runs past him and out into the parking lot to escape with the others. He finds that they have fled and he knows more police officers will be along in seconds. He turns and runs back inside. Walter, lying huddled on the floor in the fetal position, manages to grip his radio and transmit, "Help me, I've been shot." Those of us who hear those words on the radio don't recognize the voice, we only feel the terror and the pain. We rush headlong toward the scene.

Alvin kneels beside Walter and demands the keys to the police cruiser. Walter, through clenched teeth, tells him which pants pocket to dig into. Alvin gets the keys. Then he rips Walter's .38 service revolver out of the holster, places the barrel just behind Walter's ear and fires one shot.

Alvin makes his getaway in the police cruiser, and the first officers to arrive at the scene find Walter dead.

There is the inevitable violent surge of police activity, and all four suspects are eventually captured.

Walter is buried with a quiet private service. The court system plods along, and Alvin's three partners are given life sentences. Alvin is sentenced to death. Now he sits on Florida's death row, and even though well-meaning or publicity-seeking lawyers have appealed his case in every way, his sentence stands. The governor has signed the warrant.

Alvin has waited to die in the electric chair for more than ten years. Those trying to save him claim that he is mentally ill—that he sees space beings and talks with God. The court is pondering whether or not we can put to death a man who is now insane, though he was sane at the time of his crime and conviction. But for now, the sentence still stands: Alvin must die for what he did.

If it were possible, I would travel to where Alvin is today, and I would watch as he was strapped into the chair, and I would pull the switch myself.

Seriously.

"Hey, honey, I'm home. Sorry I'm late—had a bunch of paperwork to do. We still going out tonight?"

Silence.

"Hey, you OK? How was school today—learn some good stuff?"

"Have you seen the newspaper? The story about what happened yesterday? The *front-page* story?"

"Yeah. Crazy paper went wild with it, didn't they? It's—"

"It's a front-page story about how you and your partner beat up this poor kid after he had an accident in his car! Of *course* they went wild! Witnesses said the kid was just walking away. You were seen beating him after he was handcuffed, with your radio! *Jesus!*"

"Don't drag him into this—"

"Oh, it's something we can joke about, right? Do you know my mother has already called me, she's so upset?

"And my *friends*! They already ask me how I do it, and after this—"

"After this, *what*? Honey, it's just a newspaper story. Sure, it's front-page stuff now, but only because they've got it all bent out of shape! Six weeks from now, after the department review board and the state's attorney's office clear me, the story will cover maybe two lines on the last page. Don't worry about it."

"Oh, you're going to get away with this one? What if you get time off without pay? What's it going to cost us?"

"*Goddamn it!* Did the paper mention that the kid crashed a stolen car into a house? Did they mention that he was coked out of his skull, that he has a record for auto theft and battery on a cop? If I break my police radio, I have to *pay* for it! You think I'm gonna chance that on some scroatbag's head when I can do a better job with my hands? Listen, honey, the paper doesn't have the whole story, and they don't *want* it."

"Your name—and *my* name now—is still spread all over the front page, and you sound like every other overly aggressive cop out there, like a monster. Why can't you just take it easy?"

"Officer, tell us again how you came to stop the defendant in the first place. I mean, what did he do that made you feel you could detain him and 'check him out,' as you say?"

"Well, sure. I was talking with some of the guys coming off the midnight shift and they told me to look for him, because they were pretty sure he had done the smash-and-grab at Davie Boulevard and Twenty-Seventh Avenue."

"They were 'pretty sure'?"

"Yeah, you know, they had seen him in the area earlier, and they know the way he usually works."

"Now, wait a minute, Officer, all this is hearsay. How much of this do *you* know personally?"

"Well, I know who he is and I know he is one of the neighborhood burglars."

"And just how do you know that? Have you ever seen him burglarize anyplace?"

"No, I haven't. But, hell, everybody knows he's been into this stuff since he was a kid. He even used to be on a list that the juvenile squad put out."

"Do you have that list with you?"

"No."

"OK, please go on. Tell us why you stopped the defendant."

"Like I said, the midnight guys told me to be on the lookout for him, and a little while later, I observed him scootin' through an alley. His hair was longer then and he was wearing jeans and a windbreaker. He kept lookin' all around, you know—*hinky*."

"Hinky?"

"Yeah, hinky—acting nervous, not right. So I told him to stop and he looked like he was gonna rabbit, so I—"

"Hold it, Officer. How far from him were you when you first saw him?"

"Across the street."

"And from there, you could tell he was, as you say, 'hinky'? From there, you could tell he was going to, as you say, 'rabbit'?"

"Yeah."

"How could you tell these things, Officer?"

"You know, the way he looked. I could just tell, that's all."

"So you decided to accost him there in the alley—stop him, detain him, force him to submit to a search? Is that right?"

"Yeah. That's right."

"And you claim he had a camera under his jacket? And a bag of what you claim to be marijuana in his pants pocket, right?"

"Well, yeah. I was told to look for him. I saw him. He was hinky, so I patted him down, you know, for his protection and mine. That's when I found the camera—it could have been a weapon under his jacket. And the bag of grass made a bulge in his pants pocket, so I thought I'd better check it out. The camera was stolen during the smash-and-grab."

"Do you know where the defendant got the camera? Didn't he tell you he found it in the alley?"

"Well, sure, but—"

"But nothing, Officer. I have no further questions of this witness, Your Honor. And at this time, I would like to ask that the court consider the facts: that, in actuality, this officer had no real basis—legal or otherwise—to stop and detain the defendant. Then he illegally searched him and charged him with possession of narcotics and of stolen property. At this time, I ask the court to find that these charges stem from the product of an illegal search and that they should be dropped immediately."

"The court concurs, Mr. Counselor. And before we adjourn, I want to take a moment to warn you, Officer, that what you do out on the street must conform with the law. You can't just do what you please out there. You must work within those guidelines so clearly set out for you. Don't get so carried away with trying to do the right thing that you violate a man's rights, as you have in this case.

"Well, Officer, don't you have anything to say?"

I'm exiled to the Communications Center again. I languish there for a couple of months, waiting impatiently to be reassigned to the street. The incident this time involved what is termed "excessive use of force" and "falsifying a police report"—meaning I beat some dirtbag's ass and disputed his version of it in my report. The dirtbag's parents complain, and rather than get into a costly investigation, the easy way is taken: "severe disciplinary actions."

I'm going through the motions, biding my time, and I begin to notice some things about myself that worry me. I admit to myself that I've known this for some time, and I've been ignoring it, and it has festered and inflamed like a wild case of emotional acne.

I tell the communications sergeant that I think I need help; he immediately refers me to the chief's office. I say that I am mentally injured as a direct result of my job, and the help I need should be funded by the city. The city agrees, and I'm given a series of appointments with a psychiatrist.

The chief makes me promise to comply with the doctor's final evaluation and recommendation. If the doctor thinks I can be a cop, then I can keep my job. The doctor's letter to the chief is six pages long and a masterpiece of ambiguity. There is some question that I *should* be a cop, he says but there is no question that I *could* be a cop. I can do the work, but I'm probably not cut out for it.

The chief shrugs his shoulders and tells me that he'll take the chance on me. I can keep my job, but if I screw up again, the letter will be interpreted the other way, and I'll "be gone."

On my last visit, I ask the doctor flat out if I should be a cop. He says he understands that I could be an effective police officer but that I may pay a terrible price. He sees me as an artist, maybe a writer.

From that time on, if anyone accuses me of being crazy, all I have to say is, "I'm not crazy—and I've got a six-page letter to prove it."

The strip on New Year's Eve.

The very same part of the beach I used to come to as a kid with my parents. We would get cherry Cokes at the drugstore fountain and waffle ice-cream sandwiches down the street near the old Casino Pool.

It was clean then, sunny and nice. The people were different, we were all different. The beach was a nice place for the family to go on a weekend to be together and enjoy what Fort Lauderdale was supposed to be all about.

The strip on New Year's Eve is nothing like that. I'm leaning against the wall, in uniform, watching the people drift by.

Drunk, dirty, drugged, nasty, filthy, spaced out, leering, laughing, giggling, spitting, cursing, crying, shrieking, stumbling, falling, pushing, fighting, gaggles of street types making their abrasive way from one end of the strip to the other. Happy New Year. We're all assholes and we're going nowhere.

I don't want to be here, obviously.

Anyway, here I am, trying to stay out of the way and just make it through the night. I'm at the entrance to a video-game arcade when it happens.

Clinging hands clutch at my ears, wet lips press against mine and a slick, rubbery, darting, probing tongue invades my mouth and penetrates almost into my throat. I push away with my hands and jerk my head back hard. The tongue and lips and hands fall away.

Shocked, I look down at my attacker.

There, standing in front of me, is an honest-to-God *primo* example of a female street maggot. She is not very tall, not very old and not very clean. Her long, greasy brown hair clings to her bare shoulders. She wears a silver metallic-looking tube top with no bra, and it is easy to see that when she takes it off, her still-young but oh-so-old breasts will sag against her pudgy belly. She has stuffed her heavy thighs into dirty jeans, and her feet are black with street filth. Her face is painted with glitter eye make-up and rouge, and she has thickened her pouty lips with a heavy layer of greenish lipstick. Her oily, sweaty skin—even on her shoulders—is pocked with acne.

And she smells *bad*.

She stands there looking up at me with a leer on her grotesque-pathetic face and her hands on her hips. She sways slightly on her spread legs, giggles and blurts out, "*Happy fucking New Year, piggly-wiggly!*" Then she sticks out her tongue and, with a wink, adds, "And if you think you can handle it, little policeman, I'll show you *another* place where I'm pink on the inside!" Then she turns away, looks over her shoulder at me, gives her greasy hair a toss and walks off, blending in with the crowd and disappearing quickly.

I stand there, wiping her spit off my face, thinking about gargling and wondering where I'm going to find a quart of penicillin mixed with paint thinner.

"It's stupid."

"Because I'm hurt on the job, that's stupid?"

"It's stupid to punch someone in the mouth with your fist. It doesn't help in the arrest, and it only proves you're not as tough as you think you are. The dirtiest place on this planet is someone else's mouth. Punching someone in the teeth is a guaranteed way of getting infected."

"What if I'd been shot, or run over again, or stabbed again, or hit with a bottle again? Would that be better?"

"It's still stupid."

"Jesus, honey, getting hurt is one of the things that happen sometimes with this job; you know that."

"I know that other cops go thirty years without firing their guns, without shooting and killing someone. Other cops don't get gangrene from punching other people in the mouth. They don't get stabbed or run over, either. They get promoted, assigned to inside jobs, jobs where they use their heads. And they don't do the job, job, job and forever the job all the time! And they don't use their bodies like some kind of *macho* sacrificial weapon to accomplish their mission! There are other people out there doing positive things with their lives, living *real* lives, in peace."

She bites her lip, close to tears. I sigh. We look into each other's eyes.

"I didn't purposely go out to get hurt," I say quietly. "But it happens in *my* real world. Next time, I'll try to get hurt in some acceptable way, all right?"

"It's still stupid. This life *we* live is stupid," she says, and walks out.

I'm standing in the sun, looking at her driver's license and feeling the heat rise from the rough pavement of Seabreeze Boulevard. The photo shows me one of those beautiful, healthy surfer-type girls—you know, with the long, straight blonde hair and the glowing, tanned face with perfect white teeth, full soft lips, a cute nose and big, lovely blue eyes. It's a picture of a teenage girl trying hard to be a woman, and I want to smile at the doubt in the young eyes staring at the camera.

She lies on her back on the cruel hot street, her legs spread and her arms flung outward. Her hands are balled into loose delicate fists. She has been covered with an old Army blanket by a guy who will later become a cop but who now just sits on the curb, staring at the sun.

She had been riding on the back of her boyfriend's motorcycle, in jeans and a tube top, wearing a helmet she hated because it made her face look too small. They had waited in the sun at the top of the causeway bridge, and when it finally closed and the gates went up, they had come charging toward the beach, leading the pack. Her boyfriend could handle his bike, and he roared over the small bridge east of Pier 66 and then leaned it over nicely into the first curve on Seabreeze.

The curve is not banked, and her boyfriend had suddenly realized that speed and centrifugal force were working against them, so he tried to slow down as they drifted toward the curb. He almost made it. But as he leaned into the curve, that same centrifugal force made her lean the other way, out toward the sidewalk and the concrete light poles. The front tire of the motorcycle ripped into the unforgiving curb, the bike bounced once and went down and her boyfriend was scraped and scratched up pretty good as he slid several feet on the rough asphalt.

At the same instant the bike went down, the right side of her face hit the brutal edge of a concrete light pole, her helmet exploded and she cart-wheeled off the bike. As her body slid on the asphalt, her tube top was peeled down and, when she finally stopped, her breasts were exposed to the sun.

The guy who would later become a cop told me that was why he had covered her with his old Army blanket. He had been a Beret in Vietnam and had seen blood—that didn't bother him.

What bothered him was that her breasts were exposed. He was embarrassed for her, because people were standing around and driving by slowly and they were all staring at her breasts. No one had tried to cover her. They just stared.

I look at her license photo again, then I bend down and lift the top corner of the Army blanket. Some parts of her lower jaw and her left ear are still there. And her left eye is still in its socket, but it's impossible to tell what color it is. The skin is peeled back from her shattered facial bones and skull—it lies wet and bloody against the blonde hair fanned out behind her.

The rest is gone. I try mentally to reconstruct her face. I can't. It's gone forever. The only tangible evidence that it ever existed is that awkward, doubting, sad little face on the driver's license.

We roll code-three on a statistic.

The nine-year-old had gone next door to the eight-year-old's house to play. The eight-year-old proudly showed his friend his dad's high-caliber hunting rifle, which had been standing behind the door in the bedroom. They took it out into the back yard to play, excited and happy. The nine-year-old turned to say something to the eight-year-old, who held the rifle waist high. The roar of the rifle going off could be heard for blocks.

When we arrive, we run into the back yard and find the nine-year-old sitting on the ground, the eight-year-old kneeling beside him. The eight-year-old still holds the hot-barreled rifle, his face ashen. The bullet had exploded into the nine-year-old's stomach, causing most of his intestines to be blown back out of the entry wound. The nine-year-old sits there, holding his insides in both hands, crying. As I kneel beside him and place my hands on his shoulder to lay him down, he says to me quietly, "I don't want to die. Can you put me back together?" The eight-year-old looks at his friend and then down at the rifle. He understands everything.

The nine-year-old dies.

The divorce is quick, friendly and brutal. Our small home goes up for sale, proceeds are split and we both move out and go separate directions.

She is gone. I am a divorced cop. And I drive around town in my new *macho* Firebird with tinted windows, feeling a hard, cold aloneness creep into me. I feel tickled by a curious freedom, but I'm not sure if I will fly or just withdraw into myself, peeking out only occasionally to examine, with skepticism, anyone peering in at me.

The chase ends about seven blocks north of Sunrise Boulevard. The Cadillac with that dirtbag Aconomie and his two partners has screeched to a halt in a cloud of dirt and dust and blue smoke. Aconomie has the gun.

Now we'll see about shooting a cop.

Paul slides his patrol car to a stop almost directly behind the Caddy. I swerve to the right and stop 30 feet behind and to the right of it. As we open our doors, I see a sweaty black arm flick out of the right front window, holding a gun. It fires toward us once, and then the arm is drawn back quickly inside the car.

Paul, using his door for cover, begins firing at the guy in the back seat. He hits the trunk of the Caddy and then the rear window, and one of the slugs crashes through the glass and hits the guy in the face. He goes down.

After firing at us, Aconomie crouches down on the seat behind the door of the car, knowing that we will hide behind our car doors and yell for him to give up. But that's his fatal mistake, because when he raises up quickly to see where we are, he's looking into the eyes and gun of a cop running straight at him.

A cop had been shot, a cop had been shot, a cop had been shot—and now these bastards had shot at *us*, and now *I was going to kill them!*

I had killed in Vietnam the same way—charging forward, leaning toward my target. I know he is going to come up. I'm less than three feet away, and with my service revolver tight in my hands, pointing right at him, I scream and fire twice—point-blank—into his face. One slug hits the top of the window edge and breaks up before spinning into his skull like shrapnel. The other takes him dead on, between the eyes. His body punches backward and he is gone.

Now other units start sliding into the area and other officers are running up. The driver gets out with his hands up. Then there's the usual craziness and shouting and orders and confusion; bright lights, ambulances and captains.

As Paul and I reach in to pull the two fluid bodies from the car, all rubbery and loose-limbed as they slide onto the dirt, the scene suddenly becomes juxtaposed in my mind with the bodies of North Vietnamese soldiers: long-sleeved dark-green shirts, small backpacks, rubber sandals. . . .

I have relived that shooting in my mind many times since that night. I can still feel myself running toward the car, leaning forward with my gun, coming down on Aconomie to kill him. He shot a cop and I killed him. And I'd stand in front of you or the face of God and say, "That's right, I did. *I did!*"

Working the streets for you and knowing the truth took its toll on me. I had the same problem many cops have: I believed in what I was doing. I would go out at night in my marked cruiser. I'd have a radio so I could hear you when you called for help. When it was *happening*, you didn't call an attorney or a reporter or a judge or a city administrator or an influential person. You called me. I had a flashlight, the better to see you with, and I had a gun, because that's what the world has come to. I went out looking for those who would steal from you, or hurt you.

You slept, and just outside your bedroom window were people who would violate your wife. They would steal your little girl and leave her body in a canal. They would smash their way into your business—where you had worked so hard to make a living—and take your tools. They would go into your house, your castle, your sanctum, and after they took what they wanted and smashed the rest, they would defecate on your kitchen floor.

Who was out there to stop them? Me.

When you were afraid, I felt the fear. When you cried out, I felt the pain. When you bled, I cried. I stood in your living room and felt your loss. The color TV, your mother's ring, your daughter—she was only 17. When you were violated, *I was violated*. When you were dying on the hard pavement, I knelt over you to keep the sun from your eyes. I wore your powerful tin badge on my chest and it gave me reason.

Often, I was criticized or reprimanded for my actions. I kept on, though, because I learned that my critics were hollow relics of what I represented. They fulfilled themselves vicariously through my courage, and the paper projectiles they hurled in response to my street actions were just manifestations of their desire to control me. They had never known the street I knew; they couldn't function there.

Was I a rogue police officer, a renegade? Did I turn my back on our laws, our system of rights and freedoms?

No.

I never abandoned the truth of the law. Its spirit remains pure, even as its implementation is perverted by egotistical opportunists and sanctimonious, hypocritical overseers.

I took up your sword and hurled myself against those who would hurt you. Every day, my physical and emotional reserves were a little more depleted; every day, another piece was torn from me.

Everything I did, I did for you. And I did only what I thought was right.

3

Why Cops Hate You

by Chuck Milland

"The local police department is the only governmental agency that will even answer the phone at 3:00 AM, let alone send anybody."

—Chuck Milland,
Why Cops Hate You
(1986)

Have you ever been stopped by a traffic cop and, while he was writing a ticket or giving you a warning, you got the feeling he would just *love* to yank you out of the car, right through the window, and smash your face into the front fender? Have you ever had a noisy little spat with someone, and a cop cruising by calls, everything all right over there? Did you maybe sense that he really hoped everything was *not* all right, that he *wanted* one of you to answer, No, officer, this idiot's bothering me? That all he was looking for was an excuse to launch himself from the cruiser and play a drum solo on your skull with his nightstick?

Did you ever call the cops to report a crime—maybe someone stole something from your car or broke into your home—and the cops act as if it were *your* fault? That they were sorry the crook didn't rip you off for *more*? That instead of looking for the culprit, they'd rather give you a shot in the chops for bothering them with bullshit in the first place?

If you've picked up on this attitude from your local sworn protectors, it's not just paranoia. They actually don't like you. In fact cops don't just dislike you, they *hate* your fucking guts! Incidentally, for a number of very good reasons.

First of all, civilians are so goddamn *stupid*. They leave things lying around, just *begging* thieves to steal them. They park cars in high crime areas and leave portable TVs, cameras, wallets, purses, coats, luggage, grocery bags and briefcases in plain view on the seat. Oh, sure maybe they'll remember to close all the windows and lock the doors, but do you know how easy it is to bust a car window? How fast can it be done? A ten year old can do it in less than

Reprinted from *Gallery*, April 1986.

six seconds! And a poor cop has another Larceny from Auto on his hands. Another crime to write a report on, waste another half hour on. Another crime to make him look bad.

Meanwhile the asshole who left the family heirlooms on the backseat in the first place is raising hell about where were the cops when the car was being looted. He's planning to write irate letters to the mayor and the police commissioner complaining about what a lousy police force you have here; they can't even keep my car from getting ripped off! What, were they drinking coffee somewhere? And the cops are saying to themselves, Lemme tell ya, fuckhead, we were seven blocks away, taking another stupid report from *another* jerkoff civilian about *his* fucking car being broken into because he left *his* shit on the back seat, too!

These civilians can't figure out that maybe they shouldn't leave stuff lying around unattended where anybody can just pick it up and boogie. Maybe they should put the shit in the trunk, where no one but Superman is gonna see it. Maybe they should do that *before* they get to wherever they're going just in case some riffraff is hanging around watching them while the car is being secured.

Another thing that drives cops wild is the, "surely this doesn't apply to me" syndrome, which never fails to reveal itself at scenes of sniper or barricade incidents. There's *always* some asshole walking down the street (or jogging or driving) who thinks the police cars blocking off the area, the ropes marked Police Line: Do Not Cross, the cops crouched behind cars pointing pistols and carbines and shotguns and bazookas at some building has nothing whatsoever to do with *him*—so he weasels around the barricades or slithers under the restraining ropes and blithely continues on his way, right into the field of fire.

The result is that some cop risks his ass (or hers—don't forget, the cops include women now) to go after the cretin and drag him, usually under protest, back to safety. All of these cops, including the one risking his ass, devoutly hope that the sniper will get off one miraculous shot and drill the idiot right between the horns, which would have two immediate effects. The quiche-for-brains civilian would be dispatched to the next world, and every cop on the scene would instantaneously be licensed to kill the scumbag doing the sniping. Whereupon the cops would destroy the whole fucking building, sniper and all, in about 30 seconds, which is what they wanted to do in the first place, except the brass wouldn't let them because the motherfucker hadn't killed anybody yet.

An allied phenomenon is the, "my, isn't this amusing" behavior exhibited, usually by Yuppies or other members of high society, at some emergency scenes. For example, a group of trendy types will be strolling down the street when a squad car with its lights flashing and siren on screeches up to a building. They'll watch the cops yank out their guns and run up to the door, flatten themselves against a wall, and peep into the place cautiously. Now, if you think about it, something serious could be happening here. Cops usually don't pull their pistols to get a cup of coffee. Any five-year-old ghetto kid can tell you these cops are ready to cap somebody. But do our society friends perceive this? Do they stay out of the cop's way? Of course not! They think it's vastly amusing. And, of course, since they're not involved in the funny little game the cops are playing, they think *nothing can happen to them!*

While the ghetto kid is hiding behind a car for the shooting to start, Muffy and Chip and Biffy are continuing their stroll, right up to the officers, tittering among themselves about how silly the cops look, all scrunched up against the wall, trying to look in through the door without stopping bullets with their foreheads.

What the cops are hoping at that point is for a homicidal holdup man to come busting out the door with a sawed off shotgun. They're hoping he has it loaded with elephant shot, and that he immediately identifies our socialites as serious threats to his personal well being. They're hoping he has just enough ammunition to blast the shit out of the gigglers, but not enough to return fire when the cops open up on him.

Of course if that actually happens, the poor cops will be in a world of trouble for not protecting the "innocent bystanders." The brass wouldn't even want to *hear* that the shitheads probably didn't have enough sense to come in out of acid rain. Somebody ought to tell all the quiche eaters out there to stand back when they encounter someone with a gun in his hand, whether he happens to be wearing a badge or a ski mask.

Civilians also aggravate cops in a number of other ways. One of their favorite games is, "Officer, can you tell me?" A cop knows he's been selected to play this game whenever someone approaches and utters those magic words. Now, it's okay if they continue with, ". . . how to get to so-and-so street?" or, ". . . where such-and-such a place is located?" After all, cops are supposed to be familiar with the area in which they work. But it eats the lining of their stomachs when some jerkoff asks, "Where can I catch the number fifty-four bus?" Or, "Where can I find a telephone?"

Cops look forward to their last day before retirement, when they can safely give these douche bags the answer they've been choking back for 20 years: "No, maggot, I can't tell you where the fifty-four bus runs! What does this look like, an MTA uniform? Go ask a fucking bus driver! And, No dogbreath, I *don't* know where ya can find a phone, except wherever your fucking eyes see one! Take your head out of your ass and look for one."

And cops just love to find a guy parking his car in a crosswalk next to a fire hydrant at a bus stop posted with a sign saying, "Don't Even Think About Stopping, Standing, or Parking Here. Cars Towed Away, Forfeited to the Government, and Sold at Public Auctions," and the jerk asks, "Officer, may I park here a minute?"

"What, are ya nuts? Of course ya can park here! As long as ya like! Leave it there all day! Ya don't see anything that says ya can't do ya? You're welcome. See ya later." The cop then drives around the corner and calls for a tow truck to remove the vehicle. Later, in traffic court, the idiot will be whining to the judge, "But Your Honor, I asked an officer if I could park there, and he said I could! No, I don't know which officer, but I did ask! Honest! No, wait, Judge, I can't afford five hundred dollars! This isn't fair! I am not creating a disturbance! I've got rights! Get your hands off me! Where are you taking me? What do you mean, ten days for contempt of court? What did I do? Wait, wait. . . ." If you should happen to see a cop humming contentedly and smiling to himself for no apparent reason, he may have won this game.

Wildly unrealistic civilian expeditions also contribute to a cop's distaste for the general citizenry. An officer can be running his ass off all day or night handling call after call and writing volumes of police reports, but everybody thinks their problem is the only thing he has to work on. The policeman may have a few worries, too. Ever think of that? The sergeant is on him because he's been late for roll call a few days; he's been battling like a badger with his wife, who's just about to leave him because he never takes her anywhere and doesn't spend enough time at home and the kids need braces and the station wagon needs a major engine overhaul and where are we gonna get the money to pay for all that and we haven't had a real vacation for years and all you do is hang around with other cops and you've been drinking too much lately and I could've married that wonderful guy I was going with when I met you and lived happily ever after and why don't you get a regular job with regular days off and no night shifts and decent pay and a chance for advancement and no one throwing bottles or taking wild potshots at you?

Meanwhile, that sweet young thing he met on a call last month says her period is late. Internal Affairs is investigating him on fucking up a disorderly last week; the captain is pissed at him for tagging a councilman's car; a burglar's tearing up the businesses on his post; and he's already handled two robberies, three family fights, a stolen auto, and a half dozen juvenile complaints today.

Now here he is, on another juvenile call, trying to explain to some bimbo, who's the president of her neighborhood improvement association, that the security of Western Civilization is not really threatened all that much by the kids who hang on the corner by her house. "Yes, officer, I know they're not there now. They always leave when you come by. But after you're gone, they come right back, don't you see, and continue their disturbance. It's intolerable! I'm so upset, I can barely sleep at night!"

By now, the cop's eyes have glazed over. "What we need here, officer," she continues vehemently, "is greater attention to this matter by the police. You and some other officers should hide and stake out that corner so those renegades wouldn't see you. Then you could catch them in the act!"

"Yes, ma'am, we'd love to stake out that corner a few hours every night, since we don't have anything else to do, but I've a better idea," he'd like to say. "Here's a box of fragmentation grenades the Department obtained from the Army just for situations like this. The next time you see those little fuckers out there, just lob a couple of these into the crowd and get down!"

Or he's got an artsy-crafty type who's moved into a tough, rundown neighborhood and decides it's gotta be cleaned up. You know, "urban pioneers." The cops see a lot of them now. The cops call them volunteer victims. Most of them are intelligent, talented, hard-working, well-paid folks with masochistic chromosomes interspersed among their otherwise normal genes. They have nice jobs, live in nice homes, and have a lot of nice material possessions, and they somehow decide that it would be just a marvelous idea to move into a slum and get yoked, roped, looted, and pillaged on a regular basis. What else do they expect? Peace and harmony? It's like tossing a juicy little pig into a piranha tank.

Moving day: Here come the pioneers, dropping all their groovy gear from their Volvo station wagon, setting it on the sidewalk so everyone on the block can get a good look at the food processor, the microwave, the stereo system, the color TV, the tape deck, etc. At the same time, the local burglars are appraising the goods unofficially and calculating how much they can get for the TV down at the corner bar, how much the stereo will bring at Joe's Garage, who might want the tape deck at the barbershop, and maybe mama can use the microwave herself.

When the pioneers get ripped off, the cops figure they asked for it, and they got it. You want to poke your arm through the bars of a tiger cage? Fuck you! Don't be amazed when he eats it for lunch! The cops regard it as naive for trendies to move into crime zones and conduct their lives the same way they did up on Society Hill. In fact, they can't fathom why anyone who didn't have to would move there at all, regardless of how they want to live or how prepared they might be to adapt their behavior. That's probably because the cops are intimately acquainted with all those petty but disturbing crimes and nasty little incidents that never make the newspapers but profoundly affect the quality of life in a particular area.

Something else that causes premature aging among cops is the "I don't know who to call, so I'll call the police" ploy. Why, the cops ask themselves, do they get so many calls for things like water leaks, sick cases, bats in houses, and the like—things that have nothing whatsoever to do with law enforcement or the maintenance of public order? They figure it's because civilians are getting more and more accustomed to having the government solve problems for them, and the local P.D. is the only governmental agency that'll even answer the phone at 3:00 A.M., let alone send anybody.

So, when the call comes over the radio to go to such-and-such address for a water leak, the assigned officer rolls his eyes, acknowledges, responds, surveys the problem, and tells the complainant, "Yep, that's a water leak all right! No doubt about it. Ya probably ought to call a plumber! And it might not be a bad idea to turn off your main valve for a while." Or, "Yep, your Aunt Minnie's sick all right! Ya probably ought to get her to a doctor tomorrow if she doesn't get any better by then." Or, "Yep, that's a bat all right! Mebbe ya ought to open the windows so it can fly outside again!"

In the meantime, while our hero is wasting time on this bullshit call, maybe someone is having a *real* problem out there, like getting raped, robbed or killed. Street cops would like to work the phones just once and catch a few of these idiotic complaints: "A bat in your house? No need to send an officer when I can tell ya what to do right here over the phone, pal! Close all your doors and windows right away. Pour gasoline all over your furniture. That's it. Now set it on fire and get everybody outside! Yeah, you'll get the little motherfucker for sure! That's okay, call us anytime."

Probably the most serious beef cops have with civilians relates to those situations in which the use of force becomes necessary to deal with some desperado who might have just robbed a bank, iced somebody, beat up his wife and kids, or wounded some cop, and now he's caught but won't give up. He's not going to be taken alive, he's going to take some cops with him, and you better say your prayers, you pig bastards! Naturally, if the chump's armed with any kind of weapon, the cops are going to shoot the shit out of him so bad they'll be able to open up his body later as a lead mine. If he's not armed, and the cops aren't creative enough to find a weapon for him, they'll beat him into raw meat and hope he spends the next few weeks in traction. They view it as a learning experience for the asshole. You fuck up somebody, you find out what it feels like to get fucked up. Don't like it? Don't do it again! It's called "street justice," and civilians approve of it as much as cops do—even if they don't admit it.

Remember how the audience cheered when Charles Bronson fucked up the bad guys in *Death Wish*? How they scream with joy every time Clint Eastwood's Dirty Harry makes his day by blowing up some rotten scumball with his .44 Magnum? What they applaud is the administration of street justice. The old eye-for-an-eye concept, one of mankind's most primal instincts. All of us have it, especially cops.

It severely offends and deeply hurts cops when they administer a dose of good old-fashioned street justice only to have some bleeding-heart do-gooder happen upon the scene at the last minute, when the hairbag is at last getting his just deserts, and start hollering about police brutality. Cops regard that as very serious business indeed. Brutality can get them fired. Get fired from one police department, and it's tough to get a job as a cop anywhere else ever again.

Brutality exposes the cop to civil liability as well. Also, his superior officers, the police department as an agency, and maybe even the local government itself. You've seen those segments on *60 Minutes*, right? Some cop screws up, gets sued along with everybody else in the department who had anything to do with him, and the city or county ends up paying the plaintiff umpty-ump million dollars, raising taxes and hocking its fire engines in the process. What do you think happens to the cop who fucked up in the first place? He's done for.

On many occasions when the cops are accused of excessive force, the apparent brutality is a misperception by some observer who isn't acquainted with the realities of police work. For example, do you have any idea how hard it is to handcuff someone who really doesn't want to be handcuffed? Without hurting them? It's almost impossible for one cop to accomplish by himself unless he beats the hell out of the prisoner first—which would also be viewed a brutality! It frequently takes three or four cops to handcuff one son of a bitch who's absolutely determined to battle them.

In situations like that, it's not unusual for the cops to hear someone in the crowd of onlookers comment on how they're ganging up on the poor bastard and beating him unnecessarily. This makes them feel like telling the complainer, "Hey, motherfucker, you think you can handcuff this shithead by yourself without killing him first? C'mere! You're deputized! Now go ahead and do it!"

The problem is that, in addition to being unfamiliar with how difficult it is in the real world to physically control someone without beating his ass, last-minute observers usually don't have the opportunity to see for themselves, like they do in the movies and on TV, what a fucking monster the suspect might be. If they did, they'd probably holler at the cops to beat his ass some more. They might actually want to help!

The best thing for civilians to do if they think they see the cops rough up somebody too much is to keep their mouths shut at the scene, and to make inquiries of the police brass later on. There might be ample justification for the degree of force used that just wasn't apparent at the time of the arrest. If not, the brass will be very interested in the complaint. If one of their cops went over the deep end, they'll want to know about it.

Most of this comes down to common sense, a characteristic the cops feel most civilians lack. One of the elements of common sense is thinking before opening one's yap or taking other action. Just a brief moment of thought will often prevent the utterance of something stupid or the commission of some idiotic act that will, among other things, generate nothing but contempt from the average street cop. *THINK*—and it might mean getting a warning instead of a traffic ticket. Or getting sent on your way rather than being arrested. Or continuing on to your original destination instead of to the hospital. It might mean getting some real assistance instead of the runaround. The very least it'll get you is a measure of respect cops seldom show civilians. Act like you've got a little sense, and even if the cops don't love you, they at least won't hate you.

4

Cop, Killer: A Real-Life Dirty Harry (Norm Nelson, LAPD) Pulled the Trigger 32 Times

by Jason Harper

"The pressure from above was always the worst part. I felt exposed, criminally and civilly."

—Norm Nelson
LAPD

A real-life Dirty Harry. Pulled the trigger 32 times. Norm Nelson is one of the most notorious shooters in LAPD history. And still, he has no regrets.

"I was always the most easygoing cop. But get me pissed and I was a 415 officer—I wanted to kill somebody." (Four-fifteen is the police code for disturbing the peace.)

It sits on the kitchen table, the blueing around the barrel and cylinder worn away from years of being tucked into the front of his waistband. It's small, heavy, made of steel. Six semi-jacketed hollowpoint bullets—a man-killer configuration, they punch through skin and then expand—are gathered in a neat cluster next to it. Norm Nelson bought the .38 Colt Detective Special in 1973 for $76 as his backup weapon. Now he keeps it in his bedroom, half for self-defense, half because he can't quite give it up.

Nelson never used the revolver on another person—it was always his everyday .38 or a .12-gauge shotgun instead.

"Everything I've done in the line of duty, I'd do exactly the same way," the 56-year-old retired Los Angeles cop says in his homey, friendly voice. Nelson fired on another human nine times in eight incidents, killing three, seriously injuring four, grazing one. No one keeps statistics on the national percentage of officers who discharge their weapons in the line of duty, but in 1999

Reprinted from *Gear Magazine*, June 2000.

in L.A. there were 59 shootings among 9,500 officers, and just 6.4 percent of New York City officers have fired their weapons during a crime.

Eight shootings is a hell of a number.

Norm Nelson was a shoot-first, answer-investigators'-questions-later type. At least that's the legacy he took with him when he received a "stress" pension in 1991 after 17 years on the LAPD. (He spent five years as a volunteer sheriff deputy before that.)

Nelson is adamant that all his shootings were good. "In policy" is the police parlance: when a reasonable person could reasonably assume that his or someone else's life is in danger. At one point, softly, Nelson says, "Maybe I did pull the trigger too quickly, I don't know. I just never wanted to be the one lying on the ground. I wasn't going to die for the city. Fuck the city. I didn't want a fancy funeral."

During a blustery day in late March, we're on his Arizona ranch (which Nelson named "Luck of the Draw Ranch") discussing the arc of his career. We have our feet up on his handmade kitchen table and, during our long hours of talk, drink Coors Lite (cans) and coffee. Nelson seems forthright, unflinching. "That's just what happened," he'll say.

He has the handsome, crevassed looks of a Marlboro man and lives like one, too. Nelson's home is near a tiny town two hours outside Phoenix, with no neighbors to speak of. For company, he has Faye (wife No. 4), Chopper (dog), Curly and Black Beauty (bulls) and Tomahawk (horse). There's a five-mile dirt road to get to Nelson's double-wide trailer, which is filled with all things cowboy, including a large collection of hats hanging on a rack of antlers.

He's ridden bulls since '82, pursued the senior championship since '92. Most riders retire at 30: he *started* at 41, so far collapsing both lungs, breaking all of his ribs, twice smashing in his face, and herniating a disk in his neck. He traded the danger and macho camaraderie of the streets for the danger and macho camaraderie of riding 1,700-pound bulls.

We discuss the three police shootings of unarmed blacks in New York City in the last 14 months. Nelson usually feels bad for the cop. "That officer is going through hell. He's done something that's going to be scrutinized and that he may go to jail for. He probably believes deep in his heart that he was doing the right thing."

Nelson wants to explain how, when capers go bad and bullets fly, the officer gets tunnel vision, how the world blinks out. Cops aren't taught to shoot at an arm or leg. "You only see the largest mass of body."

How many bullets did he fire in his 22 years? He extends a finger for each incident. "Parkin, four—Granville, five—bar shootout, one—Tatum, five—Marie Callendar's, four—Bustamante, five—Cubans, three." He looks at his seven outstretched fingers. "Wait, I missed one." He goes back through them. "Oh, Russians, five."

Thirty-two shots. "I was always at the wrong place at the right time." His friend and former partner Cesario Reyes says, "No doubt about it, he's an s.m.—a shit magnet."

Says Nelson: "In 1980, I told a sergeant, 'Man, I had a bad year.' He said, '*You* had a bad year? What about all those people you shot?' Years later, he told me, 'I'll give you this: you're an equal opportunity shooter. You've shot whites, blacks, Mexicans, Russians and Cubans.'"

He wasn't even supposed to work the night of May 1, 1973. Nelson, an ex-Marine from Wisconsin, had made his way to California to pursue a pop singing career (dismal failure), and signed on as a reserve sheriff deputy, earning one dollar a year. A friend asked him to fill in on patrol on a Tuesday night, and at about 10:30 P.M., Nelson and a sergeant received a "shots fired" call at a residence. A woman answered the door and said her husband had a gun, but was gone. Nelson checked the backyard. It was dark as hell, and he peered through a large hole in the wooden fence. He gingerly stepped through—and a shot zipped by his head. "It was like the air had been sucked out in front of me, the bullet went by so fucking close," he says now. The husband was crouching in the shadows with a .45.

It was the first time the anger would come upon Nelson, the incredulity and insult that someone was trying to kill him. "That's one thing I always used that makes me work. When I get in one of those situations I go, *motherfucker*, I want to kill your ass. You may kill me, but the best you're going to do is break even."

Four-shot Ithaca pump shotgun in hand, Nelson chased the suspect along a wall until the perp reached a car lot on the corner of Hawthorne Boulevard and 166th Street and ducked behind an old Dodge. A woman was talking in a phone booth and Nelson yanked her out—a bullet sliced through the glass seconds later. Nelson went to one knee and fired all four double-ought rounds. His partner ran up and also snapped off a shot. The husband went down, all limp hands and feet, bleeding from the shoulder, chest, leg, hand. Nelson's shotgun pellets also hit a passing car, but missed the three women and baby inside. Another shot busted out a window in a furniture store.

David Paul Parkin, 33, was taken to the hospital with severe artery damage to his chest. "He came to court in a wheelchair," Nelson says, sipping coffee back at the ranch. "It seems a lot of my victims ended up like that." He adds, "The thing is, when a shooting's over, you're happy. It's selfish, but you're just glad it wasn't you. Glad you survived and they died."

Nelson got a commendation.

After graduating from the LAPD Academy in 1975, Nelson landed at the 77th Division—South Central. It was almost completely black. The force wasn't. "There were five black officers in the division and, like, 500 white ones," Nelson says. The veterans would take new recruits out to the oil rigs and initiate them by making them climb onto the arm of the pump as it pendulumed up and down. Nelson climbed on top and stood up, surfing. "You're one crazy motherfucker," the officers called out. Nelson fit.

"There was this one dude known as Sugarbear who used to hang out at a bar called the Suicide Club. We'd take the new recruits out there and start shit with him. Sugarbear was in on it—we'd slip him $5 afterward. We'd tell the new recruit to take care of him. In those days you pretty much did whatever your training officer told you to. If he didn't choke Sugarbear out, we knew he was no good. There was one new white cop who wouldn't do it. 'No man, I don't have a problem with him.' I wrote him up a bad recommendation. The other guys said, 'Oh, Norm, he's all right.'

"We'd throw a initiation party for all the recruits when they passed their year probation period. We'd go out to the oil rigs and drink. There was this girl, we called her Bobbin' Robin, and she'd give all the guys blowjobs. She weighed, like, 180 pounds. This same white cop was like, 'I'm not letting her suck my dick. She's already done two other guys.' So we grabbed and cuffed him, and she gave him a blowjob. When we let him go, he went for his gun. He was going to shoot somebody. We had to take it away from him. I said, 'See, I told you he was crazy.'"

A vigilante justice ruled South Central, both on the street and in the force. There were lingering resentments between police and residents left over from the 1965 Watts riots, an event sparked after a routine traffic stop of a black man escalated into 34 dead and 4,000 arrested. It was in this environment, for better or worse, that Nelson learned his craft. Cesario Reyes, who partnered with Nelson at the 77th and was involved in three of the shootings, says, "A lot of stuff we did then, you'd get fired for today." About Nelson, he says, "The people who say he was trigger-happy, they're going by the number of shootings Norm was in. Those same people, if their daughter or son was kidnapped, they'd thank God knowing Norm was on the job, because he was a bulldog. He can sift through dangerous situations so quickly. A few times, if Norm hadn't acted that quickly, he'd have been dumped [killed]."

Whenever Nelson tells a story, it's "this black dude," or "a white cop," "black victim . . ." It seems less than pejorative, more than qualitative. I ask him about the racism on the force. Did he arrest mostly blacks? "No, I worked all divisions." And the word "nigger?" "I used the word. I didn't know a cop who didn't. It wasn't a term that was used that way, it was like 'asshole.' There's an asshole of every color. I did hear it used that way by some cops, and it wasn't cool." Would he use it around black cops? "No. Well—yeah, if we knew the guy. The black cops themselves would use it all the time."

Is it still in common use on the force? "No. Mark Fuhrman killed the word nigger." Nelson knew Fuhrman, thought him a good cop. "He was trying to do a movie script, and that did him in. Language was the only thing they had against him."

In January of '79, Nelson got in three separate shootings in two weeks, two on consecutive days. He was about to earn legendary status.

According to Nelson, he and Reyes responded to a call in Watts. Gun drawn, Nelson rushed inside the house to find Jerome Granville sitting on a chair, an automatic weapon on his knees. Nelson told him to drop it. The guy stood up. Nelson fired.

One round struck Granville in the hip. He sat back down, the gun falling to the floor. He was taken to the hospital in good condition. Three days later, though, he fell into a coma. The bullet had splintered off the bone and ricocheted—taking a course to his heart. He survived the open-heart surgery. "How the hell did you manage to ricochet it into his heart?" someone asked.

Two weeks later, Nelson and Reyes responded to a call of three guys shooting up the Melody Room bar. Arriving to a guy running out the door brandishing a gun, Nelson took a shot, hitting the door of a Cadillac. The perp threw away the weapon, giving up. Another officer joked, "That bullet that hit the door of the Cadillac, I bet it ricocheted into the carburetor."

"I came to work that next day and the sergeant said, 'Hey Norm, you were up all night with that shooting, you want the night off?' I said fuck it, let's go to work. I had the chance to go home, I shoulda taken it. It was a Saturday night, already dark, and six of us went out in two cars. We picked up a sandwich and headed to catch the bus on the western bus lines. We'd patrol the buses in plainclothes. Usually everyone knew who we were—we were the only white people getting on.

"I was wearing a short-sleeve shirt, and a long plaid shirt over it, so it'd cover my .38. We didn't have radios except in the cars back then. We turned off Vermont onto the Imperial Highway in South Central; the Power Gas Station was to the side. It had a little pay booth in the center. Cesario says, 'There's a guy in that gas station with a shotgun.' We turned around, parked and the three of us deployed from the vehicle. My gun was drawn. Then I saw him: a large black man, had a coat on. He was approaching the door of the booth with a shotgun by the side of his leg. We yelled, 'Police! Freeze!' and he turned and pointed the shotgun at us. As soon as he spun around, my instinct was *fire*. We believed he was a robbery suspect. We all fired. He went into the booth and ducked down.

"I ran to change position. There was a Pontiac Firebird in front of the booth with two women inside who had been buying cigarettes or something, and over its hood I could see into the booth's open door. He was ducking down, still looking the way the shots had come. I yelled 'Police—freeze—drop the gun.' That's when he turned toward me with the shotgun and I fired four rounds.

"It hit him, I think, in the chest, stomach, pocket, chest. I go inside the booth, pick up the shotgun and place it outside. I roll him on his stomach to cuff him and he says, 'Why did you shoot me? *I work here.*'

"He was the gas station attendant. We thought he was robbing the place. I asked, 'Why'd you point the gun at us?' He said, "I don't know." I walked out with a look like somebody had just slit my throat. 'This guy works here,' I tell the guys. They're like, '*What?*' It was a pretty depressing scene.

"The whole thing from start to finish probably didn't take more than 15 seconds. Drive up— get out of car—'police, freeze'—boom boom boom—I change positions—'drop the gun'—boom boom boom boom—that's it.

"There'd been so many robberies at the station that he was worried, so he brought the shotgun . . . that's what we found out later."

The attendant was 42-year-old Cornelius L. Tatum. He was paralyzed from the waist down. Just as Norm Nelson wasn't supposed to be working the night of his first shooting, so, too, Tatum was filling in for someone else.

In March of 1980, the district attorney charged the three officers with assault with a deadly weapon. The LAPD's Chief of Police Daryl Gates claimed the prosecution was politically motivated—the case was filed the same day as a congressional committee began hearings on police shootings in Los Angeles. The officers passed a lie detector test on the events of that night.

The lead D.A. on the case was Jay Lipman, but another ambitious D.A. also contributed— Johnnie Cochran. Tatum's and one of the cigarette-buying women's testimony was radically different from the officers'. At trial, both said that Tatum had gone into the booth, laid down his shotgun and was reaching for cigarettes when police opened fire.

Defense attorney George Franscell cross-examined the female witness, asking why she waited more than a year before saying that Tatum had been unarmed when police opened fire— a claim made only *after* Cochran reinterviewed her. Originally, she told investigators she was digging in her purse for change and saw nothing. A reporter asked Franscell if he was suggesting the witness was coerced by Cochran. Franscell replied: "I'd rather not answer that."

Robert Hilleary, the now-retired district attorney investigator who spent almost two years on the case, and who accompanied Cochran during the interview with the woman, says, "It seemed awful coincidental to me, especially with later developments in the O.J. trial, when she switched testimony shortly after Cochran arrived at her doorstep." (Cochran could not be reached for comment.)

Nonetheless, Hilleary believes that Tatum *was* unarmed when police fired. "The thing that sold me on Tatum's version was where the bullet holes were located in the booth—by the cigarette rack. There were none by the door where he was supposed to be with his shotgun pointed at the officers."

Hilleary says, "Norm Nelson did the coup de grace. The officers were behind the gas pumps, pumping away shots, and when Tatum was already down, Nelson fired a few more gratuitous rounds."

Lipman, still a deputy D.A., says, "We called him Stormin' Norman. It ended up being a question of credibility. The officers said Tatum pointed a shotgun at them. They were lying."

Nelson says, "I never questioned what happened that night. I know exactly what happened. I said on the stand, "I'm totally sorry for the situation, but I don't apologize for my actions.' My lawyer asked, "Officer, if you were confronted with the same situation, what would you do?' "I'd shoot Mr. Tatum again. I believed he was a robbery suspect."

The trial lasted two weeks. "After Lipman did his closing, even I thought I was fucking guilty," says Nelson.

"I got up and started going crazy, like in a movie," Lipman says. "I was calling them judge, jury and executioner, waving my hands around. It felt good."

Nelson says, "One cop came to court the day of the verdict with five guns on him. He said, 'If they find you guilty, we'll shoot our way out.' We just laughed at him." Says Lipman: "The place was packed with blue suits. I thought I was going to die."

The jury was out for four days. Cesario Reyes and Officer Harrell Compton were acquitted. The jury was hung on the charges against Nelson, 9-3 in favor of acquittal. However, in a written statement, the jury said: "We do not believe . . . the police conducted themselves with due concern for the lives of the persons who could have been seriously injured. Two women in a vehicle, almost in the line of fire, were disregarded by the officers." The D.A. didn't refile. "The thing that hurt me and my career through the years was they didn't find me not guilty," Nelson says "I didn't get that cleansing."

Tatum filed a civil suit, and the city settled, awarding $687,000. Tatum's then-lawyer, Irwin Evans, says today, "My opinion of Mr. Nelson is that he was a shooter. I don't think he had a lot of conscience about it. With the number of shootings he's done, there's something scary about that statistic. I don't think the shooting was justified."

Nelson's personal life soon disintegrated. Married with two boys, he and his wife of 14 years divorced just before the trial. "There was no way to relate," he says. (His current wife, Faye, says, "I don't think I could have been with you then." Nelson replies, "I was a different person.")

Even before the Tatum shooting, Nelson was always partying with his cop buddies at cop bars. "I had a lowrider Harley and one night I drove home so drunk I drove right into the garage door. The bike fell over on me and I lay there till morning. You spend so much time with your partners, they become more important to you than anything else."

After the trial, Nelson was transferred out of the 77th to West L.A.—"the nice part"—as a uniformed day watch officer. Still, the next shooting came swiftly. Nelson took an extra job providing security to a restaurant, Marie Callendar's, on the weekends. It was averaging a robbery every couple of weeks.

Nelson was sitting at a table in plainclothes on a Sunday night, the end of September, 1980, when two guys held up the eatery. He sat it out until they walked, cash in hand, out the door. He followed. "I was going to back-shoot the guy with the gun, but an old Jewish couple got in the way." Nelson yelled "Police!"—the guy turned around and capped off two shots, hitting a metal sign over Nelson's head. Bystanders scattered and Nelson fired four times. One hit the guy's stomach. Nelson grabbed the unarmed accomplice, put the gun to his head, and forced him onto the ground—using him as a shield. The armed suspect fired twice more, crawled into the getaway car and screeched away. He was found in the hospital the next day.

Holy hell rained down upon Nelson—the brass had had it with his shootings. "One captain said, 'You're a fucking dinosaur.'"

Nelson spent the next two years in cop purgatory, giving lectures to high school kids. He didn't shoot anyone. But in January of '82 he got an offer to go to the Westside Major Crime Violators Task Force (MCVTF), a sort of über-proactive group made up of different agencies in the city. Crime was up, and the idea behind MCVTF was to slap the criminals down—hard. According to Nelson, he was called up by a head of the task force, whom he'd prefer not to name, who said: "Look Norm, we've had a lot of chances to kill bad people, and we haven't. I need somebody who'll drop the hammer on bad guys."

Nelson says, "He didn't mean like executions or anything, but he wanted people who—if shootings went down—could handle it." Nelson jumped at the chance.

Richard P. Bustamante, 27, and David Hydro, 26, (known as "Shotgun" because he often carried one) had pulled a string of heists in Venice Beach and West L.A., and Nelson wanted them bad enough that he flew home two weeks early in July from a vacation in Wisconsin with his sons to get in on the bust. "They robbed anything and everything," says Nelson. "Bustamante was one stone-cold motherfucker."

Nelson and a team tailed the pair for two weeks. "They'd go buy dope, fuck around, go pick up their girlfriends. Nothing was happening," says Nelson. "It's bizarre: you watch them get up, put them to bed, watch them eat, watch them make love to their girlfriends, and then watch them die. Pretty profound.

"We had an old black van, a Dodge, and we'd sit in that thing for 10 to 12 hours a day. We'd pee in a can and dump it out the side door, chew tobacco all day. With two guys in there all day, you'd stink, you'd smell, you'd fart—it was hideous. It had shit-color brown curtains. You'd wake up and say, "Oh no, it's 100 degrees. I can't do the van today." It would slowly cook you like a pork chop.

"One day, we just knew it was going to be the day—the hair on the back of your neck stands up. Bustamante and Hydro picked up their dope, dropped off their girlfriends and changed cars, getting into an El Camino. They drove to a small overnight store named Carl's Market and parked two blocks away.

"I was in an old Thunderbird, a '74, and parked nearby. They were in the market a few minutes, and I was approaching when a gal ran out of the store. She yells out that they're robbing the place. They made everyone get on the floor and were taking wallets. I radioed in that it was going down.

"Just as I did, Bustamante and Hydro exited the store. Bustamante had a bag of money in his left hand and a 9mm Luger in the right. He looked right at me. I don't think I got more than 'Police!' out of my mouth when he turned toward me and I fired. The first round hit him in the left shoulder. Hydro took off running. I was so locked in on Bustamante that if Hydro had carried a shotgun like he normally did, I'd have been in big trouble. But he had a knife that night. Go figure.

"I fired again, and it entered Bustamante's right knee, blowing out the kneecap. He stumbled and hit the shopping carts with his left shoulder. It spun him around so that we were standing face to face not more than 10 feet away. He had the Luger pointed at me, trying to shoot, but the safety was on. He was fumbling to get it off. I shot him and he winced, dropped the bag of money and grabbed his stomach. The second round went into the back of that hand. Another officer fired and it hit him in the side. This whole time, he's trying to pull the trigger on the 9mm. The rounds stunned him, but I could see it in his face, trying to shoot me.

"He fell. As Hydro was running away, another officer took off the top of his head with a shotgun.

"The thing I notice . . . Richard was a stone-cold killer, but as I handcuffed him and rolled him over, he was crying for his momma. That killer look he always had, that smirk—it was gone. He looked boyish. The killer look, it had come onto me, like it was reversed, and *I* was the killer. Before he died there on the street, it transferred. It was weird, but that's how it felt."

When the shooting investigators arrived, they took away Nelson's gun at the scene. (Officers involved in shootings where there is a "hit" are given three days off and their weapon is taken for testing—but never in public.) "The guy thought I was far too aggressive," says Nelson. "There was a 24-hour, grueling, grueling, grueling investigation."

Cesario Reyes says Nelson called him that night. "If the phone rang at two or three a.m., it would be Norm, involved in a shooting. It was traumatic for him: he'd tell me what happened, take a deep breath while laying it out. During the course of battle your adrenaline is going, but later it really sets in how much at risk you were."

The shooting was deemed "in-policy," but a LAPD superior complained about Nelson being in on another incident. "After a week or two as the phone bitch, I was kicked back on the street," Nelson says.

After the Bustamante shooting, Nelson's ability to keep it all together slipped. He was partying all the time, spending precious little time with his second wife, and emotionally breaking down. "They give you the three days off after a shooting to become 'normal,' but it's never really normal after that," he says. "I was an aggressive cop, and I paid for it physically and emotionally."

It was at this point that Nelson started riding bulls. "At first, I probably did it because I was hoping one of the bulls would kill me. It would have been honorable . . . I couldn't do it myself." Every Tuesday, he'd leave work at 3 p.m., drive 200 miles to the north, ride bulls, drive back, and get up at five in the morning to start the next shift. "It was the only thing keeping me afloat," he says.

In September, 1982, MCVTF was working a Russian gang that extorted money from immigrants. A victim went to the cops and a sting was set up. After fake money was dropped, the cops would arrest whomever picked up the money. It went awry: the Russians rammed a sergeant's car with their own, and a bunch of cops emptied their guns into the older-model car. Just before the Russians rammed the police car again, Nelson emptied his own gun. One bullet hit the driver in the arm.

The gang was caught, but, again, the brass were livid. "They thought it was overkill. I sat on desk for more than six months—riding the pine. Hey, I can see their point, that was my seventh shooting. But I always loved the street. *Loved* the street." Eventually he was turned loose from the desk and, in August '83, started working a group of Cuban robbers who were knocking off gay bars. After weeks of stakeouts, police got word the gang was going to rob a liquor store.

Nelson was purposefully put in the back of the operation. He was a mile away when a shootout began between the Cubans and police at Crown Liquors on Melrose Avenue. One suspect was killed, two escaped in a stolen car. Nelson got a radio call: go find that car. As they headed toward the scene, the driver looked in the rear-view mirror. "The Cadillac—it's behind us."

The suspects took a right turn, speeding, and Nelson's car gave chase. The two Cubans, Sergio Collazo and Ivan Cosmeme, both in their 20s, abandoned their car and fled into a parking garage underneath an apartment building. The cops parked outside and Nelson pulled out a shotgun. "After Bustamante, I didn't give a fuck. As I went into the garage with the Cubans, I already made the decision one of us is gonna die. I didn't really give a fuck who," says Nelson. "I told one officer to take the back. He always said I sent him to the back so I could shoot the guys."

The Cubans couldn't escape—the exit was covered by a remote-controlled gate. Nelson found them behind two cars. "I shot the nearest one once, and then I shot again. When he fell, he was already dead. Then I saw he had no gun. I whipped around as the second suspect was felled by shots from the other officers, and I shot again. Neither had a gun."

The second Cuban had been shot several times by the other cops, but Nelson's shotgun blast finished him off. (A paraffin test was done on the dead men's hands and tested positive for gunpowder, confirming that they'd fired shots at the previous scene.)

To shoot two unarmed suspects . . . sipping a beer, I ask, how does it happen? "After I shot the guy the second time and I saw he didn't have a gun, I thought, Oh God," says Nelson. "But it was one of those things. These guys had already committed the crime, tried to get away and already shot at other officers. There's a big difference between a guy who's guilty and someone who's innocent. It doesn't give me the right to be an executioner, but that's the way things happened."

Does he look for the gun? Or just assume? Nelson pauses, long, deep, tilting in his chair. "Maybe the truth of the matter is, when cops look at a guy and he does something abnormal, and he continues to do it, the cop automatically thinks he must have a gun, and instead of playing catch up, he's ahead of the game—already shooting."

And the Cuban shooting? "In all the other robberies, all the suspects were armed. You just assume. I just assumed." He wasn't looking for a gun? "No, you're looking at the whole moving target coming at you."

After the final shooting, a superior told him, "If you get into another shooting, you better be in a hospital full of holes and breathing your last."

In '87 he transferred to the gang unit, but in '89, he put in for a stress pension, effectively retiring. "The pressure from above was always the worst part. I felt exposed, criminally and civilly. I took the stress pension, because what were the chances I wouldn't get in another shooting with my record? Slim to none," he says.

I ask Nelson if he thinks about Cornelius Tatum, sitting, somewhere, paralyzed for life. Nelson shakes his head. "You just can't. You can't do that." We sit in his house quietly for a while, drinking the last of the beer. It's after 3 A.M. We're talked out and exhausted.

"If I were to write this story, I'd title it 'The Tail,' which is what we called roll call. It would be about a bunch of good cops who went out and did a good job, but ended up becoming just like the people they hunted. We turned into drunks, our lives fell apart. My personal life was a tragedy. It wasn't just me, but a lot of guys I knew. The only thing that got us through was each other: 'If you come to work tomorrow, I'll come to work tomorrow.' The camaraderie was all that mattered.

"We became the killers. Like when I was standing over Richard Bustamante, and his killer look came onto my face and transformed me, just like a whore. Maybe it's a lesson that no one should ever hunt another human, no matter what—I don't know. One day at a bar, I asked my partners, 'How did we become *them?*'

"After all these years, it's something I've never been able to let go. I used to sit out here late at night, and Faye would come out and ask what was wrong. It was the dreams. There were always all these ghosts at the foot of the bed—the people I shot, like Richard.

But, finally, the ghosts and I, we aren't fighting anymore. At the end of the night, one of us goes to sleep . . . and it's okay."

5

Cop Diary

by Marcus Laffey

"There are things you've done and places you've been (as a cop) that no one else has had to do or see in quite the same way."

—Marcus Laffey,
Cop Diary

Marcus Laffey is a pseudonym for New York police officer Edward Conlon, who writes a regular column for the New Yorker. *His accounts about policing the city offer a window on work that is sometimes horrifying, sometimes funny, and sometimes sad.*

Over the past year, more than a hundred people have worn my handcuffs. Not long ago, in a self-defense class, I wore them myself. There was a jolt of dissonance, like the perverse unfamiliarity at hearing your own voice on tape. Is this me? They were cold, and the metal edge pressed keenly against the bone if I moved, even when they were loose. The catch of the steel teeth as the cuffs tighten is austere and final, and never so much so as when it emanates from the small of your back. I thought, Hey, these things work. And then, Good thing. Because their intransigent grip means that, once they're on the correct pair of hands, no one should get hurt. Barring an unexpected kick or a bite, the story's over: no one's going to lose any teeth or blood, we're both going safely to jail, and at least one of us is going home tonight.

The handcuffs are a tool of the trade and an emblem of it, as are the gun and the nightstick. People—especially children whose eye level is at my equipment belt—stare at them, sometimes with a fearful look, but more often with fascination. Since I hold them from the other end, I regard them differently, just as surgeons don't feel uneasy, as I do, at the sight of a scalpel or a syringe. Police work can look ugly, especially when it's done well: you might see a man walking down the street, untroubled, untroubling, when two or ten cops rush up to him, shouting over sirens and screeching tires, with their guns drawn. You haven't seen the old man rocking on a

Reprinted from *NYPD: Stories of Survival from the World's Toughest Beat*, edited by Clint Willis (2002), Perseus Books Group.

stoop three blocks away with one eye swollen shut. You haven't heard his story, his description of the man being handcuffed: coat, color, height, the tattoo on his wrist.

The transformation from citizen to prisoner is terrible to behold, regardless of its justice. Unlike my sister the teacher or my brother the lawyer, I take prisoners, and to exercise that authority is to invoke a profound social trust. Each time a surgeon undertakes the responsibility of cutting open a human being, it should be awesome and new, no matter how necessary the operation, no matter how routine. A police officer who takes away someone's freedom bears a burden of at least equal gravity. Let me tell you, it's a pleasure sometimes.

I walk a beat in a neighborhood of New York City that is a byword for slum. Even if the reality of places like the South Bronx, Brownsville, and Bed-Stuy no longer matches the reputation, and maybe never did, these bad neighborhoods are still bad. Children still walk through three different brands of crack vials in the building lobbies. People still shit in the stairwells. Gunshots in the night may have become less common in my precinct, but many people, young and old, can still distinguish that hard, sharp crack—like a broomstick snapped cleanly in half—from fireworks or a car backfiring.

The genuine surprise is how wholesome and ordinary this neighborhood sometimes seems, with its daily round of parents getting kids ready for school, going to work, wondering if a car or a coat will make it through another winter. Life in the projects and the tenements can be just the way it is in suburbia, except that it takes place on busier streets and in smaller rooms. Sometimes it's better, in the way that city life, when it's good, is better than life anywhere else. In the summer, you can walk through the projects beneath shady aisles of sycamore and maple, past well-tended gardens and playgrounds teeming with children. There will be families having cookouts, old ladies reading Bibles on the benches, pensive pairs of men playing chess. Once, I went to the roof of a project and saw a hawk perched on the rail. Always, you can see Manhattan in the near distance, its towers and spires studded with lights, stately and slapdash, like the crazy geometry of rock crystal. There are many days when I feel sorry for people who work indoors.

The other revelation when I became a cop was how much people *like* cops. In safe neighborhoods, a cop is part of the scenery. I used to notice cops the way I noticed mailboxes, which is to say only when I needed one. But in bad neighborhoods I notice people noticing me, and especially certain classes of people—older people, young kids, single women, people dressed for work or church. They look at me with positive appreciation and relief. I am proof that tonight, on this walk home, no one's going to start with them. Sometimes they express that appreciation. The exceptions are groups of young guys on the street (older, if they're unemployed). Sometimes they're just hanging out, sometimes they're planning something more ambitious, and you're a sign that this wild night's not going to happen—not as they hoped, not here. Sometimes they express themselves, too.

When I'm working, I wear a Kevlar vest, and I carry a nightstick, pepper spray, a radio, a flashlight, two sets of handcuffs, and a gun with two extra fifteen-round magazines. A thick, leatherbound memo book has been squeezed into my back pocket, and leather gloves, rubber gloves, department forms, and binoculars are stuffed in various other pockets. When you chase someone in this outfit, it's like running in a suit of armor while carrying a bag of groceries. But I'm safe, and it's only very rarely that I feel otherwise. All the people I've fought with were trying to get away.

I walk around on patrol, keeping an eye out and talking to people, until a job comes up on the radio. The radio is constant and chaotic, a montage of stray details, awful and comic facts:

"Respond to a woman cornered by a large rodent in her living room."

". . . supposed to be a one-year-old baby with its head split open."

"The perp is a male Hispanic, white T-shirt, blue jeans, possible mustache, repeat, possible mustache."

The appeal of patrol is its spontaneity and variety, its responsiveness to the rhythms of the street: there will be long lulls and then sudden convulsions as pickup jobs and radio runs propel you into a foot pursuit, a dispute, or a birth. When the action's over, the world can seem slow and small, drearily confined. And then you have to do the paperwork.

When you arrest someone, it's like a blind date. You spend a few hours with a stranger, a few feet apart, saying "Tell me about yourself." You ask, "How much do you weigh?" and "Are you a gang member? Really! Which one?" And you hold hands, for a few minutes, as you take prints—each fingertip individually, then four fingers together, flat, and the thumb, flat, at the bottom of the card. A lot of people try to help you by rolling the fingers themselves, which usually smudges the print; sometimes that's their intent. Crack-heads often don't have usable prints: their fingers are burned smooth from the red-hot glass pipe. Junkies, as they're coming down, can go into a whole-body cramp, and have hands as stiff as lobster claws. Perps collared for robbery or assault may have bruised, swollen, or bloody fingers. You try to be gentle, and you wear latex gloves.

When you print a perp, you're close to him, and because you're close you're vulnerable. You take off the cuffs and put your gun in a locker. Once, I was printing a guy as he found out he was not getting a summons but, instead, going through the system. He became enraged at the desk sergeant, screaming curses and threats, and I wondered if he'd make a run at him or, worse, at me. But I was holding his hands and could feel that they were as limp and loose as if he lay in a hot bath—as if his body were indifferent to the hatred in his voice. So I went on printing as he went on shouting, each of us concentrating on the task at hand.

The paperwork involved in policing is famously wasteful or is a necessary evil, sometimes both. Often, it reaches a nuanced complexity that is itself somehow sublime, like a martial art. If, for example, you arrested a man for hitting his girlfriend with a tire iron and then found a crack vial in his pocket, the paperwork would include a Domestic Incident Report (for follow-up visits by the domestic-violence officer); a 61, or complaint, which describes the offense, the perp, and the victim; and an aided card, which contains information on the victim and what medical attention she received. The 61 and the aided are assigned numbers from the Complaint Index and the Aided and Accident Index. The aided number goes on the 61, and both the complaint and the aided numbers go on the On-Line Booking Sheet. The O.L.B.S. provides more detailed information on the perp; it has to be hand-written, and then entered into the computer, which in turn generates an arrest number.

You would also have to type two vouchers—both of which have serial numbers that must be entered on the 61 and on the O.L.B.S.—for the tire iron and the crack vial; affix a lead seal to the tire iron; and put the crack vial in a narcotics envelope in the presence of the desk officer, writing your name, your shield number, and the date across the seal. You also fill out a Request for Lab Exam (Controlled Substance and Marihuana) and attach it to the envelope. Next, you run a warrant check on the computer, take prints, and bring the perp up to the squad room to be debriefed by detectives, who ask if he knows of and is willing to tell about other crimes.

The prisoner is then searched again and delivered to Central Booking, at Criminal Court. There he waits in a holding cell until he is arraigned before a judge. At C.B., you photograph the prisoner and have him examined by the Emergency Medical Service, interviewed by the Criminal Justice Agency for his bail application, and searched yet again. Only then is he in the system, and out of your hands. Next, you see an assistant district attorney and write up and swear to a document that is also called a complaint. The entire process, from the arrest to the signing of the complaint, usually takes around five hours—if nothing goes wrong.

There are arrests that cops hope and train for like athletes, and in this felony Olympics, collars for homicides, pattern crimes, drugs by the kilo, and automatic weapons are considered gold medals. But the likelihood that things will go wrong with arrests seems to escalate with their importance: a baroque legal system, combined with the vagaries of chance, provides an inexhaustible source of misadventure. You feel like a diver on the platform who has just noticed that all the judges are Russian.

There was my rapist, a match for a pattern of sexual assaults on elderly women. My partner and I responded to a report that a suspicious person was lurking in the stairwell of a project, one floor up from the latest attack. When the man saw us, he ran, shouting, "Help me! Get a video camera!" We wrestled with him for what seemed like ages; he was limber and strong and sweat-soaked, as slippery as a live fish, and was chewing on a rolled-up dollar bill filled with cocaine. He looked just like the police sketch, and also had distinctive green eyes, which victims had described. He had been staying on that floor with his girlfriend until he beat her up and she threw him out, on the same day as the last attack. He was the rapist, beyond a doubt.

At the precinct, he collapsed, and he told the paramedics he'd ingested three grams of cocaine. At the hospital, his heart rate was two hundred and twenty beats per minute, and he was made to drink an electrolyte solution and eat activated charcoal, which caused him to drool black. He was handcuffed to a cot in the E.R. while the midnight pageant of medical catastrophes was brought in. There was an E.D.P. (an emotionally disturbed person) who had bitten clean through his tongue, clipping into it a precise impression of his upper teeth. Another E.D.P., an enormous drunk picked up from the streets, was writhing and thrashing as a diminutive Filipina nurse tried to draw blood: "Now I prick you! Now I just prick you!" An old man threw up, and another prisoner-patient, handcuffed to the cot next to him, kindly handed him the closest receptacle he could find—a plastic pitcher half filled with urine, which splashed back as he vomited, and made him vomit more.

I'd worked almost twenty-four hours by the time we got back to the precinct, when a detective from Special Victims called to say that my perp had already been taken in for a lineup, a few days before, and had not been identified as the rapist. This meant that we had to let him go. I'd felt nothing toward my suspect throughout our ordeal, even when I fought with him, although I believed he had done hideous, brutal things. But now, suddenly, I hated him, because he was no longer a magnificent and malignant catch—he was just some random asshole who had stolen an entire day of my life.

A few days later, I saw him on the street, and he said hello. I didn't. A few days after that, he beat up his girlfriend again, then disappeared. The rapes stopped.

"Whaddaya got?" This is what the boss—usually a sergeant—asks when he arrives at a scene, to make a decision or review one you've made. You tell him, I got a dispute, a matched pair of bloody noses, a shaky I.D. on a chain snatch; I got a lady with a stopped-up toilet who thinks I'm gonna help mop the bathroom; I got an order of protection that says I have to throw the husband out of the house, but he has custody of the three kids because she's a junkie and they have nowhere to go; I got twenty-seven facts in front of me, too many and not enough, in a broken heap like they fell off the back of a truck, which left yesterday.

When you arrive at the scene of an incident, you have a few seconds to take stock—to make a nearly instantaneous appraisal of a jumble of allegations concerning injuries, insults, histories, relationships between neighbors, brothers, lovers, ex-lovers, lovers again—all this with roots of enmity as tangled and deep as those among Balkan tribes. You say, "No, I just need to know what happened *today*." The outpouring of stories can move like a horse race—a hectic and head-long jostling for position, yet with everything moving in the same direction, toward the same end. Or it can turn out to be like a four-car crash at an intersection, where all the drivers sped up to lay triumphant claim to the right of way. Brawls often conclude with such a profusion of contradictory stories that you simply take the losers to the hospital and the winners to jail.

When we answered an emergency call from a woman whom I'll call Jocelyn (all the names in this piece, including my own, have been changed), her complaint seemed to be a simple case of assault; her assailant, George, who was the father of her infant daughter, had already left the scene. Jocelyn moved stiffly and was covered with scuffs and scratches, and one earlobe was notched where an earring had been pulled out. She was surrounded by a phalanx of female relatives who let out a steady stream of consolations and curses, all attesting to George's history of violence. I asked her about her earlobe, and she said, "Oh, that's old," and, looking closer, I saw that it was, and so were many of the marks on her. But then she lifted up her pant leg and showed me a fresh red scrape that covered most of the kneecap, and the course was clear. I asked for a detailed description and got one: "He's about five-eight and two hundred pounds, a lotta muscles and a bald head. Gonna take a lotta you cops to lock him up, 'cause he on parole for armed robbery and he say he ain't goin' back for nothin'!"

"Does he have a weapon now?"

"Wouldn't be surprised."

When my partner spotted him on the street, I called him over to us, and he came, without delay. "You George?" I asked, and he said that he was, in a clear, precise diction that was unusual for the street. He'd spent his time upstate well. I asked if he'd fought with Jocelyn, and he seemed mildly embarrassed, as if he had found out that they'd awakened the neighbor's baby. "Yeah, we did argue, over some stupid little thing."

"Tell you what," I said. "Take a walk with us up there. Let's straighten it out." The only matter to be straightened out was the "confirmatory identification," a procedural nicety in which I was glad to have his innocent cooperation. His lack of concern was disconcerting, and suggested either that her story was shaky or that his reflexes and instincts were wildly askew.

Upstairs, Jocelyn made the I.D. I discreetly put my location and condition—"Holding one"— over the air and gently asked George for a lengthy, time-killing version of events. Even when plentiful reinforcements arrived, and his alarm became evident, he didn't give up, but pulled back as someone tried, gently, to take his arm. Given his strength and the dimensions of the cinder-block hallway where we had gathered, no one wanted a brawl. He began to shake, and to bellow "I did not hit her!" and "I am not going back to prison!" We managed to coax him into restraints while he continued to shout, calling for neighbors to tell us what was really going on.

As we took George downstairs, he began to pitch his version of events: Jocelyn was a crackhead; he had custody of their infant daughter; he was angry at Jocelyn because she left the baby alone; her marks were from a fight she had yesterday; lots of people had seen her attack him earlier that day, and would testify that he had never raised a hand against her. On the street outside, one woman—who looked like a crackhead herself—said she had fought Jocelyn last night, and a man said he'd seen George endure Jocelyn's beating him without protest. Toni, whom George referred to as his fiancée, and who also had a child by him, happened by and joined in, shaking her head in disapproval of Jocelyn. But I still had a complainant, an I.D., a fresh injury, and no choice. And when George admitted that he "might have knocked her down" I didn't feel bad about bringing him in.

At the precinct, George alternated between brooding reveries on injustice and civil, reasonable explanations of his predicament. Then he suddenly assumed a soft-voiced and menacing tone, so that I couldn't tell if he was putting on a mask or dropping one. "I did time, man, time," he murmured urgently. "I know people who rob every day. I know people who sell guns, sell machine guns. I know people sell you a grenade man, I could help you out."

Short of gunfire, nothing has as strong an effect on a cop as the word "gun." Guns are unique in their ability to change nobodies and wanna-bes into genuinely bad men in an instant. And while there is nothing more serious than apprehending a dangerous criminal, it also seems like boyhood itself when you can spend your days trying to get the bad guys. That was why, if I almost believed George when he told me about Jocelyn, I almost loved him when he told me about the guns.

I tried not to let it show, though. I didn't want to get greedy—to let the balance tip from buyer to seller. Not long before, a similar story—completely detailed, wholly plausible, legally sworn—had led me, along with thirty other cops, some equipped with full-body armor and shot-guns, to raid an apartment where we expected to find a crate of semi-automatics but instead found a dildo and ten thousand roaches. I knew that if George meant it he'd say it more than once, and for his information to be useful he'd have to be willing to keep talking when he wasn't wearing my handcuffs. So I treated him with consideration—"You got change? I'll get you a soda"—and continued to process the arrest.

As it turned out, however, nothing came to pass. Jocelyn dropped the charges, and even came down to Central Booking to take George home. He was elated as he left, telling me, "Watch, I'm gonna get you a gun collar!" Laughing, I called after him, "Give me your number," and waited to see his reaction. He hesitated, then came back and gave me his beeper number. "I'm telling you," he said.

For a while after that, whenever I ran into George on the street, he would talk to me. The information was always good but never quite useful: he confirmed things I knew, and told me about witnesses to assaults and robberies who wouldn't come forward. I called him once or twice, and my call was never returned.

You often start with these cheesy collars: dice, blunts, trespass. It's not what you signed up for, being a glorified hall monitor, if "glorified" is the word. "Public urinator at two o'clock! Let's move in!" But it's part of the job, so you do it—preferably with the discretion you are empowered to exercise. If a group of guys are hanging out smoking marijuana and I'm walking by, one of two things tends to happen. Either I hear a rapid apology, the blunt is tossed—and if it's down a sewer there's no evidence to recover and no basis for a charge, you follow me, guys?—and the group gets a stern word of caution. Or someone decides to lock eyes with me and take a drag, and someone else calls out some cute remark, like "Fuck the police!" and they decline to heed my word to the wise: "Break out, guys. Bounce!" No? And in seconds, or in a minute if I decide I want backup, they're all up against a wall. I start going into their pockets, taking names.

If someone has I.D., I might run a name over the air, and if there's no warrant out for this person's arrest he'll get a summons for Disorderly Conduct at the scene. But most guys like these don't carry I.D., and you take them into the precinct to search them thoroughly, run the checks, and write the summonses. Often, someone will have drugs on him, or a stolen credit card. One in five will have an active warrant, in my experience, and fully half will come up on the computer as "Robbery Recidivist" or as "Target Narcotic Violator," which means that they have a number of convictions for mugging or dealing. Maybe they were just hanging out tonight, but, as far as I'm concerned, tonight they've lost their street-corner privileges. And now and then you find a prize, like a hard-core felon hiding behind a bottle of Bacardi.

For the most part, the time you spend with people you like and respect occurs at a low point in their lives: they've just been robbed, their child is missing, or their husband has collapsed from chest pains. You are less the bearer of bad news than the proof of it. More often, you become bound up in lives that are dismal and grim: parolees and their teen-age girlfriends, thugs, drunks, and junkies, E.D.P.s taking too much or too little for their pain. Other people you never get to know, even after you've spent some time with them.

The old man lived alone and died crumpled on the floor in a little alley between the bed and the wall. He was wearing a dirty shirt and no pants. His apartment was small and cluttered, and all his clothes were in old suitcases, or were stacked beside them, as if he were packing for a long trip. There were two televisions—one old, one brand-new. A manic kitten darted amid the piles of clothes and rubbish around the old man's body. Because he lived alone, we had to search for valuables, in the presence of a sergeant, and voucher them at the precinct. We found his military discharge papers, his false teeth, and stacks of pornography. The other cops left, and I stayed. It was my turn to sit on the D.O.A., waiting for the Medical Examiner to have a look, then for the morgue to take him away.

A man knocked at the door and said, "I took care of him. I'm his stepson. He wanted me to have the TV."

I told him to get some proof, and said that until then he should take the kitten. He left—without the kitten—and I turned on the television.

Less than an hour later, he returned with a lady friend. Both were completely drunk, and demanded in unison, "We loved him! We was his family! Let's have that TV!"

I closed the door on them and sat back down. There was a phone call. I waited, then picked it up, hoping that no one who cared for him would learn of his death by accident, from a stranger.

"Is Mr. Jones at home?"

"No, he isn't."

"Is this . . . Mrs. Jones?"

"No." But thanks for asking.

"When will he be available?"

"No time soon."'

"When should I call back?"

"Can I ask who this is?"

"Mr. Jones had recently expressed an interest in our low-cost insurance policies, and—"

"He's not interested."

"'And who, may I ask, is this?"

"The police. Mr. Jones is dead. That's why I'm here."

"Well, do you think—"

"Dead."

"There may be some—"

"Dead, dead, dead. He's stuck to the floor six feet away from me, guy. No sale."

"Have you considered whether you have all the coverage you need, Officer?"

I hung up and went back to watching television.

Most of the time, the enforcement of the law follows a simple moral algorithm—the sum of what you should do and what you can. If the perp is there, you make an arrest; if he's not, you make a report. If he runs, you chase. If he shoots, you shoot back. The facts, rather than your feelings, dictate the course of action, but the close correspondence of the two is a satisfaction of the job. Sometimes, though, the victims are less sympathetic than the offenders, and an odd bond develops between cop and perp which can emotionally skew the equation.

One woman called to say that her thirteen-year-old son had locked her out of her house; she had obtained a Family Court order that allowed her to call the police whenever she couldn't control him. For over an hour, we knocked, reasoned, and threatened, and fiddled with the locks. We had ample time to find out about the family.

"Is there anyone—someone he isn't mad at—who could talk to him, get him to open the door?" I asked.

"Oh, he's not mad at me," she said. I let it go.

"Maybe a friend from school?"

"I been tellin' him to go to school since last year," she said, adding that he stopped because the other kids beat him up. Asked why, she said that he wore makeup and women's clothes. My partner went to get a coat hanger, to see if he could work the door chain off. The woman went on about how the boy's father left her, how she worked, how the boy stayed out till dawn. She paused a moment, as if she'd just remembered, and said, "I had a three-year-old—she died. She was pretty." She paused again, then said, "I wish that faggot never was born."

My partner got the door open. The thirteen-year-old, a light-skinned black boy with hair dyed a sunny yellow, was dozing. I told him to get some things together, because he was going to a juvenile holding facility now and to court in the morning. By his bedside I saw a list of around twenty names—all men's, and all but a few with beeper rather than phone numbers. His mother picked up a skimpy pair of gold satin shorts, held them up to her substantial waist, and said, "Who wears these? Not me!"

What friendly or fatherly advice was there to offer? "I didn't peddle my ass when I was thirteen, young man, and now I have a cushy civil-service job"? We drove downtown without saying much, and I haven't seen him since.

Another day, on the street, I noticed that a middle-aged woman was staring at me, in the throes of indecision about whether to approach. I went over to her and asked if I could help. "My husband, he beats me, he beats me very bad," she said. I pressed her for details, telling her how, even if I couldn't make an arrest, she could get an order of protection, but she brushed me aside: "No, no, that's all no good. My daughter, she says she's just gonna get somebody to take care of him."

I told her that if he was beaten he'd probably take it out on her anyway, and again she saw I didn't get it. "I don't mean beat him up," she explained. "I mean take care of him. You know!" She raised her eyebrows, like she was letting me in on a sweet deal. "What do you think?"

"Lady, you noticed that I'm wearing a blue hat, badge, the rest? That I'm a cop? And you want to know what I think about having your husband murdered?"

Before she could ask me to quote a price, we parted, each convinced that the other had only a flimsy grasp of reality. A few hours later, another officer and I responded to a call of a "violent domestic dispute." A burly, middle-aged man answered the door and allowed us in. He was in his underwear and seemed at ease, smiling as he showed us around: there was no one else there, and no sign of a struggle of any kind. Even so, I didn't like him, and the female cop with me had the same reaction, but stronger: he had a corrupt and military air, as if he were an aide to some South American President for Life. As we left, I noticed a photograph of the woman I had spoken with earlier hanging on the wall. She was trying to win our argument, it seemed to me, saying, "Look at him. Look. If this one ended up dead, would you really come after me?"

I continued to have hopes for George. I didn't know if he was much more than a corner hoodlum, but the corners he favored were hot ones. And then he came to my attention again, formally, when he beat up his fiancée, Toni. The night before, she told me, George had knocked her down, shoved her against a wall, and confined her in a bedroom when she threatened to call the police. He'd slept at the door of the room, on the floor, to prevent her from escaping. The next morning, he went out and brought her back breakfast, drew her a bath, and then walked her up to her mother's house, where she called the cops.

When I came for George at his job, his rebuttal was as edgily eloquent and semi-plausible as the last time: Yes, they argued, but, no, he didn't hit her ("Did you see a mark, a single mark on her?"), and if he shoved her once it was because she said she'd have him arrested if he ever left her. A cop witnessed that, he added, and we'd have to find him. He had a letter, in which she made that threat: we'd have to find it. I told him that I still had to take him in. He shrugged his acceptance, and we left for the precinct.

For the past year or so, it's been procedure to debrief every prisoner who comes into the precinct. Most perps won't talk, and many are as ignorant of the local underworld as they are of portfolio management. A detective asks, "Do you have information about robberies, homicides, guns, arson, hate crimes, chop shops, terrorism?" I've had people say, "Chop-chop? What chop-chop?" But when George's turn came he said, "Yes," "Yes," "Yes," "Yes," "No," "Yes," and "What was the last one?"

As it turned out, my prisoner was the Rosetta stone to scores of violent felonies, past and planned. George told us that people approached him to do hits and robberies almost every week. The narcotics king of Atlanta wanted to open night clubs in the city, for dancing and dealing, and had been asking George to run them. A robbery at a bodega was supposed to take place a few hours from now, and he knew the two guys who had planned it, what kind of gun they'd carry, how they knew the owner's brother, a pockmarked Dominican who carried a .357, and how he was the one to watch, to take out if he moved. One of the two had robbed a meat market a few months ago of five thousand dollars, with at least a grand in food stamps, which they moved through a Chinese restaurant. Most important, he knew about another planned hit—on a Brazilian man, a witness in a state case. He wouldn't say more.

It was as if George spread the deck and asked the detective to pick a card, any card—but only one. The detective chose the robbery planned for that night. The exchange was remarkably businesslike: if the bodega robbery occurred and arrests were made quickly, that would be good; if it could be prevented, that would be even better; and either result should be enough to secure George freedom. Though it seemed shabby, and even dangerous, to bargain Toni's distress against the safety of a grocery store, it was just that—a bargain. What was left unmentioned was that George would, in all likelihood, be freed by the judge at his arraignment. Toni's case was weak, even terminal, and if history served as a guide the charges might well be dropped. (I had even found the cop who'd witnessed Toni's threats to have George arrested if he left her.) But George was back in the cage now, and he would do what he could to get out of it. It was a line of thought we encouraged.

As calls were made, and the hours passed, George explained that he had no problem giving up people who weren't close friends and who were going to hurt people. He had hurt people himself, and, while it didn't keep him up at night, he thought it a better thing if people didn't get hurt during jobs. George's efforts at moral understanding had a rote, calisthenic quality: "You think, What if it's your brother, your girl who gets shot in a holdup—how would you feel?" What really bothered him was that here he had information of great value, and he'd had to squander it on an domestic-violence charge. "I'm not gonna say all I know," he told me. "What if they grab me with a gun sometime, what am I gonna have left to give?"

It was after dark by now, and the bodega would be open for only a few more hours. There were countless reasons for the robbery not to take place then: a hangover, a date, the flu, an argument, a bad horoscope, or an arrest. The next night was Halloween, when the robbers could even wear masks without attracting notice. The detective passed the information to the borough robbery squad and sent us on our way to Central Booking.

The password had been spoken, but the gates remained shut. I hadn't quite expected that, and neither had George. This meant that he would have to spend the night with the losers, with their foul smells and sad stories, their tough-guy sneers and choked-back sobs. As I put him in the holding cell, George leaned close to me and whispered that he wanted to talk. "About the Brazilian?" I asked. "About the Brazilian?" he said. I loved that part; it was just like the movies. As they say, this is no job for a grownup.

There may be no crime more destructive to the criminal-justice system than a hit on a witness: if witnesses won't work, the system doesn't. For several hours, I pursued district attorneys and detectives to peddle my murder conspiracy, but there didn't seem to be a buyer. After midnight, I went home, determined to keep trying in the morning.

Toni arrived at court in the morning looking fresh and rested, and she remained resolute in her desire to press charges. When we were finished, I was taken aback at the vehemence of the assistant D.A.'s reaction. "Did you see that poor woman? I've never seen such fear!" she said. "I really want to put this guy away!" She had tears in her eyes.

Ordinarily, I would have been delighted with the response. Time after time, I've brought in assault cases, from domestic violence more often than not, and seen them dealt down to next to nothing. At last, I'd met a blazing champion of the downtrodden, and it couldn't have happened at a worse time. My peculiar mixture of motives made me uneasy, but I genuinely felt that her reaction was naïve and awry. There are times when my heart breaks for people; this wasn't one of them.

After Toni signed the complaint, I spoke to another supervising D.A., who sent me to another detective. This time, however, the detective reacted as I hoped, saying that we had to move, immediately, and do whatever possible to get to the Brazilian. But when I retrieved George from his holding cell, it looked as if the case had, again, fallen apart. He'd barely slept or eaten, and he was talking in crazy circles, saying that he could go back to jail and wouldn't care, and then that he'd never go back because he hadn't done anything. Once, he broke down—crying, with his face in his hands—and I thought we had lost him. We moved between paying him sympathetic attention and allowing him moments of privacy; we fed him; we let him call his sister to talk. "Think about your children!" I said. Let me tell you, we were ruthless. Finally, he came around and told us what he knew.

George didn't know if the Brazilian had testified or was scheduled to; if he was an informant or was just suspected of thinking about turning. The Brazilian ran narcotics for another dealer, who was in prison; the dealer suspected that his employee had betrayed him, and had ordered the hit. The fee would be six thousand dollars—half on agreement, half on completion. George also knew the name and address of the Brazilian, because he'd seen a video as a kind of prospectus for the hit: footage of the block, the apartment building, the apartment. In the last ten seconds, the Brazilian himself appeared in the video, stumbling unsuspectingly into the frame on his way home. All this George knew because he had been asked to do the hit.

Throughout the afternoon and into the evening, we worked on the deal. The D.A. wanted to know if anyone could I.D. the Brazilian as a witness or an informant; calls went back and forth between cops and prosecutors, word went up the chains of command, across agencies and jurisdictions. We were determined to prevent a murder, but the D.A., in particular, was terrified of another one, whose headline would read, "D.A. FREES PAROLEE, GIRLFRIEND SLAIN." He had Toni brought back in, to see for himself how she felt, how badly she was hurt, and if she was afraid.

George would not give the Brazilian's name without a promise from the D.A. that he himself would be out, today. The D.A. eventually agreed that it would be enough if the name checked out. George gave up the first name, which was all he remembered anyway—Kari. With this shred of evidence, the detectives started calling around and reporting back to us whatever they turned up.

"The D.E.A. has a Bosnian named Kiri, wants to know if it's your guy."

"'F.B.I. has a Corio, from Naples.'"

"Naples, Florida, or Naples, Italy?" Never mind, forget it, but keep taking anything close—Brazilian Kari might be Jamaican Kelly after how many guys are passing along the name."

By sundown, there had been no confirmation, but the D.A agreed to let George out that night, in exchange for the Brazilian's address, with the stipulation that he accept the terms of the order of protection, enter a batterer's program, and agree to bring them the videotape the next morning. George gave an address in Manhattan, and a half hour later D.E.A. agents were on a cell phone from a car. No one was home, but neighbors confirmed that a Brazilian man lived there, and several said he was a drug dealer. They had a name. The Manhattan D.A. confirmed that he was a defendant in a drug case and a witness for the prosecution in a kidnapping: his own. The hit had been scheduled to take place that very night, it turned out, but the killers were spooked by the police presence.

And so it finally proved to be a good day's work, though not without its questions and compromises. A life was saved, by freeing the man who'd been asked to take it. The intended victim was the kind of person I'd just as soon arrest as rescue. But he was alive—at least for a little while longer—and George was his unlikely and reluctant savior.

George picked up his life more or less where he left off. Toni decided to drop the charges, and Jocelyn became pregnant by him again: "Gotta keep trying till I get a son," he said. Every week or so, I still run into George on the street, and we say hello. I like him, as far as it goes. The feeling is as mutual as it can be, I think, between two people who wouldn't hesitate to shoot each other. As he's a hit man and I'm a cop, the odds of such an occurrence are less remote than they might be otherwise.

It was near the end of my tour of duty, and I was headed back to the precinct when an aided case came over the air. Aideds are among the most frequent jobs, usually entailing an escort of E.M.S. workers to the scene of an illness or injury. When I arrived in the apartment, I could tell from the smell why someone had called. As I walked down the hall, past what seemed to be numerous, spacious rooms, the rank, ripe odor of decomposition grew stronger, and when an expressionless teen-age girl directed me to the last bedroom I was thrown less by the sight of the still, frail old Puerto Rican woman in bed than the four emergency medical technicians working around her. Two were crying.

The old woman was naked, lying face down, stuck to plastic sheets that made a crackling sound as she was unpeeled from them. She had once been a hefty woman but now looked less slimmed down than deflated: her breasts were empty, pressed against her chest, and the bones of her hips and thighs were plainly visible, draped with loose, lifeless skin. Maggots crawled on her, inchworming along, and popping off like broken watch springs. There was rodent excrement in the bed with her, and one E.M.T., examining her legs, said, with a horrified intake of breath, "Those are rat bites! Whoever did this to her should go to jail!"

The old woman let out a breathy moan as she was rolled over, feeling pain wherever her body was alive. This woman was dying; parts of her were already dead. And she didn't live alone. I turned away, and went to talk to the teen-age girl: "Who takes care of this lady?"

"Well," she said, with a pouty, long-suffering tone, "I'm the one who does most of the work."

"Who lives here? How old are they?"

"Me and my sister and my grandmother. My sister's twenty-three, but she's out now."

"Can you tell me why you didn't feed her?"

"She said she wasn't hungry."

"Why didn't you call a doctor?"

"I'm the one that did."

"Before now, why didn't you call?"

"My mom said not to."

She said that her mother lived in another part of the city. I told her to call her and tell her to go to the hospital. I asked what they lived on, and she said her grandmother got checks and her sister cashed them to run the household. Ordinarily, E.M.S. prefers to have a relative ride in the ambulance with the aided, but when the teen-ager approached the door a no-longer-crying E.M.T. told her, curtly, "You want to visit Grandma? Take the bus."

Back at the precinct, it took some time to figure out how to write the complaint—for, while there are many laws regarding the care of children, the elderly are less explicitly protected. I found a misdemeanor in the Penal Law called "Endangering the welfare of an incompetent person," and named the adult sister and the mother as perpetrators. Since there were checks coming in, "Investigate larceny" was added. And that, I realized, without satisfaction, explained the family's nearly homicidal neglect. The old woman was the keystone of a tidy edifice of subsidies: a large apartment, Social Security, welfare for the teen-age girl. If she went to a hospital or a nursing home, all these benefits would vanish from their pockets. People talk about living from paycheck to paycheck; this family almost let a woman die that way.

Every cop has his gripes and jokes, his epics and anecdotes about life on the job. I grew up hearing them. My great-grandfather was a sergeant, in Brooklyn: a dapper, dangerous figure from the Jazz Age who became Mayor Jimmy Walker's driver. My father was a police officer—briefly, before moving on to federal law enforcement, a law degree, and an M.B.A.—and his brother was a police officer for thirty-three years. My father died before I went on the job, but I think that my decision to become a cop would strike him as an affront to how far we've come from the hardscrabble west of Ireland and the docks of Hell's Kitchen. For the next generation to pound a beat might mean that his grandchildren would not try cases in the Supreme Court but instead make their livelihood digging potatoes with a stick by the crossroads outside Ballinrobe. Ah, acushla machree.

Now, after a few years on the job, I have my own war stories. On weekends, I'll sit back, lift up my feet, and tell my girlfriend, "I took a bullet out of a lady's living room. It must have been shot from Jersey. It went through the glass, and stopped on the sill. It landed there like a sparrow." Or "I talked a runaway into coming home. She was fourteen years old. All I had to do was tell her I'd lock up her boyfriend's whole family if she didn't." At times, the point of the job seems to be to make it home with an intact skin and a good story. The stories are a benefit, like the dental plan.

And you need them, like your handcuffs or your vest, to control events when you have to, and to cover your back. If you're a cop, you need a quick tongue, to tell the victim, the perp, the crowd, the sergeant, the D.A., the judge, and the jury what you're doing, what you did, and why. Are you ready to make a statement? No? Then you just did. You told me you weren't ready. "Police were unprepared to answer," says the lead in the morning paper. Or the gossip in the locker room, or the word on the street.

I also hear more than my share of stories. And so, aside from the odd Christmas party or fund-raiser, I don't hang out with cops from the precinct. My friends who are cops were friends of mine before I went on the job. And most of the people I see regularly have nothing at all to do with police work. The job has enough of me. For five days a week, I stay off the streets unless I'm working them. And when I'm not in uniform I'd just as soon not see blue.

But I also notice that when I'm out on weekends and there's another cop there—at a wedding or a cookout or a club—I'll often spend most of the time talking with him. There are things you've done and places you've been that no one else has had to do or see in quite the same way.

6

My Life in the NYPD: Jimmy the Wags

by James Wagner

"At this point, I'd been on The Job only a little over three years, but even six months in the Ninth Precinct was like a lifetime anywhere else . . . My life was changing a little at a time, but I failed to notice, and neither did my family."

—James Wagner,
My Life in the NYPD: Jimmy the Wags

Kenny and I were never what you would call good friends. We trusted each other with our lives, but our personal lives never intertwined because of our divergent lifestyles.

Kenny was a terminal partyer, currently on wife number three, and a Vietnam veteran who couldn't forget the war. I found my thrills in being home with my family, never thought once about divorce, and couldn't handle more than two drinks. The closest I ever came to fighting a war was being on patrol in the Ninth Precinct.

Partners don't last long together if their personalities clash. We got along well, but our relationship ended after work or after a few cocktails at Cal's.

Still, I knew him almost better than I knew my wife. Spend at least eight hours a day in a radio car with a guy for years and you can read his mind.

It was during the mad minute, one cool September night, before the rush of calls for service on a four-to-twelve tour. We had just turned out and were in the car by the park gulping coffee when I noticed something was wrong with Kenny. He was unusually quiet and withdrawn. Kenny's normal state was manic, particularly on a four-to-twelve, when our adrenaline was pumping and we could expect anything in the way of assignments.

Despite the workload—we usually handled anywhere from thirty to forty jobs a tour, as compared to three to five for a quiet precinct—Kenny would always manage to squeeze in at least

Reprinted from *My Life in the NYPD: Jimmy the Wags* (2002), by permission of Dutton Signet, a division of Penguin Group, Inc.

a few bad jokes. He had a remarkable memory when it came to jokes. I never recall hearing the same one twice.

He would come up with something like, "The Lone Ranger and Tonto are sitting in a bar. A stumblebum cowpoke comes in and tells the Ranger his horse, Silver, collapsed in the street. The Ranger says, 'Shit, I forgot to water him before we came in here. Tonto, would you give him something to drink and run him around in circles for a while? It'll cool him off.' Tonto says, 'Sure, kemosabe.' Twenty minutes later, another cowboy comes in the bar, asks the Ranger if that's his horse out there running around in circles. The Ranger says, 'Yep.' The cowboy says, 'Well, you left your *Injun* running!' "

I would say, "Kenny, you're a riot," and usually yawn. It was either listen to lame jokes or watch him tell the performing mimes in Tompkins Square Park that they had the right to remain silent.

Today, however, no jokes.

"What's the matter, run dry?" I asked.

Kenny was lost in thought. He snapped out of it. "Huh? What?"

"No jokes today? I need something to put me to sleep."

"Uh, not today. Say, Wags, let me ask you a question: You still love your wife?"

I looked at him. "What kind of question is that? Of course I love my wife."

"Yeah, okay, I'll accept that—"

"Gee, thanks."

"But are you still . . . you know, attracted to her?"

"Are you serious?" He was staring at me intently. He *was* serious. I thought about it for a while.

"I'll tell you a story. A couple of weeks ago I'm almost home after a day tour and realize I'm out of smokes. So I'm passing the neighborhood Pathmark Supermarket, decide to get a carton. I go in and as soon as I get inside, I see this woman way across the other side by the produce. She has her back to me. Short skirt, great legs, phenomenal ass. I go out of my way to get a look at her. Turns out it's my wife. That answer your question?"

He snorted. "Yeah."

There was a moment of awkward silence. We had about three minutes before the dispatcher would start spitting out jobs. Our division dispatcher was good; he empathized with us street scum, probably did his time in some hellhole, and would hold back jobs for the first ten minutes of a tour so the troops could have their coffee.

"Okay," I said, "talk to me."

Kenny ran his fingers through his hair. "My wife caught me in bed with another woman."

"Oh, shit, Kenny. Man, I'm sorry."

"Sorry for what? That I got caught or that I was fucking around?"

"Sorry you may be chalking up another bride. What happened?"

"She was supposed to be out of town visiting her sister. I picked up some young broad in a bar after work, brought her home. We fell asleep. Eight o'clock Tuesday morning, Kathy walks in. She came home a day early. She missed me." He was looking out the window at three Hispanic kids climbing a tree in the park.

"I probably know why I did it. Me and Kathy, we've been sorta drifting apart, you know what I mean?"

"Couldn't you have drifted over to the girl's house? What were you thinking?"

"I dunno; maybe I wanted to get caught. You think?"

I didn't know what to think. Pat and I had a good marriage because we worked at it. I never took advantage of her by using The Job as an excuse. I can't tell you how many overtime tours, midnight grand jury appearances, and off-duty arrest excuses are used by cops—all cops, not just NYPD cops—as excuses to cheat.

To my way of thinking, The Job provided enough stress without having to live a double life at home. My home and family were my escape, the only place where I could be myself, unwind, and relax. I didn't need the worry of some bimbo I banged showing up on my doorstep.

"So what did you do when she walked in on you?"

He shrugged. "I denied it."

I was puzzled. "I thought you said the girl was in your bed."

"She was. Kathy flipped, the girl panicked, grabbed her clothes and ran out the door. I told my wife to calm down. Told her she was seeing things."

"But she caught you red-handed. How the hell do you talk yourself out of that?"

"For the last two days I've been telling her she imagined it."

"What're you hoping for, to drive her crazy? I saw a movie like that once. Hitchcock, I think. Guy tries to convince his wife she's imagining that someone's trying to kill her. Figures she'll flip out, he'll commit her and get all her money."

"I saw the same movie."

"Apparently."

The dispatcher chimed in. "Holding forty-one jobs in the Ninth."

"Jesus," Kenny said, and we poured our remaining coffee out the window. We tossed the Styrofoam cups onto the backseat, where they joined their brethren.

I grabbed the portable radio. "Sector Frank, Central, what've you got hot?"

"Let's see, I'm holding a maternity—don't think that can wait. I've got a bleeder from a knife fight, perp fled the scene, the loser's already at the hospital. And I've got a report of a vampire at three-twelve East Thirteenth Street, apartment Four-Boy. Nothing further on this one."

A word about delivering babies: I helped bring six children into this world over the course of twenty-two years in uniform. There's nothing remotely readable about delivering a baby. Actually, other than the various odd locations where I helped deliver these kids (elevator, car, restaurant bathroom), maternity cases are all the same. Babies deliver themselves. I stood there like Johnny Bench, sans catcher's mitt, and the tykes shot into my hands. Had a breech once, but by that time the ambulance had arrived. Every now and then a roving reporter from the *Daily News* picked up the radio run and took a picture of me holding a newborn that looked like a boiled chicken. Don't even want to mention the blood and accompanying mess.

I'd like to say there's at least one Wags Gonzalez running around the Ninth, but despite what mothers tell you about how grateful they are that you helped bring their future little mugger into the world, it's rare that a cop gets a namesake.

So . . .

"We'll take the vampire, Central."

A chorus of verbal jabs from other units followed. "Bring a crucifix." "Stop off for some garlic," and a poor Bela Lugosi imitation, "I vant to sock your blood!"

"Yeah," Kenny mumbled, "sock this."

I peeled into traffic.

The complainant who made the 911 call was an elderly Hispanic male with a neck like a turkey. He was waiting in front of the building, a ratty tenement of mostly abandoned apartments known to harbor junkies who used them as shooting galleries.

Directly across the street, a squat, dark-haired man was on his knees in front of another tenement. Beside him was a bucket. He appeared to be scrubbing the sidewalk with a wire brush. We made eye contact and he smiled and waved. I waved back. Wags is my name; community relations is my game.

Our complainant frantically flapped his arms to get our attention. "There's a vampire on the top floor," he told us as we got out of the car. He made the sign of the cross.

"Oh, yeah?" Kenny said. "How do you know it's a vampire?"

The complainant's eyes went wide. "She pays the junkies five dollars to suck their blood. Up there"—he pointed—"in her apartment."

Kenny and I looked at each other and rolled our eyes. "What does she do, bite their necks?"

He nodded. "Yeah, yeah. Sometimes she'll suck their fingers or their arms after she cuts them with a knife."

"She's been doing this how long?" I asked.

"About a year."

"So why call us now?"

"I just heard someone scream for help in her apartment."

It was late afternoon, and the light was dimming fast. The top floor of the building was almost dark, the soot-smeared window at the end of the hallway blocking out what was left of the natural light.

The complainant had told us that the vampire's name was Helen; that's all he knew. As we neared Helen's apartment we heard a muffled scream.

Without exchanging a word, Kenny and I took our places on opposite sides of the door. "Your turn to knock," I said. We drew our guns.

Kenny rapped on the door. "Police, open up!" Another scream, this one louder.

"Your turn to break down the door," Kenny said. So I did.

Old tenement doors are usually very thick and sturdy, but the jambs are less than substantial. One kick and the door went flying.

The fair-size room was black—not unlighted, mind you, just black. Illumination was supplied by a bare bulb, also painted black. The walls and ceiling were painted a matte black, and a black blanket was draped across the window. I could vaguely make out two figures in front of me. Fortunately we came in from a dim hallway and my night vision kicked in almost immediately.

A skinny woman dressed all in, you guessed it, black was hovering over another, even thinner woman tied to a chair with thick rope. She was stripped to the waist, her bra and sweatshirt were on the floor, and her left arm was bleeding. The woman over her appeared to be sucking her victim's arm.

Our supposed vampire straightened up and growled at us. Her teeth were filed to points and blood dripped from her mouth. She wasn't carrying any weapons. This had to be Helen.

"Back off!" I shouted.

Kenny said, "Jesus, look at this nut."

Helen hissed. I guess she thought the growl wasn't effective. Her prisoner screamed. I holstered my gun.

"Okay," I said in a calm voice, "back up against the wall." Kenny was maneuvering behind her.

Helen said, "Fuck you!"

"Hey," Kenny said, sounding offended, "a vampire's not supposed to say that. Be nice and go up against the wall."

Helen flashed her nails, also filed to sharp points and at least two inches long. She hissed again. The prisoner flipped the chair over trying to get free from her restraints.

I had no desire to get close to those nails. I sighed. "I've had enough of this shit." I took three giant steps to Vampira and laid her out with one slap from a spring-loaded sap.

End of problem.

A weepy, undulating autumn rain was falling as we watched an ambulance take Helen's victim to St. Vincent's Hospital. "I guess she didn't need the five bucks," I said.

Helen was secured inside a straitjacket for her trip to a padded room. Her last name was Rosen, she was thirty-nine, and according to her, she had been a vampire ever since getting bitten on the neck by a rabid wolf while journeying through Transylvania in search of Dracula. The closest I thought she'd ever come to being bitten on the neck was getting a hickey from a horny fifteen-year-old boy in Canarsie High School. Helen had some identity problems. I was certain Bellevue would set her straight or hang her from her ankles so she'd feel right at home.

We had a pile of paperwork to write. "C'mon," Kenny said, "we'll pick up some Chinese before we go to the house."

No one would be looking for us for a while, so a detour to Sam Wo's in Chinatown sounded reasonable. Sam Wo's was virtually unknown to anyone other than Chinatown residents and cops until Woody Allen mentioned it in his movie *Manhattan*. After that it turned into a must-see for every tourist from Westchester who wanted to be a real New Yorker. Happily, we were still a few years away from that.

What surprised me about crazy Helen wasn't so much that we faced down an honest-to-God vampire (well, sort of—the woman drank at least a quart of blood a day), but that the whole episode didn't faze me.

At this point, I'd been on The Job only a little over three years, but even six months in the Ninth Precinct was like a lifetime anywhere else. I also had no compunctions about hitting a woman, even though I wouldn't have put Helen in the same category as June Cleaver. My life was changing a little at a time, but I failed to notice, and neither did my family. When I was home I was a different person.

"Hey, Wags," Kenny said as I slipped the car into gear, my stomach growling and bird's nest soup calling my name, "what's with this guy?"

Our squat friend was still across the street scrubbing away despite the fine mist of rain. "Wanna see?" I asked.

"Sure, why not?" Kenny said.

The man with the wire brush looked up from a kneeling position and smiled. He was wearing a bulky sweater and khaki pants, both soaked through, and GI jump boots. "Good evening, Officers."

"Yeah, good evening," I said. "May I ask what you're doing?"

"Preparing."

Kenny said, "Preparing what?"

"Preparing for the end." Despite being olive-skinned and swarthy, he had the brightest blue eyes I'd ever seen. He saw that we were puzzled. He grinned.

"Allow me to introduce myself," he said with a flourish and a half-assed bow. "My name is Oric Bovar, and I'm the pastor of the Church of Everlasting Life. This is our place of worship." He gestured toward the building behind us, which looked to me like every other tenement on the block, although with cleaner windows.

"We believe that the end is near, and we are readying ourselves for that eventuality. Cleaning our living and working area is part of our preparation." He explained that he had just thirteen "parishioners" and they all lived in the tenement. I was thinking maybe Helen was one of Bovar's followers.

The rain came down harder. I'd heard all I wanted to hear; one nut was enough for the tour. "C'mon, Kenny," I said. "Sam Wo's awaits." Bovar smiled serenely. It could have been raining pigs for all he cared.

As we neared the radio car Bovar called, "Kenny," just loud enough to be heard over the common noise of the city. He sounded like he'd known Kenny for years, rather than having heard his name for the first time just minutes ago.

We turned to find Bovar back on his knees, brush in hand, a radiant smile on his face. He had dazzling white teeth and they glistened through the falling rain.

"Yeah?" Kenny said, slipping into the front seat.

Bovar pointed toward the low-slung clouds. "Death from above."

Kenny said nothing. I rolled my eyes and we drove out of there. I hadn't gone three blocks when I had completely forgotten about Oric Bovar and his Temple of Doom or whatever the hell he called his church.

Kenny was closemouthed. I figured he was still stressing over his wife catching him in bed with the bimbo and the distinct possibility that he'd just written off marriage number three.

I was willing to talk with him, offer advice, do whatever I could to help him, but I wasn't about to volunteer my services until I was asked.

When we reached the narrow streets of Chinatown, Kenny said, "Hey, Wags, this guy Bovar, he gives me the creeps." He was staring straight out the windshield, his voice flat.

I almost said, "Bovar who?" Thoughts of one from Column A and one from Column B occupied my mind. "What about him?"

"Death from above. You know what that is?"

I double-parked in front of the restaurant. Sometimes The Job has its benefits. "Yeah, the ramblings of a nut."

"I was in the First Cav in Vietnam. We were an airmobile unit. 'Death from Above' was our motto."

THE RUNAWAY AND THE HELL'S ANGELS

Kenny became obsessed with Oric Bovar. Whenever he was driving, he made sure to pass Bovar's building. Sometimes we'd do this five, six times a day. He couldn't get "Death from Above" out of his mind. More than once he asked Bovar what he meant by the remark. Each time, Bovar smiled that mystical smile of his and changed the subject or ignored Kenny completely. It drove my partner nuts.

"How'd he know I was in the Cav? Huh? I ask you, how'd he know?"

"What makes you think he knew you were in the First Cav or the friggin' first grade? C'mon, Kenny, that coulda meant anything, like a flowerpot was gonna come down on your head, the sky's falling, anything. The guy's a whack."

"I dunno about that."

Kenny's wife had left him. I thought he was losing it. He had no appetite, had gotten thinner, and had stopped ironing those military creases in his uniform shirts.

It was a little after eight P.M. on a November night and autumn was making a frigid exit. Still, there was Bovar under a streetlight on the sidewalk in front of his building. Only now, instead of scrubbing the sidewalk, he was painting it.

"What's he doing?" Kenny asked for the second time as we passed the little guy with his paintbrush in hand.

"Kenny," I said, a little exasperated, "who gives a damn. He's painting the sidewalk. Who cares?"

"I gotta know." We got out of the car and walked across the street.

"Good morning, Kenny, Wags." We were on a first-name basis by this time.

"I don't suppose you want to tell us why you're painting the sidewalk?" I said. He had painted a neat red circle, about the size of basketball, right in the middle of the sidewalk.

"Pre—"

I raised my nonshooting hand, "Yeah, I know, preparing. C'mon, Kenny."

Kenny stood his ground. "So when's the end coming?" He tried to make the comment light, but I read something much deeper into it. Kenny wanted an answer.

"When I decide. I'll go first, then come back and tell my flock they have nothing to fear from death."

There was a moment of silence. I thought Kenny was about to ask Bovar a question when the portable blared.

"Sector Charlie available?"

Kenny keyed the radio. "Charlie."

"We've got numerous reports of a fight at the Ritz. Hell's Angels may be involved."

The Ritz was a nightclub located on Eleventh Street, between Third and Fourth avenues, and was a popular watering hole for the Hell's Angels.

Normally the club policed itself, hiring enough bouncers to nip any fight in the bud before it got out of hand, but you can have a bouncer contingent larger than the First Panzer Division, and it's going to do you no good when the Angels get frisky.

Even if just two Angels cause a ruckus and get tossed out of a club, you can bet that those two will return, bringing forty of their biker buddies to level the place.

The cops of the Ninth Precinct and the Angels maintained a grudging respect for each other. A lot of the Angels were Vietnam vets (some went back to the Korean War), as were quite a few cops. And cops, for the most part, are very orderly, regimented people who adhere to a list of rules that would make a dominatrix proud. Angels, too, live by a strict code, and despite what the press led readers to believe, the Angels were for the most part law-abiding citizens. Except when you fucked with one of them.

They didn't bother us and we didn't bother them. When Kenny and I drove by their club-house (which is still there, by the way) we'd wave and they'd wave back. Very civil.

We pulled in front of the Ritz with four sector cars, sirens blaring, right behind us for backup. Since this was a fight possibly involving the Hell's Angels, we could use all the backup we could get.

There were three bodies on the street, bruised and battered, but breathing. These were the bouncers, big, muscle-bound, and unconscious. Inside the foyer, two more bouncers were nursing head wounds, and the manager, a tall, well-built guy with a neck full of gold chains, was arguing with six burly Angels, one of whom had to weigh four hundred pounds. The big guy was wearing a leather vest with no shirt, sporting full-sleeve tattoos.

When the manager, a mob-connected wanna-be with slicked-back hair that looked like it was brushed with a buttered roll, spotted me, he began screaming. "I want these motherfuckers arrested! They wiped out my security team!" He ranted for a minute about the murderous Angels whom he wanted to get locked up for life (if not longer). "They attacked my men with no fucking provocation!"

The gorilla in the vest, who introduced himself as Big Vinny, calmly explained the Angels' side of the story.

"That's not how it happened, Officer. The shithead outside with the black jacket cornered one of our brothers in the john and started pushing him around." He indicated a smaller (by comparison) Angel who was wiping blood from his forehead with a cocktail napkin.

"Yeah, that's what happened," the head bleeder said.

"So we found the mutts," Big Vinny said, "and defended our friend. Simple street justice. You gotta lock us up, do what you gotta do."

I was impressed that the Angels had stuck around. Had they gone to the clubhouse, it would have taken a frontal assault by a regiment of cops to extract them.

We were twelve people, including the backup cops, jammed into a small foyer. Since my sector had the job, we had to make some kind of a decision as to who was getting locked up, if anyone, before the fight resumed.

I grabbed the manager by the arm. "Can I talk to you alone?" I asked. I ushered him into the street without waiting for an answer.

"Listen," I said. "We lock these guys up then your guys go, too."

"I don't give a fuck!" He was hot. "I'll have my men out in a few hours. These assholes gotta learn a lesson. Bust up my men, no fucking way."

I put my arm around him and took him out of earshot of passersby. "You're not thinking. They're gonna get out, too, you know? You want these guys coming back? Maybe with their friends? Besides, who was wrong here? You know, me and my partner, we've got better things to do than break up fights. Maybe next time we'll take our time getting here. Get my drift?"

He thought about it. "Yeah, yeah, okay."

We went back into the club. Kenny gave the Angels a half-assed dressing-down—in private. They left, and we went back on patrol.

An hour later we were in Ya Ya's, a coffee shop on Fourteenth Street where you could get a decent burger without going into cardiac arrest. As I was paying the check, I heard the ear-splitting and easily identifiable roar of Harley-Davidson motorcycles.

Outside at least a dozen chopped bikes were pulling up on either side of our parked radio car. The riders wore the unmistakable colors of the Hell's Angels. They cut their engines and sat on their machines, waiting.

The handful of patrons in the coffee shop stopped what they were doing and looked at us, then the Angels, then back again. Like a tennis match.

"Oh, shit," Kenny said. "I think we've got a problem." He reached for the radio. I stopped him.

"What're they gonna do, kill two cops in uniform in front of witnesses?"

"Maybe just fuck us up a little. These guys don't give a shit about anything."

"C'mon, let's see what they have to say." I unlocked my revolver from its safety holster, just in case.

We went outside and stood on the sidewalk. The bikers stared at us. The whole spectacle was surreal, like a scene from the movie *High Noon,* magnified.

One of the bikers dismounted and walked toward us. I put him at about thirty, a little under six feet tall, wavy black hair, and built like a bodybuilder. His denim jacket was opened, stretched at the shoulders.

"You guys handle the Ritz thing?" he asked calmly. He was almost nose-to-nose with Kenny.

"Yeah," Kenny and I said in unison.

The biker extended his hand. "Name's Chuck Zito." Handshakes all around. "I want to thank you for treating my brothers like gentlemen. It doesn't happen too often."

"Just doing our job," I said. John Wayne, or what?

"I think it was a little more than your job. You need a favor—anything—you call me." He handed me a card. "Anytime." With that he got back on his bike, and the outlaws screamed down Fourteenth Street.

We stood there a few seconds. Kenny broke the ice.

"See, piece of cake."

"Turned out better than I thought."

Kenny said, "You can trash that card. If we ever need those guys, we've got a problem."

It turned out we did indeed end up needing the Hell's Angels' help despite Kenny's thoughts to the contrary. Fortunately, I held on to the card.

About a month later, close to Christmas, we were turning out for a four-to-twelve, and Sergeant Reddy had just finished conducting the roll call. As was department policy, he read us a list of unsolved crimes, wanted persons, and other items of interest to conscientious, intelligent, caring cops. And us, too.

In recent months we'd been getting a lot of reports of runaways. After a while they all sounded the same: female, white, fifteen to seventeen years old, from some tiny town in the Midwest, ran away after telling friends she was headed for New York, where she would live among the flower children, protest the war, and get high. Didn't sound like too bad an idea.

Anyway, New York City is a big place. The odds of finding one of these waifs was infinitesimal. The case Sergeant Reddy was telling us about, however, was different.

It started out the same, female, white, etc., but that's where the similarities ended.

"This kid," Reddy said, referring to his report, "is Lisa Anderson." He passed around copies of Lisa's picture, a fresh-faced kid who made Doris Day in her prime look like a slut. "She called her mom in some town called Milton Freewater, Washington, two days ago saying she was being held prisoner in a building on Thirteenth Street in Manhattan. Then she was cut off. We don't know if it's East or West Thirteenth, which would put her in the Sixth Precinct, but we gotta check East Thirteenth, which is ours. Talk to your snitches; see what you can find out. Take your posts and, hey . . . Be careful out there."

During the course of the tour we talked to the street people, who seemed to know everything about everybody within their own little world. We never expected to find out anything useful; we were just doing our job.

"Yeah, I seen her," said a junkie with the street name of Charcoal, so named because of his unwashed face. "Somewheres over on Thirteenth Street."

My adrenaline began pumping. "Where exactly, Charcoal? You gotta be specific."

He stroked his stubbly chin. "I dunno . . . hold it, it was three-twelve, yeah, three-twelve, that was it."

Helen the Vampire's building.

I rewarded Charcoal with three bags of the finest confiscated China White and we raced to the tenement.

Oric Bovar was sitting on his stoop admiring his handiwork. The red circle on the pavement was now surrounded by a blue circle. It had taken him a month to paint the latest addition to his work of art. A real perfectionist. Also a goddamn polar bear. It had to be twenty degrees and he was wearing his now-familiar sweater and khakis with the same boots.

"Hey, Oric," Kenny said, "you seen this girl?" He waved the picture out the window. Bovar ambled over like he was marching up the aisle with a new bride.

"Oh, certainly, Kenny. She lives across the street. Don't know what apartment, though."

We knew the building was full of junkies. "Seen her lately?"

He shook his head. "Not for at least a few days. Kind of cold, you know? These people don't have much money for clothes."

Yeah, I thought, all their money goes for heroin. "She seem, you know, under restraint, like she's a prisoner?"

"Now that you mention it, I've never seen her alone. She's always with someone, always a man. Could be she's being held against her will."

I called for Sergeant Reddy. He met us around the block. No sense in alerting the enemy.

"Goddamn building," he said. "All the years I've been here it's nothing but trouble. Stabbings, shootings, ODs—"

"Let's not forget the vampire," Kenny said.

We formed a plan of attack. Sergeant Reddy assembled those who were available from the remaining sectors, which included Foster and Laurie and Frank Moran, who was still wandering around the wrong foot post.

"Okay," Reddy said, "it's gonna be a full-frontal assault." Foster and Laurie took the first floor; the sergeant and his driver, Glover, took the second floor; and Kenny and I took the third and fourth floors. Moran went around back to the alley to scoop up any escapees.

While this was the dawning of the era of guarding one's constitutional rights, cops from the Ninth generally ignored the first several amendments when dealing with junkies or violent felons. We hadn't the time to apply for search warrants or play nice-nice with whomever might be living—if you could call it that—in those crash pads and shooting galleries. A kid's life was at stake; screw the Constitution.

Kenny and I broke down doors like Patton invading Italy. Out of four apartments on the third floor, one was vacant and the remaining three were littered with passed-out junkies, lying amid used spikes, twisted bottle caps, spent matches, and the occasional cast-aside condom. We left the nodding junkies to their heroin-induced dream states and tossed the lucid junkies into the street, but not before showing them a picture of Lisa Anderson.

One strung-out hophead admitted seeing her on the fourth floor, but gave that information up only when I gave him a nickel bag of smack from the stash in my memo book. Who knew if he was telling the truth.

We scored in the first apartment we hit on the fourth floor. The one-bedroom pad hadn't been legitimately rented in years. The one window in the bedroom had been shattered during the Kennedy administration, and a cable ran from a nearby lamppost on the street through the window to pirate city power for light.

A lone dim bulb swinging from a rope in the center of the ceiling cast eerie shadows across the room.

The only piece of furniture was a beat-up brass bed with a sagging bare mattress at the far end of the room. On that bed, facedown, naked and unmoving, was a young woman.

She was on her stomach and tied with rope sideways across the bed. Her arms and legs were secured to opposite ends of the rusted metal bed frame, her legs spread wide enough to kick a field goal through.

Blood and dry, caked semen adhered to her buttocks and thighs. Her back was scratched; dry scabs ran down its length. The picture we had of Lisa showed her with long, flowing auburn hair, shiny and healthy. Now her hair was matted and dirty. Someone had butchered her long tresses with what might have been nail clippers. Her hair was chopped, short and uneven.

I turned her head to one side to see if she was breathing and saw the remnants of semen caked on the side of her face.

Lisa Anderson was being used as a sex receptacle for any junkie who passed through the apartment.

"She's alive," I said, as if her current state could be called living.

"Jesus fucking Christ," Kenny said.

A cop sees a lot of misery during the course of his career, and I'd seen my share, but the sight of this kid—that's all she was, a kid—sexually abused and debased in this shithole, when she should have been going to high school dances in her small town of Milton Berle, or wherever the hell she lived, incensed me.

"Check the other room," I told Kenny. I was mumbling a tirade of "motherfuckers" and worse as I cut the kid free with a pocketknife.

"No one here," Kenny reported back. He got on the portable. "Central, Nine Charlie. Send a bus to three-twelve East Thirteenth Street, top floor, ASAP. We've got an unconscious white female, about fifteen, the victim of a gang—" He stopped and chose his words carefully. ". . . sexual attack. Fast, Central, okay?"

Cops began to fill the room. I brushed by them after blurting out, "Crime scene!" and headed for the last occupied apartment we'd found. I was livid, and the junkies were going to pay. Sergeant Reddy was right behind me.

He spun me around as I reached the stairway. "Where the hell you going?"

I yanked my arm away. "I'm gonna throw a junkie out a fucking window." I got one step before the sergeant grabbed my pistol belt.

"Oh, no, you're not. What's that gonna solve? You kick some junkie's ass, maybe kill him, you go to jail. For what?"

"Sarge, the kid—"

"Yeah, yeah, I know—the kid. I've got kids, too." He backed me up against the wall. "There's always a better way. Think."

So I thought.

* * *

Kenny and I accompanied the ambulance to Bellevue. The girl was as yet officially unidentified, and we had a pile of paperwork to do. We needed a preliminary diagnosis from a doctor.

A young female intern, visibly shaken, met us in the hallway outside of the ER.

"Her insides are ripped apart. Multiple contusions, vaginal wall tears. Jesus, she's a mess. Someone apparently held her mouth open with a tool, might be pliers, and three of her teeth have been knocked out."

She talked; I wrote and kept quiet. I was formulating a plan, and the only person who was going to share in it was Kenny. "She gonna be okay, Doc?"

The intern snorted. "The vaginal damage was inflicted with something other than the male penis. We're still checking for further abuse. She'll make it—physically. I gotta get back."

I found a pay phone in the lobby and called the Angels' clubhouse on East Third Street.

Chuck Zito met with Kenny and me by Tompkins Square Park. He was on foot and alone, per my request. A thundering herd of Harleys wasn't conducive to keeping a low profile.

I told him the story.

After a few dozen expletives he finally said, "You believe this? My teenage daughter's name's Lisa. Fucking junkies—I hate 'em."

"Listen," I said, "we need a favor. What they did to that girl—"

Chuck held up a hand attached to a sinewy forearm. "Don't say anything; you'll be hearing from me." And with that he turned and left.

Two days later, Kenny and I were doing our last four-to-twelve. It was getting close to quitting time during what had been a particularly busy tour. Nothing like the approach of the holiday season to bring out the murderous inclinations of New Yorkers, at least in our little end of the city.

Our radio beeped three times. A dispatcher will utilize beeps only when the next job is serious and he needs to get everyone's attention. Immediately.

"Units in the Ninth Precinct, we've got a report of a gang fight on Thirteenth Street between Avenues C and D. At least five calls on this, reporting numerous bodies all over the street."

The Ninth Precinct is small. As soon as the call came over I heard blaring sirens, converging from all sectors in the command. Sector Adam was the first to respond. "We're going, Central." All other sectors that weren't out on jobs backed up.

"Nine Charlie's backing, too, Central," I said and flipped on the turret lights.

"Gee," Kenny said, "wonder what this could be?"

The street looked like a battle zone. There were fifteen unconscious men and women littering the gutter. All had taken bad beatings, some worse than others, but would live, if you can call going through life with two broken kneecaps living. The winners were nowhere to be found. These beatings were administered by professionals.

A thick-linked chain coupled by a padlock the size of a corn muffin secured the front of building number three-twelve.

"I guess these folks are the former tenants," I said.

Kenny shook his head. "The streets of Saigon looked better after Tet."

Ambulances were pouring into the block; cops were canvassing for witnesses. Across the street, Oric Bovar was in his usual spot on the sidewalk, this time without his can of paint.

"I gotta ask, Oric, you see anything?" I said.

He looked at me, unsmiling. "It pains me to witness such violence, Wags."

"That mean you saw something?"

"See what?"

The building stayed chained and vacant. The victims of the assault suffered amnesia as part of their injuries, undoubtedly induced by promises of things to come.

The police—that would be us—professionals that we were, established that four males wearing long leather dusters marched into the building and began throwing out the non-rent-paying residents shortly thereafter.

Rumors to the effect that members of the Hell's Angels had been involved in the massacre were proven to be unfounded. No one saw any motorcycles, and what self-respecting Angel would be without his bike or his colors?

So what became of those involved? Lisa Anderson was taken home by her family. Neither she nor her family ever contacted us, and Lisa was unable to identify her assailants. We weren't looking for thank-yous. We're cops. The last person to thank us did so after being shot only once, instead of a dozen times.

Later, Chuck Zito became an actor and could be seen playing the part of Pancamo in the hit HBO series *Oz*. He was a damn good actor, and there was talk of his getting his own television series. You could hear him occasionally on the Howard Stern show, too. He'd found his niche.

Big Vinny is no longer with us, having succumbed to a heart attack in the early '70s. He had one helluva send-off. The funeral was held at the Provenzano-Lanza Funeral Home on Second Avenue.

Over a thousand Hell's Angels from all over the world attended the funeral, and FDR Drive had to be closed from Houston Street to the Bronx to accommodate the mass of motorcycles.

Big Vinny's bike was driven right into the funeral home and parked next to his casket. A mural of Vinny, painted by Zito, adorned the wall of a tenement next to the Angels' clubhouse for years, until the building was demolished. A memorial beneath the painting read, *In memory of Big Vinny. When in doubt, knock 'em out.*

And Oric Bovar? He was to change my life dramatically.

THE SQUAD, PART III: KENNY KENRICK

One day Frank Moran vanished.

He had shown up straight from Cal's for a day tour, drunk but able to navigate. It seemed that the only time he wasn't drinking was when he was boxing. He would stay sober for two days prior to a bout, for which he didn't train. He would invariably lose, getting his brains further scrambled in the process. The last we saw of him that fateful morning, he was strolling toward Third Avenue to walk the foot post of his choice.

The prevailing attitude on The Job back then was to protect drunks as long as they weren't hurting themselves or anyone else. These days, if a cop shows up for work smelling of Listerine someone will turn him in.

But with Frank Moran, there was little the bosses wanted to do with him, other than protect his job. Sympathy for the death of his brother and how it had affected him had taken priority over their responsibility to the citizens of New York. Besides, cops and bosses from the Ninth stuck together. It was bad enough the rest of the world was trying to bump us off; at least we had each other.

Frank had been a damn good cop at one time and everyone liked him. Now that his retirement was but a few years away, no one saw the need to jam him up. If he was crying for help it would have been a different story, but he was content to survive day to day, wandering around the precinct on foot and handling minor street altercations.

Initially, it was thought that he was off on a bender somewhere, but when hours led to days and then to weeks, a natural alarm was sounded. Was there a new terrorist group out there targeting cops? Did they assassinate him? Kidnap him?

Kenny and I had our own theories. If Moran was a victim of BLA-like terrorists, whether as a murder or kidnap victim, someone most certainly would have claimed credit, because that's what terrorists do. To terrorize, one must publicize (thank you, Johnnie Cochran).

"He probably kept walking west and fell into the Hudson. Bet he washes up during the spring thaw," Kenny said. The emergence of spring invariably brought numerous bodies bobbing to the surface. You could set a watch by it.

"I think he just got fed up and took off," I said. "Enough is enough. Too much death in this precinct."

We were both partially right. After two weeks, the FBI got involved because of the possible terrorist angle. If it happened once with the BLA it could happen again.

They traced Moran to Cooperstown, in upstate New York. Turns out he headed north, as Kenny had predicted, and chose Cooperstown as his new home because the Baseball Hall of Fame is located there. It seems Moran was a fan. Enough *had* been enough, as I'd predicted, and he'd just boogied.

He was charged with being AWOL and quitting The Job without the permission of the police commissioner, both serious offenses. You can't take a piss on The Job without the PC's okay. Moran was fired, losing all pension rights.

Funny thing is, he could have fought the charges. His alcoholism and the death of his brother may have caused a mental breakdown, thereby resulting in his aberrant behavior. That angle would have at least saved his pension. But he chose not to have anything further to do with the NYPD, took his punishment, and settled into a new life upstate.

Kenny and I were the last of the original Sixth Squad. Of course, replacements were immediately assigned as our numbers dwindled, but we didn't get friendly with the new troops. This was a subtle, subconscious way of avoiding undue grief should something happen to them.

Kenny figured it out. "Did the same thing in Vietnam," he told me one night. "You've got your inner core of friends within an infantry squad, usually your assistant gunner and ammo bearer if you were a machine gunner like me, but you kept your distance from the rest of the platoon. If you don't know them that well, you can't be too broken up if they buy it."

Kenny was still struggling with his inner demons. His appearance, while by no means sloppy, was decidedly unmilitary. He still wore his jump boots, and they were always polished, but they didn't blind you with their usual spit-shine. His shirts were ironed, but without the razor creases he'd sported when I had first arrived in the command.

I don't subscribe to the Vietnam vet theory that was, and still is, popular in this country. Anytime a veteran of the Vietnam War begins to act weird, his troubles are usually automatically attributed to his combat experiences.

While any war recollections can be disturbing, I can name numerous friends who survived the Vietnam War, and its unpleasant memories, and went on to live normal, productive lives.

Kenny's funk, I believe, had more to do with the police department and what he'd seen on the mean streets of New York over an extended period of time. His street experiences had directly contributed to his failed marriages. His Vietnam memories, if anything, were a crutch on which he relied for escape from the frustrations of the present. Most cops get divorced, but most cops didn't fight in Vietnam. To Kenny, the military was a symbol of order, with clearly defined rules and authority. The streets of the EVil were just so much disarray.

One of the reasons a person becomes a police officer is because crime offends his or her sense of order, and the military is the quintessential orderly lifestyle. The inability to create order out of the chaos puts some cops over the edge, particularly those with a military background. Kenny followed that pattern.

On a brisk March night there was a break in the action.

"Pull over; I want to talk to this guy," Kenny said. He pointed to a skinny white male, about twenty-five, in jeans and an army field jacket, complete with buck sergeant's stripes, unit patch (First Infantry Division), and a Combat Infantry badge. He was unshaven, his hair was long and scraggly, and he carried a crudely scrawled cardboard sign that read, VIETNAM VET NEEDS FOOD AND SHELTER.

We'd seen this character standing on a corner near Tompkins Square Park for about a week. At his feet was an upended U.S. Army dress cap, an invitation to contribute money.

I pulled the car over. GI Joe threw back his shoulders and flipped us a sharp salute, but not before scooping a pile of bills out of his hat. "Evening, Officers." His eyes sparkled with a joviality that belied his appearance.

"Yeah, good evening," Kenny said. "You been to Vietnam?"

"Yes, sir. Big Red One, sixty-five to sixty-six. You guys, too?"

"Just me, First Cav. My partner's a draft dodger." Kenny and the former GI laughed. "Boonie humper?"

"Did my bit as an Eleven-B-Ten—rifleman with the Sixteenth Infantry."

"Hitting on hard times?" Kenny inquired.

"Some. You don't mind if I try to hustle up some dough, do you? Got nowhere to live; my wife threw me out. Need some seed money. You know what I mean?" He winked.

"Yeah," Kenny responded, "I know what you mean. You take it easy, okay?"

"Yes, sir." He got another highball salute, sharp and crisp.

We got back in the car and drove in silence for a while; then Kenny said quietly, "Drive by the house, would you, Jimmy?"

"You feeling okay?"

"Yeah. I just want to test Sergeant Rock back there. Need to get something."

"You don't think he's on the level? He seemed to have all the right answers."

Kenny snorted. "He had the answers, but not the eyes."

"Meaning?"

We pulled in front of the station house. "Meaning the Thousand-Mile Stare. He don't have it."

The Thousand-Mile Stare is the look a combat veteran will get when he's seen too much death. It's a dull, vacant expression that extends outward from the eyes—the true definition of a poker face. I knew this because more than a few of the cops in the Ninth had that look. They could be recognized as cops from a considerable distance. I practiced in front of a mirror to avoid getting "the look," with only moderate success. I think I'm the proud owner of a Five-Hundred-Mile Stare, but I'm working on it. I still have it, even after ten years of retirement. Kenny had a Two-Thousand-Mile Stare.

Kenny went into the station house while I monitored the radio. The Ninth was backed up over ten jobs, and I was getting more than a little fidgety when Kenny finally emerged, carrying a piece of rolled-up cardboard.

"What's that?" I asked.

"Tell you later."

"C'mon," I said, "we've gotta take something; Adam's picking up our jobs."

"Okay," Kenny said, settling in. He keyed the radio and picked up a past burglary on Avenue B. "Back to our friend first. The burglar's long gone; the complainant can wait a few minutes."

I humored him and made for the park. The ex-soldier, or whoever he was, still stood on the same corner. We waved; he saluted. I pulled the radio car to the curb in front of him. We got another smile.

"Back so soon, Officers?" There was a wariness in his voice despite his outward conviviality.

Kenny unrolled the cardboard. With a felt-tip black marker he'd written, *I CORPS*. He turned it so that the panhandler could see it. "Tell me what this says."

The ex-soldier laughed nervously. "What's this all about?"

Kenny smiled, but I saw no humor in his eyes. "My partner and I are having a little disagreement. Maybe you can help us out. What's this say?" The last sentence was forceful, the friendliness gone.

The panhandler stepped back from the car and examined the sign, brows knit. He licked his lips. "Uh, it says, 'One Corp.'" He said it with a hard P.

Kenny turned to me. "See, numbnuts, I was right."

I played along, mystified. "When you're right, you're right."

The former soldier seemed to deflate. He smiled. Kenny smiled.

"You hang in there, buddy," Kenny said. "We gotta go."

We got another salute, and I pulled out.

"What the hell was that all about?"

"He failed the test." Kenny pointed down the street. "Stop around the corner and park."

"We're on the clock, Kenny . . . the past burglary."

"Fuck the past burglary; pull around the corner." There was fire in his eyes.

I was getting hot, too. "We're going to the goddamn job." I accelerated. He grabbed my arm. His voice softened. "Jimmy, please, a few more minutes, okay?"

There was pleading in the request, an urgency. I pulled around the corner.

It was a little after ten o'clock. The streets around the park were dark and nearly deserted. Junkies don't like the cold. The few stragglers still out and about were waiting for a late delivery from Junkies R Us.

Kenny opened the door and looked at me, grinning. "I'll be right back, dear; keep a light on." Manic. Panicked one second, jovial the next.

As I watched him walk away, curiosity got the better of me. I got out of the car and poked my head around the corner.

Kenny ambled up to the panhandler. They talked, but I couldn't hear what they were saying. Kenny pointed across the street to an alley and they both walked toward it. They had left my field of vision, so I crossed the street for a better angle.

Kenny backed the veteran into the mouth of the alley, out of the glare of the street's only lamppost. What the hell was Kenny doing?

Then I saw the gun.

Kenny had drawn his service revolver and stuck it in the soldier's gut. I looked around to see if anyone else had seen it. Other than a few nervous, strung-out, oblivious junkies looking for their connections, the block was empty.

The soldier was giving Kenny money, emptying his pockets in furious movements, while Kenny stuffed his pockets with cash. After what seemed like an eternity, the soldier held up his hands. Kenny reared back and laid the barrel of his Smith & Wesson across the panhandler's face.

Blood spattered from his nose and he went down. Kenny holstered his gun and started for the car. I ran across the street and cut him off, grabbed his shoulder, and spun him around.

"What the fuck did you do?"

Kenny's eyes were wild. "In the car, in the car." He broke loose, walked rapidly toward the radio car, and got in. I climbed in after him, envisioning a small army of bosses from Internal Affairs at my doorstep in the morning.

I left rubber and made for the East River, the past burglary we were supposed to be handling a distant memory.

We drove in silence. I slammed the car into park after I backed onto a secluded, deserted pier. "Talk to me."

"The cocksucker was a liar." Kenny was breathing heavily, his eyes wide as hubcaps, his head nodding. "He's never been to Vietnam."

What was happening? "A liar . . . what liar? You held the son of a bitch up! At friggin' gunpoint!"

"The sign," Kenny said, calming down, "it says *Eye Corp,* like eyeball, and a soft P. Every soldier that ever passed through Vietnam knows that. It's the northernmost sector—"

"I don't give a fuck!" I was livid. "You stuck him up, for crissakes. We lock people up for that." Kenny exploded.

"That motherfucker has no right! He has no right! Soldiers died; they died!" He spun in his seat, facing me. "Cops're dying, too, man; there's nobody left. That cocksucker is disgracing every cop and soldier who ever wore a uniform!"

I tried to be calm, the voice of reason. "Kenny, he's a con artist; the uniform's got nothing to do with it. Next week he'll be a priest or Ronald McDonald. You can't take this shit personally. You should know this by now."

"Oh, yeah? What happens if next week he's a fucking cop? What happens if next week he's wearing Rocco Laurie's fucking shield number? Huh? What then?"

Kenny was making absolutely no sense. At least not to me. A few seconds later he began pounding his fists on the dashboard. Tears came to his eyes; then they unleashed in a flood— tears for every cop and soldier who was ever killed, tears for his inability to maintain a relationship, tears for the hopelessness of it all.

I let him cry. After a while I put a hand on his shoulder. I hoped that my presence wasn't embarrassing him. He didn't seem to notice.

We never handled that past burglary. Kenny had me drive to a church off Broadway, where he gave all the money he'd just stolen to an astonished priest. I put us out of service, drove to the station house, and Kenny went sick. He headed straight to the locker room to change while I checked in with Sergeant Reddy.

"What's wrong with your partner?" Reddy asked.

"Something he ate, Sarge. I've got some time on the books; can I follow him home, make sure he makes it?"

Being stupid is not one of the prerequisites for becoming a sergeant. Sergeant Reddy knew something wasn't right, but in the Ninth we stuck together.

"No problem. Call me if you need anything."

My calls to Kenny's apartment went unanswered. After two days I drove by his building and found his car parked around the corner. I debated knocking on his door and decided to come back later that day. After dinner I went back and found that his car had been moved to the front of the building. I went home.

Kenny stayed out for the rest of the set. He came back to work after the swing.

It was a new Kenny Kenrick who came through the door of the station house for our first day tour.

"Yo, Jimmy, how's it hanging?"

He was smiling from ear to ear. His formerly dead eyes sparkled.

"You high?" I asked, only half joking.

"Yeah, buddy, on life." And with that he bounded up the stairs toward the locker room, his uniform slung across his shoulder in a garment bag.

Kenny stood roll call like part of the honor guard for the Unknown Soldier. His boots were polished to an eyetearing shine.

"How the hell do you do that?" Jim Liedy asked, admiring the best spit-shine I'd ever seen.

"Cotton balls, tap water, shoe polish, and six hours," Kenny said.

Liedy shook his head. "I think you gotta get laid more."

"Job's fucked me enough," Kenny said, and laughed. The military creases were back. Even his pistol belt, cuff case, and holster were spit-shined.

Kenny took some good-natured ribbing. Even Sergeant Reddy doled out a few shots.

"Wags, Kenrick, Sector Charlie, thirteen hundred meal. Kenny, *GQ*'s outside; they wanna do a spread."

Kenny grinned. "Spread this."

I was glad to see him back from the brink. Whatever transpired during the time he was out would forever remain a mystery. I didn't ask and he didn't volunteer any information.

Kenny was positively effervescent in the car. Shortly after the tour began, we found ourselves rolling down St. Marks Place. Kenny pointed to a garishly dressed hippie.

He beckoned him over to the car. This was a young kid, maybe nineteen, wearing blue-and-white bell-bottoms, an orange pirate-type shirt, and a tie-dyed denim jacket. His Mohawk "'do" sported a red-and-purple dye job.

The kid was scared. "Yes, Officer?"

Kenny said, "I had sex with a parrot once, thought maybe you were my son."

I cracked up, the kid caught on and laughed nervously, and Kenny waved him off.

We were pulling off the block when we heard the familiar radio beeps. Five in a row. Trouble. I had my usual testicular tightening. "Oh, shit."

Central: "In the Ninth, we've got a jumper. Front of three-fifteen East Thirteenth Street. Units?"

Kenny keyed the radio. "Frank, central. Victim down or threatening?"

Central: "Off the roof, sidewalk in front of."

It took a moment for the address to register. It was Oric Bovar's building.

We'd seen Bovar in front of his church over the last few months, still painting his sidewalk. Kenny was nervous around him and steered clear when he was driving, and I managed to stay off the block entirely unless we had a job there.

"That's Bovar's—" I started.

"I know," Kenny said ominously.

An ambulance was already on the scene, a crowd just beginning to gather.

Oric Bovar's body, clothed in its usual attire, lay supine in the middle of the sidewalk. He seemed oddly intact, considering he'd made the leap from atop a five-story building.

His eyes were open, and he lay on his back, arms outstretched. Crucified without a cross. A small halo of blood was forming around his head.

"Anyone see this?" I asked the crowd.

Five people stepped forward. All described Bovar on the roof, seemingly praying before he did a swan dive toward the pavement, twisting in midair to land on his back.

I began moving the crowd back. Kenny was shaking his head.

"Jimmy, check this out."

I looked at the body, not realizing what he was referring to. Then I spotted it.

Bovar had landed smack in the middle of his artwork—a bull's-eye.

All those months he'd been painting a goddamn bull's-eye to jump into.

"Jesus Christ," I muttered. I heard more units responding, sirens screaming.

We finally got to see Bovar's church. Six of his "disciples," four men and two women, admitted us after Bovar's body had been carted to the morgue. No tears among the flock, just serenity and good fellowship.

"He had been planning this for months," a young woman with waist-length, raven-colored hair told us.

"He'll be back, you know," another said.

"Back where?" Kenny asked. He seemed to be taking the suicide pretty well. We hadn't been there fifteen minutes and he'd already come up with a lame Bovar joke. (It's a bird, it's a plane . . .!)

"He will rise from the dead," Raven Hair told us.

"Oh, yeah?" Kenny said "When he comes back tell him to give me a call. I want to tell him he was right."

Now it was my turn. "Right about what?"

Kenny smirked. "Death from Above."

Old Oric turned out to be a pretty popular guy. He was laid out in a funeral home on Tenth Street, and it was standing room only. Of course, his followers attended, but a surprising number of politicians and celebrities showed up also. I recall seeing John Belushi and a few *Saturday Night Live* players, plus a few local musicians.

We passed the funeral parlor on the second day of the three-day wake.

"Wanna go in?" I asked Kenny.

"Nah, I'll catch him when he comes back."

Out of the mouths of cops . . .

Bovar did come back.

Bovar's body vanished from the funeral home the following night. We picked up the "missing body" job and went right to Bovar's church.

Sure enough, reposing in a makeshift coffin in an apartment on the top floor, basking in the glow of candlelight and surrounded by a dozen chanting devotees, was Oric Bovar, dead guy.

"Okay," Kenny announced, "you're all under arrest."

"What for?" one of them asked.

"Harboring a dead body," Kenny responded, sounding officious. "It's a misdemeanor."

"But he's not dead," a woman said (she actually looked worse than Oric). "He's in a state of transposition. He's returning."

"Good," I said, "then he'll be here when you get back."

We called the morgue wagon, booked the kooky cluster ("See," Kenny said, "smooth foreheads."), and repaired to Cal's for a few cocktails.

It was like old times. Kenny's return to being Kenny seemed like a permanent thing, and I couldn't have been more pleased. For a while there I'd begun to worry that he was losing his sanity.

The bar was packed with expectant cops—all expecting to get drunk and most well on their way.

I'd reached my two-drink limit. Kenny saw that I was getting restless.

"Looking to go home?"

"Yeah, Pat waits up on the four-to-twelves."

"You're lucky, you know. Got a wife, a kid—a little boy. Nice having someone to go home to," he said wistfully.

I wanted to break the mood. "You will, too, Kenny. Sometimes it takes time to find the right girl." I looked at my watch and stood. "Hey, gotta go." He grabbed my arm.

"One second, one second. I ever show you this?" He opened the top buttons of his shirt and pulled out a gold dog tag suspended around his neck on a thin golden chain.

"I've seen it in the locker room, sure."

"My most cherished thing in the world." He fingered it lovingly. "I melted down four eighteen-carat gold rings, made my own mold, and poured it myself. Used my real dog tag, imperfections and all. Had to take it to a jeweler to smooth it out, though. Didn't have the tools. Here, check it out." He removed the dog tag from his neck and handed it to me.

I felt odd touching it, like it was something real, alive, and it had seen much more than I ever had. What could anyone possibly buy in a jewelry store that would have more value than this flat piece of gold?

"It's beautiful, Kenny." I handed it back gingerly.

He looped it back around his neck. "Something happens to me, Wags, I want you to have it."

"What? Kenny, come on, nothing—"

He held up a hand. "Nothing's gonna happen? C'mon, this is the Ninth Precinct," he said with a laugh. Then quietly he said, "Anything could happen."

I left him at the bar. As I hit the street I heard his hearty laugh and a chorus of guffaws right behind it. Kenny Kenrick was working the room.

Kenny was late for our first day tour.

"Where's your partner?" Sergeant Reddy asked me as I stood by watching the rest of the platoon file out into the street.

"Hey, Sarge, I don't know. He was gonna be late he'd call. I—"

A clerk hollered from the desk. "Wags, Kenny's on three."

I smiled at the sergeant. "See, car probably on the fritz."

I picked up the phone and the clerk punched me through. I heard traffic noise.

"Wags?"

"Kenny? Where the hell are you?"

"Goddamn car broke down four blocks on the wrong side of the Brooklyn Bridge."

"You stay there; I'll pick you up."

"Nah, I'll grab a gypsy. Hey, there's one now." He yelled, "Over here!"

"Okay," I said, "I'll be out front picking up the jobs." I started to cradle the receiver.

"Yo, hey, Wags!"

"Yeah, Kenny?"

"Take care, okay?"

"I think I can manage for ten minutes." But he'd already hung up.

> *Five minutes after speaking with his partner, Police Officer James Wagner, on the telephone, Police Officer Kenneth Kenrick, while off-duty and on his way to work in a livery cab, asked the driver to stop in the middle of the Brooklyn Bridge. When the driver complied, Police Officer Kenrick exited the vehicle, placed his off-duty revolver to his head, and pulled the trigger, killing himself instantly.*
> —Excerpted from the official NYPD Unusual Report.

SUICIDE

In addition to being totally shocked and grief-stricken, I had a thousand questions.

Kenny's suicide came seemingly out of nowhere. He'd seemed so up, so animated. Did Bovar's suicide drive him over the edge? If it did, he'd disguised his true feelings pretty well.

A cop killing himself is not a rare event. Law enforcement professionals alternate with dentists as the top two jobs that provoke the most suicides. It's a rare cop who doesn't know someone who ate his or her gun. Kenny was the first of my friends to take that final drastic step, but by no means the last. While males lead the pack, the number of female cops who end it all is rapidly rising.

Although self-destruction is almost commonplace, The Job still stigmatizes the act. Often a suicide is disguised as an accidental death resulting from a gun-cleaning mishap, usually explained as a dropped pistol that landed on its hammer, thereby firing a round. This is virtually impossible because of the automatic safety bar that separates the hammer from the firing pin in police-issued firearms. The only way a cop's gun fires is when the trigger is pulled, and that takes thirteen pounds of pressure. Difficult to do accidentally.

Funerals of suicides are always guilt-ridden affairs. Everyone blames themselves for not seeing the signs, but the major guilt falls on the partner. In this case, me.

Kenny was in great spirits. What signs had been evident? The guilt was killing me. Why hadn't I seen *something?*

"It wasn't your fault, Wags," Sergeant Reddy said at the funeral.

Kenny's was not a line-of-duty death; there were no politicians in attendance, no brass, just the cops of the Ninth Precinct, reeling from yet another brother's violent end.

I took a week off. My dad and I took a ride upstate, just to get out of the city and look at the early spring scenery, away from the squalor and smell of death.

We stopped in a little town, Roscoe, in the Catskills and had lunch in a tiny diner. I hadn't mentioned Kenny for the entire two-hour ride. My father broke the ice.

"They're happiest when they know they're gonna do it, you know."

I was lost in thought, hands wrapped around a steaming cup of coffee. "Huh?"

"A suicide. Cops particularly. Once a cop makes the decision he's gonna kill himself, his whole attitude changes. He goes from morose to positively tickled."

"Really?" I said. I shook my head. "That makes no sense."

"Does if you think about it. Kenny wrestled with his demons, probably for a long time; you said so yourself."

"Yeah."

"He was melancholy, erratic—he *looked* like he was gonna eat his gun. Had you worried, remember?"

"So you're telling me once he made his mind up to do it, *that* put him in a good mood?"

"Sure. He'd fought the urge; now the fight was over. He was relieved."

"You've seen this?"

My father snorted. He looked a lot older than his forty-nine years. Over the last few months he'd dropped some weight ("No good places to eat anymore; Staten Island's going to hell."), and virtually quit drinking hard liquor. He still rode with Dave Ballantine, but they were dinosaurs, unable to comprehend the speed at which the world was changing. Their little fiefdom in Stapleton was being invaded by the marauding hordes, and they were overwhelmed. Still, they were fighting the good fight, although outgunned and branded pariahs by the people they served in a place where at one time they had been both loved and feared.

"Seen it? Jimmy, have I got stories for you."

A desk lieutenant, my dad told me, had signed himself out for meal, gone downstairs to the supervisor's locker room, opened up his locker, sat in it, pulled out his gun, and shot himself in the head.

"We heard the report. Loud as a son of a bitch. It was in Midtown South; Dave and I had a parade detail. Ran downstairs; there he was." He smiled ruefully. "I was about your age. It was the first time I'd ever seen a dead cop. What shocked me wasn't so much the suicide but how he got his fat ass in that locker." He spread his hands. "Ass as wide as the dashboard of a Buick— took the Jaws of Life to get him out."

I had to smile. Cops have an odd sense of humor. Keeps us going. Most of us.

"Why'd he do it?"

My dad shrugged. "I heard later he was named in a corruption case, but only as a witness. Real reason? His father was a chief, worked for the PC in the Puzzle Palace. Broke his son's balls, wanted him to be a superchief, continue the family legacy. The story around the precinct was that he never wanted to be a cop in the first place. Even if the kid was called before a grand jury for something he had nothing to do with, it's a career killer."

"That bothered him? Couple of years, it would have been forgotten; he would've been back on track."

"His old man didn't see it that way. The kid killed himself because he embarrassed his father."

We drove up what a city boy like me considered a mountain, meaning a hill higher than the escalator at Grand Central Station.

We followed a winding tree-lined road that meandered past horse farms, a country club, and wooden firetrap resorts all named Something Manor or Lodge. After about twenty minutes the road widened, the trees thinned, and we found ourselves next to a lake.

"Remember this place?" Dad asked. "Tanana Lake?"

"No, should I?"

"I guess not. You were young, maybe five, six. We came up here one day with Dave. Went fishing."

It was an overcast day. Pillows of diaphanous fog settled over the lake. Summer cottages hugged the shoreline, abutting rotting piers suspended on rickety pilings. Nearby, off the main road, was a cluster of nursing homes. Some of the residents were in wheelchairs, blankets across their laps, facing the water, heads drooping, eyes unseeing, abandoned by their caregivers to enjoy the view. My father looked at them, then quickly turned away.

"Don't ever put me in one of these places, okay, Jimmy?" he said.

I felt myself flush. "Hey, Dad, I would never—"

"I hope not." He rubbed my shoulder. "Let's get off this grim subject and talk about something different." He smiled. "Wanna hear some more suicide stories?"

I did. Call it morbid fascination, but I had to know what drove a cop to kill himself. I wondered if what I feared most was that one day I'd be in a state of mind where I'd be pondering the ultimate solution.

The New York City Police Department Museum is recognized around the world as an achievement in recording the history not only of the NYPD but of the city itself.

Until the 1980s the museum was housed in the Police Academy (it was eventually moved to 1 Police Plaza) and run by one cop. Not a cop of high rank, just a patrolman (as police officers were known in the seventies) with a penchant for collecting NYPD memorabilia.

I'm specifically not naming the officers who committed suicide here. Their families have suffered enough. So call this cop Officer Al.

Officer Al was more an academician than a cop. He was an extremely smart man in his thirties who collected, cataloged, and pampered artifacts from the earliest recorded period of The Job.

Officer Al spent a lot of his own money procuring NYPD memorabilia, items that he then altruistically donated to the museum.

He also gave enlightening guided tours of the museum to visiting politicians and dignitaries. His knowledge of the history of the NYPD was awe-inspiring. Yes, Officer Al was definitely a genius. But he had one failing.

"He couldn't pass a sergeant's test. He failed five of them," my dad recounted.

To get promoted in the NYPD, a cop has to pass civil service examinations. The only exception is promotion to the rank of detective. That is often a tenuous position where you serve at the discretion of the police commissioner. Besides, some cops aren't meant to be detectives. For them, it's the civil service route, sergeant being the first hurdle.

Officer Al, despite his superior intelligence, couldn't pass the damn test, and it bothered the hell out of him. It was all he talked about. To be fair, it's a difficult exam, and it's geared more toward the street cop rather than the academician.

One day, while tending to his trophies, Officer Al shot himself in the head. The cops who heard the shot raced to the scene to find the dead cop slumped over behind his desk, gun in hand.

"His death went down as an accident," Dad said. "An accidental discharge while cleaning his service gun. Oddly enough, the responding detectives found an open gun-cleaning kit on his desk." Dad snorted. "Gee, I wonder how it got there?"

"The cop was fighting with his wife," my dad was explaining. "He was the type who liked to do a four-to-four tour."

A four-to-four is Job parlance for a cop who goes to a bar after a four-to-twelve tour. Bars in New York close at four A.M. Do the math.

"So this goes on for months. Finally he trips home drunk for the umpteenth time, just as his bride is making breakfast. The kids are already on their way to school.

"Him and his wife get into a heated argument over the breakfast table, he flings a bowl of Cheerios to the floor, says something like. 'I'll show you, you cunt,' whips out his gun, and kills himself."

"He showed her, all right," I said, finding the whole thing hard to comprehend.

My father and I were in the middle of the lake in a rented rowboat. The fog had burned off and the sun reflected off the water. We had also obtained two beat-up fishing poles and a tin of worms from the old man who rented us the boat. So far no luck, but I was more interested in my father's stories than in fishing.

"Worked with a guy named Miller once. Quiet cop, bright guy, on the sergeant's list, single, kept mostly to himself. One day I'm off and I had this burning desire to see the movie *Al Capone* with Rod Steiger." Dad rubbed his chin. "I guess this was in 'fifty-seven, maybe 'fifty-eight.

"I'll never forget this as long as I live. So I take the ferry—this was a few years before the bridge—and two trains to the Victoria Theater on Broadway and Forty-seventh. The movie was only playing in Manhattan, no multiplexes back then.

"I just made the start, settled in with a bag of popcorn, and enjoyed the show. Afterward, the lights come on and who do I see but Miller, sitting by himself about six rows down. He spots me, all smiles. We leave the theater together, walk across the street to check out the pimp clothes in Leighton's, and wind up in Jack Dempsey's saloon for a few cocktails.

"We got a little fucked up, five drinks or so each. Miller turns out to be a regular guy, good sense of humor. Maybe the booze loosened him up a little, who knows.

"Anyway, I wanna get home in time for dinner and Miller wants to check out another movie. Okay, I leave." His pole was yanked into the calm lake water. "Hey, I got one!"

Dad landed a trout. We marveled at what a great fisherman he was and he threw it back. Live and let live.

"So what happened with Miller?"

"Oh, yeah." He baited the hook and tossed the line over the side. "Next day, I walk into the precinct and the whole place is buzzing. Miller wound up under a downtown A train an hour after I left him."

"Wow. Could've been an accident." I said. "He was drinking; maybe he fell."

My father turned to look at me; then his eyes grew distant, searching the past.

"Maybe."

We got off the subject. We called it a day after three hours in the boat, my father's trout the only score.

When we settled into the car he asked, "Want to grab something to eat?"

"Sure."

"I know a place."

The joint was the Skytop Lodge. I remember because it burned down the next day and the story made the *Daily News*.

We ate fresh grilled catfish and baked potatoes, washed down with a few beers. Over dessert and coffee my father said, "I've got a few more. Up for them?"

I knew what he meant. I could've heard a dozen more stories. "Yeah, sure."

He told me about a cop he'd worked with when he first came on The Job. Young guy, seemingly stable, good family man.

"His father dies, not unexpectedly, cancer or something. At the grave site, as they're lowering the casket into the ground, this cop pulls out his gun, shoots himself in the head, falls into the hole with his father's coffin."

"Jesus."

"Sergeant and his driver patrolling the Two-Six Precinct in Harlem. Sergeant was a friend of Dave's. A few hours into the tour the cop driving the boss needs to use the head. The closest place is a construction site with those portable johns. The cop wanders off into the site while the sergeant catches up on some paperwork in the car. After a while, still no cop. The sergeant gets concerned, goes looking for him. Finds him on the bowl, pants down, gun in his hand. Shot himself in the head. DOA."

He saw the concern on my face.

"Look, Jimmy, I know what you've gone through with Kenny and all. What I'm trying to tell you is that you or me could've been Kenny or any of these other guys."

I liked to think that I was a pretty stable person, and I conveyed that to my father.

"I bet Kenny thought he was a stable person, too," my dad said. "So'd all those other guys. What it is, is the availability of the gun."

I was listening.

"My theory, but I think a valid one: Firemen see much the same kind of shit we do, sometimes worse. How many firemen do you know who kill themselves? Almost unheard-of. Bet if they carried guns they'd be right up there with us."

"Not too easy to off yourself with a hose, huh?"

He smirked. "Exactly. It's a spur-of-the-moment thing. The world gets to be too much for a cop, the fancy hits him, he pulls out the gun, boom! He can't say then, 'Aw, shit, I didn't mean to do that.'"

We drove home in a sleek rain. Talk was kept to a minimum. What little we said was mostly commentary on the weather and traffic.

As we paid the toll on the Verrazano Bridge, I asked him if he wanted to come by my house to see Pat and my son.

"Not today—your mother's been cooking something special." He seemed pensive for a moment, lost in thought, perhaps pumping life into old ghosts.

"Jimmy, I want you to think about something, okay?"

"Yeah, sure, Dad. What?"

"Retirement."

I laughed. "Hey, Dad, I've got thirteen years to go before I pull the pin."

He touched my shoulder. "We live fast lives, Jimmy, cops do. Twenty or more years of adrenaline racing on a day-to-day basis. Then you retire and it stops. We're not 'us' anymore, not a member of the fraternity. We're 'them,' part of the problem, a civilian."

This, he confided, was one of the reasons retirement scared him. How do you go from the excitement of police work, seeing all we see, to having to listen to your relatives bitching about crabgrass or the price of tomatoes?

"You know, who gives a fuck about this petty shit? I know I don't." He looked at me. "You don't either."

He was right. Time spent with someone who hadn't handled a quadruple homicide was like being with someone who lived in a bubble. I never took The Job home with me, never discussed it with anyone but my fellow cops, but I liked being *around* others who'd lived on the edge.

"It's worse for the war veterans who become cops," Dad said. "Years of maximum velocity to a dead stop. Some don't make it to retirement."

I thought of Kenny.

"The average cop has very little tolerance for civilians," he added. "Most haven't seen anything in their lives, and what's important to them bores the shit out of us. I don't really give a damn about my neighbor's tough day at the phone company. Can't relate. I dread the day when I gotta pull the pin."

"It's a while off yet," I said.

"Not too far off. You'll have that fear, too, that fear of being bored, of knowing exactly what you're gonna do every day." He shuddered. "Man, that's gotta be the worst feeling in the world." His eyes became distant again. "You know, a lot of guys leave The Job, sit home, and watch soap operas. Suicides happen more after retirement. You don't wanna hear about those."

We pulled up in front of his house, the home I grew up in. He got out of the car, leaned in the window, and kissed me on the cheek.

"You get out, Jimmy; go with something that won't make you bored. It's a death sentence. Plan for it now; think about the future." He smiled.

"What're you gonna do when you retire?"

He laughed and shrugged. "Who knows? But you can bet your ass it'll have some variety." I watched him walk into the house.

I think Oric Bovar's death was the last straw for Kenny. He was fragile to begin with, and Bovar represented a slim thread of reliability because Bovar knew what he wanted. While Kenny's world was crumbling around him, he saw in Bovar a man who believed in something, no matter how aberrant. Bovar believed in his own destiny and had the will to convince himself that he would return from the dead.

Kenny admired Bovar's strong beliefs in a world where he saw no order, no absolutes. While outwardly scoffing at Bovar's "church," he admired the man's conviction and inner strength.

If Oric Bovar could make the ultimate decision, take the ultimate step, so could Kenny Kenrick.

In the end, I couldn't take the dog tag.

Kenny had been wearing it when he shot himself. It went with him to the grave. Amidst all his pain, one of the few times I saw warmth in Kenny's eyes was that day in Cal's when he caressed that hunk of gold.

I wasn't going to deny him that.

7

Blue Blood

by Edward Conlon

"I enjoyed patrol as I hadn't in a while. As theatre, there is no match for it, and even the way you engage the spectacle is like something a kid would invent—you knock on a door and someone has to tell you a story."

—Edward Conlon,
Blue Blood

When I went to work midnights, it was discovered that I didn't have a nickname. You need one, for patrol, to talk casually over the radio: "Stix, you getting coffee?" "Chicky, did you check the roof?" "OV, T, GQ, can you swing by?" Nicknames never stuck to me, for some reason, and I always thought that nicknaming yourself was like talking to yourself, something that made you look foolish if you were overheard. So the Hat, Hawkeye, Hollywood, Gee-Whiz, Big E, the Count, Rollercoaster, and the rest pitched a few:

"Hemingway—nah, they'd know it was you."

"Ernest is better."

"Or Clancy—he'd be a good one to have."

"What about Edgar?"

"What from?"

"Edgar Allan Poe."

"What about Poe?"

Poe it was. As I thought about it, the fit was neat: Poe had worked midnights, too, weak and weary, upon a midnight dreary, in his most famous poem. He moved to New York City in 1844, the same year the legislation that created the New York City Police Department was signed. He wrote the first mystery story ever, called "The Murders in the Rue Morgue." I don't mean to spoil the ending for anyone, but the killer turns out to be a demented orangutan with a straight razor. There is a brilliant detective, an earnest sidekick, a mood of languor and gloom—all the hallmarks of a genre that has endured for a century and a half. No one else has done much with

Reprinted from *Blue Blood* (2004), by permission of Riverhead Books, an imprint of Penguin Group, Inc.

the crazy ape. Poe spent his last years in the Bronx, living and working in a cottage that is midway between where I lived and where I worked. I was a police officer in the Bronx, where some kids called the cops "po-po." Was it all coming together? Give me a minute.

Midnights for Poe seemed less a time than a territory, a place of woefully distant vistas, as if he were stargazing from the bottom of a well. A lot of that has to do with needing sleep, I think. Everyone lacked sleep on the midnights, and it may have been this state of worn-out wakefulness while the rest of the world was dreaming that lent itself to thoughts that meandered roundabout and far. Each precinct has a list of "cooping-prone locations"—out-of-the-way places, under bridges and by rail yards and the like, where bosses are supposed to check to make sure patrol cars haven't stopped in for a nap. The list is posted, and when you look at it when you're tired, it seems like a recommendation, a Zagat's guide for secret sleep, as if it might say: St. Mary's Park, with its rolling hills and abundant trees, offers superb concealment in a pastoral setting—we give it four pillows! On the midnights, we talked about sleep the way frat boys talked about sex. Did you get any last night? How was it? Nah, nah, but this weekend, believe me, I'm gonna go all night long! Though I asked practically everyone on the tour how long it took for your body to adjust to an upside-down life, only three people gave precise answers:

"Two weeks."

"Four months."

"Never."

Nevermore . . . Uncle Eddie finished his thirty-three years as a cop working midnights in the Bronx, and he would have told me, I know, that he liked it because they leave you alone. That's why I went. I would wait until Narcotics called, or Vice, away from the storms of SNEU. Stix would wait with me, until the Captain understood what had happened, or the Sergeant was thrown out, or enough time passed for no one to care anymore. We would have time to think and breathe. I didn't look forward to coming in to work, but I didn't hate it—root canal no longer rated as a relative pleasure. Stix said that his wife, Anna, thought that he seemed better, too.

We would be partners in Squad A, and Sgt. Yolanda Gonzalez was our boss. Sgt. G would be retiring in the spring, and the precious closeness of her departure, coupled with twenty years on the Job, gave her steadiness and perspective. Sgt. G was pretty and proper, sweet-natured as a schoolmarm, and the cops looked up to her and looked out for her, as if they were reform-school boys who'd found a sudden inspiration for homework. Since she was a veteran of the military and also of undercover work, the protective sense that she inspired in her cops might not have been entirely necessary, but it was certainly good to see. Of the handful of cops in the command who were closer to the end of their careers than the beginning, most of them—Linda McLean, Timmy Anderson, Mike Moxom, Harry Thompson—worked the midnights. They looked at us with sympathy and something akin to bemusement—what we'd been through might have been bad, but no one had been indicted or killed, and so tragedy-wise, we were still a little light. Years before, I'd been surprised to see Timmy Anderson, in the daylight and wearing a suit. He was heading to court. "Someone had the bad taste to die while they were wearing my handcuffs," he said wearily, cutting to the nub of a longer story he told me later, of a perp whose cocaine psychosis led to cardiac arrest, and who would haunt Timmy as a litigious ghost for long after. Did we have problems? *Lemme tell ya about problems.* . . . If nothing else, our SNEU saga made us part of the hard-luck fraternity of the NYPD, and the midnight cops welcomed Stix and Poe as the newest old-timers.

Still, it was a difficult adjustment, for Stix especially. He was so fastidious that when he ate a sandwich, he held it in a paper towel. Once, when he was getting dressed, he dropped his uniform shirt on the floor of the locker room, and promptly threw it back into his locker to take it home to wash.

"The floor is covered with toejam," Stix said.

"Your partner, he's a real perfectionist," observed another cop, dressing by his locker.

"That's one word for it."

Stix found it hard to get used to eating and sleeping on our new schedule, and he was often nearly delirious with exhaustion. In the first week, I think he asked me a dozen times: "Do you wake up at night and have breakfast? And do you go home in the morning for dinner? How can you have eggs at night, or pasta when your wife is having eggs?" For me, a perversely ordered life was somewhat better than the old chaos, but it was still hard. Though the schedule was not kind on either of our digestions, I grew weary of his reaction whenever we encountered any foul odor—he would wrinkle his brow, glare, and ask, "Did you fart?" Quite often, I had not.

On our first night, Stix and I guarded an empty apartment. A woman had made a complaint about her ex-boyfriend, and he had come back and fired a couple of shots at her. For an indefinite period, two cops would be stationed outside her apartment, twenty-four hours a day. Though she had been staying with relatives for some time, Stix and I didn't object to the assignment, and we devoted the tour to reading and the discussion of breakfast philosophies. We were assigned there another night, and then another. The silences grew longer and more leaden.

"Did you say something?"

"I didn't even *think* anything."

A cop from the four-to-twelves who was also on the Captain's shitlist had spent a lot of time there, until he got into even more trouble by bringing in a chaise longue. It made sense to me. A lieutenant from the Inspections Unit made periodic checks on us, I suppose to make sure we were doing nothing. On other nights, we were detailed to guard hospitalized prisoners, or to work inside, handing out radios or working the "T/S," the telephone switchboard, behind the desk.

I had never worked inside, and I didn't think much of the cops who chose to—who would want such a dull and easy assignment? I didn't change my mind about the "dull" part, but "easy" was revised after my first tour on the T/S, when I developed my first case of writer's cramp since college. It was well after four when I was able to look up from the "daily summons recap," which consisted of indexing and cross-referencing the five-digit control number for each day's master sheet with each summons. On the master sheet, I'd write the cop's name and six-digit tax number, the date of issue, and then the ten-digit summons number, and then the plate number if it was a parking summons, or the person's name, address, and date of birth, if it was a criminal-court summons, or the plate number, name, address, and date of birth, if it was a moving summons. Seventy-three summonses had been issued in the past twenty-four hours at PSA-7, and I learned each of them intimately. Then I had to count them again and break them down: back copy for us, front for court, each in its own envelope, with separate envelopes for the two summonses that were turned in a day late. When I finished, Sgt. G politely explained that I'd written the control number on the wrong part of the summons, on the tear-off strip on top that would be thrown away. "Forget it, don't worry about it," she said consolingly. "I don't know who looks at this stuff anyway."

One night, when Stix had a hospitalized prisoner—a seventeen-year-old asthmatic crack dealer—he got the perp to give up three spots, one with a gun, which he'd been inside within the last twenty-four hours. When he came in for meal, we ran the checks and IDed all three players—each with felony narco raps, one on parole. Stix talked to Timmy Anderson about it, and Timmy suggested that we take it up with the Lieutenant, who was usually gung-ho for this sort of thing. But when Stix approached the Lieutenant to say that we wanted to look into something, the Lieutenant laughed and shook his head. "It's a waste of time," he said. "They're never gonna let you guys do a warrant. Tell you what—instead of trying for the warrant, why don't you just run into that wall as fast as you can. Maybe that'll get it out of your system."

After a couple of weeks, Harry Thompson, who was the PBA delegate on the late tour, took us aside. "You guys might have noticed you've been getting shitty assignments."

Yes, we had.

"What happened was that your old boss reached out to fuck you guys. But if you guys write some summonses, get some collars, whatever, Sgt. G is gonna be in a better position to tell them that she won't."

"How are we supposed to get collars on a fixed post or T/S?"

"That's the thing."

It was the thing. Sgt. Gonzalez later had a word with us, as well. "Here and now," she said. "This is a clean start. Whatever happened in SNEU is past—I won't hold it against you."

"What did you hear that happened?" I asked. If I had to write a complaint for the "suspicious DOA" of the SNEU team, Stix and I would have been listed as the complainants instead of the perps. It was disquieting to hear that the common understanding might be otherwise.

"I don't know what happened," she said. "I heard it was something about a warrant. . . . I don't know, and it doesn't matter to me."

Stix said, "It wasn't like that, Sarge."

She nodded. "Like I said, this is a fresh start."

I would have liked to think so. Rumors in the precinct buzzed around like microwave signals, in high volume and low quality—various cops had told me, with utter confidence, that the Captain was beloved by the bosses downtown and had a limitless future; that he was hated and was on his way out; that he hated the Job and would leave the instant he was eligible; that he never wanted to leave and was desperate for promotion to deputy inspector; that the promotion was due any minute now; and that it was a flat-out impossibility, because—and this is on the highest authority, so don't tell anyone—no one in Housing would be promoted. Sgt. G's reference to the warrant had an understated accuracy in my case, but it had nothing to do with Stix. It was little wonder that the rumor mill did less to clarify than to confuse.

The degree of confusion became apparent when a cop informed me matter-of-factly that it wasn't the Sergeant who'd thrown Stix out, but the new lieutenant—who had gleefully sent us on patrol when the Sergeant was out, and who now was the precinct Integrity Control officer—on the grounds of "chronic lateness." Stix had been officially late once, when there was a hurricane. The new lieutenant put him in the Minor Violations Log, and the Sergeant wrote "counseled for tardiness" on his evaluation. It was the only recorded infraction in his career, since the Sergeant's later charges of insubordination were bluntly dismissed by Lt. Johnson. But other cops picked up the theme of the story, passing along remarks to the effect that no one liked the new ICO, and that he was bound to cause trouble. Finally, cops from SNEU told us that the Sergeant now claimed that he didn't throw Stix out, to anyone who wasn't in the room when it happened—"I fought to keep him, there was nothing I could do . . ."—which was a rather grand lie. Since Stix and I had eight hours and thirty-five minutes a night to think about it, I came to speculate that the Sergeant and the ICO spun the story together, since it suited one to look like a nicer guy than he was, and the other to look tougher. It deepened our mistrust of the bosses, and made gestures of support from other cops all the more touching.

When Angelo Ricci, one of our PBA delegates, heard that we were both out of SNEU, he marched in to the Captain to confront him. The Captain said that Stix and the Sergeant "had been butting heads for a while," and that I was trying to transfer just about anywhere, but it wasn't happening because "nobody trusts him." Angelo said, "What are you talking about? Everybody loves him—he's a great cop and a great guy, one of the best cops in the command."

"Well, maybe it's the supervisors who don't trust him."

Angelo left the office, saying, "You just flushed two great cops down the toilet."

As part of my escape plan, I wrote up the bribery collar and the last warrant for department recognition, to get the points for the transfer. I was given bars for Meritorious Police Duty and Excellent Police Duty, respectively. An EPD is the most basic police commendation, and an MPD, which was a step above, was the conventional award for a bribery collar. The bribery collar took a couple of hours, and it sidelined a junkie for a couple of months; the warrant took six weeks, and it disabled the operation of serious criminals, even if the effects were more partial and temporary than they should have been. It didn't make sense, but I made nothing of it. And then Sgt. Clark, who headed the precinct awards committee, told me, "I put you in for a Commendation"—one level above an MPD—"but the Captain said you didn't deserve anything. He said it didn't happen the way you wrote it up, and Narcotics did all the work. He didn't want to give you anything—I had to fight with him to get you the EPD."

Though we were free of the Sergeant completely, and I'd rarely see the Captain, their enduring reach rankled nonetheless. It was not right that such small people had such a large influence in our lives, and similar revelations spurred many cops into devoted study for the sergeant's exam and beyond. Things were bad-marriage bad between us, with the kind of intensity that depends on an element of mutuality. Time and distance might provide a better perspective. The Sergeant was eagerly friendly to me again when we saw each other, as he had been on the first days on the team. I was not friendly in return, but I did wonder whether, if he'd been a cop with us, instead of our ostensible leader, his shortcomings would have been so pronounced. He was a bad fit for us, but not a bad man, at least at first; most people have a breaking point, and we were his. He reminded me of certain clients from my defense days, who were decent enough people as long as life treated them decently, but whom three bad weeks in a row would send into coke binges and liquor-store stick-ups. For the Captain, it was harder to guess—if the Inspector hadn't canceled one warrant, or he hadn't canceled three, or my book news had stayed hidden for another week, or he'd been at the command longer . . . Then again, I thought, the hell with both of them. In one year, I'd made more collars than either had made in his career. For the past eleven months, I had done backflips for them; the next jump would be out. Stix and I resolved that if one of us were hurt, the other would keep them both out of the hospital; if it went worse for us, they were to be banned from the church.

The Sergeant and the Captain cost us faith, time, and needless aggravation, but the worst you could say of them—arguably, at the farthest reach—was that certain criminals owed them their freedom, since they had kept us from working as we should. To encounter people who were genuinely evil, we would have to leave the precinct. We didn't have to go far away. When we finally got out on patrol, we were out for an hour before we were called in for another fixed post, at a crime scene. There had been a rape at one of my old buildings on Washington Avenue, on a stairwell in Morris Houses. The scene encompassed three flights of stairs and the elevator that the perp had taken to escape. The victim's clothes had been thrown all over the stairs: a scruffy brown leather jacket and an orange sweater on one landing, tan pants and a pair of aqua-and-blue-striped gym shorts on another. Her shoes were there, too—gray leather ankle-high boots, each still laced up and tied. There was a condom wrapper on my floor and a condom two flights up. I had the bottom of the stairs, Vinnie Commisso had the top, and Stix had the elevator. I asked about what had happened, and a sergeant casually threw out a couple of details. My job was to stand guard over a pair of shorts, and it didn't really matter what I knew. I overheard that there were inconsistencies to the woman's story: she said she was going to the store, but she didn't have any money and never left the building. One detective on the canvass muttered that she must have been hustling on the stairwell: "We're gonna lock this guy up for Theft of Service." I told Stix, "You're gonna wait here for an hour, and then Crime Scene's gonna show up and say, 'We're not gonna get a print off an elevator button,' and walk away." That happened, only it took longer.

I stood next to a door covered with gang graffiti—"031" and "Tre 9 Bloods"—the babel of proclamations of who was a lover, who was a fighter, and who just was. I was careful not to lean on the wall because of the roaches, and then I wondered idly why there were so many flies in the hall, especially near the clothing. Two detectives from the Crime Scene Unit came and asked what we had, and I told them what I knew. Per their request, I called upstairs, "Hey, Vinnie, is the condom full?" They shone UV light on the clothes, which illuminates body fluids, but there was no evidence of semen. They bagged some of the clothes, and then one of them went to pick up the condom wrapper.

"Uggh, there's shit on it. Check the shorts," he said.

"You check 'em," said the other.

He did, and found they were full of excrement. Did it matter if she was a whore? Maybe it had started as a conversation about a deal, and maybe it hadn't. However it had started, he tried to move her to the roof, and she didn't want to go. They were in a public area in the middle of a sixteen-story building with eight apartments per floor. She had been stripped naked, and even forced to take off her shoes. Whether she lost control of her bowels out of pure terror, or in a desperate gesture to repel her attacker, she was raped as she sat in her own shit, and she ran home dirty and naked.

Moments like those cleared your mind of office politics, at least for a while. Not every job on the midnights was as heavy as that, but the jobs tended to be substantiated: "shots fired" on the four-to-twelves often meant someone wanted to clear out the kids in the lobby; "shots fired" on the midnights usually meant shots had been fired. At least half of our homicides were on the midnights, but a higher percentage of those were the "misdemeanor murders," the perp-on-perp hits. When Stix and I went to one, in the lobby of 180 Brook, the body had already been removed, but there were blood and brains all over. White feathers were also strewn about, and they began to drift away in the breeze, except for where they were stuck in the red pools and gray piles.

"What happened here, a pillow fight?"

"Nah, he had a down jacket, EMS had to cut it open to work on him. . . ."

In the lobby of a project on Webster Avenue, a member of the Bloods was ambushed by Crips and shot five times: in each hand, the chin, the belly, and the balls. An elaborate shrine had been set up for him, of candles, beer and brandy bottles, wilting flowers, and scribbled notes and pictures. The notes were from adults and teenagers, but the writing—penmanship, spelling, and everything else—were like kids' letters to Santa. One of them said more than the others:

2 guns up
Shawny AKA
Shady AKA
Waterbug
Let me drop some knowledge on you
I'm sure (God) will make sure that they 'pay' 'how' nobody knows he may send them to 'jail to life' or he may choose to deliver them to his dogs, dogettes, b-brothers and sisters
Much love Dutchman RIP
13 murders finest

Was God a Blood or a Crip? I wondered. Did they think of Him as the Original Gangsta? Too often in the projects, the knowledge was promised but never dropped. Two buildings away, a night or two later, we had another gun run—"Male black, dark clothes . . ."—in a lobby where there were eight or so guys hanging out. I knew at least two of them as dealers. We approached with holsters cracked, our voices reasonable at first—"Guys, lemme see your hands"—and several complied, and then the voice harsher—"Up, I said. Hands up!"—and the rest followed, except for one. He sat listlessly and stared at me, and Stix covered the rest as I closed the gap between us. He didn't move—*Get your fucking hands up!*—and I grabbed him, flipped him around and pushed him against the fence, twisting an arm behind his back. The guys on the wall began to shout: "Hey! Take it easy on him!"

"Go easy!"

"That's my cousin, he's retarded!"

"Hey, he's retarded, yo!"

I shifted tone, reassuring him that I just had to check, I was sorry, it would be okay. I patted him on the back as I continued to check for the gun. I felt bad for him, but if they knew what they were doing, the gun wouldn't be on the big guy, or even the shooter. It would be in any of the places the cops don't want or think to look: under the colostomy bag of the guy in the wheelchair, or in the baby carriage, or in the young girl's knapsack. You want to know why I roughed up the retarded kid? *Let me drop some knowledge on you . . .*

At the daylit end of one tour, a woman hailed us to point out white smoke billowing from the top window of an old three-story house with a mansard roof on Courtlandt Avenue. We rang the bells and banged on the door, and then we kicked and kicked and kicked. It was a steel door but we were almost through when a man sleepily stuck his head out from the second floor.

"You all right?" we asked.

"Yeah, don't worry about it—it's just the radiator. This is a city building, nobody's here but me and I don't know how to shut it off. The Fire Department knocked the door down last week to get in, that's why there's a nice new strong one. Thanks anyways, guys."

Both Stix and I were downcast. "I was thinking of the Commissioner," Stix said. "Him saying, 'You saved their lives, where do you want to go?'"

"I was thinking the same thing."

Such were our thoughts, and we didn't lack time to think them. There were fewer jobs than during the day tours, and far less than on the four-to-twelves. Even on the weekends, they tended to taper off after two or three in the morning. You had more time on your own than on any other tour. It felt odd to be back in the bag, back on patrol, at this hour and at this time in my career. When I thought about my past and the past of this place, as we drove and the late hours drifted on, I wondered where I was going. It often brought on a terminal feel, which I would sometimes try to cure by looking at the cause.

One night, Stix and I drove to the corner of 132nd Street and Lincoln Avenue—a cooping-prone location, in fact, though it wasn't the intention for the visit—a dead end at the very bottom of the Bronx, with a warehouse on one side and a parking lot on the other. Across the black shimmer of the river, you could see Harlem and the salt piles along the highway. When I was young, my father told me that kids from Harlem had died playing in the piles, and each time I'd see them I'd think of the little black boys drowning in the white salt. The Bronx began here, physically, and it began here in history, too, when Jonas Bronck built his farmhouse. Not much is known about him: he was a Swedish sea captain who was induced to settle the area by the Dutch West India Company. A peace treaty was signed at Bronck's house between the Dutch and the Weckquasgeeks, who lived in what would become the Bronx and upper Manhattan, ending years of sporadic but bloody skirmishes. Bronck didn't have much to do with it, but his house was the only one around.

"When did he move?" Stix asked.

"I don't know, probably when they built the projects."

It was a funny question, anyway, because it made me think that the Bronx is a place people come from, and not where they go to and stay, if luck is on their side. It was also a place of slow beginnings: Bronck came here in 1639 to homestead, and at the beginning of the twentieth century there was still farmland in the South Bronx; it only became citified as they built the subway. A person alive today could have witnessed its entire metropolitan career: two generations as a vibrant, blue-collar boomtown, and one as a slum so ravaged and riotous that when people from outside struggled to describe it, they compared it to Berlin and Hiroshima at war's end, a place so defeated that its enemies felt pity. They also compared it to the moon.

Stix and I cruised up to 142nd Street between Willis and Brook avenues, a block with a row of little houses on one side and a school on the other. We had chased a lot of junkies down that street, when they bought heroin with the brand name "President," among others, from the projects on the corner. One hundred years ago, stonecutters from Pisa named the Piccirilli brothers had a studio there, where they carved the Lincoln Memorial, but I don't suppose the dope was named in any commemorative spirit. Four blocks up and two over, Mother Teresa's order had a mission. The work they did was holy and noble, but there was also something a little embarrassing about it, to have nuns reassigned from leper duty in Calcutta to lend us a hand here. There was a picture in the *Daily News* a few years back of Mother Teresa and Princess Diana, visiting together, and Smacky was there, standing guard, just out of the frame. A little farther out of the frame is the building where Rayvon Evans died. He was a little boy whose parents kept his corpse in the closet until it seeped through to the floor below and the neighbors complained. John had driven the Lieutenant there when the job first came over, and they looked at both apartments, but the family had already thrown Rayvon's body out the window. The parents were never charged with murder because there wasn't enough of Rayvon left to tell how he died. When it was on the news, I saw Sammy and other cops from the PSA in the footage, in the hallway of the apartment and on the street, but I was glad that wasn't my job. There is a garden dedicated to the little boy, but there is no sign of the stonecutters, the princess, or the rest. Memory is short here, but the past is transparent, and you can look back as far as you want, until the present compels you to see what's happening now. It can take time for your eyes to adjust.

Midnights magnify things, sets them in sharp relief against the empty night, like gems on black velvet cloth. You answer jobs for lonely people who seem more lonely at midnight, more solitary and sorrowful, like the chubby little woman who reclined in her armchair like a pasha after attempting suicide by taking three Tylenol PMs. Or the woman whose close-cropped, dye-drowned blond hair was going green, who denied trying to hurt herself, but whose boyfriend confided that she had tried, by slapping herself, hard. Domestic disputes are all the more squalid and small-hearted when they take place at five in the morning: two middle-aged brothers at each other's throats, hours before their mother's funeral. The place stank and the walls seethed with roaches. One brother had a weary and beaten dignity, and he sat on the couch with his overcoat and an attaché case, like a salesman who had just lost a commission. The other brother shouted drunkenly, jerking and flailing like a dervish because of some unknown neurological misfires. They had argued because he had started drinking again, with a friend, who had called to report the sober one for his lack of sympathy. I took the jerky one aside, to let him ventilate a little. In his room, which was littered with cans of malt liquor, certificates from the Army and alcohol rehab were on proud display, taped to the wall. As he punched his honorable discharge to emphasize that his had been a life of accomplishment, a sunburst of roaches shot out from beneath it. I wanted to punch his rehab diploma, to show that he still had some work to do, but I thought better of it. We knew that we would be back if we left them there, and we dreaded the idea of having to lock someone up before the funeral, so we asked the sober one if he would mind leaving for a while. He agreed that it was the best thing to do; we agreed it was deeply unfair. He used to work as a security guard and he had a business card, which he offered to several cops—on the midnights, cops back each other up more often—and I took it without looking at it. "If there's anything I can do for you gentlemen . . ." he said, and then he went out to walk until daybreak.

If some people call because they want someone, anyone, to talk to, there are others for whom we are the last thing they want to see. For them, we arrive the way the Bible says judgment will: like a thief in the night. It felt like that when we took a woman's children away. With Stix, Sgt. G, and her steady driver, Louie Malagon, I escorted two caseworkers from the Administration for Children's Services who had a court order to remove the one-, two-, and three-year-old kids of a crackhead named Pamela into their care. The midnight visit was a sneak attack, as she had dodged the caseworkers during the daylight hours. Our part was to be—not to put too fine a point on it—hired muscle. These jobs are always awful, even when they run smoothly, and this one did not begin well: when we knocked, a woman answered— "Who?"—and then delayed ten minutes, muttering excuses—"Hold on," and, "Let me get something on," and then, "Who is it, again?"—before surrendering to threats to kick the door down. She was just a friend, she said, helping to clean up—probably in anticipation of such a visit. Pamela was out, she said, and there were kids in the back, but they were Pamela's sister's kids, and the sister was out, too. As we went to see the children, another woman came out from a back bedroom. Three kids were there, sleeping, who looked as if they might have been one, two, and three. But the second woman was coolly adamant: "Those are my kids, and I'm not Pamela, I'm her sister, Lorraine! I can show you, you're making a mistake!" I thought, what are the odds, two sisters, each having three kids the same ages? Somewhat high, and then the sexes—girl, girl, boy—and the odds were a little more comforting—a long shot multiplied by eight, to be precise—but I was still glad it was ACS's call, not mine. We grilled both women but they never broke from their story, and we could find no baby pictures or prescription bottles or anything else that would tie these children to the case—there lingered a twinge of doubt. And so when Lorraine said she could prove it, if we'd let her call her mother to get their ID, we agreed, as it would clearly demonstrate whether we were professional public servants doing a difficult job well, or dim-witted repo men hauling off the wrong crackbabies. But Lorraine didn't call for ID, she called for reinforcements, and the apartment was soon flooded with angry women. Lorraine wouldn't give up her kids, clutching the oldest two, while we had the baby boy, and then another neighbor took a girl, and then Lorraine tried to get out with one kid, walking down the hall. More cops came, and one told her to stop, but a neighbor woman blocked him when he went to follow, then blocked him again when he tried to step around. She howled: "Call the cops! Call the cops and have him arrested! He ain't leaving till the cops come and arrest him!" It looked like it was about to boil over, when even more cops came, two of them running up twelve flights of stairs, and one had to lie down when he got there, and the other was rushed to the hospital with chest pains just after. The press of angry bodies made the apartment hot, and some women yelled for everyone to calm down, and some women yelled the opposite, and as we tried to dress the crying kids, some women tried to help, in earnest, finding their jackets and socks, while others were plainly angling to shoplift them. Lorraine had her last child taken, and she took a swing at a cop but one wrist was grabbed, then the other when it followed, and her friends took her aside, and after a few more eruptions of screaming, we got the kids out. One woman yelled, "This is why people hate the cops!" And though I thought very little of her and the rest of them, the Mothers United for Narcotics and Neglect, she had a point, because no one likes people who steal babies in the middle of the night. Although I was confident that we had done right, it felt wretched, and I didn't want to dwell on it. We had just started our tour.

THE MIDNIGHT TOUR IS ALSO CALLED THE FIRST PLATOON, the second and third being day tours and four-to-twelves. You begin at 2315 hours and end at 0750. There are three squads for each platoon, working five days on, two days off, five days on, three days off, so that there are two squads on patrol every tour. The five days are the "set," the two or three the "swing." If you have Tuesday and Wednesday off one week, say, you have Tuesday, Wednesday, and Thursday the next, and then Wednesday and Thursday the week after that. It takes some getting used to, because if you're working a Friday, you don't come in Friday, you come in Thursday night. Another depressing thing about midnights is that when you finish work, at ten minutes to eight in the morning, you don't say, "See you tomorrow," which would seem soon enough; you say, "See you tonight." Tonight began yesterday and tomorrow begins tonight, and the days become one rolling night.

You lose track of time on this schedule, much more than on any other. I started out on steady four-to-twelves, Sunday to Thursday. You could lead a more normally regimented life. For my first two years at the Morris Houses, I was busier than on the midnights, when I might cover an entire precinct. The crime rate hadn't fallen as far as it later would, and the hours weren't as late. I knew less local history then, and the landmarks I navigated by were of recent relevance: the pawnshop to check after a chain-snatch; the crackhouse where the baby had overdosed; the rooftop where they fought pit bulls, sometimes throwing the loser to the street below. Sometimes Stix and I covered that area on the midnights, but even with a better grasp of the place and more time to think about it, I still wondered why things had turned out as they had.

Morris Houses were named after Gouverneur Morris, a Revolutionary War hero and coauthor of the Constitution who served with Washington at Valley Forge, and who later established the decimal system of U.S. currency, inventing the word "cent." His half-brother, Lewis, was a signer of the Declaration of Independence, and he tried to get the Founding Fathers to establish the Capitol on the family estate, though the idea was more or less a non-starter. The Morrises owned most of the South Bronx from 1670, and their name is everywhere: the neighborhood called Morrisania, in the Four-Two, where my beat was, and Morris High School, which graduated the industrialist Armand Hammer and Secretary of State Colin Powell, not to mention dance-school impresario Arthur Murray. The neighborhoods of Morris Heights and Port Morris are named for the family, as is Morris Avenue, although Morris Park, which was built over the racetrack where they once held the Belmont Stakes, is named after someone else. Yet I couldn't say they mean much to anyone here; Morris Houses was the place where the kids Bernhard Goetz shot came from—four thugs who approached the wrong lunatic on a subway, in 1986. One remained confined to a wheelchair, and I'd sometimes see him around. I locked up another one's sister for robbery, after a nasty girlgang fight, and I can't imagine their mother said, upon each of her children's return from jail, "Gouverneur Morris and his half-brother Lewis must be rolling in their graves!" The Morrises made this place and helped make this nation, but they might as well have knocked up some local girls after a one night stand, leaving nothing but their name.

It's hard to think of how things could have gone worse, though they certainly could have. On a map of what might have been, I could point out the spot where someone planned to shoot Franklin Delano Roosevelt during a campaign visit. It isn't far from where the ransom was paid for the Lindbergh baby, though the child had been dead a month by then. I could show you the spot on Bryant Avenue where Popeye and Sonny recovered eighty-eight pounds of French Connection heroin, though I wish I could drive by and say, "This is where we won the war on drugs." There are other local monuments to lost opportunity that are not all cause for regret, however. A few blocks away, at 1522 Vyse Avenue, Leon Trotsky lived for a year before returning to Russia for the role that fate had assigned him. When the story broke, the headline of *The Bronx Home News* read, "Bronx Man Leads Russian Revolution." Imagine if he had stayed here. John

F. Kennedy lived in the Bronx for a year as a child. I wonder what he would have sounded like, if he'd stayed: *Ax not what yiz can do for ya country* . . . Lee Harvey Oswald lived in the Bronx as a young teenager, in Highbridge and Belmont. But JFK returned to Boston, and Oswald was sent to the Youth House, for psychiatric evaluation, and they would not meet for years, and not here, and they would not know that they had the Bronx in common.

When the time dragged, these scraps of fact that jammed my head like a junkshop's clutter tended to pop up more often. The Russian theme reemerged one night, when it was so slow that three patrol cars showed up for a dispute between two crackheads over a lost shopping cart. To pass the time, we conducted a thorough investigation, asking pointed questions: *What color was the cart? Do you have a receipt?* It was cold, and after a while, one of the cops said we should leave. But I was bored enough to want to talk to the crackheads, who relished the attention. I said to the cop, "They have issues, we can help them work through them, the relationship can come out even stronger than it was before." He looked at me and said, "Hey, I'm no Dr. Zhivago, let's get out of here."

On the midnights, there is a risk of drifting within yourself, trailing off on your own weird trains of thought, so that when the even weirder world intrudes, it is hard work not to laugh. In short, you get a little punchy sometimes, I felt bad after one job, for a few reasons. It was a sad case and they seemed like good people, an old man and his sick wife. He had an upright, military bearing, and she was a stick figure, with plum-colored bruises all over, gasping through her nebulizer, "*Ayúdame, ayúdame, ayúdame. . . .*" We made small talk, in broken English and Spanish, while waiting for EMS. There was a picture of a young man in a police uniform, and the old man said he was his son, a cop in San Juan who had died at the age of thirty-four, from cancer. The entire apartment was a Santería shrine: cigars laid across the tops of glasses of clear liquid; open scissors on dishes of blue liquid; dried black bananas hanging over the threshold; tarot cards, change, and dice before a dozen statues of saints, including a massive Virgin Mary with a triple-headed angel beneath. They struck me as objects of pity and power at once. I wondered if it was the woman or the man who was trying to stack the supernatural deck in their favor, if disaster, past or impending, could be renegotiated with the spirits and saints. And then I thought, *They keep the place up, but it's more House Voodiful than House Beautiful.* The line wouldn't leave my head, and I started to break up. I had to pretend to cough and walk outside, while Stix gave me a funny look.

You get in the habit of reading these scenes for signs, forensic or sacramental, as they both make the same point about sin and struggle in the fallen world. In Santería, shrines of candles and other offerings are often placed in the corner of a room, near the entrance; and in just that spot, in one apartment, there was a black-handled butcher knife, and blood that had not just pooled but piled, it lay so thick on the floor. There were dark sedimentary layers, and a clear overlay like varnish, which I was told came from the lungs. The woman whose handiwork it was explained what brought her to this sacrifice at the household altar: "Two years ago, my brother broke my leg in five places. I came in tonight, he sold my couch. He killed my mother. Well, she died from him and all his nonsense." She stopped talking for a moment, and tried to shift her hands in her cuffs, as EMS took him out in a wheelchair, pale and still. "I didn't stab him," she went on. "He stabbed himself by accident, in the back, in the tussle." Some objects tell simple stories of fierce violence, like the two-by-four, so bloody it looked like it was dipped in the stuff, used to collect a fifty-dollar debt one woman owed another. Others are more subtle and tentative, like the open Bible in the apartment of a woman whose brother, just home from prison, suffered some sort of psychotic break. "He sat there reading the Bible for a while, and then he just looked up and said he was going to kill me," she said. The Bible was opened to the first page of Proverbs, which says, in Chapter 1, Verse 18: "These men lie in wait for their own blood, they set a trap for their own lives." Maybe he only read the first part of the sentence. The woman's husband had just died, and beside the Bible was a sympathy card from someone named Vendetta.

As a cop, you look for patterns, for context and connections that tell a fuller truth than a complainant may be willing to tell. But sometimes the patterns themselves are deceptive; there are parts that belong to no whole. So it was with a matched pair of attempted robberies, twenty minutes and four blocks apart. Each perp was a male Hispanic, tall, slim, and young, in dark clothes (all brown in the first case, all black in the other), with a razor blade. In the second robbery, the perp wore a bandanna over his face and a wig, and the victim was cut in the hand with a razor. We packed up the complainants and canvassed the park that lay between the crime scenes, and we stopped a tall, slim, male Hispanic in his twenties, in all-black clothes, and when I searched him, I found a wig, a bandanna, and a razor in his pocket. If there was some doubt that the perps were the same, there was little that I'd found the guy responsible for one of them. Both complainants were sure, however, that he wasn't the perp, and we let him go. Since the weapon was a razor, maybe I should have remembered Poe and gone to look for the orangutan.

That was one kind of mystery, the puzzle of whodunit, which has a solution that is out of sight but within reach, like the winning card in three-card monte. There are other mysteries that raise questions that are far older and more open, and if there is a hint of a game in what unfolds, you feel more like a piece than a player. One night we went to a routine Aided case, an old woman with a history of heart trouble, whose breath was rapid and shallow. She moaned, "*Mami!*" as she sat on a red velvet couch, flanked by her young teenage granddaughters, and as she left with EMS, Stix told me that the old lady took care of the girls. We drove around for a while, and then we had another Aided case, a "heavy bleeder." When we went inside, a woman said, "She's in bed," and, "It's in the tub," and we checked on the teenage girl in the bedroom, who said she was fine, and then looked in the bathtub, where a fetus the size and color of a sprained thumb nestled in the drain. The head was turned upward and the eyes were open and dark. When the EMTs came—they were the same guys as at the last job—they asked for some plastic wrap or tinfoil, and they were provided with a sandwich bag to pick it up. As we helped them put the teenage girl in the ambulance, the EMT told me that the old lady had gone into cardiac arrest and wouldn't make it. Nothing else happened that night, and as we drove I thought about the two jobs, what they asked and answered, and what went through my mind was that for every one that dies, another one never is born. It was late but not late enough, not yet time to go home.

. . .

OCTOBER PASSED, AND THEN NOVEMBER, AND CHRISTMAS approached. In the beginning, especially, it didn't seem that John and I worked at the same job: I was a security guard, and he might spend a night drinking, going to bars where an underage police cadet would attempt to be served, or to see if he could buy a drink after four a.m. He was getting paid to drink beer. Technically, he was an undercover, but the assignments were not 007 stuff: he'd go to bodegas and try to buy loose cigarettes, or to Yankee games to scalp tickets. They locked up old men in social clubs for having a case of beer in the back room, or old ladies in bodegas for having policy slips or a joker poker machine. At first, I was jealous of the ease of his life, but later on, when I was back in the street, he was jealous of the stories of real police work. When people asked us where we worked, I noticed that he began to say he was in the Organized Crime Control Bureau instead of Vice.

Nonetheless, the time counted for his shield, and there were other perks. John was trained in the use of the "asp," the new, telescoping nightstick, which you'd extend with a flick of the wrist, and perps would run at the sound of it. He was sent to a day-long course on eavesdropping technology, where they gave out tote bags that were emblazoned SECRET SERVICE NYPD ELECTRONIC CRIME SEMINAR. He came home beaming, holding it up.

"How do you like it?"

"The logo's cool. It's just a shame they decided to put in on a purse. You're probably tough enough to get away with carrying it around, but you could also give it to your sister."

As Vice grew less attractive to me, it was becoming clear that the distaste was mutual. John asked the Vice captain about me a couple of times, and then he stopped, as the answer of "Soon, I think" grew testy and cool. More temps came into the office, and I came to suspect that this constant flow of new people was someone's idea of an integrity tactic, so that the cops wouldn't trust one another enough to steal. John worked often with another temp named Chris Verdejo, and we went out for dinner one night. Chris had just made a case that was featured on the front page of the *Times* sports section, when he took down a major counterfeiter of pro sports tickets. Chris had worked a Yankee game for scalpers, and he picked up a perp who had counterfeit tickets. Even the "legit" scalpers, who after all sold a real ticket, hated the counterfeiters. Chris developed his perp as an informant, and it led to a print shop where tickets for hockey, baseball, and basketball teams all across the country were produced. George Steinbrenner had assisted the police in the investigation, and it got great press. "I'm the flavor of the month!" Chris laughed. The Vice captain told him he could stay permanently, if he wanted, but later on said he couldn't manage it. Some inspector's nephew would be getting the spot. It reminded me to call Inspector Mullen, and offer myself up for adoption. At Central Booking one night, I noticed a cop from the Four-Seven eyeballing me, after which he asked if I knew Mullen. I said I did, but when he scrutinized my name tag, he shook his head and said, "I thought you were his son." If only that cop worked in the personnel office.

And then John received another unexpected notification. He was called up for the Fire Department, from a test he had taken five years before. The rumor was that the old list was resurrected because the son of one of the big bosses was on it. My cousin Brian had also been called. Both of them were the sons of firemen—my cousin Gerald, Brian's brother, was also on FD—and John's father had worked until he had a heart attack in the firehouse, refusing to go to the hospital until he was carried out. Mr. Timpanaro loved his job, as most firefighters did, while John's love of police work was a rarer and more complex commodity. A lot of cops went over to FD, like my friend Tommy Killian, but you never heard of firefighters who switched over to become cops, except for one or two who traveled from PD to FD and back, and were considered oddballs by both departments. Firefighters could arrange the schedules so that they worked two or three days a week; the camaraderie was legendary and the politics were minimal, next to our job; the public loved them. They died more often than we did, but they killed themselves less. For most people, there was no hesitation to transfer; for John, there was. John was not afraid of many things, and to date I was aware of two of them: he dreaded roaches, and he lived in fear that I might use his toothbrush and not tell him. I was *gabbados* and a *stunad,* thickheaded, but more important I was a *gavone,* a slob; he was a *skeevats,* who saw messy things as positively menacing. His skeeve-levels were nearly as high as Stix's, in the avoidance of doorknobs and of handshakes from bums, and once when I told him I was returning a pair of his underwear—washed, of course—he looked at me with unabashed horror and said, "Keep them." But the third thing he was afraid of was fire, I learned.

"If I see a guy with a gun, I chase him. I know the risks but I'm not afraid—I know I'm smarter, stronger, and faster than him, and that I'm a better shot. I've been trained in tactics, and he hasn't. In my gut, I know I'm gonna win. But with a fire, none of that matters—a fire cares about me less than even the worst perp, and all I have to go against it doesn't matter. As a cop, I work in the worst part of the city, and the part I love best is the gun collars. If I went to FD, I'd go to the quietest corner of Staten Island, where I can work out all day and help cook and get a cat out of a tree once a year. I don't like fire."

And yet he decided he would accept the job. He went through another interview and medical, and was told he'd get a call on a particular Friday or Monday. The days passed, but then he was told the date had been postponed. When the next date passed without a call, he knew that the job wasn't there for him. My cousin Brian became a fireman, and John stayed a cop. I think he was relieved as much he was disappointed, but I was angry that the NYPD was such that even people who loved it would leave for work they hated, because there were so few real or rational reasons to stay.

Stix and I had begun to find our stride on the midnights, becoming a familiar team like Moxom and Parisi, Otero and Garcia, Flower and Thompson. We collared, and learned how to work an odd little cat-and-mouse OP for 175 Alex, handicapped as we were by uniforms and a marked car, available for jobs at any moment. The building had a back door, so we'd have to wait for someone to walk out in order to make a sneak attack on the dealers in the lobby. One night we had an inspiration to send in someone to open it up for us. We drove a few blocks away, to the prostitution strip on Jackson Avenue, and made the acquaintance of two ladies named Melissa and Snake. Snake explained that her boyfriend lived in the building and that she couldn't go there, but Melissa figured that opening a door for five bucks would be the easiest money she made that night. But we waited in vain—Melissa went to the wrong building, and Snake marched straight to 175 Alex to warn the dealers.

"What's the world coming to, when you can't trust a whore named Snake?"

We sometimes slipped in to work with Eddie Fackler and his conditions team—Eddie Wynne, Dennis Koesterer, Scott Griszcewicz, Chris Barry, and Danny Campagna, who set up like SNEU each night to collar. Eddie Fackler could "smell a gun," and his team brought them in routinely. I doubted that either of us would be able to join conditions, but to jump in with them to hit a set or chase a gun was exciting and nostalgic at once. We'd forgotten that the Job could be fun. If the midnights were never quite normal, they began to feel a little more familiar—we were in the streets, at least, and that was good. As the holidays drew near, Sgt. G organized a Christmas party, where each cop had to bring in a dish from where their family came from, and that night we answered jobs from the precinct, like firemen, around tables of pasta, empanadas, and fried chicken.

Two days before Christmas, Stix was out, and I worked with a new guy named Tommy Rendo. We had a job for a smoke condition, from a fire that had been put out on the four-to-twelve, when someone lit up a couch in a project basement. A few people were gathered outside, unable to return to their homes because the building was still choked with smoke, and we sent a couple with a baby to the hospital for smoke inhalation. Though the Fire Department had come and gone, the building still seemed unsettled and unsafe. We propped the front doors open and waded through the ankle-deep sludgy water of the basement to open more doors, and then we walked up ten stories to open the roof doors—the elevators had been shut down—so the building could ventilate. On the walk up, the smoke was so thick we could barely see in front of us, and we had to wait on the roof for a while to catch our breath, dizzy and coughing. On the way back down, we checked each apartment, but we had to go back to the roof a few more times for air. I was ambivalent about leaving, though the firefighters knew what they were doing and we didn't. After talking to the people outside to find out which elderly tenants might be at risk, we knocked on a few more doors and then we left.

We had to do a "vertical patrol" at a particular building, and we drove there, a little dazed and short of breath, stinking of smoke. The door was locked, and we sat in the car for a while, waiting for someone to come out. There was a recent decision to make verticals "activity," as a formal and quantifiable unit of work, like a summons or an arrest, and now every cop had to perform several each night, in designated buildings, and to notify the dispatcher at the start and finish of each. I suppose it made some cops walk when they would have preferred to sit, but it struck me as still more pointless and wrong-headed bureaucracy—would beat cops have to fill out reports for how many times they said hello to people, and whether they got a pleasant response? Why didn't they just put pedometers on our feet, and count how many steps we took at the end of the month? At roll calls, a lieutenant said, "Listen, the most important thing is to just put them over the air, so we get credit for them," with the plain message that seeming to do them was more important than anything else.

Finally, a woman walked out of the building and said hello to us—for a point maybe, on the new scale—but we didn't feel like moving just then. Tommy and I had a cigarette, to get the old smoke out of our lungs, and then we waited awhile longer. Finally, I said, "The hell with this," and we drove off. A few minutes later, the ICO raised us for a scratch, and twenty minutes later, we were called back to the command—he had been watching us, with binoculars, and had seen that and we hadn't gone into the building. He called me into his office, and gave me a speech about how shocked and disappointed he was: "I can't believe this! People say good things about you here! How could you do it, when you've got a rookie with you, who doesn't know any better? If Inspections caught you instead of me, this would have been a serious hit! What if there was a homicide in that building, and you put over the air that it was OK? I'm thinking about just writing the CD and getting it over with!"

As he spoke, he huffed up his sense of indignation, until he almost believed it himself. I knew it didn't matter, and I knew that neither of us really cared. I was on midnights in the South Bronx, on punishment posts more often than not, and there was little else that could be done to me. I also knew that he had me, dead to rights. I'd radioed that we'd gone into a building, and we hadn't.

I said, "What can I say? It won't happen again." Tommy and I went back out on patrol and checked the building, which of course was empty. Though I wasn't much concerned about the ICO, I told Tommy about a recent experience Stix and I had with him, when we were called in for a GO-15—an official department hearing, with union representatives—over a dent in the car. When we were assigned the car, Stix inspected it—checking the back seat for contraband, looking at the fluid levels, and so on—and he noticed a crimp on the passenger side, where the door hinge met the front panel. Every time you opened the door, the crimp got bigger, and after trying a few times, the two-inch gap became a three-inch gap. Cars pick up all kinds of nicks and scratches, and sometimes if cops dent the car more seriously, they'll pay a body shop to pound it out, rather than going through the fuss of the paperwork, or losing the car for weeks to the police mechanics. Once the accident is reported, the last cops to use the car are responsible for the damage; in this case, Comparetto and Clifford might catch a little grief, since someone gave it a kick on their watch. We were reluctant to report it, but we'd had enough trouble for ourselves, and the senior cops we talked to said we had no choice. The lieutenant at the desk said he'd have a look at it, as the ICO was walking by.

Had you seen the ICO look at the car door, you might have thought that he'd found a murder weapon; had you heard him, you might have thought that the homicide was of his twin brother. "I bet they were in a hit-and-run!" he said, as Stix and I stood by, unable to share in his mounting excitement. "There was a pursuit in the Four-O on the four-to-twelve, I bet they were in it and hit somebody! Let me see if they put it over the air that they were there!" and he raced back to pull up the printout of the job, certain that he was closing in on the culprits. Comparetto and Clifford, who each lived more than an hour away from the precinct, were summoned back at two in the morning. If they weren't so tired and enraged, they might have felt sorry for the

ICO. As it was, they were informed of their rights to union and legal representation. The Accident and Investigation Section of the Highway Unit was called in, to photograph the dent and dust it for prints; the District Attorney's Office was notified of the possibility of criminal prosecution; a team from Inspections arrived to conduct the formal interrogation.

Lt. Mahoney, who had the desk that night, said, "Leave it to the Police Department to turn a hundred-dollar dent into a ten-thousand-dollar investigation."

And so it was with a mix of false confidence and real indifference that I put my thoughts of the ICO aside, when we went back in for meal at five. When we left, an hour later, Tommy told me that the ICO had decided to write us up for Command Disciplines. I said, "Turn around, I'm gonna talk to him, we'll say we didn't go in on my account." Tommy began to protest that whatever we did, we did together, but I said forget about it, let's just settle this, and we headed back. As soon as I walked into the ICO's office, he said, "Where were you? You stink!"

If anything, we smelled better than the first time around, and I told him about the fire. I said that we could have gone to the hospital and gone sick for the next couple of days, but we were the only Housing car covering the Four-Two, and that wasn't the kind of cops we were. My diplomacy was not what it might have been, but he'd left me with the clear impression the reprimand would be man-to-man. He hemmed and hawed, saying that he had to write me up because he'd talked about it in front of another cop, whom he *really* wanted to get—and eventually would, for taking days off while claiming to be in the military. Finally, he told me, "Don't worry, you're one of the Captain's best guys, you won't lose any time."

"I don't think it's right," I said, and I walked out. It was the morning before Christmas Eve, and I'd have the holiday off for the swing. When I went back in, the day after Christmas, our PBA delegate Harry Thompson told me that the Captain wanted to take three days, and it was non-negotiable. The CD, for "improper patrol," would remain on my permanent record. My great-grandchildren would be able to look at the citation, much as I had been able to look at Pat Brown's. At the roll call, the lieutenant bellowed about what a fuck-up I was, and he sent Stix and me on another fixed post, for another threatened witness who wasn't home. It was more than a mile away, near Hunts Point, and the rest of the cops were ordered explicitly not to drive us there—we would take the bus. As we waited at the bus stop, for fifteen minutes, twenty, half an hour, the other guys kept driving up to us and saying, "C'mon, get in." "Forget about it," we said. "If they want us to take an hour to get there, it'll take us an hour to get there. If somebody gets killed, we'll be glad to explain why."

That would be my post for the next two weeks, sometimes with Stix, and sometimes with Parisi, who also had run afoul of one of the bosses. I sat there and read. One night, Eddie Fackler, Eddie Wynne, Chris Barry, and Dennis Koesterer got a gun, from a pistol-whip cab robbery. The perp hid in the bushes, reaching down to his ankle as they saw him. At the precinct, Koesterer yelled at him: "What the hell is wrong with you! I could have killed you!" "I had to straighten my sock," said the perp. Louie Malagon and Sgt. G got a gun, from a robbery at 169 and Cypress. Alex Otero and Louie Garcia got a gun, and Chicky got a gun with Sgt. Toth. Chicky had also come to mid-nights, a month after we did. He was tired of the fighting, too.

I called Inspector Mullen, and he said that Narcotics should come soon, not long after the New Year; I shouldn't worry about the CD, he said, but I had to have it adjudicated before the transfer. Harry Thompson was able to negotiate down so that it would be removed from my record if I stayed out of trouble for six months; my dark secrets would remain hidden from my descendants. I took the three days and signed the CD. The Lieutenant apologized for blowing up at me, and said that it was the Captain's orders. Once the two weeks were up, I could go back to work with Stix again on regular patrol.

On New Year's Eve, I was assigned to guard the PSA parking lot, and it was there that I greeted the new millennium. After five years of hard work in the NYPD, I was sent to stand there, freezing amid the empty cars, as the fireworks erupted somewhere out of sight, and the gunshots rang out, a little closer. I was with a new guy named Ullman—since he'd seen combat in the Israeli Army, "rookie" seemed patronizing—and we bullshitted away the hours. I tried to say what I liked about the Job, but it was hard to come up with anything. I didn't want to come off as a hairbag, though it wasn't far from what I felt. The Captain and the ICO both paid me visits, to make sure I was at my post. I think I said "Happy New Year" to them, but I don't really recall.

8

Turnpike Trooper: Racial Profiling and the New Jersey State Police

by John I. Hogan

"The power and prestige that are bestowed upon New Jersey Troopers is over-whelming, especially to an impressionable new, young recruit who waited a life-time to don the blue and gold. To put it bluntly, John I. Hogan #5068 ate, slept, and breathed the culture of the New Jersey State Police."

—John I. Hogan,
Turnpike Trooper: Racial Profiling & the New Jersey State Police

As my graduation day approached, the only problem was that I didn't know the first damn thing about being a cop. I could shine shoes, polish brass, whisk toilets, and make a floor look like glass using a mop; but I had no concept of what being a police officer was all about. At the most, we had a few hours of actual hands-on police training such as handcuffing or making motor-vehicle stops. I was in great shape, was confident about not getting my ass kicked, had all my leather uniform gear highly polished; but I didn't know the first thing about being a trooper.

As talk of our commencement began, I was excited but nervous. For nearly five months, my classmates and I had accepted, endured, and passed every challenge thrown at us. None of these tasks, however, really had anything to do with actual hands-on police training. Though it wasn't discussed, I would like to think my fellow classmates felt the same way.

Our Christmas present came in the form of learning what our badge number would be. On our last day at the academy before the Christmas break, I learned that I was to be Trooper John I. Hogan, badge no. 5068. We were informed that no matter what, no other person in history will ever have that number again! I recall Sergeant First Class Bernard telling us, "Even if you quit

Reprinted from *Turnpike Trooper: Racial Profiling and the New Jersey State Police* (2005), by permission of TPR. John I. Hogan, #5068-NJSP.

or get fired, that number is yours for life. No trooper will ever be assigned the same badge number." I remembered thinking to myself, *Fired after what I went through to get here! No way would I ever jeopardize my new career and lifelong dream!* We were also introduced to and given a block of instruction from the NJSP's Employee Assistance Program (EAP). It was during this block that we were all assured that any physical, mental, or other permanent ailment suffered by a trooper during an on-duty altercation (right or wrong in his actions), the state would be responsible for paying that trooper's permanent-disability status if forced to resign as a result. *Whatever! Why are they telling us this bullshit! What's with all the information relating to alcoholism and depression? Do some cops have problems?*

Christmas came and went, as did New Year's Day. On the first morning back to the academy after the New Year, we were treated to a fourth surprise: urine-sample test. We were now just two weeks from graduation, which was slated for January 15, 1993, and the thought of a urine test seemed absurd to me. All I could think about was finally putting on that uniform and marching into the Trenton War Memorial and saluting before Colonel Justin Dintino who would hand me badge no. 5068, which was soon to be mine for life.

The week before graduation came and went, and it was all a matter of routine now. I left on that Friday for the last time, knowing that when I come back to Sea Girt as a recruit on Monday, January 11, 1993, it would be for the last time. The weekend dragged on as I couldn't wait to go back. My class, which had dwindled to ninety-four recruits since arriving that dreadful August afternoon, was ready to take on the world. *Wow, fifty people quit or were forced to resign, and I could probably only name five!*

Monday morning, graduation week, was finally here. The 113th class assembled on the fire line for our last week of training. Instead of the normal "Welcome back, scumbags," Trooper Kilmurray yelled, "Recruit Russano, what's your badge number?" Andrew Russano replied, "Five-zero-nine-four, sir!" "Not anymore, Russano. You are now no. 5-0-9-3. Recruit Maloney post on me!" *What in the hell? How can someone get kicked out five days before graduation?*

With that, Recruit "*Stephen Maloney*" was gone, never to be seen or heard from again. After twenty-two weeks of hell, the former local police officer allegedly tested positive for cocaine on the last urine analysis and was immediately dismissed. That was probably the largest dose of reality I had been hit with in my young life. After the shock of Maloney's dismissal wore off, I settled in for my last week, and before I knew it, Thursday night had arrived. I was going to bed as a civilian for the last time, but sleep was an afterthought for me on this night. The fact that in less than twenty-four hours I was going to be a New Jersey state trooper kept me awake all night. Was I more excited about graduation, or was I more nervous because I knew deep down that I didn't have the faintest idea on *how to be a trooper?*

Friday, January 15, 1993, arrived, and together as one unit, the improbable 113th NJSP Recruit Class marched into the Trenton War Memorial. To say the least, it was the happiest and proudest day of my life. Though the ceremony was a blur, numerous dignitaries and politicians were there and spoke of pride; tradition; and, most importantly, *honor, duty,* and *fidelity.* After the ceremony, we were handed our badges, weapons, and bullets. This would be the first time I ever possessed a weapon without supervision as I posed for pictures with my parents, family, and friends who attended.

As I drove home from Trenton in full uniform by myself, with a loaded weapon on my hip, I recalled a million "what if" scenarios popping into my mind. I was truly at a loss as to what I'd do if confronted with a situation during those twenty minutes. I did it! I made it! My high-school-yearbook prophecy had now been fulfilled. I was indeed a New Jersey trooper but only because the certificate and badge said so. What do I do now? Aside from putting on the uniform, I sure as hell don't know how to be a trooper!

PLAYING A TROOPER

"You stay down here, and I'll take the upstairs," the senior trooper whispered to me in a dead-serious tone. With that, he pulled his weapon and entered through the unlocked front door of the large white colonial home we were dispatched to. Mentally, this burglary call just took a real-life twist. Initially, as we sped to the residence, I was excited but nervous. It was roughly 10:30 PM, and the rural roads of Millstone Township were pitch-black as a misty rain fell onto our windshield. I could feel my entire inner-self shaking but needed to prove to my new partner that I was calm; cool; and, above all other things, a trustworthy and reliable colleague. As we neared the property, the senior trooper turned off the lights of our marked New Jersey-trooper car. I assumed we did not want the potential burglars to be aware of our arrival. *Ah, the element of surprise . . . I remember them talking about this tactic in the academy.* Once we parked in front of the totally darkened home, no other cars or persons were visible. We quietly exited the troop car and briskly walked to the front door. The burglar alarm that had sounded, prompting us to respond, was loud and annoying. This deafening high-pitched noise only added to the tension I already felt throughout my entire body. As I watched the senior trooper remove his gun from its holster and approach the house, the reality of what was transpiring smacked me right in the face.

At twenty-three years old and just a few weeks removed from the academy, I was now thrust into real-life action for the first time. To worsen this predicament was the glaring fact that I had no idea what to do or how to act, let alone be a "squared away" trooper. *I wish I were back at the academy, scrubbing toilets.* Following my partner's lead, I too grabbed my weapon. The black metal was cold and intimidating. With my left thumb, I wearily unsnapped the button that secured my gun to my holster. I then hesitantly removed my Heckler & Koch 9-mm semiautomatic pistol with my left hand. My body and hands trembled. *Shit, did I remember to fully load my ammunition clip? Is there a live round in the chamber?* My palms were sweaty. My breathing was erratic. It was early February, very damp and cold; but my body temperature was overheating from nervousness, anxiety, and anticipation.

In the academy, instructors advised that if we were lucky, we would never have to draw our weapons throughout our career. Statistically, I recall them telling us a very, very slim percentage of police officers across the country ever have to use deadly force. Ironically, the probability of the same officer using deadly force twice in his career is very improbable. *Great! Here I am with less than a fucking month on the job, and already, I am put into a situation where I am drawing my weapon.*

A possible burglary in progress was the call received from dispatch minutes ago. The thoughts and ideas that ran rampant in my mind were endless and incomplete as the senior trooper drove to the scene. *How great would it be to catch the burglar in action,* I thought to myself. Personally, this was what I had waited a lifetime for. To be "on the job" as a New Jersey state trooper was my sole dream, but as this scenario unfolded before me, I was now unexpectedly confronted with numerous circumstances I never gave much thought to.

Could I really shoot somebody? Would I panic or overreact? Will my actions get my partner shot, even killed? Will the burglar overpower me and take my weapon, then kill my partner and me with my own weapon? What if I shoot an innocent person or the homeowner? Even worse, what if a little kid comes running around the corner, and I shoot him or her? Mentally, I was at a loss and realized I had never given much thought to the seriousness and irreversible impact my actions could have. *This is it. I just know I am going to screw something up, and someone will get hurt because of my actions.*

Once we were on the porch, no sign of forced entry was visible as I stood behind my partner. We quietly entered the unlocked home, and straight ahead of us was a beautiful hardwood staircase that wrapped around to the left. My partner went straight up the steps and immediately disappeared. I was alone, confused and at a total loss at what to do next. *What in God's name do I do now?* My weapon was in my left hand, but it was far from steady. I stood frozen in time for the next few seconds. It was eerily quiet.

As I struggled internally to regain confidence and composure, I leaned up against a wall and slowly peeked left into the living-room area. Barely able to control my breathing, I exhaled deeply when I saw no one was present. As I hesitantly went from room to room, no sign of forced entry or theft was present. The tension and anxiety that controlled my body slowly ceased. Gradually, I began to regain my poise as I checked the home farther, room by room. Within minutes, my partner and I were reunited on the first floor and concluded that the call was a false alarm. Once back in the troop car, we notified dispatch of our findings, and I immediately handwrote the operations report. Much to my disliking and embarrassment, my hands were still shaking, but I did my best to conceal it from the senior trooper, who appeared completely unfazed by what just transpired. I already loved being a trooper, but as I sat there, writing the report, I prayed that would be the last time I ever had to draw my weapon in a real-life scenario.

While most may not admit it, I feel every police officer, at some point in their career, will second-guess themselves and their abilities. Taking someone's life or being confronted with a situation that could result in your own death is not something that was ever discussed at the barracks. We all knew the dangers of being a police officer. It's been my experience that most cops enjoy living on the edge. The adrenaline rush we get maybe five, six, or even seven times a day is, to say the least, extremely addictive. The power and prestige that are bestowed on New Jersey troopers is overwhelming, especially to a impressionable new, young recruit who waited a lifetime to don the blue and gold. To put it bluntly, John I. Hogan #5068 ate, slept, and breathed the culture of the New Jersey State Police.

In retrospect, our preparation to the realities of being a trooper is hard-core: mentally and physically exhaustive. The body, mind, and soul are transformed during this insanely intense training. You leave the academy with a sense of invincibility. With credentials in his or her hand, its then up to each individual trooper to withstand the daily unknowns that confront every police officer across the country. Only the individual officer knows, deep down, if he or she has what it takes to adapt, interpret, and react in a split second to any given situation.

What weighed most heavily in my mind on a daily basis was whether I could rise to the top if I had to. If I failed, I would ruin what the instructors ingrained in us to be the only and most important thing we had going for us upon graduating from the academy: ***our reputation.*** Repeatedly during our training, instructors alluded to the importance of not getting "labeled" because once a junior trooper was in bad standing, life at the barracks could be miserable for that individual. Hopefully, statistics will be on my side, and I won't ever be in that miniscule percentage who will ever be confronted with a deadly-force situation or other critical incident, but what if I'm not so lucky?

Over the course of the next few months, I settled in and learned what being a trooper was really about while at my first assigned post: the Hightstown Station. Situated on the southbound side of Route 130 in Middlesex County, this barracks was older and run-down in appearance. Surprisingly and most upsetting to me, however, was, unlike what was preached in the academy, the most palpable observation was the lack of camaraderie at the barracks. Prior to exiting the academy, Trooper Kilmurray assured us every trooper would have our back, be our "brother," and give their life for one another but, apparently, not at this barracks.

Needless to say, from an outsider's perspective, there were kinks in the armor at the Hightstown Station. Unexpectedly, the "brotherhood" at this barracks I was now a part of was more equivalent to a halfway house. Among our eight-person squad were unique personalities who refused to ride with one another, barely spoke to certain squad members, and definitely didn't party or hang out after work ended as I hoped. I was fortunate, however, to have a very good "trooper coach" named Leslie "Rob" Bice. At five foot eight and around one hundred and fifty pounds, Trooper

Bice was far from the mean, nasty-dispositioned individual I assumed would be my mentor. A very mellow and soft-spoken gentleman, Trooper Bice's biggest accomplishment was to never have had an Internal Affairs Bureau (IAB) complaint during his fifteen-year career. He taught me the correct way to speak to motorists and the importance of avoiding verbal confrontations that could only escalate into more problematic situations. His motto was simple—"The power of the pen"—meaning, write your ticket and send the motorists on their way without disputing the issue.

Trooper Coach was an eight-week crash course in how to actually be a trooper. During this time, I continuously rode with Trooper Bice or other senior troopers and experienced arrests for driving while intoxicated (DWI); investigated motorvehicle accidents; and handled various complaints such as alarms, trespassing, and other minor infractions. While working the midnight shift on the coach program, I was also fortunate enough to make an arrest for what I really wanted to concentrate on and practiced so often in my parents' basement: *drug possession!* Admittedly, though, after completing the volumes of paperwork and required reports that came with these arrests over the course of several hours, I swore I never wanted to make another criminal arrest again.

With a decent foundation to now work with, I almost felt like I knew what to do as my two-month "trooper coach" orientation concluded. In mid-March 1993, I set out on duty for the first time by myself. I arrived to the barracks an hour early, as was customary, to do the dishes, empty the trash cans, and maintain the overall cleanliness of the barracks, as was every junior trooper's job. Once dressed, I inspected the interior and exterior of my assigned marked troop car, loaded the shotgun, tested my radar, and pulled out of the Hightstown Station. Alone in the troop car for the first time, I was the happiest and proudest human being alive. Each time the dispatcher came over the airwaves, I was hoping to be detailed to a serious crime or traumatic situation so I could prove that I could handle anything. Even if they didn't like one another, my peers' opinion of me was paramount in my mind. Being "squared away" was what I strived for, and I refused to become one of those guys that other troopers didn't want to ride with. Now that I had the uniform, the car, the badge, and the mentality, everything else was up to me; and I strived to become the most squared-away trooper I could be.

As was tradition with new-recruit classes, our first assignment was short-lived and, we rotated stations as a class, according to troops. The state police was divided into three areas: Troop A (south), Troop B (north), and Troop C (central). Graduated recruits were disseminated among the stations that made up these three troops. The other (2) troops that comprised the state police were Troop D (New Jersey Turnpike) and Troop E (Garden State Parkway).

My second assignment landed me at Troop C's most notorious barracks: Fort Dix. Located in Wrightstown, just outside of the Fort Dix and Maguire Air Force military installations, this barracks was the exact opposite of Hightstown. From day one, Sgt. Billy Vowell spoke of squad loyalty, unity, and *insisted* that we have squad outings that came to include fishing expeditions, overnight stays in Atlantic City, picnics and parties, lots of parties, where drinking, joking and having fun were rampant.

This was the trooper lifestyle I always heard stories about and couldn't wait to live. Work hard and play even harder—this was the mentality at Troop C's busiest barracks. Fort Dix was synonymous with, and often called, the Wild West. This well-deserved reputation was not because of the disgusting walls, floors, lockers, or fact that the water was not consumable or even suitable for showering. Instead, it was dubiously named so because of its proximity to the military bases, where several section 8 housing complexes were situated, and trust me, the inhabitants of these "projects" were always up to no good. At Dix, drunk driving and warrant arrests were very easy to come by, and they quickly lost their luster to me. Even more importantly, I almost felt hypocritical arresting "DUIs," knowing I was guilty of this offense from time to time.

As a trooper, the "system" stated locking up drunks was just something we had to do (on the average, one a month), but to separate yourself and be considered a "squared away" trooper, you had to make drug arrests, and despite the volumes of paperwork it entailed, this was my burning desire and true reason for wanting to be a trooper.

While at Dix, in hopes of garnering and solidifying my reputation to my peers, I began to quiz the minds of senior troopers assigned there, many of whom I respected and looked up to because they had already done the ultimate "time on the Big Road," also known as Troop D—the New Jersey Turnpike.

Just as I had been instructed to do in the academy, I tried to learn something—good or bad—from every trooper I came in contact with. For example, while at Hightstown, I learned *not* to "hawk bars" in hopes of making DWI arrests because the douche-bag trooper, who was infamous for having a "heavy thumb," was disliked by everyone for this inexcusable activity. At Fort Dix though, the troopers were all great guys and talked from experience. Jerk-offs were not permitted at Dix; and if they surfaced, they were quickly identified, singled out, and sent packing! Through conversations with experienced senior troopers, I learned little tips like observing a subject's body and eye movements when being questioned; finding the places either in a vehicle or on a person where contraband may be concealed; and knowing *everyone,* no matter what or why, lies to the police.

With each passing day, my confidence and abilities in becoming a good trooper increased. My level of awareness to my surroundings and the subjects I was now dealing with on a daily basis was at an all-time high. Making good, quality narcotic arrests and the paperwork that came with it quickly became second nature as everyone on the squad chipped in, and then once the "perp" was dropped off at the county jail, our squad would most often go to a local bar or hang in the rear of the barracks for hours of "debriefing."

After spending nearly a year at my second assignment, prior to leaving Fort Dix, I had made the largest seizure in recent memory: two pounds of marijuana. Though the issue of "profiling" had never surfaced either in the academy or at my first two assignments, I did learn the equivalent to "reverse profiling." Much like in Camden City, North Philadelphia, or other predominant minority areas, I was subjected to an area known as Sunbury Village in Pemberton Township, Burling County. It was in this area where Caucasian motorists were often singled out and stopped if motor-vehicle infractions were observed and questioned about their presence in this area. These routine stops often lead to arrest for narcotics, weapons, or other contraband. *So much for common stereotypes!* I was no longer naive and felt ready for the place I dreamed of patrolling since I was a child: the New Jersey Turnpike. Unfortunately, due to the dangers and complexity of incidents that occurred on the turnpike, only troopers with a minimum of sixteen months' service could be assigned to "the Big Road." Though I was willing, eager, and ready, the turnpike would have to wait, and the third and final rotation for the 113th Recruit Class landed me at the Wilburtha Station in West Trenton.

Situated at the base of the hill leading up to Division Headquarters, the Wilburtha Station, with its fresh and friendly atmosphere, was unlike any other barracks I had stepped into. Complete with an actual jail cell as opposed to the normal "handcuff locked to a bench" that served as a cell at most stations, Wilburtha was neat, clean, and properly outfitted with all basic necessities. Unfortunately, even though we were "state" troopers, we were forbidden by our superiors to patrol Trenton City, so there was no use for any of this great equipment. In a nutshell, my time at Wilburtha was an abysmal tour.

Upon meeting my new sergeant for the first time, I was poignantly advised to steer clear of Trenton. I was further informed that if I chose to go into the city and got involved in something, I was on my own. *What a pussy this guy was!* With one of the highest crime rates in New Jersey, I was incensed that we were not allowed to patrol Trenton. Personally, I thought the superiors who ran the station were cowards for not insisting we go into the city and aggressively patrol for criminal activity as was the case when Colonel Pagano was empowered to lead the ranks.

Instead, day shifts were wasted with junior troopers, like myself, acting as overpaid delivery persons. At least twice a day—if not more, we did "package relays" between the Division Headquarters and Troop C headquarters, which was located on the southbound side of Route 1 in Princeton. With no specific area of responsibility, troopers from Wilburtha patrolled Interstate Highways 95, 195, and 295. As known by most New Jerseans, these roads are mainly comprised of business commuters. The mundane, daily practice of writing speeding tickets to decent, hard-working citizens going to work bored the hell out of me. I did not join the state police to write tickets to commuters who would then be forced to pay the ridiculous insurance surcharges that New Jersey is nationally infamous for.

To put it mildly, I couldn't wait to leave Wilburtha. With the exception of occasionally "sneaking" into the inner city streets of Trenton on midnights with K.C., time stood still, and each day brought more bullshit as we served as gophers for the pompous division personnel. Finally, my sixteen months of service arrived, and I was now permitted to request a transfer. Without hesitation and despite the lecturing of my boy K.C., who nearly got jammed up on the 'Pike years previously, I submitted my paperwork requesting an immediate transfer to Troop D. I couldn't wait to be identified as a "turnpike trooper"!

Forever resentful of the fact we weren't permitted to patrol Stuyvesant, Oakland, Perry, or other "mean streets" of Trenton, once on the 'Pike, I could do what I truly joined the state police for and be a real "trooper." In December 1994, my transfer request was granted, and with just less than two years of active duty, along with my classmate Joe Sansone, we were the first troopers from the 113th Recruit Class to be assigned to the enigma known as the New Jersey Turnpike.

THE BLACK DRAGON

Reporting to the storied New Brunswick Barracks for my first day of duty was more intimidating than day one at the academy. Decades of state police lore; stories of wild chases, shootings, murders, massive contraband seizures and pandemonious, theatrical-like events gave the infamous New Jersey Turnpike its well-deserved reputation. This roadway is commonly known by most motorists as Interstate 95 or "the road that connects New York City to Philadelphia," but throughout the Division of State Police, because of its aerial structure and demonic reputation it is referred to as the Black Dragon.

At first glance, the circular-shaped barracks located within the Turnpike Authority Building on the southbound side of exit #9 gives off an unassuming persona to the millions of motorists who pass it daily. Nestled back on a hilltop and barely noticeable from the roadway, most passersby probably had no idea this structure doubled as a state-police barracks.

For me, however, in addition to the fears and apprehension I already had for the potential dangers that lie ahead, after hearing numerous gut-wrenching stories of the unbelievable and tragic incidents that previously occurred on the Big Road, I had chills as I approached the legendary barracks for the first time.

Once inside, my eyes shifted quickly, and I tried to take in as much as possible but was fearful that one of the senior troopers who was present may chastise me. As I looked around, I couldn't help but to mentally relive the numerous dramatic events that transpired within the confines of this infamous building.

Dingy walls and less-than-desirable flooring covered the small outdated dispatch area that sat to the left. On the opposite side of this wall was a single warped wooden bench with (2) sets of handcuffs locked to it. Next to this "cell" was a fingerprinting station; and I immediately wondered if Joanne Chesimard, Yu Kikumura, or other high-profile criminals were processed on the same fingerprinting board I now hoped to use.

Mentally, I was overcome with an eerie feeling of "if these walls could talk"! On the backside of the main corridor was a prisoner cell, and I was disappointed to see that it was empty during my initial venture into the barracks. Peering around and trying to remain unnoticed, I could sense the high level of activity that this station was notorious for. During this brief encounter, the phones were constantly ringing, the trooper who was serving as the dispatcher barked details over the radio, and I could sense the likelihood of utter chaos breaking out at any given minute.

After all, this was the very place where Trooper Werner Forrester was stationed when he was murdered by the members of the Black Panthers, including the most sought-after fugitive to date in New Jersey: the aforementioned Joanne Chesimard.

Even more menacing than the structure and aura of the New Brunswick Barracks were the troopers I initially encountered. As I carried the mounds of uniforms and gear I had down the spiral staircase that led to the "round room" where our lockers were located, each trooper I passed seemed more muscular, intimidating, and unapproachable. My "How are you, sir?" was continuously ignored by senior troopers, and in most cases, I was given a dirty look for even speaking to a turnpike trooper. Rumored as being a little meaner and crazier than the rest, troopers assigned to the 'Pike received a certain distinction throughout the Division of State Police. It was deliberated that no trooper's career was complete unless he or she did time on the Big Road, but as we all knew, there were a certain percentage of troopers who would never consider doing turnpike time.

Fitting in and being accepted by the likes of Billy Klimek, Dave Maruca, Sean Boero, and Kevin Goldberg was my ultimate goal. These guys were notorious throughout the division as the top "lock up" guys, and unbeknownst to them, I strived to join them at the top. Fortunately, I was assigned to squad #6, the same squad that Trooper Klimek was on. This, or so I thought, was my in. All I had to do was ride with and observe Trooper Klimek in action, and I too could soon become revered throughout the division for drug interdiction. The problem was, Klimek—like all the other squared-away troopers who I wanted to be like—wouldn't even acknowledge my existence let alone trust me enough to go on patrol with them.

My first three days on the turnpike were spent working day shifts and riding with Trooper Russ Gutter. With nothing other than mile markers and U-turns to learn, the only tricky part was determining what township you were in when making a motor vehicle stop. Trooper Gutter was extremely knowledgeable regarding turnpike policy and also served as our union representative. Unfortunately, Russ was the last person I should ride with if I were to be criminally active. He knew that and never pretended to be anything other than a good guy who liked to challenge the system. Russ was a great resource for everything except investigative questions and was one of the few senior troopers who were friendly to me from the start.

After my customary three days of authorized duty leave (ADL), I returned to work and was assigned my own car, equipment, and area of responsibility by Sgt. Jeff Suarez. When I pulled out of the barracks to go on patrol alone for the first time, I was alarmed at the speed in which traffic flowed. Previous to this assignment, I had only been on the turnpike in my personal car a few times, and now, here I was, in charge of an entire assigned area of the busiest roadway in all of New Jersey, perhaps the nation. Regardless of what happened in my area, I had to handle it—alone; "One job, one trooper" was the motto on the Big Road. I knew the only way to impress my new squad mates and prove that I was squared away was to handle all jobs quickly, efficiently, and without help. Keeping traffic moving was the underlying responsibility for troopers on the turnpike. If the traffic stopped, so did the toll revenues. With the exception of fatal accidents, *nothing* stopped traffic from flowing on the turnpike. Using high visibility with both marked and unmarked trooper cruisers, we tried to control the speed of traffic, but regardless of the number of troopers assigned to this roadway, the average speed at which the traffic flowed was still roughly seventy-five miles per hour on any given day despite all signs indicated the limit at 55 MPH.

With the traffic flowing continuously, troopers who were criminally active could then concentrate on what the Big Road was notorious for: guns, drugs, money, and bad-guys!

As my first few weeks of assignment on the 'Pike passed, frustration set in as I persistently tried to make an arrest. *I had to prove myself!* Then, to make matters worse, while alone on patrol, my classmate Joe Sansone made a narcotic arrest, and the razzing began. "Hey, boot, when are you going to be like your classmate and start bringing in some weight [referring to narcotics]?" or "Hey, troop, isn't it about time you stop being dead weight around here [referring to my lack of arrests]?" As hard as I tried to show my squad and other members at the barracks that I was going to be a "lock up" guy, I continued to fail. In reality, I was shy, timid, and even intimidated by the persons, mostly out of staters, I was stopping during the course of my shift. I quickly realized I was not confident, and I did not know the first thing about highway drug interdiction. *It all seemed so easy in my parents' basement!*

In the meantime, I handled my jobs, cleared accidents as quickly as possible, and did everything I could to try and fit in. None of this, however, was going to help get me noticed by the troopers I envied; then the unthinkable happened and forever changed my life and career path.

PART II

Deadly Force

It's pitch-black outside, and I'm awakened by my alarm clock blasting rap music from Power 99 FM. Outside of my covers, I could feel the brisk, cold air that swirled from the combination of the ceiling fan centered above my bed and the preset thermostat temperature in my house being kept at sixty-two degrees, even in the winter. *I have to be cold when I sleep!* The only heat I felt was from the internal heater of my king-size water bed as I lay there, struggling to prevent myself from falling back to sleep. It's 4:35 AM, and I had to be out of the house by five. *Day shifts suck!* From 6:00 AM to 4:00 PM on this day, March 23, 1995, a section of the New Jersey Turnpike would belong to me. With slightly more than two months of experience on the 'Pike, I was still struggling to fit in; make my first individual arrest; and, most importantly, earn the respect of the senior troopers assigned to the New Brunswick Barracks.

As usual, I got to the station around 5:30 AM so I could take out the trash, clean the dishes, make coffee, etc. At twenty-four years old, I was the youngest and, along with Sansone, the most junior guy on the turnpike. If I am labeled "salty," my reputation—as well as my entire locker, uniforms, gear, and even my personal vehicle—could have been destroyed by the infamous Phantom. (Part of state-police folklore, the phantom routinely preyed upon any trooper believed to be too salty or for failure to adhere to the numerous unwritten rules or codes of conduct at any given barracks.)

When I completed those menial duties, most of which I split with Sansone, together, we trekked down the spiral staircase and entered the circular locker room. Lined with aging dark brown cabinets that served as lockers, a massive weight room anchored the middle portion of this room and was frequently used by the numerous muscle-heads that were currently assigned to New Brunswick.

As we began to dress in our class A winter uniform, Sergeant Jeff Suarez arrived and promptly advised that I would "have the book" or serve as the administrative trooper for the day. Additional responsibilities for the "bookman" consisted of doing computer checks, logging motor-vehicle stops, and running criminal-history or background checks of any prisoners that were locked up during our shift. I immediately advised Sgt Suarez that I had a grand jury at 10:00 AM for an arrest that was "TOTed" to me (turned over to) by Trooper Mark Wondrack because, as everyone knew and constantly reminded me, I had yet to make a solo arrest! Upon learning this, Sgt. Suarez told me to disregard and assigned this duty to my classmate Joe Sansone.

After our squad briefing, I was assigned to patrol the "south," which was from milepost 61 to 73 or exits 7A to 8A. Since this area was closest to my residence, I was more familiar with this territory and, for obvious reasons, preferred this assignment. Plus, being further south meant less traffic which was critical as I was still adjusting to the unbelievable speed and volume of traffic that flowed daily on the 'Pike. Because seniority ruled on the Big Road, I became very familiar with the southern area since Troopers Busz, Gutter, Klimek, and Vona always had first preference and consistently selected the more northern territories that made up the New Brunswick Station.

Upon completing my equipment and vehicle inspections, I departed the parking lot of the barracks at roughly 6:20 AM. I immediately headed southbound and drove around in a sleepy funk for most of the morning. After stopping for breakfast and doing a final "loop" of my assigned area, I headed off Interchange No. 9 en route to Middlesex County Courthouse for a grand jury, which was a formal hearing where a prosecutor walked you through the events that led up the arrest. The civilians that made up the "jury" then voted whether or not to indict the arrested individual.

This particular hearing was for an arrest made on the midnight shift while riding with Trooper Wondrack. A routine motor-vehicle stop of a rental car from North Carolina was conducted, and though he assumed the role of the lead during this stop, he was good enough to give me credit for finding the loaded 9-mm pistol that led to this arrest. This, or so I hoped, would lessen the ridicule I currently faced from other station personnel for my lack of criminal activity.

Once I finished testifying before the grand jury, which took roughly ten minutes, I drove through the center of New Brunswick and headed back to the turnpike where I resumed my area of responsibility. Mentally, I wasn't in the mood to work, and before I realized it, lunchtime was quickly approaching, and I hadn't done a freaking thing all day. Once at Interchange 7A (milepost 61), I turned around at the toll plaza and headed northbound. Still in a sleepy funk, I observed no motor-vehicle infractions to enforce and was now growing concerned because I had absolutely no activity written on my daily patrol log.

Within minutes, I swiftly reached and entered the milepost 75 U-turn, which is a service ramp that crosses over the entire turnpike and is off-limits to the public. As I headed down the ramp to travel southbound, I encountered a white Volkswagen Jetta that was occupied by two black males sitting in their car, just at the base of the ramp. Identical to the Volkswagen I drove in to the academy with Brice for twenty-three weeks, it was facing northbound and had come to a stop. *No big deal. They're probably just lost or perhaps contemplating making an illegal U-turn.*

Facing opposite their vehicle, I pulled my marked troop car next to the driver's side window of the Volkswagen. As I hit the automatic window button to put mine down, I motioned to the driver to roll his window down. It was a bright, sunny, crisp, and cold day; and the sky was cloudless. As the sun's glare pierced my eyes, I asked the driver what he was doing. Without looking at me, he immediately stated that he was lost and needed to turn around. His breath dissipated in the cold March air, and I could tell he was very nervous for some reason.

Less than five feet apart and face-to-face while seated in our vehicles, I advised him that it was illegal for him to utilize this ramp. Sensing his heightened sense of nervousness, I asked the driver, a black male in his late twenties with close-cropped hair, if he had his driver's license. Almost as if he purposely ignored my question, he hesitantly replied, "It's not my car!" With this response, a lump began to form in my throat, and an uneasy feeling overcame my body. My sixth sense, which I started to question because of my lack of arrests, told me this guy wasn't your ordinary knucklehead.

As this encounter unfolded, the passenger, a thin, black male in his late twenties, remained motionless, looking straight ahead the entire time and never once acknowledging my presence. Lastly, I could tell the driver was extremely jittery and at times even observed his hands shaking. *This dude looks like me the first time I had to draw my weapon, shaking like a crackbaby!* I ordered the operator to stay put and cautiously turned the troop car around to pull behind the white Volkswagen. Keeping a close eye on the car and its occupants the entire time, I then called the stop in to the bookman at the New Brunswick Station, Trooper J. Sansone.

Once completing this standard operating procedure (SOP), I exited the troop car and briskly walked up to the driver and asked for his license, registration, and insurance. After erratically explaining to me that the car was his uncle's and he didn't have any identification or paperwork for the car, I asked the operator to step out. With my trooper hat pulled down over my eyes, the driver—who was about six feet three, dark skinned, and appeared to have a muscular build hidden by the brown leather bomber jacket he was wearing—towered over me. *Oh Christ, I don't like this.* Fighting my own fears and emotions, I attempted to maintain control of the scene as he immediately began rambling on about being lost and just needing to turn around. In my best command voice, I directed the driver, "Just chill out, relax, and hang on a second!"

A quick pat down for weapons revealed a glass crackpipe on the inside-jacket pocket of this individual, who now identified himself as "John Smith." (If that doesn't set off bells, you shouldn't be working in law enforcement!) The transparent pipe was shrouded in a dirty white paper towel and gave the impression of frequent use. Burn marks covered the entire length of the glass pipe, and the operator immediately stated, "Man, that shit ain't mine! I don't fuck wit da rock!" As I further patted down this subject, I continued to question him as to where he was coming from and where he was headed in addition to whose vehicle it was. During this encounter, John Smith constantly fidgeted and refused to look at me as his head appeared to be on a swivel. Aside from realizing the obvious—that this guy had a suspended license and maybe a stolen car, I had no idea what was about to happen. Growing up in quaint little Florence Township just didn't prepare me for this, and I had no idea of just how "green" I truly was.

As much as I wanted to, I knew I couldn't lock up this scumbag for just a crack-pipe. The guys at the station would hound me mercilessly. It was an unwritten rule that you never arrest a "2B" (black male) unless you had at least an ounce of coke; bullet of heroin; loaded weapon; or, at the minimal, a pound of marijuana. Sadly, white folks, on the other hand, got locked up for anything more than a roach. Pathetically, it was a numbers game that we were all aware of, and as unfair as it was, we had to play along to keep the stats even-keeled. These unwritten policies were never explained to me, nor did I understand or question them; it was all just a part of being a turnpike trooper!

When no further contraband was found, I immediately focused my attention to the passenger. Prior to approaching the passenger's side of the vehicle, I ordered John Smith to sit on the hood of my troop car and not move. He had a jagged, glazed look in his eyes and continued to peer everywhere but at me. Reluctantly, he leaned back on the hood of my troop car as ordered, but I was far from convinced that the remainder of this encounter was going to go smoothly.

The ill feeling I had in the pit of my stomach just kept getting worse by the second. Being new and trying to prove my mettle, as much as I wanted to, I just couldn't call for backup! I had no choice—one job, one trooper!

I now quickly attempted to walk up to the individual seated in the front right passenger's seat. As I turned my back, John Smith immediately got up and began to walk hesitantly back toward the driver's side of his car. I screamed for him to stop and sit back down. After bouncing left and right on his feet a few times, he obeyed my command. The same exact scenario played out as I again tried to reach the passenger. "Move again, motherfucker, and I will lock you up for obstructing! I'm not playing with you, asshole! Sit down! Don't move or talk!"

I was hoping this idle threat would at least keep John Smith seated momentarily. I was now caught in a cat-and-mouse game, and the bad guy was getting to me. I had to maintain control of the scene! I was in a zone, and the chatter that blared from the portable radio that was connected to my side was inaudible to me. I was focused but scared. Nothing else in life mattered at this point except finding a way to keep these thugs from overpowering me. I knew shit was fucked up, but I didn't know to what extent. *Goddamn it! Why didn't I have the balls to call for backup? Screw pride! This was my life!*

On my third attempt, I finally reached the passenger's window, and just as I did, John Smith leaped from the hood of the troop car and bolted directly to his door. Before I knew it, he was inside the Volkswagen, which had been running the entire time. In less than a few seconds' time, he was seated, the door was shut, and the car was in gear. I heard the engine roar as he accelerated rapidly in first gear. *What in the fuck do I do now?*

I was caught flat-footed between the Volkswagen and troop car. Instinctively, I chased the driver and reached his window just as he began to accelerate. Running alongside the Volkswagen, on impulse, I reached through the partially opened window, attempting to grab the keys and turn off the car's ignition. As long as the passenger, who I never got to pat down, didn't have a gun and blow my freaking head off, I figured this was the logical split-second thing to do.

My breathing had all but stopped. The next few seconds were a blur. I didn't hear anything and only saw the driver's entire body leaning forward as if to make the car go faster. Both his hands were on the wheel, and I could see his knuckles turning white from the death grip he had on the steering wheel. At last glance, the passenger appeared to be screaming, his mouth was wide open, but all sounds evaded me. As he banged his hands on the dashboard, everything appeared to be in slow motion. Fear left my body and was replaced by a desire to live.

Everything was happening so quickly but yet appeared to be occurring in fragmented intervals, step by step. Would I rise to the top or fall flat on my face? Concerns over reputation and doing the right thing gave way to sheer primal instinct.

At this point, I was running alongside the Volkswagen with my right arm inside the window. The driver was attempting to hit my hand away as I reached for the ignition keys. Suddenly, due to the speed at which I was running as I tried to keep up, I lost my balance. Falling straight down, my right arm clutched the interior of driver's door, and my right tricep and armpit banged down on the window. Supporting all of my weight with this one arm, both legs were now being dragged along the ground. As I held on for dear life solely with my right arm, I struggled to regain my footing.

As the milliseconds passed, my right leg was under the car as my left shoe dragged on the blacktop. I screamed for him to stop the vehicle. Instinctively, without thought, I grabbed my gun. With my left hand, I removed my weapon from its holster and pointed it directly at the head of John Smith as I held on to prevent myself from falling underneath the car. "Stop the fucking car or I am going to blow your fucking head off!" is what I think I screamed from this most precarious position.

The last thing I recall seeing was John Smith's right hand come off the steering wheel and grab the barrel of my weapon. *FUCK!* I thought to myself. Not only am I holding on for dear life here, now this cocksucker is attempting to steal my weapon and possibly use it against me. I knew my only other option was to let go and sacrifice the possibility of allowing my legs and lower extremities to be run over by the Volkswagen. At all cost, I had to retain possession of my weapon.

As we fought for control of my weapon, his right hand tugged at, twisted, and turned the barrel of my gun, hoping to pry it from my death grip. Getting run over just wasn't how I wanted this day to end. *Christ, I wasn't even supposed to be out on the road today! All this shit because of stupid grand jury for an arrest that wasn't even mine!*

Could I really shoot someone if I had to? Was it the right thing to do? What if the driver was truly a good guy and just panicked? Does he have children, a wife, and parents? What are the repercussions if I fire? Can I lose my job? Will I go to jail if I am wrong? What if he gains control of my weapon? Does the passenger have a gun? Is there a gun under the driver's seat? Would these guys be able to shoot me, a police officer in full uniform? Why is he attempting to flee?

In the academy, we were instructed that if you are in a situation and have the luxury to ask yourself. "Should I shoot?" then the answer is no. Dangling precariously from their vehicle and within inches of losing my weapon and possibly my life, I did not have to ask myself or the Lord for forgiveness of the inevitable. My will to survive took over.

I have no recollection of seeing or hearing the rounds go off or where they went. When I fell off and rolled backward, I knew I had shot the driver, banged the hell out of my head, and somehow avoided being run over. Uncertain if the adrenaline was preventing me from feeling any serious injuries, I recall just lying on the ground with weapon in-hand, unaware of how many shots I fired and what was now transpiring around me. I had no idea how or what stopped the fleeing Volkswagen, but up ahead in the distance, I observed it at a standstill. Having yet moved a muscle, I recalled seeing a pair of feet exit the passenger's side of the Volkswagen; and a black male ran right past me, down the ramp, and toward the southbound lanes of the turnpike.

Before I knew it, troopers were everywhere. Trooper Justin McCarthy helped me to my feet and positioned me upright in a seated fashion on the silver, metal guardrail. I recall hearing someone say that backup was en route because the car came back a "signal 18" or stolen motor vehicle. Before paramedics arrived, I just had to walk up to the Volkswagen and see for myself what just occurred. Not knowing the consequences of what I was about to see, as I approached the Volkswagen, I observed the operator, John Smith, still seated in the driver's chair. His upper torso had fallen to the right, near the area where the passenger was previously seated. Blood filled the entire center's console area and was splattered about the passenger's seat and floor area. I remember hearing him gurgle from all the blood he was swallowing. Mentally, I was overcome with anxiety and emotion, and I immediately began to dry heave. Almost in tears and nearly vomiting, I couldn't help but to think that the man who, seconds ago was trying to get my gun, now begged for help. I wanted to help him. I needed to save his life! A group of troopers wisely removed me from the area as other troopers and a local policeman from Medford Township who witnessed the entire tragedy began lifesaving first-aid treatment on John Smith.

One second, you are fighting for your own life; the next, you are trying to save someone else's—this is just one example of the immense and traumatic adrenaline swings a police officer must endure. As they all sped to my assistance, the troopers probably could care less about the occupants of the stolen vehicle; now they were administering medical treatment to save the life of an individual who, quite possibly, could have taken the life of one of their own. This mentality, I believe, is why it takes a special person—a rare, unique breed of human being—to wear a law-enforcement uniform.

Seated again on the cold guardrail, I continued to dry heave. *Would he die? Did I just kill some-one? How many rounds did I fire? Was I justified? Am I going to jail for murder? I'm going to lose my job and go to prison!* Unknown to me, these "thoughts" were being said aloud in-between my attempts to throw up.

Trooper McCarthy grabbed me and shouted, "John, I saw the whole thing! You didn't do any-thing wrong! Stop talking like that!" As this transpired, I observed the passenger, who was now handcuffed and surrounded by troopers, being walked back to the scene. As he stood approx-imately ten yards away, he repeatedly screamed, "I'm shot! I'm shot!" *How in the hell did he get shot?* I wondered to myself.

In an instant, the scene became movielike. Helicopters from both the State police and local news stations were flying overhead. Detectives and troopers were everywhere, setting up a crime-scene perimeter. Ambulances, with sirens blaring loudly, raced to the scene. Traffic had slowed, and witnesses came to a stop on the shoulder. Within minutes, a simple motor-vehicle stop was turned into what appeared to be a multimillion-dollar movie production, only this wasn't Hollywood or New York City; this was the New Jersey Turnpike!

Within minutes, I was whisked from the scene by superior officers and taken back to the New Brunswick Barracks. Before going to the hospital, I gave a brief statement of the incident to investigators from the NJSP's Major Crimes Unit. Once at Saint Peter's Hospital in Edison, I was treated for overall body soreness and deep bruises on my right arm and triceps. I also had a bad bump on the back of my head, a sore left ankle, and a damaged shoulder, which would eventu-ally require surgery as a result of being dragged.

Once released from the hospital after refusing to be admitted for further observation, I was transported back to the New Brunswick Station. As I entered, it appeared as if everyone was just staring at me. Two turnpike-authority workers were present, wearing full-bodied wet suits, and a strong bleach-like odor permeated the barracks.

Led into a private room by members from Major Crimes, I was informed that in addition to not having a driver's license and possessing a stolen motor vehicle, John Smith and his coun-terpart were both fugitives. From the passenger, it was learned that they met earlier in the day in Jersey City where they both resided, After smoking crack cocaine together, they reportedly committed a burglary in the Jamesburg area. While traveling back to Jersey City on the turnpike, they realized they were headed in the wrong direction and were trying to turn around when our most unfortunate encounter unraveled. *How's that for timing?* As it was then explained to me, the turnpike workers wearing the chemical suits were cleaning the station's cell because to top it all off, both subjects were believed to be HIV-positive. As a result of being exposed to their blood, I then underwent two years of continuous HIV testing to ensure I had not been infected. *Talk about a burdensome cross to bear at twenty-four years of age!*

Most people probably think this type of thing can't happen in broad daylight. Something this unbelievable can only take place in a big city or in the middle of the night. The truth is, the gen-eral public has no clue as to the dangers that exist on the New Jersey Turnpike or the unreal-istic volumes of weapons, drugs, and contraband that flow daily. The mystique of the Black Dragon is what separated turnpike troopers from the rest of the Division. Those of us who worked on the Big Road did so by choice. We didn't get paid more or have special privileges. As turnpike troopers, we just took more pride in "doing the job and making the big grab."

The day following the shooting, a member of the NJSP's Employee's Assistance Program visited me at my residence. I was asked about the incident and if I felt the need to drink alco-hol, stay with family as opposed to remain home alone, and a bunch of other routine, generic questions by the counselor. Fearful of opening up my true emotions from this incident, I fool-ishly downplayed the totality of this tragedy and the repercussions I was currently enduring, both physically and psychologically. Before leaving, I was deemed "fit for duty" by the counselor and he offered me two tickets to the Philadelphia 76 ers' basketball game that night. Though appreciative, I declined the offer, and we mutually agreed to remain in contact to address the possibility of me suffering posttraumatic stress syndrome.

Two days later, like a good soldier, I suited up and reunited myself with Squad Six. Patrolling the Big Road was where I wanted to be, and no one tried to hold me back. Oblivious to what was really going on internally, I just assumed the repetitious nightmares and flashbacks of the incident were a normal reaction. Eventually, they would stop! After all, I was a turnpike trooper—fearless and unflappable. I wanted everyone to respect and like me. I couldn't show weakness! *What would my peers or, even worse, my class-coordinator Trooper Kilmurray think of me if I stated I wasn't mentally prepared to return to full duty? Troopers are hard! No emotions allowed! Plus, like Kilmurray said, troopers never let one another down, and if I didn't return to work, my squad would be short-staffed.* In my mind, it was my only option.

In exchange for all the emotional and physical trauma of nearly taking a life and perhaps giving my own, I was awarded with a plaque during a luncheon hosted by the Middlesex County 200 Club Award, a small consolation for the lifelong psychological scars this incident left me with.

9

E-Man: Life in the NYPD Emergency Services Unit

by Al Sheppard (with Jerry Schmetterer)

"When people need help they call the police; when the police need help they call Emergency Service."

—Al Sheppard,
E-Man: Life in the NYPD Emergency Services Unit

In January 19, 1973 I was a still wet behind the ears young cop. On the 19th of that month I was working a 4 p.m. to midnight tour, 4 by 12 in station house jargon, in a radio car in the 81st precinct, a fairly busy house in the Williamsburg section of Brooklyn.

The station house was an old one, even by New York standards. It was more than 100 years old. During the Civil War the building was rumored to be a military hospital, so it had seen its share of bloodshed and tears and if its walls could talk there would be some stories to be told. But none would be as dramatic, or heartbreaking as the tale that was to unfold that night in Williamsburg.

The 8-1 was a busy precinct known as the "Hole in the Donut" in the vast patrol area known as Brooklyn North. The area got its nickname because it was a relatively decent part of Brooklyn as inner city ghettos go, surrounded on the north by run-down Brownsville, industrial Bushwick to the east and dangerous Bedford-Stuyvesant to the west. Williamsburg with its mix of Orthodox Jews, Hispanics and Blacks who had lived there from the end of the World War II was in the southern end of the precinct.

My partner Billy Smith, one of the most veteran Black police officers at the time, and I were assigned to sector Adam. The sector bordered the 83rd, 79th and the 90th precincts.

These were the years when domestic terrorist groups were beginning to make themselves known to the American public. I'm not talking about the college based groups such as the Weathermen or Students for a Democratic Society. What the urban police forces of America were

Reprinted from *E-Man: Life in the NYPD Emergency Services Unit* (2007), Rooftop Publishing, by permission of Al Sheppard.

beginning to deal with in these years was the FALN, the Puerto Rican separatists and the Black Liberation Army and Black Panthers. Not long before this night the Panthers actually attacked a police station in Oakland, California, a desk sergeant died in the battle, and many police departments felt under attack. This threat was on the minds of every state trooper stopping a car and every undercover cop buying illegal weapons.

One summer night in those years a mob, led by the Panthers, marched on a Brooklyn precinct, giving the cops a choice of opening fire to save themselves or retreating behind closed doors and large steel shutters pulled down to cover the windows. This being New York, the cops, press and civilians barricaded the station house doors and called for help by the Tactical Patrol Force. In fact the station houses all over the city instituted plans to hold off an attack. At the time J. Edgar Hoover called the Panthers the greatest threat to freedom we had ever faced. This of course was before Al Qaeda.

In NYC we lost several officers in cowardly ambushes. One was a very good friend and classmate in the Police Academy named Gregory Foster. He and his partner Rocco Laurie were on foot patrol in the 9th precinct on the lower East Side, when they were fatally ambushed, gunned down by automatic weapons. They were simply walking their beat. Foster was a Black man but I guess that didn't matter.

The Black Liberation Army sent out a communiqué saying that they were both enemies of the people and part of an occupying army. That could not be further from the truth. Both were devoted to the community. Laurie even paid, from his own pocket, for one local kid to get methadone treatment.

A few months later two members of the BLA, Woody Green and Avon White, would be shot and killed in the Big T Steakhouse on Broadway in the 81st precinct by detectives from the Major Case Squad when they resisted rather than go for questioning in connection with a robbery. The BLA maintained its war chest by pulling off large scale robberies and that's why they were under suspicion. They were guilty!

The media was having a difficult time connecting all these various robberies and shootings. I do not believe the public, up to this point, really had an understanding of the mood in the streets, especially in the mean, inner-city, neighborhoods.

While no smart cop ever took his patrol for granted, there was an especially tense feeling as we slowly cruised down a street crowded with beat up cars abandoned in front of once proud apartment buildings where many of the city's leaders as well as prominent people in any field, sports, entertainment, politics, had grown up safely in the 40's, 50's and even into the 60's. By the early 70's in New York City, such neighborhoods were war zones where drugs were the currency and hate was the politics.

But I was a young cop, a combat vet, full of piss and vinegar and not afraid of anything. I yearned for hot calls over the radio. I wanted action. I wanted to work. I thought I wanted to make things better for the kids I saw playing in the trash strewn streets; running errands for drug dealers and staring blank-eyed into space when we came into their apartments to investigate the drug overdose of their mothers whose bone-thin bodies would be sprawled in the next room on a bed made of cardboard.

This night was a typical January, cold and wet. As we settled into our tired green and white Plymouth our ears tuned to the static-scratchy voice of the 14th Division dispatcher. In these Divisions, covering the kinds of precincts we worked, the dispatcher was a constant companion for eight hours. Night after night she assigned patrol cars to cover jobs generated by 911. We heard everything from a kid with his head caught in a fence to shots fired, report of officer down. This night was no different: *shots fired in the 8-3, man with a gun in the 9-0, stabbing in the 9-4*—on and on it would go all night long as it did every tour in Brooklyn North. Violence and despair ruled these streets. But for me being a cop was still about helping people. I still had the image from my youth of cops coming to the rescue. So, when I looked at the downtrodden in my patrol area, I thought with pride that I was on their side. My job was to help them.

We had handled several routine runs prior to our assigned meal hour. The most exciting involved a dispute between an elderly woman and her grandson who she said was stealing money from her purse to buy drugs. He took offense at the allegation and punched her in mouth. He had left before we got there or we might have administered some "street justice." We referred the case to Criminal Court, but as I left their apartment I had the thought that someday that addict would kill his grandmother for a taste of dope.

Those kinds of runs ate up time and seemed to take forever. I hated standing in the crowded apartments, feeling so out of place with my gun and nightstick. I thought, "Oh Shit! It's going to be a long night." Nothing made the time drag on more than sitting in a radio car filling out forms of past crimes, complaints against landlords or husbands. No action, all paperwork, made for eight hour tours that felt like 80 hours.

When lunch hour came, because there was no decent place to even get a sandwich in the 14th Division, we snuck over the borough line into Queens to pick up food, and then went back to the precinct to eat it. After we had eaten we had barely started the engine of the RMP, the Radio Motor Patrol car, when we were assigned a 10-30 in a liquor store, a robbery in progress.

The location was not in our sector, but due to a backlog we were "IT." The store was right off Broadway, no, not the Great White Way in Manhattan. This Broadway was the real street of Broken Dreams. It was littered with garbage, dead rats, broken beer bottles, hypo needles dropped by heroin addicts, and some trash that was just indescribable.

Traffic was heavy. We hit the lights and siren, then, as per procedure, we shut it all down a few blocks from the location. No need to advertise our arrival to the bad guys.

For some reason, I remember thinking at that time of my first month in the precinct about two years earlier, when my partner and I turned a corner into a shooting.

We were on our way to a 10-52 domestic. Turning off of Broadway at Chauncey Street a man shot another man in the head right in front of us. The victim literally fell onto the hood of our RMP. The street was full of people and dozens of children were running in all directions. We jumped out of the car and with guns drawn took cover behind its doors. We shouted to the man with the gun to "drop it."

We were in a Mexican Stand Off. But the rules were unfair; we couldn't fire because of the chance of hitting a civilian. It lasted maybe a minute, but it felt like an hour until he attempted to fire. But his automatic pistol jammed. We were on him like stink on shit. We took him down hard to the street, all to the cheers of the crowd.

We later learned that killing involved a decades old dispute between two cousins. One ended up dead, the other did hard time upstate.

That was a routine call that ended in terror filled moments. We were headed for the same thing tonight, only I did not know it yet. Of course, I would welcome any action, the more dangerous the better. Or so I thought.

As we approached the location we saw "Old Sal" waving his arms. He had the usual cigar clenched between his teeth. Sal was a tough old Jewish man from Brownsville. It was rumored that he had been associated with Murder Inc. the prohibition era mob run by the likes of Meyer Lansky, Lucky Luciano and Bugsy Seigel.

I loved learning about guys like "Old Sal" because I have always been a student of New York history, especially its criminal history. Murder Incorporated began as a murder for hire outfit where the young Jewish mobsters earned their spurs working on retainer deals, getting paid while they waited for assignments. Eventually it earned its rep under the leadership of Albert Anastasia who was shot to death sitting in his barber chair and Louis "Lepke" Buchalter who died in the chair at Sing Sing.

Despite his notorious background, Sal was a super guy and always happy to see the cops. The clerk in the liquor store told us the perp was long gone. My partner, Billy Smith, as I have said was an old timer, one of the first Black cops to be assigned to a radio car beat, and he knew the clerk. They greeted each other by first names. Billy who had maybe 20 years seniority on me told me to go back and sit in the RMP. I took his cue, recalling how my Platoon Sergeant in 'Nam would always take control of situations the same way.

In the car I lit a cigarette and sat back and listened to the nonstop voice of the dispatcher. No doubt about it, things were heating up. This might be a busy night after all.

Looking into the liquor store, through its large windows, I saw Sal smiling and the clerk and my partner in a brotherly bear hug.

The radio droned on, job after job, shots fired in the 8-3, a recorded hold up alarm in the 9-0 at John & Al's Sporting Good Store. Not an unusual call, we got them all the time like clock work.

Then, in a moment that has stood still in my memory all these years I heard a voice gasping for breath and trying to scream over the radio, "*10-13, 10-13 officer shot, Myrtle and Broadway.*" I could actually hear gunfire in the back ground. Shit that's our sector where it bordered the 90th Precinct. That's where the sporting goods store was.

I jumped out of the RMP and ran into the store yelling "We got a cop shot at Myrtle and Broadway!" As we ran back to the car my heart was beating as if it was going to explode from my chest.

We did what dozens of cops throughout Brooklyn were doing at that very second. We hit the lights and siren and raced to the scene. But unlike most of those other cops we were close, only about eight blocks away. Not unexpectedly, Billy was a great driver. It is drummed into you in driver training; don't make things worse by getting into a crash on the way to the crime. We were there in a minute or so, but it seemed longer.

We pulled into the northeast corner of the intersection facing against traffic. Gunfire was sounding through the streets. Unbelievably we were taking rounds into the RMP, so both of us bailed out the driver's side door on to the wet cold street. I crawled under the car and emptied my service revolver in the direction of the store. Maybe it wasn't the smartest thing to do since I had no idea of who was shooting at who but I did not want anyone thinking of me as an easy target.

My combat vet instincts told me these were high-powered rounds being fired at us. Looking around I could see there were three officers down, wounded and unable to get to cover. As I surveyed the scene I also saw at least six other radio cars, with cops pinned down at all of them.

A subway train went rumbling overhead adding to the nightmare. More and more cops were arriving but unable to get past the police cars already there. One cop was brave enough to stand up and wave to the others to stop. Over the radio I could hear another cop from my precinct trying to explain to dispatch what the hell was going on.

"*Multiple officers down, we need Emergency Service, we need buses (ambulances in police jargon), perps barricaded in Al's . . . 10-13, 10-13,*" he barked.

Another cop, had the presence of mind to clear the street of civilians, he was using his body to protect them as they ran down Broadway, across the street from Al's.

Meanwhile central dispatch was trying to get some handle on the situation.

"*Any unit in the 8-1, how many down, how many down? How many perps? Are there civilians injured, what is the status?*"

Finally an 8-1 Sergeant got on the air and calmed the dispatcher a little.

"*This is a serious fire fight; we need citywide mobilization, alert all officers responding to use extreme caution.*"

I heard all this while trying to make myself invisible under the car.

We were in a world of shit, as the First Sgt. said during the beginning of the Tet Offensives just a few short years before.

But that was in a jungle in Southeast Asia, and our country was at war. This was happening in the middle of New York City.

During a break in the firing a sergeant yelled to me to run for cover behind the elevated subway pole in front of the Oasis Bar across from the sporting good store. Taking cover behind the RMP was now useless. The perps, who had a store full of ammo, were firing under the cars. I made a dash and sat back against the iron pole. The front door and windows of the bar were riddled with bullet holes. Billy followed and also made it.

This was the same bar used in the French Connection movie. I thought it strange, Eddie Egan—Popeye Doyle—was a detective in the 8-1 squad. And it was him who they fashioned the movie hero, Gene Hackman after. Now was a good time to reload. I still had 18 more rounds of .38 ammo, and eight .9mm rounds in my back up Smith & Wesson. Still the subway trains were rumbling 10 feet above us. We couldn't hear the radio or each other.

There it was again, the Transit Authority taking its time shutting down power. No matter what, the trains had to run. They ran for another 10 minutes while the NYPD hid under cars. When they stopped the only sounds were the sporadic gunfire that echoed through the cold night.

Still my brother officers lay in the street unable to move. Every time someone moved it was met with a burst of automatic weapons coming from within the darkened store. A voice came over the radio; a sergeant ordering us to shoot out the street light, undoubtedly the first time an order like that was ever given to a New York cop. But, we were sitting ducks silhouetted by the street lamps. As each light was shot out the thick glass crashed to the ground.

I called over to a nearby cop. If he could cover me I thought I could crawl over to the cop closest to us, and try to drag him to safety. His reply was stern: "Kid, don't be a hero; a hero is nothing but a sandwich. ESU will be here any minute."

Indeed, Truck 8 was on its way, sirens and air horns could be heard in the distance. I had no way of knowing it that night while about 50 other cops and I were pinned down under the elevated trains, but about 10 years later Truck 8 would be my last assignment in my beloved ESU.

As I looked down the street I saw the enormous truck pull to the curb. It was painted green, black, and white, the color scheme of the NYPD. Large green letters on a white back ground proclaimed "Police Emergency Squad."

Peering through the cold mist I could make out about eight men "suited up" in bulky bulletproof vests and carrying heavy weapons. They were here to save us.

It's not my original thought, but I came to live by the well known adage . . . "When a civilian needs help, he calls the police, when the police need help they call ESU. . . ." How true that was then and it remains so today with the new breed of the men and women of the finest and most diverse police force in the world. And these days their responsibilities have grown to be ready to battle international terrorists.

On that night in Williamsburg many of the police department's field commanders were Korean War veterans, some even dated back to World War II. Many of the pinned down cops, like me, were Vietnam vets. We were a seasoned bunch, even rookies like me. I watched as the commanders arrived in their bright, unmarked cars, driven by sergeants, knowing they would never venture into the ghettoes unless absolutely necessary. They had a calming affect on the whole scene. I bet even the perpetrators were glad to see a command post set up a block away. Maybe some gray haired old Irish guy who survived the Chosin Reservoir in Korea would figure a way out of this mess.

Over the years cities throughout the nation, indeed the world would develop S.W.A.T. Teams. While the NYPD, ever mindful of a liberal constituency never had such a designated unit, most of those S.W.A.T. were based on the strategy and tactics developed by the NYPD Special Operations Division, of which ESU is a Unit.

I watched, in awe, therefore, as these Emergency Service guys pulled up to the nightmarish scene. There were cops lying under cars and civilians screaming and running around in panic, while the radio chatter from the RMP radios filled the air with the urgent voices of cops and dispatchers trying to organize things until finally these ESU guys took over. Their calm, professional attitude brought some semblance of control to the scene which now covered about five blocks. They seemed to know what to do without being told and they had a beneficial effect on everyone involved. I met some of them that night, guys like ESU Captain Dennis Healy, Sergeant Ed Leighs, E-9, Jack Casey, ESS#2, Frank Gallagher, ESS#2, Ken Jaques, ESS#2, who became lifelong friends. They are people I always tried to pattern myself after as I did my job.

The ESU officers positioned themselves all around us. One of them dashed to position himself behind an elevated pole directly in front of the entrance to John & Al's. All this time gunfire continued to pour from inside the darkened store.

Then in a moment frozen in my mind forever I watched one of the most honorable actions I had ever seen unfold outside of actual war time combat. The officer behind the pole moved to his right trying to get a better angle into the shop in order to lay down some fire so the rest of the pinned down cops could scamper to cover. He took about two steps when he was gunned down, a fatal hit, no doubt about it.

His name was Stephen Gilroy. There is a plaque honoring this hero in the quarters of Truck 8. The day came when I walked past it every time I reported to duty. And every time, it would bring back the smell of that wet cobblestone street, the fear and anger that we patrol cops felt, and the frustration of watching Gilroy fall.

We were pinned down almost two hours, with the firing finally reduced to an occasional shot from the store every few minutes, when I noticed from the corner of my eye flashbulbs popping and television camera people scurrying for position. Also in the background was a rumbling sound I had not heard since 'Nam. It was coming closer.

There was no mistake about it. That was the sound of an Armored Personnel Carrier (APC), its tracks chewing up the city streets. It was a vehicle we had heard about but never seen. Not long before this night, Police Commissioner Patrick V. Murphy had announced the department had purchased a "Rescue Ambulance."

We laughed when we heard about it. The liberal Murphy would not call it an armored personnel carrier (APC), which is what it was, but in New York "Rescue Ambulance" was much more acceptable. As if that made any sense! But, no matter what you called it, it was our ticket out of harm's way.

In fairness, I have to admit that on that evening it did perform as Murphy advertised. The "Rescue Ambulance" jockeyed itself into position in front of the sporting goods store. As it blocked the windows and door, cops were able to reach Gilroy's body and the other injured officers. We pinned down cops ran along side the APC, out of the killing zone to a bank building down the street, which had been turned into a temporary headquarters. Inside I remember seeing PC Murphy. There we were in our now filthy, wet, stinky uniforms, standing in a room with the impeccable Murphy. I may not have agreed with his politics but I was impressed by his commanding figure. He was clearly in charge.

We were debriefed, by a deputy chief, and, sadly, sent back to our precincts. We did not want to leave. We had watched a fellow officer get shot to death, others were wounded. We wanted to finish the job. But the bosses said they had it under control and they knew we were fatigued. A tired cop could make a mistake that could cost him or his partner their lives.

The arrival of Murphy's tank stopped the shooting. The perps must have shit their pants thinking they could get blown away by a tank gun (they did not know there was no gun on the vehicle). The situation became a hostage negotiation that lasted through the night and for three more days.

Later we heard in the station house that the hostages escaped after ESU effected entry into the store via the roof and were able to rescue them. There to lead them to safety were the E-Men of Truck 2 led by Jack Case and Bobby Benz, some of my heroes and Frank Gallagher who drove the APC.

Now faced with cops on the roof and even more in the streets, the Sunni Muslim gunmen eventually surrendered, although reluctantly after having killed one of our own. They walked out of the store with their fists raised in defiance and that set the mood in the neighborhood for weeks to come.

As the perps were handcuffed and led away, hundreds of people began throwing bottles and breaking windows. The streets were full of hatred for the cops. The media combed the streets looking for eyewitnesses and inciting more trouble wherever they turned their flash-bulbs and camera lights. Commissioner Murphy tried to tell the story of the death of E-Man Stephen Gilroy but it was overtaken by a bullshit story of rebellion. These perps were bandits, not revolutionaries.

In the cop bars that evening and for many evenings after, we rehashed the incident. Most thought we should have just blown away the scumbags, too bad for the hostages. A lot of guys took on some anger that night and may still be living with it.

But, for me, personally I took something a little different away from that night. I knew that my future lay with the ESU.

And within two years my dream came true when I got my first assignment to Truck 4 in The Bronx.

THE CALLS

It was Just Another Day

As I have mentioned there is a kinship between cops and the other city worker types who are out there in all kinds of weather, serving the people, and are always ready to lend a hand to us. Con Ed guys, the telephone crews, bus drivers, postal workers, and even the media that follows our adventures in snow, floods, heat, smog all know what I am talking about.

One sunny March day in 1977 Gary Gorman and I were assigned to Adam 2. We patrolled the lower half of Truck 2's area, 110th St. south to 59th St., which is generally considered the geographic center of the city, and from the Hudson River on the west to the East River on the east.

We were hardly out of the garage, that day, when we heard over the radio a report of an injured Con-Ed worker at West 57 St. and 11th Ave. Technically it was two blocks south of our official patrol area, but we were available, so who was going to argue technicalities. We knew, because we filed such information away in the patrol guides of our minds, the location was of one of Con-Ed's massive generators complexes. The building took the entire city block of West 57th Street to West 58th Street from 12th Ave. to 11th. Ave. It was deceptive from the street, appearing to be an ordinary 10 story building. But it had no floors inside. It housed gigantic generators responsible for providing electrical power to much of midtown and upper Manhattan. Someone had seen what appeared to be a man dangling on the slanted roof section of the complex and called 911.

On arrival we were met by several precinct sector cars, including the sergeant. It certainly appeared from the street that this person was in serious trouble. But the only way to confirm this was to get to the roof. It was not as easy as it sounds because the building had no floors but only two 60 foot high generators. The only way to the roof was the ladders at the end of the building. These ladders rose approximately 100 feet into the air above the concrete floors. They were bolted to the brick walls. This was going to be a free climb. It was a slow and dangerous process. Furthermore we didn't know the extent of the injuries of the worker. So this meant we would also have to have our trauma kit available.

We strapped on our Morrisey Belts. We used these belts for mostly high angle rescue operations. The present ESU officers have personal life belts and nylon extenders with a large hook affixed to the ends. The Morrisey Belt was constructed of six inches of thick leather and nylon. There was a large hook attached to a steel ring at the end. This would ensure your safety by allowing the wearer to "hook" on to a fixed cable, or other stationary fixture. The belt had saved many an officer's life while fighting with a potential suicide on a bridge or roof.

This belt would allow us to periodically rest on our long climb to the top. In addition I took up 100 feet of life line. Gary waited at the bottom. This way when I reached the top I could haul up the trauma kit and Gary would follow with an additional 100 foot life line. It took me approximately 10 minutes to make the steep climb. I was sweating beneath my uniform and my arms were tired and cramped as I climbed onto the cat walk that ran around the top of the building. Once I opened the roof hatch I radioed Gary and told him I would assess the situation. He was now on his way up. I made my way onto the roof.

After a short search I found the "victim." He was startled to see me. He was sitting back enjoying a hero sandwich and a cold drink. He jumped to his feet almost falling over backwards. I explained that someone had called to report an injured man on the roof. And it really appeared from the the street that the entire roof was on a 45 degree angle, so he must have appeared like he was in trouble. We both laughed. I was relieved, he was embarrassed. I radioed Gary with the updated info, also the citywide dispatcher who was probably expecting a call for more equipment. *"Cancel all additional units,"* was the dispatcher's order.

Next was the long climb down. If not for nothing it was good practice. Just to keep things sharp ESU members train regularly on the city bridges on Sunday mornings.

Another rescue of a Con Ed worker still gives me goose bumps when I think about it. Gary and I were working an 8 by 4 tour in Truck 1 which was known as the "Hollywood Truck", because it covered the glamorous areas of Manhattan and got many high profile jobs. Day tours in Truck 1 were always busy, and you had plenty of media attention.

We had a very busy morning this one particular day. Then just after lunch we were dispatched by citywide radio to *"An injured Con-Ed worker . . . corner of Grand St. and Broadway."* That is downtown Manhattan.

On arrival we found the injured worker 10 feet down in a manhole. He had been struck by a car that ran into the Con Ed work barriers. As I looked into the manhole I could see his prone figure. He was surrounded by high voltage electrical wires that were dancing just a foot above his head. Sparks were flying everywhere. At each explosion of sparks I could see the worker was bleeding heavily from a head wound. Here again is where training and experience come into play. Instinctively Gary and I realized time was of the essence. We had to get to him, to stop the bleeding, as quickly as possible. We did not discuss this, we just knew it. It was also obvious that he had suffered additional injuries. It appeared that one of his legs was broken by the way it lay mangled in the four inch deep water and muck. I was amazed that he wasn't electrocuted when he was knocked backwards into the manhole. He had to fall in the path of the high voltage cables that were dancing like electric snakes.

The precinct cops were dealing with the reckless driver who caused the accident and were maintaining traffic and crowd control. As fast as we had to move, we also knew we had to be cautious, if we were to save his life. What good would two dead cops be to anyone? EMS was on scene, but would not enter the manhole. That was our job. As we prepared, one of the victim's coworkers told us he was set to retire at the end of the week after 30 years service with Con Edison.

I put on our heavy duty ESU rubber insulated electrical gloves. Normally, we used them on jobs when electrical poles were down to secure the live wires, and any other time we had overhead wires down. They were also needed when we had to deal with other hazardous electrical situations where electrocution was a possibility.

With the ungainly gloves firmly on my hands, I started down the ladder trying to avoid the five-inch thick cables as they shot showers of sparks in every direction. I knew that one wrong move and I would have been toast, literally. The gloves allowed me to be able to push the live cables aside, avoiding contact as I made my descent into the dark pit. After a long descent I finally reached the victim. He was bleeding badly from a serious head wound. I'd need to control the bleeding before I did anything else.

I called up to Gary to lower the trauma kit. "Slowly," I repeated, as Gary lowered it to the bottom, inch by inch. The victim was barely conscious, we did not speak and it now appeared to me that he had suffered two broken legs. This was going to be a nightmare.

I was able to control the bleeding for the head wound, using six, 4X4 compression dressings and one roll of bandage. I'd need splints for his leg injuries. There wasn't much room to work and we were in several inches of murky water. This was hell on earth; dark, smelly from burned wires and insulation, a suffering victim, and I could hardly see. It would be impossible for the victim to climb out of this potential tomb. He'd have to be raised up manually.

Normally we would use a "Stokes Basket." But in this case that would be impossible because a Stokes is made of metal and is lined with chicken wire. One contact between the Stokes and the cables would be disastrous. We'd all fry in that hole. Our only alternative would be a wooden backboard normally used to secure vehicle accident victims. That way, we could place a cervical collar immobilizing the neck and spinal column.

This was our only choice. This was going to be a tough extrication. One wrong move and we'd be goners. In order for Gary to lower the backboard I would have to make a space by securing the electrical cables. They were still arcing and showering us with sparks every few minutes.

Gary dropped a work line of one inch manila rope. Normally it was used in high angle rescues, like that "victim" on the roof. That was our work rope, never to be used to raise or lower a victim, but we'd used it to secure downed signs, or perhaps tree limbs as we cut them off a vehicle or house. Gary cut the line into four foot lengths. Using these I was able to secure the electrical cables to the metal conduits that ran along the wall making sure the exposed end were no where near the metal to complete a circuit.

Once I secured the cables Gary was able to lower the backboard. But, I needed help securing the victim to the board. So Gary had to join us in that hell that was the manhole. We barely had room to lay the board flat. Actually we had to prop it up on an angle. Our victim was obviously in a tremendous amount of pain. My heart went out to him. Having myself been injured many time I was no stranger to pain. We splinted both legs. Then we secured him with rope to the backboard.

I knew his ascent to day light would be painful. But it should take only a couple of minutes, I hoped. But we had no other choice. As Gary climbed back to the street he accidentally brushed against one of the cables. The result was another shower of sparks raining down on the victim and me. Once top side he started to pull the victim up. I carefully followed close behind, keeping the foot of the backboard from coming in contact with the cables. We finally made it to the top. Fresh air, wow, it was great to feel the sun on my face and to know we saved another life.

Sometimes, the calls were out of the ordinary as, for example, on a quiet afternoon on June 24, 1975, two p.m. or so. I was sitting on my ass in the NYPD's central repair shop in Queens. It is a cavernous place, more like an airplane hanger than an auto repair garage. A little earlier my partner and I were checking out Adam 4, preparing to bring our particular brand of police service to the citizens of the Bronx when, during a routine check, we found the emergency roof lights were not working properly. They would spin a few times, then freeze, then spin again, then freeze for a long period, then spin a moment or two, then freeze. We never liked taking out a unit that was not 100 per cent up to par. Those lights made it possible to negotiate traffic on the way to an emergency. If we got stalled in traffic we were not doing our job. If we had an accident on the way, because a civilian driver did not see us coming, well that would cost the city some moohla. So, we asked permission to bring Adam 4 in to the repair unit. I figured it just needed a signal box, a small box that controlled the electric siren and all the emergency lights that were distributed around the truck. I could have easily repaired it myself, if I had the part.

E-Men are jacks-of-all-trades. We're auto mechanics, electricians, steeplejacks, painters, typists, and also great complainers.

The citywide radio was fairly quiet. The Bronx was burning that year, but on that day, the Truck 4 units were not yet on the firing line. So we received permission from our supervisor, after I told him it would be quick and headed for the repair shop.

The enormous shop was a one stop shopping mall for any problem that could befall an NYPD vehicle. It was filled with bays that did body work on mangled police cars. The civilians who worked there were pretty good mechanics. They did routine tune-ups and complicated repairs and were better paid than patrol cops. And they were enormous pains in the ass. They had the worst attitudes. If you brought your patrol car in and said the headlights needed adjustment, after you filled out the proper paperwork, they would adjust the headlights. Now, suppose while they were adjusting the headlights, one of the lights blew out. Believe me, and those who ever went there would agree, they would totally ignore the blown light, unless you said something, and then you would have to fill out another form before they would touch it.

In a police department that prided it self on quick thinking, innovation and teamwork the repair unit stood out as place to avoid at all costs. Those guys were not typical of most civilians we worked with who were quick to help you with a problem. All had to follow the rules, and I guess they felt they were not treated with the same level of respect that the uniformed force received, although they usually made more money and they could be fairly certain they would return to their loved ones when their shift was over. In the repair shop you had to dot the "i's" and cross the "t's" and kiss the asses of a bunch of pompous pricks who made a good living doing what most teenage car freaks could do better and would be happy to do for free.

After I filled out the form saying the lights were not working and suggested it might be the fault of the signal box, the mechanic, a middle aged guy who apparently managed to perform all kinds of repairs without getting his hands dirty, farted around for about an hour, took a coffee break and finally proclaimed we needed a new signal box. We were at his mercy; we needed those lights; we loved those lights. I would always sneak a peek at them as we barreled along though an underpass or tunnel and I totally loved the way they lit up a city street, reflecting off the windows and wet pavements. It was the Hollywood screenwriter in me that would imagine it looked like a movie set.

So, with lights and siren in working order we reported to citywide that we were back in service and headed for the Triborough Bridge. We were about a mile or so from the bridge entrance ramp when the unusually quiet citywide radio came alive. "*All ESU units in Queens*" it stated and that got our attention right away even though we were assigned to and headed for The Bronx. When a message began that way it got everyone's attention. "*Report of a commercial airliner down in the vicinity of Kennedy Airport,*" citywide continued, and then there was silence as ESU all over the city absorbed the call.

This was a big one. All Special Operations Division units would be dispatched to a plane crash; E-Men from around the city, Highway Patrol, Crime Scene Units, Medical Services, Photo Units, probably some Bomb Squad guys also. The Port Authority cops whose jurisdiction includes the area's three major airports, two major bridges, and a subway system would also be on the scene. The FBI would send a team or two, the National Transportation and Safety Board would respond, of course the New York Fire Department would rush to the scene as well as the Port Authority fire fighting units. Ambulances from the city's Emergency Medical Service would join private hospital units, and the media would roll out its live trucks and every available photographer and reporter. Patty and I wanted Adam 4 to be there also. The entrance to the Van Wyck Expressway was about 1/2 mile in front of us on the way to the bridge. That would give us a direct run to JFK Airport.

Citywide: "*We're receiving numerous 911 calls, Commercial airliner down on Rockaway Pkwy. This is confirmed by precinct units on scene.*"

I gunned the engine and Patty grabbed the mike. The radio was now buzzing with reports of units on the way to the scene, the chauffeurs for all the top brass were reporting in, the police commissioner himself reported an ETA of 20 minutes. Patty joined in "citywide, *Adam 4 is in the area. We are responding.*" "*10-4 Adam 4,*" replied the dispatcher who may have wondered why we were "in the area," but being the pro he was, did not hesitate to log us in. Our supervisor also heard our response and told citywide "*ESU supervisor, read direct.*" We were on our way, all of a sudden I could care less about the asshole mechanic, the lights and siren were wailing to perfection and traveling at highway speed, in excess of 80 miles per hour would put us on scene in a matter of minutes.

My heart began to race. This was like a dust off into a hot Nam L-Z. Eight or nine gunships going in under fire. I saw a Chinook, twin rotor chopper go down under small arms fire at Khe Sahn. It totally lost its hydraulics. It was sickening to see the valiant bird twisting and turning, trying to stay aloft. When it impacted it burst into flame. Some of the 1st Cav troopers aboard got out but even they were engulfed in flame. I wondered now if this crash would have survivors.

The rush was indescribable. In ESU we always joked about the "Big Job." John & Al's The Williamsburg Siege was a big job. This would be on the list of one of the Big Jobs. Until 9/11 there were many Big Jobs. But the World Trade Center created a new base of measurement for a big job. It was the ultimate Big Job and I hope it is never exceeded.

Aircraft rescue is a part of ESU training. In my mind, as we approached, I ran through some scenarios, but most of our practice had to do with hostage rescue, not crashes. We were taught how to enter aircraft from different doors and loading areas and how to target and fire once inside the cabin. I doubted that we would have an intact aircraft to work with this afternoon.

The Van Wyck was understandably gridlocked. We approached along the grass banking along the highway until we were able to roll into an area of carnage. No rescue work to be done here. It struck me as a battlefield with dead and dying everywhere. It appeared to me that there could be no survivors. Dozens of bodies were strewn about like rag dolls waiting for a little girl to retrieve them after a day of play. Some appeared to be asleep. Some were burned beyond recognition. There were decapitated bodies still strapped in their chairs.

Despite the sirens announcing the arrival of dozens of emergency units and the screams of passersby who had rushed to help at the scene, in my mind, it was eerily quiet, like a battlefield the morning after. Within minutes units were on the scene from the FD, PD, and EMS. Then a very strange thing happened, I had a thought of the movie "Zulu" starring Michael Caine, where hordes of local residents descend on the scene of destruction following a battle, hell bent on looting the dead. They were not there to render help. No, they were there to plunder and rape the victims. People were crawling like roaches around the wrecked plane, the decapitated bodies, the burning luggage and even the bodies of young children. Within five minutes, though, the Tactical Patrol Force, elite cops who responded to major events like riots, parades and sadly, plane crashes, was on scene, led by one of the legendary Chiefs in the history of the NYPD, Ray McDermott, a true cop's cop. He gave the order "Kick ass and take names. No arrests." He would not tolerate looting of the dead. He had big balls even though he had once been demoted by Commissioner Patrick Murphy, only to return to his deserved glory. In short order TPF secured the scene, sending the cowardly looters scrambling like the vermin they were.

With a large area around the crashed jetliner secured from public view and our job of inspecting each apparent victim to make sure they either could or could not be helped, and none in this crash even made it alive to an ambulance, we began the grim task of tagging and bagging.

Each piece of a body had to be individually tagged with a 95 Tag, the official NYPD tag affixed to the big toe of a victim of a crime or death on the mean streets of the Big Apple. I know you have seen them at one time or another on A&E or some cop show when they pull the body out of the freezer in the morgue. After they open the door, it is the first thing you see as they pull the clean crisp white sheet back exposing the victim's toe. It has all the bio information of the victim including time of death, name, address, and what the ME felt was the cause of death.

Thinking back, I can still smell the stench in the Bellevue morgue. It was like a sweet smell of a melon gone bad. This was just one of many smells, depending on the stage of decomposition. The first ones are an unreal smell. But I did have numerous DOA's in the later stages. They were like leather, or a mummy.

It was a long and tiring night. Wreckage, luggage, bodies, and body parts were strewn everywhere. It was our job to put all the pieces back together.

By midmorning the next day the bodies were at the Queens Medical Examiner's Office, The Morgue. We were relieved by ESU Units from the Queens ESU Squads, Truck 10 and Truck 9. They would continue the grid search for remains, or body parts just in case we missed anything. Patty and I were heading back to the 50 Precinct where our ESU Truck 4 Squad was quartered. I decided not to go home. I would be due back for a 4 by 12 shift. It was already 1 p.m., so there was no sense driving back to Brooklyn, some 32 miles away. I took a shower then went to the corner bar. Every precinct had one. This was called Pauline's with great burgers and the coldest draft beer in *Da Bronx*. I felt I deserved a break, some down time. I ate two great cheese burgers and had a couple of drafts. The news on television was reporting that the crash of Eastern Airlines flight 66 from New Orleans was apparently caused by wind shear. All 112 aboard were killed.

I returned to quarters and sat around the gray table with the guys for a while and then took a nap. As I laid back I wondered how it must have been so difficult for the families of the victims. But I was glad on one point. They didn't have to see them as I did. I hoped for a closed coffin. As I fell into a restless sleep I wondered what lay ahead for me at 4 p.m., the start of my next 4 by 12 in Truck 4. It would be just another day in ESU.

THE LAST MIDNIGHT

Numbers on a Run Sheet

October 13, 1985 was one of those days New Yorkers call Indian summer, although that is not exactly correct. A real Indian summer comes later in the fall or early winter when Mother Nature blesses us with a few days of unseasonably warm weather.

I was still at Truck 8, headquartered behind the 90th precinct in Williamsburg, just a short distance from John & Al's Sporting Goods where I saw E-Man Stephen Gilroy die and watched the "Rescue Ambulance" come to the aid of those hostages. Thinking back, it seemed like a million years ago and every time I drove down Broadway past the sporting goods store I quietly wished to myself that I was living up to the standards set by guys like Gilroy. I hoped I was; I was an active, selfless cop, and I don't think I was kidding myself if I believed that.

But over the past year or so I had been getting down on myself; wondering if I had taken too much time away from my family, taken too many risks and wondering, as is a symptom of veteran cops, if I was appreciated at all, by the department, by my family and by the New Yorkers I served.

Brooklyn is a vast place, home to more than two million people representing hundreds of countries from Sicily to Senegal. I once heard that mass is said in 26 languages in the Catholic churches alone. Add in the mosques, synagogues, storefront churches and private homes where religion is celebrated and you have the most diverse place on earth.

Brooklyn would be the fourth largest city in America if it was a city, but it is just one of New York City's five boroughs. It was its own city until 1898 when Greater New York was formed. That consolidation took in Manhattan, Brooklyn, Queens, Staten Island, and the Bronx. At the time, each borough was actually a county with its own police and fire departments. Even today each county has its own District Attorney and Borough President.

Sometimes I felt that each county had its own separate police force. Each borough operates in extremely diverse ways. To give you just one example, in the 1970's if you were arrested for possessing a loaded gun in Brooklyn you got a $100 fine. If this had occurred in Staten Island, you were looking at serious jail time. These days Brooklyn has a special Gun Court and it is tough on anyone caught with a weapon.

Truck 8 patrolled an area covering the Brooklyn Bridge to Kennedy Airport, which is in Queens. It was also the home of *Big Bertha*. She was one of the NYPD's two Bomb/Explosive Removal vehicles. Her sister was stationed in ESU Truck 2 in Harlem.

These vehicles were tractor trailers. The trailer was constructed of wire mesh, steel cable, several inches thick. I had the privilege of driving the unit twice in my career. Once I was carrying a large pipe bomb, and once it was some dynamite. Believe me, a two hour long trip through NYC at low speeds with that baggage is no picnic. Every street intersection and every highway entrance would be closed by Highway Patrol Units who raced ahead of *Bertha*. Our final destination would be the Bomb Squad's disposal site located at Rodman's Neck in the Bronx.

Truck 8 was also home to the Air Bag Truck. This was a citywide response vehicle, which was dispatched whenever a jumper was reported. We had the same inflatable air bag used by Hollywood stunt men. This special unit was responsible for saving many bent on ending it all. Needless to say, there was never a dull moment in Truck 8, which led the city in armed barricade jobs and in execution of violent felony warrants always with a possibility of facing a combat situation.

It was not for lack of action that my attitude seemed to be changing. I was out there constantly, helping people, like I always dreamed I could do, and coming to the aid of my fellow police officers when they were in need. What higher calling is there than that! But I was losing sight of what helping was all about. People were becoming numbers on a run sheet and my family was practically a distant memory.

My assignment that night on the midnight to eight shift was chauffeur of the actual Truck 8, the big truck, which was kind of "dad" to Adam 8 and Boy 8, the smaller units that patrolled while we sat at quarters waiting for an appropriate call. At Truck 8 we did not wait long.

My partner was Detective Tony Sanpietro. Tony had a lead foot, what a driver! He hit the gas pedal and raced for every job. But I guess I'm calling the kettle black. I was also known as a guy who would "fly" to a job. Tony had a special knack of getting through intersections and red lights while barely slowing down. He scared the crap out of me at times but never committed the sin of having an accident that caused us to abort our run and call for another unit to take our place in harm's way. Other than Tony's death-wish driving he was one of the best officers in the Division.

Our tour started with the "written rule" of ESU. Always start with a dutiful inspection of all the rescue equipment on the truck by running every rescue tool, generator, saws, Jaws of Life, and checking out the weapons, trauma kit, first aid supplies, and oxygen resuscitator. You get my drift? Despite my ennui at this period of time I never relaxed my dedication to this ritual, which was being repeated all over the city in every ESU Truck garage. Who wanted to die when a subway car fell on you because a rescue tool did not perform properly? As I said in the past, the equipment was going to save a life maybe not on this tour, but sooner rather than later. Being prepared was the most important need we faced.

I was hoping for a "slow tour." I knew myself. I was burning out big time. I was weary of the smell of death, the broken and mangled bodies, the burned bodies, and the decomposing bodies. It was all starting to take effect. I always told rookies that "It's not the physical dangers in police work, but the psychological dangers that will get you."

Now I was hearing my own words in my own head. I had seen too many friends fall into the bottle, divorce, and even worse "clean their ears" or, as you would say it, kill themselves with their own weapons.

I was already at door number one, my divorce was to be finalized in a couple of weeks. I was apparent to me that I had placed my love of police work over that of my family, something I still regret.

After we finished our equipment checks, Tony and I headed upstairs to the Gray Table, the legendary place in ESU headquarters where "everything" was discussed and nothing we held back. It was where we broke bread, and on a rare occasion where tempers would flare up. Confrontations between E-Men were rare. But in ESU there were many personalities. Everyone was a star in ESU.

I had just finished pouring a cup of coffee when the citywide radio came alive. How many, many times had that happened in the past 10 years? I left many half-filled coffee cups around the city. We had speakers all over our headquarters, so there was no excuse for missing an assignment.

The female voice, cool and commanding, came over the air: "*Truck 8, Adam 8, Boy 8. Reports of a 'Man Under', Jamaica and Broadway.*" By instinct after 10 years of this service I knew the call meant someone has jumped or fallen in the path of a subway car. Sometimes a report turned out to be unfounded but the dispatcher said "reports" and that usually meant numerous calls to 911 and a confirmed job.

I thought, oh shit! The tour just started and I would have to change uniforms already. How cynical was I getting? Probably waiting for me, before my very eyes was what was left of a human of some unclear race or gender. Probably, it would be just a mass of flesh and rags lying in pieces and still smoldering from the massive shock that had been received.

A jumper in Truck 4 was my first ESU job. It was when the great Jack Shea taught me how to roll a body, twisted around a train's massive wheels, into a body bag. I had a thought as I hit the start button and the big diesel engine roared to life, which surprised even me: "I hope this is my last Man Under job."

Quickly our air pressure was right where it should be at 90 plus. I next hit the buttons that activated the emergency light and siren. Tony with his hand on the air horn was clearing the street. We turned out of quarters and headed towards Bushwick Avenue a few blocks away.

From here it would be a straight run only a couple of miles away. We should be on scene in about three or four minutes.

Bushwick Avenue is a major two-lane street. It runs from the border of Queens to the end of Brooklyn. As we raced to the job most of the vehicles in front of us pulled to the side. But this was Brooklyn North a.k.a *"The Killing Fields."* Here, there was little respect for the police, and none for an emergency vehicle with lights and sirens on rushing to an emergency. This was a place where firefighters were pelted with bottles and rocks as they tried to save life and property.

We were making great time. I could see green lights all the way. So far none of the Brooklyn North "Rocket Pilots," the drivers who steered with complete disrespect for all concerned including police and civilians alike, got in the way. Only one in 20 might have insurance. Mostly they were unlicensed, and unregistered. Their plates never matched their cars. These "Rocket Pilots" rarely stopped for red lights, and never yielded the way for an emergency vehicle. Just arriving on the scene of an emergency was a major accomplishment without having been "T" Boned as was the fate of about one precinct radio car a week. But the big truck was pretty intimidating and on this particular job we did not encounter any resistance.

As we approached the crest of Eastern Parkway and Bushwick Ave I could see several precinct units on scene. We would be getting there in a matter of seconds. I parked Truck 8 in the intersection and as the wail of the siren died down a young cop called out to me. "All ya' need is a shovel and body bag." I hated to hear a young officer talk that way. He had already lost respect for the victim.

This victim had fallen to the street 20 feet below the elevated tracks. It appeared that she had jumped in front of the lead subway car as it barreled into the station in excess of 30 miles per hour. Each subway car weighs approximately 10 tons. Several cars had passed over the victim. I could imagine the horror the motorman must have felt as he saw someone jump in front of his train. I grabbed a portable floodlight, the first thing Jack Shea had ordered me to do 10 years ago in the Bronx and walked slowly to the body lying in the street. In the dark, under the elevated train tracks, it looked like nothing more than a pile of rags that might have fallen off a passing junk truck.

But the closer I got the more I could smell that all familiar stench of burning flesh, not burned, but burning. Ten minutes ago this was living, breathing human being. Now the remains of what was once a person lie dismembered and smoldering on the damp street.

In the past I would wonder, as I approached the scene of such carnage, what could cause someone to end her life like this? How could things ever get that bad? What a waste! These days, however, I wondered more how soon I could get out of there. Bag it, tag it and get back to quarters. Not the correct attitude for an E-Man, no better than that young cop who had just advised me to grab a shovel and a body bag.

Now, standing over the body I noticed something that brought me back to the moment at large. It snapped me into the mode that had saved my life, the lives of my partners and countless souls who needed rescuing, in the past.

In the heap in front of me, almost buried in the lumpy mass of clothing I thought I spotted an infant. Was she pregnant when she jumped, was this a newborn, coming into life on the dirty streets of Brooklyn? I brought the light closer, and brushed away some of the smoldering clothing. Now digging with my hands into the remains, I was certain I saw a baby. A baby!

I shouted out to Tony to bring the trauma kit forthwith. I was operating on training and instinct. In a flash Tony, recognizing the urgency in my voice, was standing behind me. This was not a newborn, but a child of several months old, wearing a tiny Mets jacker with an arm missing. Tony, ever the cool customer was placing a tourniquet on the little limb. Amazingly the infant was conscious. There was no bleeding; it appeared that the massive wheels had cauterized the wound.

We worked feverishly to free the child from the tangled mess that was "*its*" mother. In short minutes we were able to hand the baby over to EMS and on the way to the emergency room.

It became apparent as Tony and I prepared to replace our equipment back on the truck that I wasn't myself. He asked me what was troubling me. My reply, which just poured out of my heart, surprising Tony and me was: "I'm tired of being a garbage man for society." There I said it. What had been bothering me for months, twisting around in my mind, destroying my sleep and separating me from my friends and family, was finally out.

I was tired of body bags, and torn broken bodies and dead and dying children. I could not even remember, as I wrote out the run sheet whether this child in the Mets jacket was a boy or a girl. I checked the box for "M" because of the baseball jacket. Sexist I guess, but I did not even want to take the time to call the emergency room. It was a far different feeling from the time Jack Shea and I got that kid's arm out of the meat grinder. Then I visited him in the hospital for three days.

I was tired of being the guy who had to clean used body bags, washing them with hard brushes and scalding water or taking them to the river and letting the crabs eat the human remains off of them.

Sitting at the gray table as the night past quietly, I ignored the television, Tony and the other guys. I was deep in thought upset with the realization that for too long the stench of the dead and dying has become so embedded in me that I hardly even noticed it. I knew that I had to do something or I would be no better off than being a part of the living dead.

I knew I had to make a major change in my life or I was doomed. Before the tour was over, I made a plan to go to Police Headquarters at 1 Police Plaza right after my shift ended at 8 a.m. I was going to see Monsignor Kowsky. He was the Catholic Chaplain and one of the best people I had ever met. His brother was the former Chief in charge of Safety Emergency. This was the forerunner of Special Operations Division. Chief Kowsky wore the Highway Patrol uniform, boots included. Highway Patrol was one of the units under his command. Monsignor Kowsky prior to joining the NYPD was a Vietnam combat Chaplain. He knew his men well, and he knew his cops even better.

There were several times when the legendary E-Man Paul Ragonese and I took the Chaplain to a hospital emergency room where a cop was shot. The three of us were deer hunting buddies. The Monsignor and I had become close friends. I knew he would understand. I knew he would help me. I was one of the lucky ones. I knew I was burned out; I knew I had to do something to stay alive.

I came on the PD to help people, and now it seemed that they were just numbers to me—except when it came to the children. Every cop will have the memory of a child who was killed or injured burned in their memory forever. Once you see a murdered, abused or injured child it will never leave your mind especially if you were a father. I never had a problem dealing with adults, I killed one, shot at others, arrested many who went to prison for long stretches; fuck them, they were criminals who would have killed me or another cop in the blink of an eye. They killed Stephen Gilroy and Cecil Sledge. The children, their grief, became my grief and stays with me to this day.

I had made my decision. It broke my heart, but I needed a change. I'd have to leave ESU, the job I considered the best in the entire NYPD. I would have done the job in ESU for nothing. I know every other member of ESU would tell you the same thing. I have never seen a more dedicated and unselfish group of people in my life then the members of ESU.

After a second cup of coffee I got up from the gray table to stretch a little and noticed, for the first time, my uniform pants were covered with blood and small pieces of flesh.

I was fortunate that the rest of the shift passed quietly, Adam and Boy 8 had some runs, but the big Truck was not needed by the time midnight rolled around. Mostly we spent the shift sitting around the gray table, discussing department politics, various rescues, gun jobs—the work-a-day world of cops. I pretty much clammed up. I just wanted to get out of there.

Then as soon as I could, I hopped into my old green jeep, fired her up, and hit the BQE exiting at the Brooklyn Bridge. There was a ramp there that put you smack in front of the underground parking garage at 1 PP. I walked to the main entrance of the building most active cops would just as soon avoid for the length of their career. It took me a while to get on the elevator. I had several friends on the job. And it seemed every time I was going to board the elevator a voice shouted out, "Hey Shep, or Hey Al." I cut the conversations short in response.

I knew that Monsignor Kowsky didn't hang around 1 PP very long. He had a department, unmarked car. If he wasn't out visiting injured or wounded cops, he was on patrol. I finally made it on to the elevator. I exited the car hastily, looking down and making a left all at once.

Bang, I ran smack into someone.

Not just "someone" but none other than Chief of the Department Robert J. Johnston Jr., "Patton", the highest ranking uniform member of the NYPD. I apologized, "Sorry Chief" I was in a rush." The Chief was a strict disciplinarian. Feared by many and liked by few, he expected 110% from his men. Nothing less would do. I thought he was a good boss. I had personally seen him help active cops out of jams. We were well acquainted. And he had picked me as one of the original members of the antiterrorist Team, the first in NYC in 1977. His driver Reggie Toomey was also a good friend of mine.

The Chief pulled me to the side and asked what was going on. I explained the last shift, my "Last Midnight." I was burned out and needed a change. I further explained that I was going to see Monsignor Kowsky to see if he could help me get a transfer. I sensed he seemed to be a little disappointed that I didn't go directly to him. He told me he always admired my dedication to the NYPD, and then asked me where I wanted to go? I was floored! I had never thought of where I wanted to be assigned. The Chief was pressed for a news conference at City Hall. He told me to go see the Monsignor and let him know where I'd like to be assigned.

I was lucky Kowsky was in his office. As usual I was greeted with a big smile and hearty hand shake. I related last night's shift, and how I needed a change. He agreed with me. Then I explained that I just left the Chief out in the hallway. We discussed several assignments. Then the Monsignor suggested a unit that dealt with Missing and Runaway Children. It was an investigative, plainclothes unit. It sounded good to me. It was a chance to really help people who needed it. What better then kids! Having three of my own, I knew the dangers that they faced especially in Manhattan.

The unit worked in Times Square and this was the era of the Times Square welfare hotels. Literally hundreds of hotel kids were running the streets at all hours of the night. Also more were pouring into the Big Apple from all across the country on an almost daily basis. The Chaplain and I talked for about an hour. He mentioned how he had sensed a change in me in recent months. He thought working in a unit where I could help those who really needed it would be a way to get back to my roots, the reason I joined the NYPD in the first place. I felt much better when I left and I knew I would be reassigned soon.

I never imagined how soon. I went to work that night at Truck 8 and when I got upstairs I was told. "Hey Al, you're transferred. We tried to call you. It was a telephone message right from the Chief of Department's Office." The message ordered me to report to 12 1/2 West 12th. Street in Manhattan.

My career now took a dramatic change and that new assignment became one of my most memorable ever until Major Case Squad was to follow. I went on to 10 more great years in the

NYPD, but nothing could compare to ESU. I often think back, should I have stayed? I certainly could have; others had fought off the depression and confusion I was feeling and finished their careers as E-Men. But I have no regrets. Those were great years and I hope I did my duty well. I am so proud to be a member of that fraternity. Everything in life happens for a reason. I know whatever comes my way, I will still die an E-Man.

10

Circle of Six: The True Story of New York's Most Notorious Cop-Killer and the Cop Who Risked Everything to Catch Him

by Randy Jurgensen (with Robert Cea)

"I believe TIME magazine said that if you were between the ages of sixteen and twenty-one years old, and black, you stood a better chance in the jungles of Vietnam than on the concrete corner of 116th Street and 8th Avenue (Harlem, NYC) on a Friday night."

—Randy Jurgensen,
Circle of Six: The True Story of New York's Most Notorious Cop-Killer
and The Cop who Risked Everything to Catch Him

SETTING THE TABLE

By 1968 I had eleven years on the job. The job was the New York City Police Department—homicide detective. I worked two of those eleven years in uniform in East (Spanish) Harlem. I did another four years undercover working vice and buying narcotics, guns, and whatever else the streets had for sale. It was during my undercover work that I broke a case known as the Bag Murders involving two killers who zeroed in on homosexuals. Breaking this case got me the Gold Shield. As for the last five of those eleven years, I dealt with death every morning, every afternoon, and every night, whether I was awake or asleep; I was a homicide detective. All in all, I worked eighteen of my twenty years in Harlem.

I am a white male—born and raised just three city blocks from the heart of Harlem, 125th Street and Eighth Avenue. In my time, the people of this area were always at the bottom of the ladder. Whether it was the ladder of employment, living conditions, economic opportunities, schools, or city services, Harlem and its residents were always left out—no matter gender, color, or creed. Every store on 125th Street was "white outsider–owned." The money spent and the money made in those businesses didn't come back to the community because the owners didn't live there. Most of, if not all the housing and apartment buildings were also "white owned," not to mention insufferable. They weren't maintained—there was no heat in the winter, the little running water never crawled beyond the second floor, and fires left many apartments scarred and uninhabitable. There were times when the tenants would call the police to come and shoot the rats infesting the hallways. Children returning home from school feared the vermin. Aside from rats, deplorable living conditions, and money that seemed to only go one way—out—there were drugs.

The precinct I worked at, the 28th Precinct (or 2-8 Precinct), had two distinctions. First, we were the smallest out of seventy-six others; and second, we led the city in homicides. There were three ways out of Harlem. One: as stated by Honey Combs, the proprietor of The Apollo Theatre, you could, "sing or dance your way out," like Sammy Davis Jr. who never sang or danced his way back. Two: you could join or wait and be drafted into the army, and sent to Vietnam. Three: be killed. I believe *Time* magazine said that if you were between the ages of sixteen and twenty-one years old and black, you stood a better chance in the jungles of Vietnam than on the concrete corner of 116th Street and Eighth Avenue on a Friday night.

Indeed, 1968 was a defining year.

President Nixon was in the White House. It was the apex of the Vietnam War (Tet Offensive). The city's streets were flooded with people of both genders and all colors, creeds, and religions fighting for equal rights. The Women's Movement, the Civil Rights Movement, the Columbia student riots, and of course, the explosive drug problem all crowded New York's already busy streets.

The word in City Hall was that law and order had to be restored. To that end, after years of its absence, they were going to fire up the electric chair, or *Old Sparky* as those in the know called it. But in order to sit on Old Sparky's throne, you had to have a prior arrest record.

On any given day I would look out the window of the 28th Precinct. I'd see some of Harlem's kids running in and out of the spray of a busted fire hydrant. What I didn't see was a chance in hell that any of those kids would ever be doctors, lawyers, or bankers. But given the right circumstances, which their atmosphere all too willingly provided, I saw plenty of candidates for the chair. Nevertheless hope was still alive in Harlem. But then someone killed Dr. Martin Luther King Jr.

Hope was replaced by anger and three days of fires, looting, and shooting . . . what did you expect?

The following story is true. It took place in this setting and during these trying times. Some of the names have been changed to protect the guilty.

Well, the table is set. Pull up a chair. Take a seat and indulge in some of New York City's most tumultuous history.

–New York City Homicide Detective, Randy Jurgensen *(retired)*

PROLOGUE

Wasn't that hard to make us out—three wired unshaven white guys, sipping cold coffee in a '66 Impala, middle of Harlem, 1972? Shit, we weren't trying to fool anyone. Most of the junkies, hustlers, and street mopes breezing past us that crisp Spring morning worked for me in one way or another anyhow. I was a first grade detective, Harlem's home grown *DT. Kid,* Randy Jurgensen, the omnipresent spoke on a wheel of detectives or DTs. I was part of a high-profile homicide team working out of Manhattan's *Zone-6,* affectionately known back in the day as, *The Murder Factory.*

The Zone-6 murder factory or killing field covered three of the deadliest police precincts in New York City circa 1972—the 2-8, 2-5, and 3-2 precincts. That year alone, 500 people were killed in an area no bigger than 3.4 square miles. An even broader, more staggering statistic: roughly one third of all homicides committed in New York's seventy-five precincts occurred in Zone-6. To say we officers were busy was the understatement of the decade.

My job, among many others that year, was to find those prolific murderers and bring them to justice—a job I'd grown to respect and subsequently love. My job also demanded me to know every one of those street types intimately who were scurrying past us on that severely clear April morning. Occasionally I'd have to turn to them for the info. This was all part of the game, and it would also help catch some killers. These guys, for good or for bad, were what I did for a living; my eyes and ears in a business—catching murderers—that totally relied on credible street intelligence for positive results. More than likely a few of those street mopes would turn up at the beginning or the end of my day, depending on which side of the murder weapon they were lucky or unlucky enough to be on. However, on this particular morning, I was not assigned to Zone-6 homicide. I was on loan to a newly formed furtive unit called the *Major Case Squad*. The unit's sole objective was to hunt down and arrest members of a dangerous and militant anarchist group who were calling themselves The Black Liberation Army, or BLA. The members of this group were vociferous in their threats and had murdered scores of cops across the United States during crimes such as bank robberies, holdups, armored car heists, and well-organized high-profile assassinations.

My target that April morning was as legitimate a cop killer as anyone I'd ever known, one with whom I was quite familiar—Twyman Meyers, the self-professed leader of The Black Liberation Army. Just the week before, we'd been sitting on Joanne Chesimard, "the soul of the BLA," and had missed her by six hours. Twyman was wanted in connection with the cold-blooded ambush assassination of four New York City patrolmen and the attempted murder of two other New York City cops by wantonly spraying their RMP (Radio Motor Patrol) with automatic machine-gun fire. Numerous witnesses recorded the license plates of Meyers's getaway car. He wasn't trying to hide anything. Two days after the plates of Twyman's stolen car were revealed in the news, the actual plates were mailed to *The New York Times* with this hand-written message:

May 19th, 1971

All the power to the people.

Here are the license plates sort [sic] after by the fascist state pig police. We send them in order to exhibit the potential power of opposed peoples to acquire Revolutionary justice.

The armed goons of this racist government will again meet the guns of oppressed Third World Peoples as long as they occupy our community and murder our brothers and sisters in the name of American law and order; just as the fascist Marines and Army occupy Vietnam in the name of democracy and murder Vietnamese people in the name of American Imperialism are confronted with the guns of the Vietnamese Liberation Army, the domestic armed forces of racism and oppression will be confronted with the guns of the Black Liberation Army, who will mete out in the tradition of Malcolm and all true revolutionaries real justice. [sic]

We are revolutionary justice. All power to the people.

My partner, Sonny Grosso (of *French Connection* fame), and I'd crossed paths with Meyers eleven months prior. I'd locked him up. We'd received information that Meyers was setting us up for assassination, and through some street CIs (confidential informants) we were able to get the jump on him and two accomplices before they could carry out their deadly mission—*killing us.* However, during the struggle Sonny and Twyman both fell over a banister, crashing onto a flight of stairs one-half story down. Sonny sustained injuries that would ultimately end his career. One week after our violent encounter, Twyman was bailed out of the Manhattan Detention Center, *the Tombs,* with money the BLA acquired from a St. Louis bank robbery. He was free to roam and murder again. Directly after this *jumble-fuck-of-a-release* from the Tombs, it was determined that Meyers had been party to the 1971 murders of New York City cops Joseph Piagentini and Waverly Jones. Witnesses said that Twyman Meyers danced over the fallen bodies of the two patrolmen. It was incriminating evidence, but it had come too late. The killer was long gone and had disappeared into the wind. But the scumbag wouldn't let me forget him for long. He was a son of a bitch who liked to brag. In those eleven months since we'd collared him, he'd made repeated calls to Les Matthews, a writer for *The Amsterdam News,* stating that I was at the top of his *to-be-killed* list, and that members of my family would be executed as well. Needless to say, the NYPD took those threats seriously, especially after Meyers showed up at my mother's home. After that incident, my parents received twenty-four hour, solid-gold protection and were eventually relocated to Florida and taken into protective custody. Twyman Meyers had made it personal, but so did I. I countered by calling Matthews with a message, in hopes of smoking the killer out of hiding. It was detailed, as in-depth as Meyers's rant to *The Times,* but subtly worded to get the reaction I wanted. It's a shame that the newspaper printed this watered-down version:

> *Harlem-born and reared detective, Randy Jurgensen, is looking for the young leader of the Black Liberation Army, Twyman Meyers, and his daring accomplice Robert Vickers, who are both out to allegedly assassinate the cop according to underworld sources.*

Young leader of the BLA and his daring accomplice? They weren't movie stars; they were cop killers looking to make a name for themselves. And *The Amsterdam News* had become their go-between. This only tempered my resolve to catch my would-be assassin.

In 1972 we (the NYPD) were at war with the likes of Twyman Meyers, a hostile media, and a public who, for the most part, did not trust or like what they saw as the manifestation of "the establishment." This was a brew for a hellacious and bloody year. The climate in New York was this: We cops were targeted for death. The us-versus-them mentality was a yoke on every cop's shoulder, worn like a heavy weight, carried daily with rounds and rounds of extra ammo to guard against everyone and anyone. In those mean 1972 streets, the only thing we could count on was one another—our brother cops and the superior officers we called boss. If only that held true on that particular April morning. What I and the rest of the country were about to witness would place an indelible black mark on the face of the NYPD, its uppermost echelon, the Nation of Islam, Police Commissioner Patrick V. Murphy, and Mayor John Lindsay—a dark hurtful blemish that remains to this day, one that I myself could never and will never forget. We, the rank and file, were sandbagged by our own—the hierarchy of the NYPD. One of our brother cops, Phil Cardillo, was murdered and subsequently bastardized, then hurried into the ground in a cloak of mystery and dishonor, all in an effort to cover up a purposeful negligence of duty so blatant it defies belief. In short, we were betrayed by our fathers, the police commissioner, and his deputies. It was the collusion of our own, Mayor John Lindsay, Commissioner Patrick V. Murphy, Deputy Commissioner Benjamin Ward, Chief of the Department Michael Codd, and Congressman Charles Rangel, with Minister Louis Farrakhan of the Nation of Islam—six in total—the *Circle of Six.*

To understand the backstabbing fully, we have to go back in time, back to one of the most brutal periods in New York history. Back to a time when ten cops a year were systematically executed in cold and calculated hits, back to one of the most traumatic eras in the storied New York City Police Department's past. *The place:* Harlem, New York. *The time:* April 14, 1972.

FRIDAY, APRIL 14TH, 1972–11:39 A.M.

We were set up just west of Amsterdam Avenue on 125th Street. I settled my binoculars on a clear and unobstructed view of the set. According to my information, Twyman Meyers was coming in from the north, so we felt fairly confident that our surveillance OPs (observation posts) were invulnerable to burn. I was assigned five plain-clothes cops, or anticrime cops as they were called, from the 2-8 (28th) Precinct. Two were with me in the car, while the other three were on the other side of Amsterdam Avenue. It was an unseasonably warm day, and the fact that I was wearing my army field jacket to hold ammo and conceal my shotgun made the shit-box Impala feel like a blast furnace. I was jittery and for good reason. Meyers had succeeded in doing what no other perp had done before: He'd gotten deep inside, made this a personal war. But I was a professional and didn't want emotions getting in the way of a good bust. As far as I was concerned, Twyman Meyers was about to lose his position as the head of the BLA. He had a destiny with one of two conclusions: an electric chair or a pine box. End of story.

I swept the binos over the dingy terrain and couldn't help thinking how the streets had changed. I knew the area intimately, was born and bred on 123rd Street and Amsterdam Avenue, just two blocks south of where I was sitting that very moment, trying to catch this criminal. But that was a different time and a different way of life.

My parents were the superintendents of the building, two of the few who truly cared about their residents and strived to make the conditions as nice as possible. Like most of the hard-working parents in New York City during the forties, they also took care of the neighborhood and all of its children. Now, thirty years later, I was trying to do the same, look out for the neighborhood. Though this time, so much more was at stake. The core values and very foundation that molded me into the man I was, that same foundation that once held those families, their extensions, and those tightly knit streets together, was now being dismantled by an ideology steeped in blazing hatred. In hindsight I may have been overly naive, but I truly felt that when I caught Twyman Meyers, the hatred and all the diseased thoughts that he espoused to so many young children would somehow recede, and we would all come together like so many years before. In my heart I felt that Twyman Meyers, Joanne Chesimard, and the soldiers of the BLA were the symbols of hatred that I had to do away with. Was I obsessed with my mission? You bet. My mission was to try to turn back the hands of time. I'd soon realize how ridiculous that presumption was. That day was just the beginning of five years of hell.

We were on the Zone-6 radio frequency, which seemed to erupt in a continuous cacophony of chatter between the cops of the ultra-busy Harlem precincts and Central Dispatch. It was a machine-gun ratta-tat-tat of coded numbers, legalese, and raw New York slang.

2-8 Nora, got a 52 corner of 1-2-8 and Amsterdam
Ten-four central, Nora responding, K
2-5 Adam 52 with a gun, corner of Saint Nick at 1-2-2, units to respond
Charlie, K
Adam responding
Crimes 84, K
5 Sergeant en route, K
All units in the 3-2, ten-ten reports of shots fired Broadway 1-4-0, K. Numerous calls, units to
    respond, K
3-2 Boy
Adam

Charlie's en route, K
3-2 Boy's 84, it's confirmed, get a bus, K! Get a bus, K! Guy's bleedin' like a stuck pig, K!

It was a nonstop mélange of deadly calls twenty-four seven. Shootings, robberies, assaults, murders, and of course, the end-all, ten-thirteens. *Ten-thirteen* was the code for an officer in need of help. When that thirteen alarm sounded, everything in copland stopped, all focus was on the radio for the coordinates. However, when the thirteen was phoned in via 911 emergency police operator, it often turned out to be an unfounded call. The first unit to respond would immediately contact central and designate the call as a *ninety-x-ray* (unfounded job), ceasing further response from units who were certainly traveling at breakneck speeds through harm's way to help. These fake ten-thirteens were phoned in for a number of reasons, though, generally non-malicious ones—prank callers just trying to break the balls of a few cops. Still, some had criminal intent. For instance, say an OP—like the one I was on that day—had been burned or discovered by a wanted man—like Twyman Meyers—and he needed to move from one safe house to another without being seen. He could easily call in the bogus ten-thirteen at the opposite end of the precinct and pull guys just like us off our spots. It was good business to keep the cops off guard, and most of the salty perps knew exactly where the precinct boundaries were, allowing them to send us to the opposite end of Harlem. So when Central got the call that morning, before I moved, I was going to be cock-and-balls sure that it was a confirmed ten-thirteen.

11:41:20 A.M.

A ten-thirteen call was made to the 911 operator, or Central Dispatch. What you are about to read are the identical transcripts of the thirteen in question. This was the beginning of the end for many people. One life was lost, many careers halted and destroyed, and an unbreakable bond of trust and faith shattered forever.

> *Operator: "Police operator."*
> *Caller: "Hello, this is Detective Thomas of the 2-8 Precinct."*
> *Operator: "Yeah."*
> *Caller: "I have a ten-thirteen, 1-0-2 West 116th Street."*
> *Operator: "1-0-2 West 116th?"*
> *Caller: "Right, that's on the second floor."*
> *Operator: "Second floor."*
> *Caller: "Right."*
> *Operator: "Hold on."*

The caller abruptly hung up. The operator, a uniformed member of the NYPD, immediately typed out the message and electronically sent it to the civilian radio dispatcher in an adjacent room at police headquarters. The dispatcher, or Central, immediately broadcast it over the Zone-6 radio frequency—Harlem, *my killing fields.*

11:42:00 A.M.

Central came over the air with urgency—regardless of childish pranks, call-ins do sometimes turn out to be legit and have to be taken seriously.

> *Central: "Signal ten-thirteen, 1-0-2 West 116th Street on the second floor. 1-0-2, 116, second floor, signal thirteen."*

Both the assigned cops in my car instinctively grabbed hold of their radios. I was on a *point-to-point* channel with the car across the street. The point-to-point frequency allowed us to communicate without everyone else in the zone hearing. The purpose of this was simple: Police radios were easy to come by, thus allowing the bad guys to monitor them. They could hear and know exactly what was going on. Point-to-point helped us keep them out, and the less they knew the safer we all were. Units responded to the call-in with a rush of adrenalin.

> *Unit 1: "2-8 Frank on the way."*
> *Unit 2: "David will respond."*
> *Central: "That's second floor hallway, 1-0-2 West 116, K."*
> *Unit 3: "2-8 Sergeant responding."*

I lifted up the radio and keyed the mike on the point-to-point, *"Stay on the set. Could be a ninety to pull us off."* My heart was racing for two reasons—if it was a phony thirteen then we could be very close to Meyers; however, if the call-in turned out to be legit, it would mean that a cop was in a fight for his life and we would have to pull from our OPs. Either way it was an extreme and intense thirty-five seconds. What occurred in those thirty-five seconds was a series of critical events that would alter the rest of my career. I didn't know this at the time, but I was going to find out.

The first unit to respond to the thirteen was a pair of five-year police veterans, Phil Cardillo, and his partner of four years, Vito Navarra. They were directly around the corner from 1-0-2 West 116th Street, which turned out to be the famous Mosque Number 7. Both veteran cops didn't think twice that the door to the mosque was left unattended and wide open. Why should they? They were in ten-thirteen mode—take no prisoners until the thirteen was a ninety-x or the job became a *condition corrected,* meaning: cops out of harm's way. The second car was from our sister precinct, manned by Victor Padilla and Ivan Negron. The fact that the front door to Mosque Number 7 was unlocked and unguarded was an incongruity within itself. There were never fewer than three steely FOI (Fruit of Islam) soldiers stationed at the secured doors. Their primary job was to keep interlopers out—that meant anyone who wasn't Muslim. And even if they were Black Muslims, they'd have to be members of Mosque Number 7 to be let in. Neither of the four cops fit that criterion.

All four officers, looking to help a brother in need, walked through those open doors. Once inside the vestibule, which was smallish—approximately eight feet wide by ten feet deep—they passed an empty reception desk and ran up a staircase toward the second floor. Halfway up the staircase they were met by approximately twenty Muslims, most of them FOI soldiers or building security. Two sets of metal double doors were slammed shut behind them and deadbolted from the inside. All four cops were trapped, surrounded, and becoming increasingly confused as one of the FOI men screamed, *"Allahu Akbar!"* The four patrolmen tried to gain entry to the second floor, looking for the cop in trouble. The Muslims wouldn't allow it and push came to shove. Suddenly the Muslims jumped the outnumbered cops. One of the four officers grabbed his radio and squeezed the mike in an attempt to call his own thirteen. He screamed inaudibly into it.

11:42:35 A.M.

> *Unit: [Inaudible screams.]*
> *Central: "Ten-five . . . is there a footman requesting assistance?"*
> *Unit: "—116th Street, central."*

The second I heard the screams coming from the radio, I determined this to be confirmed. I slammed the car into gear—a cop *was* on the wrong end of that thirteen. I placed the cherry light on the roof and raced east on 125th Street. I'd get Twyman Meyers another day.

There is nothing scarier than hearing the plaintive screams of a cop pleading for help over a radio. That sudden terror strikes you, like the slow motion of a tragedy happening before your eyes. Five thousand thoughts in your head all tell you to dive in the way, do whatever you can, but every sinew in your body is locked in fear. It's a crippling feeling, rushing toward a thirteen and hoping to God you're not too late. Hearing him scream over the radio, maybe the last noises he ever made, struck every cop with that same parental panic.

The four cops were beaten up and kicked back down the stairs to the first floor. The patrolmen were in survival mode as the FOI soldiers tried to rip their guns from their holsters. All they could do was cover up and wait for backup. Vito Navarra was kicked down the stairs, and Phil Cardillo was dragged down, feet first. Though he was nearly unconscious, he had the wherewithal to hold on to his weapon as a swarm of hands tried to pull it from its holster-locked position. Once on the first floor, the beating continued. That was when all hell broke loose.

I blocked everything out and focused on navigating around the traffic on 125th Street. The radio was momentarily silent, never a good sign on confirmed thirteens. I heard sirens closing in from all directions. Civilian cars heard them too and suddenly stopped. It was a bottlenecked mess on both sides of Harlem's main drag. I had nowhere to go. I heard the female dispatcher's voice, filled with heightening anxiety. It was her job to direct every unit to the location, and it was also her job to find out who the downed cop was. That would be tough to accomplish until somebody ID'd himself or another cop got eyes on him or them. It was even tougher to coordinate when sitting behind an archaic computer screen, wearing a headset some fourteen miles south of the action.

11:44:15 A.M.

For a while, more of the same transpired—dead air.

> Central: *Any unit on the scene at the assist patrolman, 1-0-2 West 116th?*

I was still trapped in four lanes of standstill traffic. I looked at my watch, almost two minutes had expired—still no sound from the units. Central was as nervous as I was; her voice cut through the radio silence.

> Central: *"Any 2-8 car on the scene at that assist patrolman, 1-0-2 West 116th Street, K?"*

There was no answer. Where the fuck were those cops? What was happening? I was starting to hyperventilate. The agonizing radio silence allowed me to imagine all kinds of horrific scenarios. I jerked the wheel, trying to pull the car into the west-bound lane; a stopped bus blocked my way. I leaned out the window and slammed my hand into the bus, screaming, "Move forward, goddamit!" But the driver had nowhere to go.

Then suddenly the radio jumped alive. Someone called off the ten-thirteen.

> *"No further, 1-0-2 West 116th Street, scooter post two of the 2-8."*

It was called off, but something just didn't seem right.

Patrolman Rudy Andre of the 2–8 was nearby. He quickly made his way to the scene. When he arrived he found a scooter cop kneeling in front of Vito Navarra, who was bloodied outside the mosque. It was quiet all around. Rudy determined that Navarra had been beaten and thrown out. The mosque doors were locked. None of them knew that three more cops were less than twenty feet away, struggling to stay alive. Even if they had known, they would have had no way to get into the building. And unfortunately, the three heavily outnumbered cops inside had no way out. Later, Patrolman Rudy Andre stated, "Navarra was out of it, barely conscious. I assumed there were no other cops in the building, because the scooter man called off the initial thirteen to slow everybody down."

We let out a collective, though guarded, sigh of relief. I actually laid my head on the steering wheel and whispered, "Fuck, fuck, fuck." I took a deep breath. Central came back on the air, calmly took control again.

Central: Units in the 2–8 Precinct, no further, 1-0-2 116th authority 2-8 scooter patrolman on the scene, 11:45 hours.

I glanced at my watch again. Three minutes had passed and the all cops were safe, or so we all thought.

I looked into my rearview mirror. The other car was trying to pull a u-turn back toward the OP. He called over the radio, *"Randy, OP, yes?"* I gave him a thumbs-up out the window. We weren't gone that long, and Twyman Meyers obviously hadn't called this one in. We still had a chance to catch him.

Meanwhile Patrolman Rudy Andre wanted to get a lead on Vito Navarra's attackers. He ran to the front doors of the mosque to search. As he reached the two-foot square windows on the double doors, he heard a gunshot explode from within. He pulled his service revolver and was jolted by what he witnessed—FOI men stomping on three bloody cops on the floor. He snatched up his radio and screamed, *"Ten-thirteen, 1-0-2 West 116th Street!"*

I jerked the wheel to the right, gunning the engine. All eight pistons fired open. The Impala slammed into the car ahead of us, pushing it far enough to give us access to the sidewalk. The Impala's undercarriage scraped onto the curb. Central squawked over the radio, *"1-0-2 West 116th a signal thirteen, 1-0-2 West 116th, a signal thirteen, what units to respond?"*

Unit: 2-5 anticrime, Central.
Central: Ten-four. Any other units in the 2-5, 1-0-2 West 116th assist patrolman?

I had a clear easterly corridor on the southbound sidewalk. We flew off into the crosswalk of Manhattan Avenue, siren blaring, crossed over to the eastbound sidewalk, and jumped the curb banging a hard right, now heading south. Pedestrians were diving into storefronts, over fences, and back into the street where other cars were at complete standstill. Now the radio was abuzz with the noise of sirens and the jumble of voices from police units jumping on top of one another.

Meanwhile Rudy Andre tried to pull the door open; it was locked. The FOI men inside the mosque continued to stomp on the downed cops. A pool of blood started to form around Phil Cardillo. It was at this point that Officer Rudy Andre made an incredible command decision. He pulled his gun and fired through the chicken-wired glass portals of the double doors. Some of the FOI men started to scatter. He reached in, slicing his wrist on a jagged edge, and fired three more times into the mosque ceiling. This stopped the advance and further beatings by the FOI. They ran down the stairs, leaving the three half-conscious cops on the floor. Though he was losing blood from a main artery, Rudy Andre used his weapon to punch out the remaining shards of glass. Other cops gathered behind him. Ivan Negron managed to shake off the hits he'd taken and stumble to the door. When he unlocked it, a dozen cops filed into the vestibule. Rudy screamed into the radio, "*Ten-thirteen, get additional units, Central.*"

We were closing in. All of a sudden, two footmen wearing 3-2 numerals turned the corner, weaving in and out of stopped cars. They were drenched in sweat and completely gassed. They had to have been running full-bore from their precinct. A sense of pride washed over me. I looked up and saw an NYPD helicopter swooping in from the south. It quickly dipped behind a building, then yawed low and out of sight. Central had called in additional units off of the next zone, meaning we were in the middle of a citywide ten-thirteen. Any available unit within earshot was to mobilize immediately to the location. It also meant that we were heading into full-blown chaos. I keyed the mike, "*Central be advised, two units from the Major Case Squad are responding, K.*"

She acknowledged the fact that we were arriving in plain clothes. In the midst of battle, during an all-out thirteen, we could have easily been mistaken for perps. I'd seen it happen all too often, and I didn't want to fall to friendly fire.

That was around the time Rudy Andre heroically led the charge into the mosque and found Phil heading toward death. He didn't realize Phil had taken a bullet. The shot that Andre heard from behind the locked doors had come from Phil Cardillo's own gun. One of the FOI men had ripped it from his holster and fired one round into his sternum. Andre ran past, assuming Phil's mouth was bleeding because of the kicks he'd taken to the face. Andre led a group of cops down the steps to apprehend whomever they could find. A breathless and sweaty man, Bobby Hopes, dressed in suit and bowtie, charged up the steps toward Andre. No questions were asked. Without hesitation, the cop brought the butt of his revolver down on the man's head.

"He went down like he was shot," Andre later recounted. "I put the cuffs on him. He probably was one of the men involved in the beating. As far as I was concerned, the man was a collar. I continued down toward the basement. I was seconds behind these guys. Next thing, I see a huge man towering over me, defiantly making his way up the steps. I screamed, 'stop!' He had this look of determination on his face, but before he reached me, I hit him too. He fell back down the stairs where I followed him."

Later this was going to prove to be powerful information: The man's name was Lewis 17X Dupree.

11:46:20 A.M.

Suddenly the radio erupted again, though this time the voice seemed to be drowned out by a thousand echoing screams. It was a unit calling in from ground zero, with the last thing any of us wanted to hear, "Shots are being fired, Central!"

> Central: *Shots fired, shots fired, shots fired. 1-0-2 West 116th, repeating units responding, 1-0-2 116th shots fired at this time.*

My blood froze. Cops were being fired upon. It couldn't get any worse than that. Manhattan Avenue had become an impenetrable wall of vehicles. All of the crosswalks were congested. We were wedged between a light post and a truck. *Fuck it*—I left it idling. The car was the last thing on my mind. I jumped out and started to run.

As I was zigzagging between cars, I tried to place the building; after all, this was my precinct, my neighborhood. I'd played stickball tournaments on these streets as a kid, played Ringolivio and Johnny Ride a Pony. Why wasn't 1-0-2 West 116th computing? Maybe I was in denial of what lay ahead. Another voice screamed over the radio, "*Patrolman shot, Central . . .*"

This transmission brought my two guns out of their holsters. With me were five other officers. Pedestrians saw us coming and dove behind cars or back into buildings. We were six wild-eyed white men, cocked and loaded, running toward the blue insanity that was engulfing Lenox Avenue.

Patrolman James Kenney of the Manhattan North Task Force was one of the first cops to enter the mosque along with Rudy Andre and a few other patrolmen. First thing he noticed was all the blood splattered on the walls. Bloody footprints and streaks of blood trailed from the stairway to the middle of the hallway where Victor Padilla and Phil Cardillo lay. The blood trailed down to an adjacent stairway, which led into the basement where sixteen suspects were presumed to be hiding. Jimmy Kenney's one and only objective was to pull the wounded from location. He ran to Phil Cardillo, grabbed him underneath his arms and started to pick him up. Kenney slipped in the puddles of blood and screamed, "Someone help me get him to an RMP!" Three uniforms ran to his aid. They lifted Phil, who was fading from blood loss.

Jimmy Kenney remembered hearing a weak moan from the cop. He'd seen downed victims before, the gray pall that crept across their face's just before they expired—Phil's babyface was slipping into that dark oblivion. "I felt myself falling into a state of shock. You have to remember, this was a cop, and it was the first time I'd witnessed another cop shot and mortally wounded."

He didn't care about the perps in the basement or the growing mob outside the mosque or the burning garbage flying off the rooftops at the cops below; all he cared about was getting Phil Cardillo out of harm's way. He needed to get Phil to an RMP where he could stem the bleeding and get to a hospital.

11:47 A.M.

I was nearing Lenox Avenue. I looked above and saw as many people on the rooftops as there were down on the streets. Noise was coming from the windows to the rooftops, echoing down the streets and back onto the sidewalks and into the vast alleyways that Harlem was famous for. The entire area was wired and ready to blow—the perfect mix for absolute mayhem—something that I had witnessed before. I knew it could only get worse.

I finally reached Lenox Avenue and 116th Street—the scene of the crime; only then was I able to place the address—Mosque Number 7. The reality of it hit me in the face. I realized the magnitude of the situation and the backlash we'd be facing. This was Minister Louis Farrakhan's militant house of worship.

Harlem always had its share of crime—assaults, street robberies, drug dealing, shootings, murder—but the mosque had never been caught in the fray. People just knew to steer clear. If you took pushpins and marked all the criminal activity on a map of Harlem, the one empty patch would be the real estate surrounding Farrakhan's mosque.

For example, during one Harlem protest, 800 windows had been shattered. Every business, apartment, and car had a rock fly through the glass, all except Mosque Number 7. No one dared deface it. The presence of the FOI soldiers made it clear what the repercussions would be. And as an expert on Harlem during that time, trust me when I say, *the neighborhood took heed.*

This was as close to a riot as anything I'd ever seen. An army of civilians and cops absorbed all four corners of the lot in varying displays of anger. The NYPD helicopter hovered low; the *womp-womp-womp* of its blades swirled up dust and debris. I was momentarily transported back to a hill in Korea. I stared at the four bloodied cops being dragged and carried into an RMP or ambulance. When the crowd of onlookers saw the battered cops, they burst into a great cheer. I felt an incredible surge of anger pack into my neck. Someone would have to pay for this.

Jimmy Kenney pulled Phil Cardillo into the RMP, slammed the doors and screamed, "Go! Go! Go! He's going out of the picture; FUCKING GO!"

The driver of the RMP, a rookie who appeared no more than twenty-one turned and saw both cops covered in sticky blood. Before he turned back to the street, his foot instinctively slammed onto the gas pedal. The patrol car skidded off the curb, directly into the middle of the street. The car cut a wide path through the waves and waves of people. The guy didn't brake for anyone, uniformed or not. In the backseat Jimmy Kenney whispered to a cop he'd never met before. But they both wore blue, so that didn't really matter. "It's okay, Guy. You're okay. Gonna get you fixed up at St. Luke's. You're doing okay, brother."

Jimmy Kenney felt the young cop fall limp in his arms. He searched for the bullet hole. There were two of them running across his midsection, one from the top right of his ribcage, another from the lower left. One hole was bigger than the other, entrance and exit. He compressed both holes; blood continued to seep through his fingers. He screamed, "Hurry, god-damit, hurry!"

A band of patrolmen surrounded the mosque but gave way to a layer of rioting civilians–blue hats, swinging bats. I tucked both guns tightly against my body with the barrels pointed forward. I didn't want to be a cowboy, but I had to get through.

I pushed into the mob toward the mosque. This was dangerous. I was dressed in ratty civilian clothing, an easy target. I stopped to collect my anger and thoughts. I recognized some of the faces in the crowd, people I had dealt with on the street. The detective in me suddenly kicked in; I began to observe everything and everyone around me. I spotted most of the players—cops, bosses, some of the Muslims, and a lot of punks itching to turn Lenox Avenue into a nuclear situation. The radio jumped again.

> *Central: Any further assistance required at this time, 1-0-2 West 116th?*
> *Unit: Send Emergency Service. I understand that they have perpetrators in the building with the*
> *cops' guns.*
> *Central: Ten-four.*

In control of the cops' guns. *Guns.* That's plural? A sinking feeling. They *were* in control. They'd stolen our weapons, which in itself, was huge—we are trained to never relinquish our weapons under any circumstances. If you steal a cop's gun, then that cop is fucked. I knew we weren't leaving the building till an arrest was made and the weapons returned.

I felt, once ESU arrived, the bloody uprising would begin wrapping up. The Emergency Service Unit was the no-nonsense rescue team of the NYPD. The cops of ESU trained day and night for this type of *urban-specific* warfare—they were also trained in bomb removal, hostage removal, and barricaded perp removal—and were affectionately known amongst the rank and file as *Big Blue Sanitation.*

ESU was the last line of defense for the NYPD, and they never lost. They were the department's mechanized artillery. The mere sight of the gargantuan blue and white ESU truck, named *Big Bertha,* accompanied by smaller armored vehicles loaded with men in Kevlar helmets and flak-jackets, all strapped to the tits with fully automatic carbines and shotguns usually changed the momentum of any situation. Their MO was this: two groups of eight cops, crouched behind bulletproof Plexiglas, enter the front and rear of the building in a wedged V-formation—like a human snowplow. Anyone in the way would get wedged to the sides and disarmed. Then a second team of ESU cops would pounce, collect, and arrest. I'd seen this before and it was always an impressive show of force and skill.

Jimmy Kenney keyed the mike for the third time, giving his ETA to St. Luke's. As the young driver pulled to the front of the emergency entrance, a gurney was positioned at the end of the ramp surrounded by cops, nurses, and resident doctors. The car skidded in, and before it stopped, Jimmy Kenney kicked the door open. Outstretched arms were thrust into the RMP, securely wrapping around Phil Cardillo's limp body. One cop wailed, "Goddamit, not Phil!" Jimmy Kenney and the driver of the RMP, another guy he didn't know, watched as the gurney disappeared through the double doors of the ER. Neither cop said anything to the other.

Kenney instinctively searched the back of the RMP for anything. It would be a powder keg investigation soon. He looked for the bullet, in case it'd slipped out of Phil's wounds. He got nothing. He looked at the puddle of blood on the seat. He looked down; his dark blue shirt was black where it had been stained. The young guy who'd driven him noticed Jimmy's shirt and rushed up, "Are you hit? Are you hit?"

Kenney shook his head "no." He began to walk back to the mosque. Jimmy Kenney didn't know it at the time, but he gave Phil Cardillo five more days to fight.

By then, the cops in front of the mosque seemed to be gaining control, forming a semicircular wall of bodies at the entrance. No one was getting in—no one was getting out. News crews were charging on foot up Lenox, cameramen stumbled as they shouldered their heavy equipment

I heard Big Bertha approaching. Its bullhorn whistle reverberated throughout the cement canyons of Harlem. The cavalry had arrived. The end was near.

Unit 1: No further West 116th. That's enough units on the scene. Authority sixth lieutenant.
Unit 2: Central, has that been a definite shooting of a cop?
Central: That's affirmative. Report of two patrolmen shot at this time.

And then I saw a man walking through the crowd. His bold advance divided the masses in two. It was like Moses had appeared wearing a tailored suit. He was tall and tan with wavy salt and pepper hair. He looked like someone out of central casting, a throwback movie star from the forties. You couldn't tell who he was by his threads. Every cop he passed saluted. He was Chief of Detectives Albert Seedman—*my boss.*

He entered the mosque, followed by three other unrecognizable suits. I figured arrests would happen, order would be restored, and I'd go back to being bored and burning up at my OP.

Unit: 2-8 John to Central, K.
Central: 2-8 John.
Unit: The inspector of the division is here. They are going to set up temporary headquarters here and there have been two patrolmen shot, removed to the hospital, no further information.

11:49 A.M.

Seven minutes had passed since the ten-thirteen was broadcast. Four cops had been savagely beaten, two of them possibly shot, and there were scores of extremely violent people locked down in an overtly militant mosque. The detective in me kicked in again. I had literally passed that mosque every day for years and not once was that door ever left unlocked or unguarded. *Why was today special?* Imagination, I believe, is crucial for detective work. You have to allow the most ridiculous possibilities, because most crimes, especially murder, turn out to be far stranger than the movies. Two imaginative scenarios would lead me to the same conclusion. The NYPD had been set up. Or maybe the mosque had been set up.

This was now a working crime scene. I was still peripheral to the mosque, but I was impressed with the speed the police showed in locking down the building. Honestly, there wasn't much for me to do at the scene. The cops inside would handle the perps—the NYPD at its finest moment.

I knew the injured cops had gone to St. Luke's, a world-class trauma center—due in part to its location—Harlem. Somebody had calculated that in the year 1971, the staff of surgeons at St. Luke's had operated on more trauma patients than any M.A.S.H. unit surgeons had in all of Southeast Asia. Another thing to recommend the place was that my father was the head building maintainer at there. The boys would get whatever they needed. I also knew my father had a direct hotline to the surgeons.

I knew they could use me more at the hospital, interviewing the cops, giving blood, picking up family members, even a coffee run would be more helpful than standing outside the mosque. The thirteen had ended and I thought arrests were in the mail. But things were going to get much worse and keep on getting worse. This was just the beginning of a war—war that I was going to be directly in the middle of. This was just the beginning of five years of *hell*.

"RIOT, WHAT RIOT?"

If there were truckloads of people in the streets before, there were boatloads by the time I got back to my car to drive to the hospital. So I ran. We had another UC (undercover) car parked along Manhattan Avenue, in case one of us was summoned back to base while walking the streets. I was breathless when I reached it, thrilled that it was in one piece. As I drove, I reflected on what had just happened. It was big, bigger than any thirteen I'd ever seen. I tried to suppress the memory of Joseph Piagentini and Waverly Jones, two brother cops executed by Twyman Meyers and the BLA. I was at the Harlem morgue when the two lifeless bodies were brought in, riddled with bullet holes, covered in scorched tissue and blood. I and some other detectives had to undress Joseph Piagentini for the last time. It was a memory I didn't want to relive while driving to see Phil.

He was a friend, not only to me and the other cops of the 2-8, but also to the community. Selfishly, I didn't want those demons and nightmares again. I didn't want to face his young wife, Claudia Joy. What could I tell her? The guilt was crawling through my chest. I bit down hard and I rolled with it. This is what I did for a living, and on April 14, 1972, it wouldn't be just another day on the job.

I pulled up in front of St. Luke's. I was amazed at how many marked and unmarked cars there were. My first thought was, *who in the fuck is watching the streets*. Some cars had been left running, doors wide open, three and four deep trailing from the emergency entrance out into the street. There were RMPs from as far off as Brooklyn. I knew they were there to give blood or offer whatever assistance they could give, much the same as me.

I entered my dad's office across the street—there he was waiting for me like a beacon of hope and strength, standing tall in his starched suit and tie, not a hair out of place. I saw his shoulders slump when he saw me. It was my father who had received the erroneous telegram, all those years ago when I was in Korea, stating I was missing in action. He had lived with that devastation for thirty-six hours before they corrected the news. I slowed and smiled; my lips and chin started to quiver. I felt my throat tighten; I knew he must've been worried sick. It was no secret what my job in the street was. I picked up the pace and he opened his arms. We didn't speak for a while. I felt his strong hands squeeze at my back. We both straightened and looked at each other. He asked, "You okay, Son?" I nodded, reached in, and kissed his cheek. He continued, "Everything is set up for the mayor and the police commissioner. We have private rooms for them. We also set rooms aside for the families."

He laid his arm over my shoulder and we began to walk briskly to the triage. I was, for the moment, comforted. Cops were lined up in the long narrow hallway. Some were crying. Some were so angry they were punching at the walls. Others just stared off into space. There was a tight knot of cops standing in front of the first triage, but not inside. Dad and I both pushed our way through. It was Victor Padilla on a gurney, convulsing. Around the gurney was a doctor and two nurses trying to hold him down. Blood was cascading out of a dark blotch that was once his left eye, now gone. I noticed another cop outside the triage, staring at Padilla. He was seated on a chair, crying helplessly. Then I recognized him; it was Ivan Negron. His face was so distended with welts and bruises that I could barely tell who he was. He saw me approach and tried to stand. I urged him back down in the chair. Tears dropped down his bulbous cheeks. "They got my partner's gun, Randy. They got my partner's gun." I assumed his jaw was broken because it was slack and he winced when he spoke. The words were thick and mumbled, as if his mouth were filled with marbles. I put my hand on his shoulder. He watched Padilla flopping violently on the gurney and started crying again. "Wasn't my fault, Randy. We were jumped. They got Victor's gun, Randy!" Both cops were out of commission. There was nothing I could do. Shock had already enveloped both of them. I didn't want my dad to see any more. I moved forward to the next triage station.

A wall of uniforms from the 2-8 Precinct surrounded the curtains. Another set of cops stood nearby, beside Vito Navarra, who was sitting rigidly on a metal folding chair. He saw me approach and stood, a little wobbly. His face was bruised; one of his front teeth protruded outward. His other teeth were caked in blood. He was beaten, though not as badly as the first two. Vito pointed into the triage that was closed off with curtains. I knew the doctors were working on Phil; he'd lost massive amounts of blood. Vito continued to point beyond the curtains; he too seemed out of it, disbelieving, though somewhat more focused than Ivan. "It's Phil, Randy, it's Phil." He balled his hand into a fist and shook it at the curtains, trying to understand what had occurred, how their world had been catastrophically rocked, all within seven minutes.

I looked around the triage, then up and down the hallway. It was filled with cops as helpless as me. Once again I was transported back in time—Korea. My platoon was pinned down trying to take a key position on the side of a hill, Pork Chop Hill. We were outgunned and outmanned, surrounded by nests of machine-gunning snipers. We could do one of two things: roll over and die, or fight the hopeless fight and just maybe come out the other side. One thing was for sure; if we didn't fight, we'd be slaughtered. I was an eighteen-year-old corporal paratrooper running and gunning up that hill. I was carried down twenty-four hours later, a sergeant with a Bronze Star and a Purple Heart. General Eisenhower's words had guided me up that hill, and now those powerful words resounded in my head once again: *Failure is not an option.*

I was back in the moment, at the hospital—real time—

I shook Navarra gently, "Look at me, Vito. Look in my eyes." His sad confused eyes slowly shifted to mine. I needed to get him back to the mosque while the perpetrators' faces were still fresh in his mind. Vito was going to be instrumental in putting faces to the crimes. The longer we took with the *show-up,* the easier it would be for defense attorneys to convince juries that the injured cop's memory was tainted by hospital narcotics and other twisted angry cops.

He seemed to be looking through me. I shook him again and then pulled at my pinned shield, "You see this, Vito. Look at it."

Then I grabbed his shield. I held both of them up. "These are who we are. They're what we do, and right now, it's our job to protect these."

I pointed behind me to the room where Phil was being worked on. "We can't protect these, or him, from here. We gotta go make this right, and it ain't gonna happen at St. Luke's, *sabe?*"

The recognition of the situation seemed to flicker on. He quietly asked, "What about Phil, Randy?"

"This is the best hospital in the country. Whatever can be done will be done. We've got to get back there before anyone slips away." He slowly nodded in agreement. I exhaled and clapped his shoulders, "Good, let's go."

I grabbed a towel from a linen closet and placed it on Vito's face.

As we walked past the other officers down the hall toward the doors, I saw them, standing in the makeshift temporary headquarters; two men on the complete opposite poles of appearance, side by side, whispering, eyes shifting and probing, warning everyone to stay away. I'd met both of them sporadically throughout my career.

The tall distinguished looking man with a head full of sandy hair was Mayor John Lindsay. His suit was expensive, though understated.

From the day he was sworn in as the 109th mayor of New York, Lindsay was on a one-way street to 1600 Pennsylvania Avenue. Everything the man did or didn't do was weighed and checked by his team of blue-blood political advisors about whether or not it would help his presidential aspirations. Everything from creating policy to the color of his tie.

The short bald man—hawkish, uncomfortable in his own skin, shoulders slumped—was Patrick V. Murphy, the current police commissioner. He'd had a stint in three other cities as a commissioner or its equivalent—Syracuse; Washington, D.C.; and his previous post, Detroit, Murphy wasn't really a cop; he was a professional commissioner. He was the type of man who spoke in grand non specifics. His passion wasn't crime fighting at all; it was administration, the inner workings of a 32,000-strong work force. Crime and justice seemed to bore the man. His crime-fighting platform: *introduce modern business techniques into the New York City Police Department.*

I didn't have a problem with these two personally. Politicos and opportunists like Lindsay and Murphy weren't news to me. Except for when it came to the BLA. Both the mayor and the commissioner were adamant that the Black Liberation Army didn't actually exist. Their statements to the public said that they were a "loosely gathered band of thugs," not an organized group committing premeditated assassinations of the NYPD cops. Murphy backed it up by investigating each murdered cop case to case. They refused to admit that cops in New York City were being systematically targeted for death. Why? *Because it would be detrimental in winning the voters.* Lindsay couldn't look like he had lost control over the city. If there were coordinated cop killers out there doing *their* job—killing cops—then Lindsay and Murphy weren't doing *their* jobs. I guess we didn't have to uproot my mother and father from their home after all, because according to the mayor and the number one crime fighter in New York, the likes of Twyman Meyers and the BLA didn't exist.

I led Vito and tried to look away, but it was too late; they'd seen me. Police Commissioner Patrick V. Murphy stepped in front of us. He never looked directly into my eyes. I didn't want to have this sit-down, but I was respectful of his position. The man was my boss, and standing next to him, Mayor John Lindsay, was his boss. Shit runs downstream, as they say, and any way you cut it, I was pretty far downstream.

I told Vito to stay put. Neither Murphy nor the mayor looked twice at the beaten cop. I had to move this along; time was either going to be an asset or a major stumbling block.

Murphy's head tilted to the side, looking down the hall beyond all those crying, angry, and frustrated cops, "What's your assessment, Detective Jurgensen?"

My assessment? I wanted to grab this tiny little man who once wore the same uniform we did and shake him into the violent reality we were all knee-deep in. The fabric known as law and order, which once clothed us and kept the city safe, had been torn to shreds in the claws of human depravity. We were stomped, kicked, beaten, and shot, and he wanted an assessment of the situation? Memo to Commissioner Murphy: Hell has broken loose. But I couldn't do that. So I gave him the assessment, sugarless. "It's bad. Close to an urban war. The streets, Sir, are ready to explode."

Only then did he look into my eyes. His head shook slowly "no" as he mumbled this fragmented half-question-half-statement, "Riot, What riot? There's no riot."

I hadn't even used the word *riot*. Then he turned to the mayor, who still hadn't acknowledged either of us. "Everything is under control, Sir. The situation is being . . . handled."

See, if Lindsay wasn't told there was a riot, then there really wasn't a riot. It's called plausible deniability. So when he officially dropped his hat into the democratic presidential nominating committee, he could say during his tenure, there was never a riot in New York as there had been in Chicago and Los Angeles. In his mind, no riot meant presidential nomination, simple as that.

I didn't wait for another rhetorical question. I turned, walked back to Vito, and said, "Whatever."

In the basement of the mosque, sixteen Muslims were being detained by the police. The Black Muslim leader of Mosque Number 7, Louis Farrakhan, was there with another massive entourage to overlook the situation. The highest-ranking police official present was Deputy Commissioner Robert Daley. Daley's official position was Deputy Commissioner of Public Information, or DCPI. It was his job to relay all truthful and pertinent information to the public and the media. When he reached the mosque, his assessment of the scene was much the same as mine—riot. Locals were dancing in the streets. A female newscaster had been stomped, doused with lighter fluid, and set ablaze. She had been rushed to St. Luke's. Other reporters were also stomped and stripped of their equipment. The roofs were raining bottles, bricks, and burning garbage. Generally riotous behavior. It's important to note that the crowds outside weren't the Muslims, but angry Harlem residents.

The newscasters at the scene had falsely reported that there was an ongoing shootout in the mosque, and that there was some sort of standoff between the Black Muslims and the police. They also reported that two police officers were shot, and both their guns were missing. This brought out multitudes of restless angry civilians with one thing on their minds—to tear shit up.

All of the information up to that point was wrong. *One* cop was shot, and four others seriously injured. *One* gun was missing, and another service revolver was recovered at the scene. There was no standoff; no one was shooting at the cops, and more importantly, the cops weren't shooting back at anyone.

Daley entered the mosque lobby and was awestruck by the amount of blood on the floors and walls. Chairs and a desk were overturned, and the walls leading up to the ceiling were marked with bullet holes. He interviewed a few of the officers to catch up. By then the building had been searched and it was empty. Apparently, the attackers had run down into the basement as soon as the cops arrived. There was only one way in and out of the basement, so it didn't take a Sherlock Holmes to know Phil Cardillo's shooter and the rest of the attackers were among the men being detained. In copland we call that a *groundball,* easy to field, easy out. But you know what they say: Everything is easy till it ain't.

Chief Albert Seedman had already started interviewing the detained men in the basement, so, as far as Daley was concerned, he could go back up and tell the press they'd have suspects in custody shortly.

When he stepped out of the mosque about seven minutes after he'd stepped in, the crowd had swelled to more than 1,500 people—all within a one-block area. The police were outnumbered five-to-one. More reporters were being trampled, beaten, and robbed. Packs of teenagers were moving through the crowd squirting lighter fluid on reporters and igniting their saturated clothing. Garbage and bricks sailed down onto the masses of people, through storefronts, and car windows. A stalled bus was pelted continuously with mortar and bricks from a disassembled chimney. While the passengers screamed, burning newspapers were jammed in through the windows. The police helicopter swooped down onto the rooftops. The perps defiantly turned and began throwing bottles and bricks back up at the chopper. At the mosque entrance, Daley was surrounded by a taunting mob. He tried to scream over the din to reporters—no use. It was impossible to get the news out from ground zero. There were just too many people.

That was around the time Vito and I were driving back to the scene.

Crowds had overtaken the street. Cars were at a standstill. We saw a fireball erupt about two blocks away. It was my unmarked RMP.

I drove as far as I could till we came to a wall of civilians. I removed my police-issued *streetsweeper* shotgun. We parked and ran. I was leading with the shotgun high above my head. At that moment the only difference between Pork Chop Hill and Lenox Avenue was four streetlights and a hotdog stand.

Deputy Commissioner Benjamin Ward exited a gleaming black Mercury sedan slowly ambling his way into the melee. Ward was the first man of color appointed to that high-ranking position. He was in charge of community affairs for Harlem. His job basically was to run interference between City Hall and Harlem. He was the man tasked to *keep a lid on Harlem* during Lindsay's reign as mayor.

Ward outranked Daley with tenure and, more important, political clout; that much they were clear on. The two of them were at odds on just about everything else. Daley was never a cop, but loyal to cops; Ward was a cop, but loyal to the mayor. Prior to holding the community affairs commissioner-ship, Ward was a lawyer in the department's trial room, prosecuting cops. Daley rarely drank; Ward was known to have a drink or two. At one time he urinated into the East River out of that very helicopter now buzzing the rooftops. This riot was only going to solidify each man's hatred for the other, and the whole city would front row for the fallout.

Ward passed Daley without acknowledging him. Daley wasn't surprised but took the unprofessionalism in stride. Daley found an accessible RMP, commandeered it, and drove to St. Luke's Hospital to give statements to the press, the police commissioner, and Mayor John Lindsay.

Vito and I threaded our way toward the mosque. The crowd was beginning to loot the mom-and-pop stores. They were destroying their own food supplies. *How mad could they be,* I thought, that they were cutting and burning themselves. Without access to those stores, they'd have to travel to get anything. But as with most riots, the principle element was not giving a shit anymore.

Things had changed drastically by the time we reached the mosque. The outer perimeter was surrounded by the NYPD and about sixteen ESU cops. The inner perimeter, including the front doors, was surrounded by para-militarized Muslim soldiers. The two groups of men stood face-to-face not five feet from one another, unflinching—a standoff of the worst kind. *What happened to the police presence and where are the cops who had taken their positions at the crime scene? Where are all the uniformed bosses?* Then I noticed Deputy Commissioner Ben Ward standing on the running boards of Big Bertha. In his hand was a bullhorn; next to him was the popular black congressman from central Harlem, Charles Rangel. They were in animated conversation when I arrived. I assumed they were the leadership on-scene.

I moved in front of the Muslims with Vito behind me. My gold shield was affixed high on my jacket so there could be no miscommunication. I tried to step past one of the FOI men at the double doors. He was about six foot six, two hundred and fifty pounds, stacked like a brickyard. He stepped in my way. It was his way now. In a clipped militant tone he said, "Only uniformed presence is allowed to walk through these doors. You . . . are not in uniform."

I stepped aside, moving Vito in front of me, "He's in uniform. I suggest you let him in."

Before Vito entered I whispered in his ear, "You point out to Seedman the shooter and anyone else you saw who was involved, you hear?"

He nodded and disappeared through the double doors. I was able to peek inside the vestibule; no longer were cops guarding the crime scene. The lobby was filled with FOI men. I turned and lost my shit on that line-backer at the door. "Who the fuck are they? This is a police investigation! That's a fucking crime scene!"

This was a fucking travesty. Who touched what, who took pictures, who recovered any evidence, who received that evidence, and so on: all that has to have a chain of command. But there was no chain of command because there was no command of the crime scene. They'd taken it over. Somebody needed to give me a fucking answer. I needed to find the superior on the scene.

Daley entered St. Luke's and immediately found Mayor Lindsay and Police Commissioner Murphy. He had to brief both of his bosses with all of the pertinent information first; though, they too barely acknowledged his presence. He might have assumed both men were worried about the fallen cop, Phil Cardillo, on the operating table. He moved to them breathlessly, "It certainly was delicate out there. It came so close to a riot. So close. It was still delicate when I left five minutes ago."

Lindsay snapped his head in Daley's direction sharply asking, "Riot? What do you mean, riot? There can't be any riot. There won't be any riot. It never came close to being a riot. How can you say such a thing?"

Daley responded quickly, "I've been around riots before. This was as close to one as I've ever seen."

Lindsay shot back defiant and angry, "How many people were there? There weren't that many people in the street."

Daley stepped back. Personal agendas were at play, so he treaded lightly. "Well there are at least fifteen hundred people in the streets."

"What's a thousand people, twelve, fifteen hundred people? You can't have a riot with 1,000 people or 1,500 people," Lindsay barked.

Daley relented. There was no winning a pissing contest with the mayor of New York City. Murphy stood and walked Daley to the corner of the small room. "We had reports it wasn't so bad there." He mumbled this so low Daley had to lean in to hear him.

"It was pretty bad," said Daley.

Daley began to break down the scene for Murphy, starting with the perps detained in the basement, to the blood-filled hallway, to the tidal wave of people on the streets. Murphy held up his hands like a disobedient six-year-old, closing his eyes, shaking his head, "No, we're not sure of anything yet. We'd better check into this a little further."

Daley continued, "I interviewed most of the cops involved . . ."

Murphy again shook his head and moved to the other end of the room to quietly talk with Mayor John Lindsay. All Daley could do was back out of the room, unsure of what to do or say to the rabid news crews.

Vito stepped into the mosque basement. Several of the FOI men receded further into the rear of the lounge-type area. Chief of Detectives Seedman and the rest of the detectives immediately noticed this. So did Louis Farrakhan. He stepped forward and in an overly loud and preachy voice he exclaimed, "I cannot guarantee your well-being if you remain inside this house of worship. Neither guns nor police are permitted in this building."

Farrakhan's men puffed up behind this brazen statement. Seedman blinked slowly; he was as ballsy as he was strategic. In his gruff New York accent he countered, "Everyone in this basement, including you, is suspect in the shooting and beating of New York cops. No one other than myself will be making any decisions in regards to this case." He looked back at Vito and cocked his head at him, "You okay?"

Vito nodded and began the task of identifying the responsible men.

Congressman Charles Rangel suddenly appeared in the basement to deliver a message. He said, "Commissioner Ward wants all police presence out of the building . . . now!"

Seedman turned slightly, hesitated for the briefest of moments. "You, right now, are impeding an assault-and-attempted-homicide investigation. Leave."

Then he turned back to Navarra. Rangel lowered his voice and repeated, "Commissioner Ward wants all police presence out of the building."

Seedman got face-to-face with Rangel. "Go upstairs and tell *Commissioner* Ward that the chief of detectives is conducting a show-up."

"All due respect, Chief, something's gotta be done. Upstairs is going to be turned into a parking lot if a riot ensues. Lots of people are going to get hurt, including cops. Now, we worked out a deal that all of the detained men will be brought into the 2-4 Precinct later today for questioning, but right now our priority is the well-being of the cops and the people of Harlem upstairs."

"*We* worked out a deal? Who's we?" asked Seedman.

Rangel grinned, "You know, myself, Commissioner Ward, Minister Farrakhan, and . . ."

"And?" asked Seedman.

"Well, there aren't too many people above the rank of deputy commissioner, Chief."

Seedman was about to rip into the congressman when he heard his name over the police radio. It was Ward's voice, "Chief Seedman, ten-two the ESU truck with all units remaining in the building!" *Ten-two* meant Seedman had to go see Ward—outside.

Even though Ward was never elevated above the rank of lieutenant within the NYPD, an appointed commissionership superceded and outranked any uniformed member of the service. As hard a pill as it was to swallow, Ward was Seedman's superior.

Seedman was shell-shocked. Thirty years of hardcore policing, this was a first. A shot cop took precedence over any crime. Every available police resource was utilized until all guilty parties were brought to justice. That was because when you're risking your life out on the street every day, you need that one assurance—*cops take care of their own*. Not on April 14, 1972 they didn't. Seedman hesitated. He had the men responsible in his sights.

Farrakhan was emboldened, and so were the FOI men who surrounded him. He looked at Seedman and raised his eyebrows as if to say, *Here's your hat, and there's the door.*

Seedman turned to his men. Even he didn't believe what he was about to say. "Let's go."

Not one of the men moved, not the uniformed presence, not the detectives assigned to the Chief of Detectives' office, and certainly not the detectives from the 2-8 and 2-5 Precincts. Phil Cardillo was one of their own; the other three cops who were beaten were also among their own. All these men could ever hope for was that in similar circumstances, had they been the ones beaten and shot, those men would do the same for them. As it were, Seedman knew this was the beginning of the end. He'd been around long enough to see the shitcanning a mile away.

One of the black detectives from his office looked first at Navarra, then back to Seedman. He refused to move. He said, "There's an attempted murderer down here, and he's coming out attached to my cuffs."

Seedman looked at the FOI men. He quickly looked at Farrakhan, who was grinning, then he turned to look at Rangel for more than a few seconds. He finally turned back to the detective and slowly shook his head. He moved inches from the detective and quietly said, "Son, this is over. We leave and maybe we fight tomorrow. I promise you, you disobey that order, there'll be nothing left of you to fight. I certainly don't want to go out that way, do you?"

It was no-win. The detective would have to wait to interview each of those men at the 2-4 Precinct. He and everyone else were going to wait a very long time.

All of the cops left. The only one who didn't leave immediately was Vito Navarra. Farrakhan and the rest of his men simply stared. Navarra didn't look away, he gaped at every man's face, placing the faces in the horrific four-minute battle that he would never forget. The one that would haunt him and 32,000 other men for the rest of their lives.

The only thing that was saving the streets from erupting into absolute bedlam was the fact that the punks on the roof were blanketing 116th Street with bricks and other skull-crushing material. The tide of people would crest into the street and then a brick would explode onto the asphalt, sending the wave of people rushing back against the buildings for safety. The tide came in; the tide went out.

Ward pulled the bullhorn to his mouth and bellowed into it, "Only block cops remain on the scene."

I looked at the uniforms that surrounded me. The same confused look crept across all of our faces, "What in the fuck is a block cop?" I asked.

And then, unbelievably, I heard it a second time. Ward wailed into the bullhorn, "All *black* cops remain on your assigned posts. All *white* cops leave the scene. Return to your command forthwith."

That was real fucked up. I thought to myself about how shameful and embarrassing it was. I was embarrassed not just for me and the rest of the white cops who'd heard the order, but for the black cops as well, and the rest of the cops who made up the vast majority of the NYPD, despite race or creed. See, we were no longer the men in blue. Now we were stripped bare by a high-ranking police official under orders, stripped of our brethren and stripped of our unity. I was dumbfounded and I saw the masses of cops, black and white, turn to one another, also dumbfounded. If we divided, we knew we wouldn't stand a chance, not with this crowd, not ever. We all stared at Benjamin Ward. He was now the *black* Deputy Commissioner.

Upon hearing this command, the crowd erupted. They were going to bask in watching the NYPD break its own back. Even later Ward would never admit who gave this order, he or a superior officer but we heard it loud and clear. Back then, an order given was an order obeyed. And reluctantly, we left our remaining brother-officers to fend for themselves in the middle of a riot.

As Chief Seedman reached the lobby, he saw twenty FOI men cleansing the hallway, situating the table and chairs, mopping up the blood—Phil Cardillo's, Ivan Negron's, Victor Padilla's, Vito Navarra's, and Rudy Andre's. The crime scene was being erased with every stroke of the mop. Seedman turned to the detective and said, "This case will never be solved."

"SEARCH THOSE COPS"

I heard my name over the radio. It was the commanding officer of the 2-8, Inspector John Haugh, the twenty-five-year career cop, lawyer, teacher, mentor, and good friend. "Randy, I need you to *eighty-five* me Lenox between one sixteen and one seventeen forthwith." He wanted a *face-to-face*.

Even though I was probably thirty feet from the man, I couldn't see him over the people. I pushed my way to the middle of the block. The bricks were still being lobbed off the roof, but we were a safe distance. Inspector Haugh was a cool operator. Even in the middle of battle, he never seemed out of control, which is why I respected and trusted him. When I reached him, he was bordering meltdown. He screamed over the crowd, "Randy, someone's going to get killed."

He pointed to the roof, shook his head violently back and forth, "Get up there and take that fucking roof!"

I didn't ask questions. I searched and quickly found all the men from the Twyman Meyers stakeout. I pointed to the roof, "We're clearing that roof."

The men followed me in a close cluster as we charged into the building. We hit the stairway and I realized that we were followed in by close to thirty civilians, all wanting to be a part of the action. I posted one of the anticrime cops at the bottom of the stairway. "Gun out, nobody comes up."

That stopped the crowd. We moved up the stairs to the second floor and encountered the same; out of apartments, tenants were spilling into the hallway, wanting to follow us up. I positioned another cop on the second and third landings—no one was getting up.

Myself and two other cops charged the roof, barreling out onto the tar and asphalt. First thing I heard was the incredible rumbling of the helicopter. I was back in Korea. I had to catch my breath, because the rotors were so low it made it almost impossible to breathe. I looked up and actually saw the pilot squinting at me. I ripped open my field jacket, revealing my shield. He gave me a thumbs-up and pulled back the aircraft. I checked the roof. Approximately ten teenagers, no older than fourteen, were standing in a semicircle around a dismantled chimney. I lifted the shotgun in the air and screamed "Everybody off the fucking roof."

The kids dropped the bricks and charged off the roof, probably very happy they weren't locked up.

It was safe. I stuffed the shotgun into my hip and halfway down my pant leg. I zipped up my field jacket. With the roof completely empty, we began to clear the rest of the mortar and bricks by dropping them down into the rear courtyard.

Now that we'd stopped the hailstorm, the crowd moved into the middle of the streets, shouting like a hellish Mardi Gras. Big Bertha was pointed at an odd angle in the middle of the street, surrounded by smaller cars that led to a stranded city bus filled with screaming people. The mosque's four corners were completely ringed by FOI men dressed in suits. The police presence in front of the mosque had all but vanished.

The roof door was suddenly kicked open. The three anticrime cops emerged, followed by a very tall *black* boss in uniform, Inspector Tom Mitchelson, commander of Zone-6. We'd never met. He was a newcomer to the area. He had a uniformed driver with him, a young guy scared witless, and another black man in his late forties wearing a dashiki and two crossed saber swords over his chest. The last man wasn't a cop. He was a local rabble-rouser, Kenyatta 35X, who at the drop of a hat would stand on a soapbox preaching of the injustices inflicted upon the community by the likes of us. *Why is he with the boss of the zone,* I thought, *and more important, why was my boss with him?*

Mitchelson pointed to me and yelled over the noise, "Who are you and what are you doing up here?"

The door was still open and people from the street were slowly growing in number—bats, sticks, bottles. They formed into a semicircle behind the inspector and Kenyatta 35X. I stepped to the inspector, "I'm following orders, Sir."

He snapped back, screaming nervously, "What orders?"

"To clear this roof, Sir." More people filed onto the roof behind Mitchelson. The situation was getting tense. They fidgeted, like they wanted to be set loose to charge. Mitchelson kept eyeing us like we were the criminals launching the airmail off the roof. Everything about that day was lopsided.

Kenyatta leaned in, whispering to Mitchelson, who in turn demanded, "We need to search you. What weapons do you have?"

He turned to the young uniform, "Search those men."

I saw the uniform's knees buckle as he took the first step. That was as far as I was going to be pushed. I wasn't going to be searched under the authority of some neighborhood agitator. I took a step backward. "Sir, you're not searching me. I'll open my coat, but you're not searching me."

I unzipped my field jacket and slid out the shotgun. Kenyatta had a smug, contented look on his face. He reached in and whispered to Mitchelson again, who in turn held out his hand, "Give me that weapon."

Some embarrassing catcalls from the angry civilians, "Right on. Give up all y'all weapons mothafuckin' pigs."

I was about to hand it to him when I quickly pulled it back. The last thing I was going to do was have that street-sweeper end up in the wrong hands. Three trigger pulls and all six of us would have been torn in half. I broke the shotgun down into pieces. I handed him the stock and butt of the gun, keeping the firing mechanism and the shells.

He accepted the pieces and demanded, "What unit are you men with?"

"The Major Case Squad, Sir. We're hunting the people who are hunting us."

I never took my eye off the crowd. It was growing. People just kept shoving their way onto the roof. Mitchelson didn't see this. He was with Kenyatta 35X so he was safe. Us, we were the bad guys, at their mercy, to be made examples for the rest of the police.

"Let me tell you something. You, and the rest of these men, by tomorrow I promise, you'll all be back in uniform. Now, I'm ordering you off this roof!"

Was that a threat? Honestly I didn't think we could have left if we wanted to. We were fucked. All of the NYPD was fucked. And on that day, the city of New York was fucked. And things were only going to get worse.

Mitchelson spun on his heels and the trio disappeared off the roof. The semicircle of people closed ranks after them. They formed a wall in front of the roof door, which was one way down. The other way was a header over the ledge.

The six of us moved in very tight. I yelled, "All right, don't pull your weapons whatever you do, they'll take them. Just stay close and hold onto each other."

We dropped our heads like fullbacks, squared our shoulders, and surged forward. I led and my men followed. A corridor of people opened as we ran through. Men, women, and children started to spit at us. This was one of the most humiliating experiences of my life. I was a New York City police detective, paid to protect the very citizens who were spitting at me. We made it into the building and charged down. On the stairs and on every floor were two rows of people just waiting to give us some of their saliva. We were covered in phlegm. Then someone threw a can, hitting a civilian man in the head. He bled profusely. Days later we would be accused of causing that wound—nothing new there. The man hit the floor. Upon seeing one of their own down for the count, the people went berserk. They started to punch, kick, and claw at us. I felt a horrific sting below my shoulder. Someone had bitten a chunk of skin out of my back. The pain was excruciating. That was when I ripped what was left of the shotgun out of my jacket and began to swing it wildly back and forth like I was clearing a jungle with a machete. I swung indiscriminately high and hard. If they were in front of me, they were going to get hit. I made a few solid connections before I finally saw daylight.

We charged out into the belly of the beast, 116th Street. I didn't stop swinging. We saw an RMP in the middle of the street and we charged for it. Smoke was now blanketing the area. It was impossible to see more than ten feet in front of us. What we did see were hands scratching and feet kicking at us.

One of my cops tripped and fell. He was surrounded by ten men. I saw a clothesline rope appear in one of their hands. They were going to string him up. Simultaneously we pulled our guns, charging the group of men, who backed away. We pulled the cop to safety. More men surrounded us. It was seconds before they'd overwhelm us, taking our guns—we were group fucked. Suddenly, Louie D'Alessio, one of the 2-8 anticrime cops, raised his gun high above and let one round go. That stopped them for the time being.

We made it to the RMP, slamming the doors and locking them. The keys weren't in the car. BOOM! The windshield exploded, covering us in a million fine pieces of glass. If that wasn't enough, burning rags soaked in gasoline were tossed in. We were choking. I kicked open the rear doors and we barely made it out, gasping for air. I saw the bus. We charged it.

BOOM! Another explosion, then another gunshot, then blackness draped over me. I felt hands wrap around my midsection. And then it all came rushing back: an incredibly piercing and constant pain in my head, loud ringing and buzzing. I saw everything around me spinning. I heard myself talk, though it was slurred and incoherent, "I'm shot . . . I'm shot . . ." *Is this it? Is this the way I'm going out? My father. He's going to see me wheeled in, half my head missing. No, not dad, not dad . . .*

I heard voices and screaming and more voices and more screaming. Then I felt my feet being dragged. I opened my eyes. Inspector John Haugh was holding me, pulling me somewhere. Louie D'Alessio was to my right, also dragging me. "Louie, I'm shot, Louie. Don't let them bring me to St. Luke's . . . My father, Louie, please." (Louie was killed two years later in the line of duty.)

Then I felt the heels of my feet banging against steps. I was deposited onto a bus. I knew this because I saw the rear doors, but the doors had hands attached to them. Hands were trying to rip open the doors. The sides of the bus were rocking up and down. Nausea gripped me. I felt bile and that unmistakable metallic taste of blood in my mouth. I started to choke on it. The bus floor started to bend. *What's happening?* There were more hands tearing at the door. The bus was being shaken; people were trying to flip the bus. Still more people were trying to get into the bus through the rear doors. I pulled both pistols out and pointed them in the direction of all those clambering hands—*if those doors open I'm going to un-fucking-load.* People next to me screamed. I screamed back, "I'm a New York City police detective. I'm here to help. I'm . . . I'm . . . shot."

Louie D'Alessio appeared next to me, out of breath, shirt ripped almost off his back. He had deep scratches down his soot-covered face. I asked, "Louie, is it bad? Am I hit bad?"

I felt his hand on my shoulder. Almost in a whisper he said, "No, Rand, it's not that bad."

I was reassured by that. Or maybe I was simply comforted by the fact that there was another one of us who'd made it out alive. I was back on Pork Chop Hill with some of the lucky platoon members. Except the sad reality was that Pork Chop Hill was 116th Street and Lenox Avenue, a neighborhood street in the richest, most powerful country in the world. The very same country I almost died for, eighteen years earlier—in pursuit of the very freedom that allowed these confused protesters their right to assemble and rebel—almost killed me eighteen years later.

11

Learning Police Ethics

by Lawrence Sherman

"Caught frequently in the cross fire of equally unreasonable citizen demands, the rookie naturally reacts by blaming the public. The spontaneous reaction is reinforced by one of the central values of the police culture: the public as enemy."

—Lawrence Sherman,
Learning Police Ethics
(1982)

There are two ways to learn police ethics. One way is to learn on the job, to make your moral decisions in haste under the time pressures of police work. This is by far the most common method of learning police ethics, the way virtually all of the half million police officers in the United States decide what ethical principles they will follow in their work. These decisions are strongly influenced by peer group pressures, by personal self-interest, by passions and emotions in the heat of difficult situations.

There is another way. It may even be a better way. You can learn police ethics in a setting removed from the heat of battle, from the opinions of co-workers, and from the pressures of supervisors. You can think things through with a more objective perspective on the issues. You should be able to make up your mind about many difficult choices before you actually have to make them. And you can take the time to weigh all sides of an issue carefully, rather than making a snap judgment.

The purpose of this article is to provide a basis for this other, less common way of learning police ethics by making the alternative—the usual way of learning police ethics—as clear as possible. This portrait of the on-the-job method is not attractive, but it would be no more attrac-

Lawrence Sherman is Director of Research at the Police Foundation (Washington, D. C.) and author of *Scandal and Reform: Controlling Police Corruption.*

Reprinted by permission from *Criminal Justice Ethics* 1, no. 1 (winter/spring 1982).

tive if we were to paint the same picture for doctors, lawyers, judges, or college professors. The generalizations we make are not true of all police officers, but they do reflect a common pattern, just as similar patterns are found in all occupations.

Learning New Jobs

Every occupation has a learning process (usually called "socialization") to which its new members are subjected. The socialization process functions to make most "rookies" in the occupation adopt the prevailing rules, values, and attitudes of their senior colleagues in the occupation. Very often, some of the existing informal rules and attitudes are at odds with the formal rules and attitudes society as a whole expects members of the occupation to follow. This puts rookies in a moral dilemma: should the rookies follow the formal rules of society or the informal rules of their senior colleagues?

These dilemmas vary in their seriousness from one occupation and one organization to the next. Young college professors may find that older professors expect them to devote most of their time to research and writing, while the general public (and their students) expects them to devote most of their time to teaching. With some luck, and a lot of work, they can do both.

Police officers usually face much tougher dilemmas. Like waiters, longshoremen, and retail clerks, they may be taught very early how to steal—at the scene of a burglary, from the body of a dead person, or in other opportunities police confront. They may be taught how to commit perjury in court to insure that their arrests lead to conviction, or how to lie in disciplinary investigations to protect their colleagues. They may be taught how to shake people down, or how to beat people up. Or they may be fortunate enough to go to work in an agency, or with a group of older officers, in which none of these violations of official rules is ever suggested to them.

Whether or not rookie police officers decide to act in ways the wider society might view as unethical, they are all subjected to a similar process of being taught certain standards of behavior. Their reactions to that learning as the years pass by can be described as their *moral careers:* the changes in the morality and ethics of their behavior. But the moral career is closely connected to the *occupational career:* the stages of growth and development in becoming a police officer.

This article examines the process of learning a new job as the context for learning police ethics. It then describes the content of the ethical and moral values in many police department "cultures" that are conveyed to new police officers, as well as the rising conflict within police agencies over what those values should be. Finally, it describes the moral career of police officers, including many of the major ethical choices officers make.

BECOMING A POLICE OFFICER

There are four major stages in the career of anyone joining a new occupation:[1]

- the *choice* of occupation
- the *introduction* to the occupation
- the first *encounter* with doing the occupation's work
- the *metamorphosis* into a full-fledged member of the occupation

Police officers go through these stages, just as doctors and bankers do. But the transformation of the police officer's identity and self-image may be more radical than in many other fields. The process can be over-whelming, changing even the strongest of personalities.

Choice

There are three aspects of the choice to become a police officer. One is the *kind of person* who makes that choice. Another is the *reason* the choice is made, the motivations for doing police work. The third is the *methods* people must use as police officers. None of these aspects of choice appears to predispose police officers to be more or less likely to perform their work ethically.

Many people toy with the idea of doing police work, and in the past decade the applicants for policing have become increasingly diverse. Once a predominately white male occupation, policing has accepted many more minority group members and attracted many more women. More college-educated people have sought out police work, but this may just reflect the higher rate of college graduates in the total population.

What has not changed, apparently, is the socio-economic background of people who become police. The limited evidence suggests police work attracts the sons and daughters of successful tradespeople, foremen, and civil servants—especially police. For many of them, the good salary (relative to the educational requirements), job security, and prestige of police work represent a good step up in the world, an improvement on their parents' position in life.

The motivation to become a police officer flows naturally from the social position of the people who choose policing. People do not seem to choose policing out of an irrational lust for power or because they have an "authoritarian personality"; the best study on this question showed that New York City police recruits even had a *lower* level of authoritarian attitudes than the general public (although their attitudes become more authoritarian as they become adapted to police work, rising to the general public's level of authoritarian attitudes).[2] Police applicants tend to see police work as an adventure, as a chance to do work out of doors without being cooped up in an office, as a chance to do work that is important for the good of society, and not as a chance to be the "toughest guy on the block." Nothing in the motivation to apply for a police position seems to predispose police officers towards unethical behavior.

Nor do the methods of selecting police officers seem to affect their long-term moral careers. There was a time when getting on the force was a matter of bribery or political favors for local politicians, or at least a matter of knowing the right people involved in grading the entrance examinations and sitting on the selection committees. But in the 1980s the selection process appears to be highly bureaucratic, with impersonal multiple-choice tests scored by computers playing the most important role in the process.

To be sure, there are still subjective background investigations, personal interviews, and other methods that allow biases to intrude upon the selection process. But these biases, if anything, work in the direction of selecting people who have backgrounds of unquestioned integrity. Combined with the high failure rate among all applicants—sometimes less than one in twenty is hired, which makes some police departments more selective in quantitative terms than the Harvard Law School—the selection process probably makes successful applicants feel that they have been welcomed into an elite group of highly qualified people of very high integrity.

Introduction

But this sense of high ideals about police work may not last for long. The introduction to policing provided by most police academies begins to convey folklore that shows the impossibility of doing things "by the book" and the frequent necessity of "bending the rules."

Police recruit training has changed substantially over the past thirty years. Once highly militaristic, it has recently taken on more of the atmosphere of the college classroom. The endurance test-stress environment approach, in which trainees may be punished for yawning or looking out the window, may still be found in some cities, but it seems to be dying out. Dull lectures on the technical aspects of police work (such as how to fill out arrest reports) and the rules and regulations of the department are now often supplemented by guest lectures on theories of crime and the cultures of various ethnic groups.

But the central method of *moral* instruction does not appear to have changed. The "war story" still remains the most effective device for communicating the history and values of the department. When the instructor tells a "war story," or an anecdote about police work, the class discipline is relaxed somewhat, the interest and attention of the class increase, and an atmosphere of camaraderie between the class and the instructor is established. The content of the war story makes a deep impression on the trainees.

The war stories not only introduce police work as it is experienced by police officers—rather than as an abstract ideal—they also introduce the ethics of police work as something different from what the public, or at least the law and the press, might expect. Van Maanen recounts one excerpt from a police academy criminal law lecture that, while not a "story," indicates the way in which the hidden values of police work are conveyed:

> I suppose you guys have heard of Lucky Baldwin? If not, you sure will when you hit the street. Baldwin happens to be the biggest burglar still operating in this town. Every guy in this department from patrolman to chief would love to get him and make it stick. We've busted him about ten times so far, but he's got an asshole lawyer and money so he always beats the rap. . . . If I ever get a chance to pinch the SOB, I'll do it my way with my thirty-eight and spare the city the cost of a trial.[3]

Whether the instructor would actually shoot the burglary suspect is open to question, although he could do so legally in most states if the suspect attempted to flee from being arrested. More important is the fact that the rookies spend many hours outside the classroom debating and analyzing the implications of the war stories. These discussions do help them decide how they would act in similar circumstances. But the decisions they reach in these informal bull sessions are probably more attributable to peer pressure and the desire to "fit in" to the culture of the department than to careful reflection on moral principle.

Encounter

After they leave the academy, the rookies are usually handed over to Field Training Officers (FTOs). In the classic version of the first day on patrol with the rookie, the FTO says, "Forget everything they taught you in the academy, kid; I'll show you how police work is really done." And show they do. The rookie becomes an observer of the FTO as he or she actually does police work. Suddenly the war stories come alive, and all the questions about how to handle tough situations get answered very quickly and clearly, as one police veteran recalls:

> On this job, your first partner is everything. He tells you how to survive on the job . . . how to walk, how to stand, and how to speak and how to think and what to say and see.[4]

The encounter with the FTO is only part of the rookie's "reality shock" about police work. Perhaps even more important are the rookie's encounters with the public. By putting on the uniform, the rookie becomes part of a visible minority group. The self-consciousness about the new appearance is heightened by the nasty taunts and comments the uniform attracts from teenagers and others.[5] The uniform and gun, as symbols of power, attract challenges to that power simply because they are there.[6] Other people seek out the uniform to manipulate the rookie to use the power on behalf of their personal interests. Caught frequently in the cross fire of equally unreasonable citizen demands, the rookie naturally reacts by blaming the public. The spontaneous reaction is reinforced by one of the central values of the police culture: the public as enemy.[7]

This is no different from the way many doctors view their patients, particularly patients with a penchant for malpractice suits. Nor is it different from the view many professors have of their students as unreasonable and thick-headed, particularly those who argue about grades. Like police officers, doctors and professors wield power that affects other people's lives, and that power is always subject to counterattack. Once again, Van Maanen captures the experience of the rookie:

> [My FTO] was always telling me to be forceful, to not back down and to never try to explain the law or what we are doing to a civilian. I really didn't know what he was talking about until I tried to tell some kid why we have laws about speeding. Well, the more I tried to tell him about traffic safety, the angrier he got. I was lucky just to get his John Hancock on the citation. When I came back to the patrol car, [the FTO] explains to me just where I'd gone wrong. You really can't talk to those people out there, they just won't listen to reason.[8]

It is the public that transforms the rookie's self-conception, teaching him or her the pains of exercising power. The FTO then helps to interpret the encounters with the public in the light of the values of the police culture, perhaps leading the rookie even further away from the values of family or friends about how police should act.

The FTO often gives "tests" as he or she teaches. In many departments, the tests are as minor as seeing if the rookie will wait patiently outside while the FTO visits a friend. In other departments, the test may include getting the rookie involved in drinking or having sex on duty, a seriously brutal slugfest against an arrestee, or taking bribes for nonenforcement. The seriousness of the violations may vary, but the central purpose of the test does not: seeing if the rookie can keep his or her mouth shut and not report the violations to the supervisors. A rookie who is found to be untrustworthy can be, literally, hounded and harassed from the department.

Finally, in the encounter stage, the rookie gets the major reality shock in the entire process of becoming a police officer. The rookie discovers that police work is more social work than crime fighting, more arbitration of minor disputes than investigations of major crimes, more patching of holes in the social fabric than weaving of webs to catch the big-time crooks. The rookie's usual response is to define most of the assignments received as "garbage calls," not *real* police work. Not quite sure whom to blame for the fact that he or she was hired to do police work but was assigned everything else, the rookie blames the police executive, the mayor and city council, and even previous U.S. presidents (for raising public expectations). But most of all the rookie blames the public, especially the poor, for being so stupid as to have all these problems, or so smart as to take advantage of welfare and other social programs.

Metamorphosis

The result of those encounters is usually a complete change, a total adaptation of the new role and self-conception as a "cop." And with that transformation comes a stark awareness of the interdependence cops share with all other cops. For all the independence police have in making decisions about how to deal with citizens, they are totally and utterly dependent on other police to save their lives, to respond to a call of an officer in trouble or need of assistance, and to lie on their behalf to supervisors to cover up minor infractions of the many rules the department has. This total change in perspective usually means that police accept several new assumptions about the nature of the world:

- loyalty to colleagues is essential for survival
- the public, or most of it, is the enemy
- police administrators are also the enemy
- any discrepancy between these views and the views of family and friends is due simply to the ignorance of those who have not actually done police work themselves

These are their new assumptions about the *facts* of life in police work, the realities which limit their options for many things, including the kinds of moral principles they can afford to have and still "survive," to keep the job, pay the mortgage, raise the kids, and vest the pension. This conception of the facts opens new police officers to learning and accepting what may be a new set of values and ethical principles. By the time the metamorphosis has been accomplished, in fact, most of these new values have been learned.

CONTENT OF POLICE VALUES TEACHING

Through the war stories of the academy instructor, the actions and stories of the FTO, the bull sessions with other rookies and veterans, and the new officer's encounters with the public, a fairly consistent set of values emerges. Whether the officer accepts these values is another question. Most students of police work seem to agree that these are the values (or some of them) that are taught:

1. Discretion A: *Decisions about whether to enforce the law, in any but the most serious cases, should be guided by both what the law says and who the suspect is.* Attitude, demeanor, cooperativeness, and even race, age, and social class are all important considerations in deciding how to treat people generally, and whether or not to arrest suspects in particular.

2. Discretion B: *Disrespect for police authority is a serious offense that should always be punished with an arrest or the use of force.* The "offense" known as "contempt of cop" or P.O.P.O. (pissing off a police officer) cannot be ignored. Even when the party has committed no violation of the law, a police officer should find a safe way to impose punishment, including an arrest on fake charges.

3. Force: *Police officers should never hesitate to use physical or deadly force against people who "deserve it," or where it can be an effective way of solving a crime.* Only the potential punishments by superior officers, civil litigation, citizen complaints, and so forth should limit the use of force when the situation calls for it. When you can get away with it, use all the force that society should use on people like that—force and punishment which bleeding-heart judges are too soft to impose.

4. Due Process: *Due process is only a means of protecting criminals at the expense of the law-abiding and should be ignored whenever it is safe to do so.* Illegal

searches and wiretaps, interrogation without advising suspects of their Miranda rights, and if need be (as in the much-admired movie, *Dirty Harry*), even physical pain to coerce a confession are all acceptable methods for accomplishing the goal the public wants the police to accomplish: fighting crime. The rules against doing those things merely handcuff the police, making it more difficult for them to do their job.

5. Truth: *Lying and deception are an essential part of the police job, and even perjury should be used if it is necessary to protect yourself or get a conviction on a "bad guy."* Violations of due process cannot be admitted to prosecutors or in court, so perjury (in the serious five per cent of cases that ever go to trial) is necessary and therefore proper. Lying to drug pushers about wanting to buy drugs, to prostitutes about wanting to buy sex, or to congressmen about wanting to buy influence is the only way, and therefore a proper way, to investigate these crimes without victims. Deceiving muggers into thinking you are an easy mark and deceiving burglars into thinking you are a fence are proper because there are not many other ways of catching predatory criminals in the act.

6. Time: *You cannot go fast enough to chase a car thief or traffic violator, nor slow enough to get to a "garbage" call; and when there are no calls for service, your time is your own.* Hot pursuits are necessary because anyone who tries to escape from the police is challenging police authority, no matter how trivial the initial offense. But calls to nonserious or social-work problems like domestic disputes or kids making noise are unimportant, so you can stop to get coffee on the way or even stop at the cleaner's if you like. And when there are no calls, you can sleep, visit friends, study, or do anything else you can get away with, especially on the midnight shift, when you can get away with a lot.

7. Rewards: *Police do very dangerous work for low wages, so it is proper to take any extra rewards the public wants to give them, like free meals, Christmas gifts, or even regular monthly payments (in some cities) for special treatment.* The general rule is: take any reward that doesn't change what you would do anyway, such as eating a meal, but don't take money that would affect your job, like not giving traffic tickets. In many cities, however, especially in the recent past, the rule has been to take even those rewards that do affect your decisions, as long as they are related only to minor offenses—traffic, gambling, prostitution, but not murder.

8. Loyalty: *The paramount duty is to protect your fellow officers at all costs, as they would protect you, even though you may have to risk your own career or your own life to do it.* If your colleagues make a mistake, take a bribe, seriously hurt somebody illegally, or get into other kinds of trouble, you should do everything you can to protect them in the ensuing investigation. If your colleagues are routinely breaking the rules, you should never tell supervisors, reporters, or outside investigators about it. If you don't like it, quit—or get transferred to the police academy. But never, ever, blow the whistle.

THE RISING VALUE CONFLICTS

None of these values is as strongly or widely held as in the past. Several factors may account for the breakdown in traditional police values that has paralleled the breakdown of traditional values in the wider society. One is the increasing diversity of the kinds of people who join police departments: more women, minorities, and college graduates. Another is the rising power of the police unions which defend individual officers who get into trouble—sometimes even those who challenge the traditional values. A third factor is the rise of investigating journalism and the romantic aura given to "bucking the system" by such movies as *Serpico*. Watergate and other recent exposés of corruption in high places—especially the attitude of being "above the law"—have probably made all public officials more conscious of the ethics of their behavior. Last but not least, police administrators have increasingly taken a very stern disciplinary posture towards some of these traditional police values and gone to extraordinary lengths to try to counteract them.

Consider the paramount value of loyalty. Police reformer August Vollmer described it in 1931 as the "blue curtain of secrecy" that descends whenever a police officer does something wrong, making it impossible to investigate misconduct. Yet in the past decade, police officers in Cincinnati, Indianapolis, New York, and elsewhere have given reporters and grand juries evidence about widespread police misconduct. In New York, police officers have even given evidence against their colleagues for homicide, leading to the first conviction there (that anyone can recall) of a police officer for murder in the line of duty. The code of silence may be far from breaking down, but it certainly has a few cracks in it.

The ethics of rewards have certainly changed in many departments over the past decade. In the wake of corruption scandals, some police executives have taken advantage of the breakdown in loyalty to assign spies, or "field associates," to corruption-prone units in order to detect bribe-taking. These officers are often recruited for this work at the police academy, where they are identified only to one or two contacts and are generally treated like any other police officer. These spies are universally hated by other officers, but they are very hard to identify. The result of this approach, along with other anti-corruption strategies, has been an apparent decline in organized corruption.[9]

The ethics of force are also changing. In the wake of well-publicized federal prosecutions of police beatings, community outrage over police shootings, and an explosion in civil litigation that has threatened to bankrupt some cities, the behavior and possibly the attitude of the police in their use of force have generally become more restrained. In Los Angeles, Kansas City, Atlanta, New York, Chicago, and elsewhere, the number of killings of citizens by police has declined sharply.[10] Some officers now claim that they risk their lives by hesitating to use force out of fear of being punished for using it. Even if excessive use of force has not been entirely eliminated, the days of unrestrained shooting or use of the "third degree" are clearly gone in many cities.

The increasing external pressures to conform to legal and societal values, rather than to traditional police values, have generated increasing conflict among police officers themselves. The divide-and-conquer effect may be seen in police officers' unwillingness to bear the risks of covering up for their colleagues, now that the risks are much greater than they have been. Racial conflicts among police officers often center on these values. At the national level, for example, the National Organization of Black Law Enforcement Executives (NOBLE) has been battling with the International Association of Chiefs of Police (IACP) since at least 1979 over the question of how restrictive police department firearms policies should be.

These conflicts should not be over-emphasized, however. The learning of police ethics still takes place in the context of very strong communication of traditional police values. The rising conflicts are still only a minor force. But they are at least one more contingency affecting the moral choices police officers face as they progress through their careers, deciding which values to adopt and which ethical standards to live by.

THE POLICE OFFICER'S MORAL CAREER

There are four major aspects of moral careers in general that are directly relevant to police officers.[11] One is the *contingencies* the officer confronts. Another is the *moral experiences* undergone in confronting these contingencies. A third is the *apologia*, the explanation officers develop for changing the ethical principles they live by. The fourth and most visible aspect of the moral careers of police officers is the *stages* of moral change they go through.

Contingencies

The contingencies shaping police moral careers include all the social pressures officers face to behave one way rather than another. Police departments vary, for example, in the frequency and seriousness of the rule-breaking that goes on. They also vary in the openness of such rule-breaking, and in the degree of teaching of the *skills* of such rule-breaking. It is no small art, for example, to coax a bribe offer out of a traffic violator without directly asking for it. Even in a department in which such bribes are regularly accepted, a new officer may be unlikely to adopt the practice if an older officer does not teach him or her how. In a department in which older officers explicitly teach the techniques, the same officer might be more likely to adopt the practice. The difference in the officer's career is thus shaped by the difference in the contingencies he or she confronts.

The list of all possible contingencies is obviously endless, but these are some of the more commonly reported ones:

- the values the FTO teaches
- the values the first sergeant teaches
- the kind of citizens confronted in the first patrol assignment
- the level of danger on patrol
- whether officers work in a one-officer or two-officer car (after the training period)
- whether officers are assigned to undercover or vice work
- whether there are conflicts among police officers over ethical issues in the department
- the ethical "messages" sent out by the police executive
- the power of the police union to protect officers from being punished
- the general climate of civic integrity (or lack of it)
- the level of public pressure to control police behavior

Contingencies alone, of course, do not shape our behavior. If we were entirely the products of our environment, with no freedom of moral choice, there would be little point in writing (or reading) books on ethics. What contingencies like these do is push us in one direction or another, much like the waves in the ocean. Whether we choose to swim against the tide or flow with the waves is up to each of us.

Moral Experiences

The moral experience is a major turning point in a moral career. It can be an agonizing decision about which principles to follow or it can be a shock of recognition as you finally understand the moral principals implicit in how other people are behaving. Like the person asleep on a raft drifting out to sea, the police officer who has a moral experience suddenly discovers where he or she is and what the choices are.

Some officers have had moral experiences when they found out the system they worked for was corrupt: when the judge dismissed the charges against the son of a powerful business executive, or when a sergeant ordered the officer not to make arrests at an illegal after-hours bar. One leading police executive apparently went through a moral experience when he was first assigned to the vice squad and saw all the money that his colleagues were taking from gamblers. Shocked and disgusted, he sought and obtained a transfer to a less corrupt unit within a few weeks.

Other officers have had moral experiences in reaction to particular incidents. One Houston police rookie was out of the academy for only several weeks when he witnessed a group of his senior colleagues beat up a Mexican-American, Joe Campos Torres, after he resisted arrest in a bar. Torres drowned after jumping or being pushed from a great height into a bayou, and no one knew how he had died when his body was found floating nearby. The officer discussed the incident with his father, also a Houston police officer, and the father marched the young officer right into the Internal Affairs Division to give a statement. His testimony became the basis of a federal prosecution of the other officers.

Other officers may have a moral experience when they see their ethics presented in public, outside of the police culture. New York City police captain Max Schmittberger, for example, who had been a bagman collecting graft for his superiors in New York's Tenderloin district, was greatly moved by the testimony of prostitutes he heard at the hearings of the Lexow Committee investigating police corruption in 1893. He told muckraking reporter Linda Steffens that the parade of witnesses opened his eyes to the reality of the corruption. So he decided to get on the witness stand himself to reveal even more details of the corruption.

No matter what contingencies occur to prompt a moral experience, the police officer faces relatively few choices about how to react. One option is to drift with the tide, letting things go on as they have been. Another option is to seek an escape route, such as a transfer, that removes the moral dilemma that may prompt the moral experience. A third option is to leave police work altogether, although the financial resources of police officers are not usually great enough to allow the luxury of resigning on principle. The fourth and most difficult option is to fight back somehow, either by blowing the whistle to the public or initiating a behind-the-scenes counterattack.

Not all moral experiences are prompted by criminal acts or even by violations of rules and regulations. Racist jokes or language, ethnic favoritism by commanders, or other issues can also prompt moral experiences. With some officers, though, nothing may ever prompt a moral experience; they may drift out to sea, or back to shore, sound asleep and unaware of what is happening to them.

Apologia

For those officers with enough moral consciousness to suffer a moral experience, a failure to "do the right thing" could be quite painful to live with. "Even a bent policeman has a conscience," as a British police official who resigned on principle (inadequate police corruption investigations in London) once observed.[12] In order to resolve the conflict between what they think they should have done and what they actually did, officers often invent or adopt an acceptable explanation for their conduct. The explanation negates the principle they may have wished they actually had followed, or somehow makes their behavior consistent with that principle.

Perhaps the most famous apologia is the concept of "clean graft": bribes paid to avoid enforcement of laws against crimes that don't hurt people. Gambling and prostitution bribes were traditionally labeled as "clean graft," while bribes from narcotics pushers were labeled "dirty graft." (As narcotics traffic grew more lucrative, however, narcotics bribes were more often labeled "clean.")

The apologia for beating a handicapped prisoner in a moment of anger may draw on the police value system of maintaining respect for authority and meting out punishment because the courts will not. The apologia for stopping black suspects more often than white suspects may be the assumption that blacks are more likely to be guilty. No matter what a police officer does, he or she is apt to find *situationally justified* reasons for doing it. The reasons are things only the officer can understand because only the officer knows the full story, all the facts of the *situation*. The claim of situational expertise, of course, conveniently avoids any attempt to apply a general moral principle to conduct. The avoidance is just as effective in the officer's own mind as it would be if the apologia were discussed with the officer's spouse, clergyman, or parents.

Perhaps the most important effect of the apologia is that it allows the officer to live with a certain moral standard of behavior, to become comfortable with it. This creates the potential for further apologias about further changes in moral standards. The process can clearly become habit-forming, and it does. The progression from one apologia to the next makes up the stages of moral change.

Stages

The stages of moral change are points on a moral continuum; the different levels of moral improvement or of the "slippery slope" of moral degeneration. Such descriptions sound trite and old-fashioned, but they are commonly used by officers who get into serious trouble—such as being convicted for burglary—to account for their behavior.

The officers caught in the Denver police burglary ring in 1961, for example, appear to have progressed through many stages in their moral careers before forming an organized burglary ring:

1. First they suffered moral experiences that showed them that the laws were not impartially enforced and that judges were corrupt.

2. Then they learned that other police officers were dishonest, including those who engaged in "shopping," i.e., stealing goods at the scene of a nighttime commercial burglary, with the goods stolen by the police thus indistinguishable from the goods stolen by others.

3. They joined in the shopping themselves and constructed an apologia for it ("the insurance pays for it all anyway").

4. The apologia provided a rationale for a planned burglary in which they were burglars ("the insurance still pays for it").

5. The final stage was to commit planned burglaries or a regular basis.

These stages are logically available to all police officers. Many, perhaps most, officers progress to Stage 3 and go no further, just as most professors steal paper clips and photocopying from their universities, but not books or furniture. Why some people move into the further stages and others do not is a problem for the sociology of deviance, not ethics. The fact is that some officers do move into the more serious stages of unethical conduct after most officers have established the custom in the less serious, but still unethical, stages.

Each aspect of police ethics, from force to time to due process, has different sets of stages. Taken together, the officer's movement across all the stages on all the ethical issues makes up his or her moral career in police work. The process is not just one way; officers can move back closer to legal principles as well as away from them. But the process is probably quite connected across different issues. Your moral stage on stealing may parallel your moral stage on force.

LEARNING ETHICS DIFFERENTLY

This article has treated morality as if it were black and white, i.e., as if it consisted of clear-cut principles to be obeyed or disobeyed. Many issues in police ethics are in fact clear-cut, and hold little room for serious philosophical analysis. One would have a hard time making a rational defense of police officers staling, for example.

But what may be wrong with the way police ethics is now taught and learned is just that assumption: that all police ethical issues are as clear-cut as stealing. They are not. The issues of force, time, discretion, loyalty, and others are all very complex, with many shades of gray. To deny this complexity, as the formal approaches of police academies and police rule books often do, may simply encourage unethical behavior. A list of "dos" and "don'ts" that officers must follow because they are ordered to is a virtual challenge to their ingenuity: catch me if you can. And in the face of a police culture that has already established values quite contrary to many of the official rules, the black-and-white approach to ethics may be naive.

As indicated above, an alternative approach may be preferred. This would consider both clear-cut and complex ethical issues in the same fashion: examining police problems in the light of basic moral principles and from the moral point of view. While there may be weaknesses in this alternative approach, it may well be the sounder road to ethical sensitivity in the context of individual responsibility.

NOTES

1. See John Van Maanen, "On Becoming a Policeman," in *Policing: A View from the Street*, eds. Peter Manning and John Van Maanen (Santa Monica, Calif.: Goodyear, 1978).

2. See John McNamara, "Uncertainties in Police Work: The Relevance of Recruits" Backgrounds and Training," in *The Police: Six Sociological Studies,* ed. David J. Bordua (New York: Wiley, 1967).

3. Van Maanen, "On Becoming a Policeman," p. 298.

4. Ibid., p. 301.

5. See William Westley, *Violence and the Police* (Cambridge, Mass.: M.I.T. Press, 1970), pp. 159–60.

6. See William Ker Muir, Jr., *Police: Steelcorner Politicians* (Chicago: University of Chicago Press, 1977).

7. See Westley, *Violence*, pp. 48–108.

8. Van Maanen, "On Becoming a Policeman," p. 302.

9. See Lawrence Sherman, "Reducing Police Gun Use" (Paper presented at the International Conference on the Management and Control of Police Organizations, Breukelen, the Netherlands, 1980).

10. Ibid.

11. Cf. Erving Goffman, "The Moral Career of the Mental Patient," in *Asylum: Essays on the Social Situation of Mental Patients and Other Inmates* (Garden City, N.Y.: Anchor Books, 1961), pp. 127–69.

12. See Sherman, "Reducing Police Gun Use."

12

The Police Officer's "Working Personality"

by Jerome Skolnick

"What the policeman typically fails to realize is the extent he becomes tainted by the character of the work he performs."

—Jerome Skolnick,
"The Police Officer's 'Working Personality'"
(1966)

A recurrent theme of the sociology of occupations is the effect of a man's work on his outlook on the world. Doctors, janitors, lawyers, and industrial workers develop distinctive ways of perceiving and responding to their environment. Here we shall concentrate on analyzing certain outstanding elements in the police milieu, danger, authority, and efficiency, as they combine to generate distinctive cognitive and behavioral responses in police: a "working personality." Such an analysis does not suggest that all police are alike in working personality but that there are distinctive cognitive tendencies in police as an occupational grouping. Some of these may be found in other occupations sharing similar problems. So far as exposure to danger is concerned, the policeman may be likened to the soldier. His problems as an authority bear a certain similarity to those of the schoolteacher, and the pressures he feels to prove himself efficient are not unlike those felt by the industrial worker. The combination of these elements, however, is unique to the policeman. Thus, the police, as a result of combined features of their social situation, tend to develop ways of looking at the world distinctive to themselves, cognitive lenses through which to see situations and events. The strength of the lenses may be weaker or stronger depending on certain conditions, but they are ground on a similar axis.

From *Justice Without Trial: Law Enforcement in a Democratic Society* (pp. 41–58) by J. Skolnick, 1966, New York: John Wiley and Sons. Copyright 1994 Prentice Hall, Upper Saddle River, New Jersey. Adapted by permission.

Analysis of the policeman's cognitive propensities is necessary to understand the practical dilemma faced by police required to maintain order under a democratic rule of law. A conception of order is essential to the resolution of this dilemma. The paramilitary character of police organization naturally leads to a high evaluation of similarity, routine, and predictability. Our intention is to emphasize features of the policeman's environment interacting with the paramilitary police organization to generate a working personality. Such an intervening concept should aid in explaining how the social environment of police affects their capacity to respond to the rule of law.

This essay places emphasis on the division of labor in the police department; "operational law enforcement" cannot be understood outside these special work assignments. It is therefore important to explain how the hypothesis emphasizing the generalizability of the policeman's working personality is compatible with the idea that police division of labor is an important analytical dimension for understanding operational law enforcement. Compatibility is evident when one considers the different levels of analysis at which the hypotheses are being developed. Janowitz states, for example, that the military profession is more than an occupation; it is a "style of life" because the occupational claims over one's daily existence extend well beyond official duties. He is quick to point out that any profession performing a crucial "life and death" task, such as medicine, the ministry, or the police, develops such claims. A conception like working personality of police should be understood to suggest an analytic breadth similar to that of style of life. That is, just as the professional behavior of military officers with similar styles of life may differ drastically depending upon whether they command an infantry battalion or participate in the work of an intelligence unit, so too does the professional behavior of police officers with similar working personalities vary with their assignments.

The process by which this personality is developed may be summarized: the policeman's role contains two principal variables, danger and authority, which should be interpreted in the light of a "constant" pressure to appear efficient. The element of danger seems to make the policeman especially attentive to signs indicating a potential for violence and lawbreaking. As a result, the policeman is generally a "suspicious" person. Furthermore, the character of the policeman's work makes him less desirable as a friend, since norms of friendship implicate others in his work. Accordingly, the element of danger isolates the policeman socially from that segment of the citizenry which he regards as symbolically dangerous and also from the conventional citizenry with whom he identifies.

The element of authority reinforces the element of danger in isolating the policeman. Typically, the policeman is required to enforce laws representing puritanical morality, such as those prohibiting drunkenness, and also laws regulating the flow of public activity, such as traffic laws. In these situations, the policeman directs the citizenry, whose typical response denies recognition of his authority, and stresses his obligation to respond to danger. The kind of man who responds well to danger, however, does not normally subscribe to codes of puritanical morality. As a result, the policeman is unusually liable to the charge of hypocrisy. That the whole civilian world is an audience for the policeman further promotes police isolation and, in consequence, solidarity. Finally, danger undermines the judicious use of authority. Where danger, as in Britain, is relatively less, the judicious application of authority is facilitated. Hence, British police may appear to be somewhat more attached to the rule of law, when, in fact, they may appear so because they face less danger, and they are as a rule better skilled than American police in creating the appearance of conformity to procedural regulations.

THE SYMBOLIC ASSAILANT AND POLICE CULTURE

In attempting to understand the policeman's view of the world, it is useful to raise a more general question: what are the conditions under which police, as authorities, may be threatened? The policeman, because his work requires him to be occupied continually with potential violence, develops a perceptual shorthand to identify certain kinds of people as symbolic assailants, that is, as persons who use gesture, language, and attire that the policeman has come to recognize as a prelude to violence. This does not mean that violence by the symbolic assailant is necessarily predictable. On the contrary, the policeman responds to the vague indication of danger suggested by appearance. Like the animals of the experimental psychologist, the policeman finds the threat of random damage more compelling than a predetermined and inevitable punishment.

Nor, to qualify for the status of symbolic assailant, need an individual ever have used violence. A man backing out of a jewelry store with a gun in one hand and jewelry in the other would qualify even if the gun were a toy and he had never in his life fired a real pistol. To the policeman in the situation, the man's personal history is momentarily immaterial. There is only one relevant sign: a gun, signifying danger. Similarly, a young man may suggest the threat of violence to the policeman by his manner of walking or "strutting," the insolence in the demeanor being registered by the policeman as a possible preamble to later attack. Signs vary from area to area, but a youth dressed in a black leather jacket and motorcycle boots is sure to draw at least a suspicious glance from a policeman.

Policemen themselves do not necessarily emphasize the peril associated with their work when questioned directly and may even have well-developed strategies of denial. The element of danger is so integral to the policeman's work that explicit recognition might induce emotional barriers to work performance. Thus, one patrol officer observed that more police have been killed and injured in automobile accidents in the past ten years than from gunfire. Although his assertion is true, he neglected to mention that the police are the only peacetime occupational group with a systematic record of death and injury from gunfire and other weaponry. Along these lines, it is interesting that of the 224 working Westville policemen (not including the 16 juvenile policemen) responding to a question about which assignment they would like most to have in the police departments, 50 percent selected the job of detective, an assignment combining elements of apparent danger and initiative. The next category was adult street work, that is, patrol and traffic (37 percent). Eight percent selected the juvenile squad, and only 4 percent selected administrative work. Not a single policeman chose the job of jail guard. Although these findings do not control for such factors as prestige, they suggest that confining and routine jobs are rated low on the hierarchy of police preferences, even though such jobs are least dangerous. Thus, the policeman may well, as a personality, enjoy the possibility of danger, especially its associated excitement even though he may at the same time be fearful of it. Such "inconsistency" is easily understood. Freud has by now made it an axiom of personality theory that logical and emotional consistency are by no means the same phenomenon.

However complex the motives aroused by the element of danger, its consequences for sustaining police culture are unambiguous. It is, therefore, a conception shaped by persistent suspicion. The English "copper," often portrayed as a courteous, easygoing, rather jolly sort of chap, on the one hand, or as a devil-may-care adventurer, on the other, is differently described by Colin MacInnes:

> The true copper's dominant characteristic, if the truth be known, is neither those daring nor vicious qualities that are sometimes attributed to him by friend

or enemy, but an ingrained conservatism, and almost desperate love of the conventional. It is untidiness, disorder, the unusual, that a copper disapproves of most of all: far more, even than of crime which is merely a professional matter. Hence his profound dislike of people loitering in streets, dressing extravagantly, speaking with exotic accents, being strange, weak, eccentric, or simply any rare minority—of their doing, in fact, anything that cannot be safely predicted.

Policemen are indeed specifically *trained* to be suspicious, to perceive events or changes in the physical surroundings that indicate the occurrence or probability of disorder. A former student who worked as a patrolman in a suburban New York police department describes this aspect of the policeman's assessment of the unusual:

> The time spent cruising one's sector or walking one's beat is not wasted time, though it can become quite routine. During this time, the most important thing for the officer to do is notice the normal. He must come to know the people in his area, their habits, their automobiles and their friends. He must learn what time the various shops close, how much money is kept on hand on different nights, what lights are usually left on, which houses are vacant . . . only then can he decide what persons or cars under what circumstances warrant the appellation "suspicious."

The individual policeman's "suspiciousness" does not hang on whether he has personally undergone an experience that could objectively be described as hazardous. Personal experience of this sort is not the key to the psychological importance of exceptionality. Each, as he routinely carries out his work, will experience situations that threaten to become dangerous. Like the American Jew who contributes to "defense" organizations such as the Anti-Defamation League in response to Nazi brutalities he has never experienced personally, the policeman identifies with his fellow cop who has been beaten, perhaps fatally, by a gang of young thugs.

SOCIAL ISOLATION

The patrolman in Westville, and probably in most communities, has come to identify the black man with danger. James Baldwin vividly expresses the isolation of the ghetto policeman:

> The only way to police a ghetto is to be oppressive. None of the Police Commissioner's men, even with the best will in the world, have any way of understanding the lives led by the people they swagger about in twos and threes controlling. Their very presence is an insult, and it would be, even if they spent their entire day feeding gumdrops to children. They present the force of the white world, and that world's criminal profit and ease, to keep the black man corralled up here, in his place. The badge, the gun in the holster, and the swinging club make vivid what will happen should his rebellion become overt. . . .
> It is hard, on the other hand, to blame the policeman, blank, good-natured, thoughtless, and insuperably innocent, for being such a perfect representative of the people he serves. He, too, believes in good intentions and is astounded and offended when they are not taken for the deed. He has never, himself, done anything for which to be hated—which of us has?—and yet he is facing, daily and nightly, people who would gladly see him dead, and he knows it. There is

no way for him not to know it: there are few things under heaven more unnerving than the silent, accumulating contempt and hatred of a people. He moves through Harlem, therefore, like an occupying soldier in a bitterly hostile country; which is precisely what, and where he is, and is the reason he walks in twos and threes.

While Baldwin's observations on police-Negro relations cannot be disputed seriously, there is greater social distance between police and "civilians" in general regardless of their color than Baldwin considers. Thus, Clinton MacInnes has his English hero, Mr. Justice, explaining:

> The story is all coppers are just civilians like anyone else, living among them not in barracks like on the Continent, but you and I know that's just a legend for mugs. We are cut off: we're not like everyone else. Some civilians fear us and play up to us, some dislike us and keep out of our way but no one—well, very few indeed—accepts us as just ordinary like them. In one sense, dear, we're just like hostile troops occupying an enemy country. And say what you like, at times that makes us lonely.

Of the 282 Westville policemen who rated the prestige police work receives from others, 70 percent ranked it as only "fair" or "poor," while less than 2 percent ranked it as "excellent" and another 29 percent as "good." Similarly, in Britain, two-thirds of a sample of policemen interviewed by a Royal Commission stated difficulties in making friends outside the force; of those interviewed, 58 percent thought members of the public to be reserved, suspicious, and constrained in conversation, and 12 percent attributed such difficulties to the requirement that policemen be selective in associations and behave circumspectly. A Westville policeman related the following incident:

> Several months after I joined the force, my wife and I used to be socially active with a crowd of young people, mostly married, who gave a lot of parties where there was drinking and dancing, and we enjoyed it. I've never forgotten, though, an incident that happened on one Fourth of July party. Everybody had been drinking, there was a lot of talking, people were feeling boisterous, and some kid there—he must have been 20 or 22—threw a firecracker that hit my wife in the leg and burned her. I didn't know exactly what to do—punch the guy in the nose, bawl him out, just forget it. Anyway, I couldn't let it pass, so I walked over to him and told him he ought to be careful. He began to rise up at me, and when he did, somebody yelled, "Better watch out, he's a cop." I saw everybody standing there, and I could feel they were against me and for the kid, even though he had thrown the firecracker at my wife. I went over to the host and said it was probably better if my wife and I left because a fight would put a damper on the party. Actually, I'd hoped he would ask the kid to leave, since the kid had thrown the firecracker. But he didn't so we left. After that incident, my wife and I stopped going around with that crowd, and decided that if we were going to go to parties where there was to be drinking and boisterousness, we weren't going to be the only police people there.

Another reported that he seeks to overcome his feelings of isolation by concealing his police identity:

> I try not to bring my work home with me, and that includes my social life.
> I like the men I work with, but I think it's better that my family doesn't become
> a police family. I try to put my police work into the background, and try not to
> let people know I'm a policeman. Once you do, you can't have normal relations
> with them.

Although the policeman serves a people who are, as Baldwin says, the established society, the white society, these people do not make him feel accepted. As a result, he develops resources within his own world to combat social rejection.

POLICE SOLIDARITY

All occupational groups share a measure of inclusiveness and identification. People are brought together simply by doing the same work and having similar career and salary problems. As several writers have noted, however, police show an unusually high degree of occupational solidarity. It is true that the police have a common employer and wear a uniform at work, but so do doctors, milkmen, and bus drivers. Yet it is doubtful that these workers have so close knit an occupation or so similar an outlook on the world as do police. Set apart from the conventional world, the policeman experiences an exceptionally strong tendency to find his social identity within his occupational milieu.

Among the Westville police, of 700 friends listed by 250 respondents, 35 percent were policemen. Further, only 16 percent had failed to attend a single police banquet or dinner in the past year, and of the 234 men answering this question, 54 percent had attended three or more such affairs during the past year. These findings are striking and consistent with the idea that police officers have a strong social identity within their occupation—police are an exceptionally socially active occupational group.

POLICE SOLIDARITY AND DANGER

There is still a question, however, as to the process through which danger and authority influence police solidarity. The effect of danger on police solidarity is revealed when we examine a chief complaint of police: lack of public support and public apathy. The complaint may have several referents including police pay, police prestige, and support from the legislature. But the repeatedly voiced broader meaning of the complaint is resentment at being taken for granted. The policeman does not believe that his status as civil servant should relieve the public of responsibility for law enforcement. He feels, however, that payment out of public coffers somehow obscures his humanity and, therefore, his need for help. As one put it:

> Jerry, a cop, can get into a fight with three or four tough kids, and there will
> be citizens passing by, and maybe they'll look, but they'll never lend a hand. It's
> their country too, but you'd never know it the way some of them act. They forget that we're made of flesh and blood too. They don't care what happens to the
> cop so long as they don't get a little dirty.

Although the policeman sees himself as a specialist in dealing with violence, he does not want to fight alone. He does not believe that his specialization relieves the general public of citizenship duties. Indeed, if possible, he would prefer to be the foreman rather than the workingman in the battle against criminals.

The general public, of course, does withdraw from the workaday world of the policeman. The policeman's responsibility for controlling dangerous and sometimes violent persons alienates the average citizen perhaps as much as does his authority over the average citizen. If the policeman's job is to ensure that public order is maintained, the citizen's inclination is to shrink from the dangers of maintaining it. The citizen prefers to see the policeman as an automaton, because once the policeman's humanity is recognized, the citizen necessarily becomes implicated in the policeman's work, which is, after all, sometimes dirty and dangerous. What the policeman typically fails to realize is the extent he becomes tainted by the character of the work he performs. The dangers of their work not only draw policemen together as a group but separate them from the rest of the population. Banton, for instance, comments:

> Patrolmen may support their fellows over what they regard as minor infractions in order to demonstrate to them that they will be loyal in situations that make the greatest demands upon their fidelity. In the American departments I visited it seemed as if the supervisors shared many of the patrolmen's sentiments about solidarity. They too wanted their colleagues to back them up in an emergency, and they shared similar frustrations with the public.

Thus, the element of danger contains seeds of isolation which may grow in two directions. In one, a stereotyping perceptual shorthand is formed through which the police come to see certain signs as symbols of potential violence. The police probably differ in this respect from the general middle-class white population only in degree. This difference, however, may take on enormous significance in practice. Thus, the policeman works at identifying and possibly apprehending the symbolic assailant; the ordinary citizen does not. As a result, the ordinary citizen does not assume the responsibility to implicate himself in the policeman's required response to danger. The element of danger in the policeman's role alienates him not only from populations with a potential for crime but also from the conventionally respectable (white) citizenry, in short, from that segment of the population from which friends would ordinarily be drawn. As Janowitz has noted in a paragraph suggesting similarities between the police and the military, "Any profession which is continually preoccupied with the threat of danger requires a strong sense of solidarity if it is to operate effectively. Detailed regulation of the military style of life is expected to enhance group cohesion, professional loyalty, and maintain the martial spirit."

SOCIAL ISOLATION AND AUTHORITY

The element of authority also helps to account for the policeman's social isolation. Policemen themselves are aware of their isolation from the community and are apt to weigh authority heavily as a causal factor. When considering how authority influences rejection, the policeman typically singles out his responsibility for enforcement of traffic violations. Resentment, even hostility, is generated in those receiving citations, in part because such contact is often the only one citizens have with police, and in part because municipal administrations and courts have been known to use police authority primarily to meet budgetary requirements, rather than those of public order. Thus, when a municipality engages in "speed trapping" by changing limits so quickly that drivers cannot realistically slow down to the prescribed speed or, while keeping the limits reasonable, charging high fines primarily to generate revenue, the policeman carries the brunt of public resentment.

That the policeman dislikes writing traffic tickets is suggested by the quota system police departments typically employ. In Westville, each traffic policeman has what is euphemistically described as a working "norm." A motorcyclist is supposed to write two tickets an hour for moving violations. It is doubtful that norms are needed because policemen are lazy. Rather, employment of quotas most likely springs from the reluctance of policemen to expose themselves to what they know to be public hostility.

When meeting "production" pressures, the policeman inadvertently gives a false impression of patrolling ability to the average citizen. The traffic cyclist waits in hiding for moving violators near a tricky intersection and is reasonably sure that such violations will occur with regularity. The violator believes he has observed a policeman displaying exceptional detection capacities and may have two thoughts, each apt to generate hostility toward the policeman: "I have been trapped," or "They can catch me; why can't they catch crooks as easily?" The answer, of course, lies in the different behavior patterns of motorists and "crooks."

The latter do not act with either the frequency or predictability of motorists at poorly engineered intersections. While traffic patrol plays a major role in separating the policemen from the respectable community, other of his tasks also have this consequence. Traffic patrol is only the most obvious illustration of the policeman's general responsibility for maintaining public order, which includes keeping order at public accidents, sporting events, and political rallies. These activities share one feature: the policeman is called upon to *direct* ordinary citizens and therefore to restrain their freedom of action. Resenting the restraint, the average citizen in such a situation typically thinks something along the lines of "He is supposed to catch crooks; why is he bothering me?" Thus, the citizen stresses the "dangerous" portion of the policeman's role while belittling his authority.

Closely related to the policeman's authority-based problems as *director* of the citizenry are difficulties associated with his injunction to *regulate* public morality. For instance, the policeman is obliged to investigate "lovers' lanes" and to enforce laws pertaining to gambling, prostitution, and drunkenness. His responsibility in these matters allows him much administrative discretion since he may not actually enforce the law by making an arrest, but instead merely interfere with continuation of the objectionable activity. Thus, he may put the drunk in a taxi, tell the lovers to remove themselves from the backseat, and advise a man soliciting a prostitute to leave the area.

Such admonitions are in the interest of maintaining the proprieties of public order. At the same time, the policeman invites the hostility of the citizen so directed in two respects: he is likely to encourage the sort of response mentioned earlier (i.e., an antagonistic reformulation of the policeman's role), and the policeman is apt to cause resentment because of the suspicion that policemen do not themselves strictly conform to the moral norms they are enforcing. Thus, the policeman, faced with enforcing a law against fornication, drunkenness, or gambling, is easily liable to a charge of hypocrisy. Even when the policeman is called on to enforce the laws relating to overt homosexuality, a form of sexual activity for which police are not especially noted, he may encounter the charge of hypocrisy on grounds that he does not adhere strictly to prescribed heterosexual codes.

It is difficult to develop qualities enabling him to stand up to danger and to conform to standards of puritanical morality. The element of danger demands that the policeman be able to carry out efforts that are in their nature overtly masculine. Police work, like soldiering, requires an exceptional caliber of physical fitness, agility, toughness, and the like. The man who ranks high on these masculine characteristics is, again like the soldier, not usually disposed to be puritanical about sex, drinking, and gambling. On the basis of observations, policemen do not subscribe to moralistic standards for conduct. For example, the morals squad of the police department, when questioned, was unanimously against the statutory rape age limit, on grounds that as late teenagers they themselves might not have refused an attractive offer from a 17-year-old girl. Neither, from observations, are policemen by any means total abstainers from the use of alcoholic beverages. The policeman who is arresting a drunk has probably been drunk himself; he knows it and the drunk knows it.

More than that, a portion of the social isolation of the policeman can be attributed to the discrepancy between moral regulation and the norms and behavior of policemen in these areas. We have presented data indicating that police engage in a comparatively active occupational social life. One interpretation might attribute this attendance to a basic interest in such affairs; another might explain the policeman's occupational social activity as a measure of restraint in publicly violating norms he enforces. The interest in attending police affairs may grow as much out of security in "letting oneself go" in the presence of police, and a corresponding feeling of insecurity with civilians, as an authentic preference for police social affairs. Much alcohol is usually consumed at police banquets with all the melancholy and boisterousness accompanying such occasions. As Horace Cayton reports on his experience as a policeman:

> Deputy sheriffs and policemen don't know much about organized recreation; all they usually do when celebrating is get drunk and pound each other on the back, exchanging loud insults which under ordinary circumstances would result in a fight.

To some degree the reason for the behavior exhibited on these occasions is the company, since the policeman would feel uncomfortable exhibiting insobriety before civilians. The policeman may be likened to other authorities who prefer to violate moralistic norms away from onlookers for whom they are routinely supposed to appear as normative models. College professors, for instance, also get drunk on occasion, but prefer to do so where students are not present. Unfortunately for the policeman, such settings are harder for him to come by than they are for the college professor. The whole civilian world watches the policeman. As a result, he tends to be limited to the company of other policemen for whom his police identity is not a stimulus to carping normative criticism.

CORRELATES OF SOCIAL ISOLATION

The element of authority, like the element of danger, is thus seen to contribute to the solidarity of policemen. To the extent that policemen share the experience of receiving hostility from the public, they are also drawn together and become dependent upon one another. Trends in the degree to which police may exercise authority are also important considerations in understanding the dynamics of the relation between authority and solidarity. It is not simply a question of how much absolute authority police are given, but how much authority they have relative to what they had, or think they had, before. If, as Westley concludes, police violence is frequently a response to a challenge to the policeman's authority, so too may a perceived reduction in authority result in greater solidarity. Whitaker comments on the British police as follows:

> As they feel their authority decline, internal solidarity has become increasingly important to the police. Despite the individual responsibility of each police officer to pursue justice, there is sometimes a tendency to close ranks and to form a square when they themselves are concerned.

These inclinations may have positive consequences for the effectiveness of police work, since notions of professional courtesy or colleagueship seem unusually high among police.

When the nature of the policing enterprise requires much joint activity, as in robbery and narcotics enforcement, the impression is received that cooperation is high and genuine. Policemen do not appear to cooperate with one another merely because such is the policy of the chief, but because they sincerely attach a high value to teamwork. For instance, there is a norm among detectives who work together that they will protect each other when a dangerous situation arises. During one investigation, a detective stepped out of the car to question a suspect who became belligerent. The second detective, who had remained overly long in the backseat of the police car, apologized indirectly to his partner by explaining how wrong it had been of him to permit his partner to encounter a suspect alone on the street. He later repeated this explanation privately, in genuine consternation at having committed the breach (and possibly at having been culpable in the presence of an observer). Strong feelings of empathy and cooperation, indeed almost of "clannishness," a term several policemen themselves used to describe the attitude of police toward one another, may be seen in the daily activities of police. Analytically, these feelings can be traced to the elements of danger and shared experiences of hostility in the policeman's role.

Finally, to round out the sketch, policemen are notably conservative, emotionally and politically. If the element of danger in the policeman's role tends to make the policeman suspicious, and therefore emotionally attached to the status quo, a similar consequence may be attributed to the element of authority. The fact that a man is engaged in enforcing a set of rules implies that he also becomes implicated in *affirming* them. Labor disputes provide the commonest example of conditions inclining the policeman to support the status quo. In these situations, the police are necessarily pushed on the side of the defense of property. Their responsibilities thus lead them to see the striking and sometimes angry workers as their enemy and, therefore, to be cool, if not antagonistic, toward the whole conception of labor militancy. If a policeman did not believe in the system of laws he was responsible for enforcing, he would have to go on living in a state of conflicting cognitions, a condition which a number of social psychologists agree is painful.

13

The Police and the Public

by Albert J. Reiss

"Given their small numbers relative to the magnitude of their task, the police regard themselves as the 'thin blue line' maintaining law and order in the community."

—Albert J. Reiss,
"The Police and the Public"
(1971, p. 1)

Local police departments in the United States are part of an organized legal system of criminal justice and part of an organized community. Fundamentally, the police mediate between the community and the legal system. The police are the major representatives of the legal system in their transactions with citizens. They are responsible for enforcing all criminal laws, regardless of the willingness of the citizenry to be policed. Given their small numbers relative to the magnitude of their task, the police regard themselves as the "thin blue line" maintaining law and order in the community.

At the same time that the police enforce the law and keep the peace, they adapt the universal standards of the law to the requirements of citizens and public officials in the community. They do this primarily through their right to exercise discretion in determining whether or not violations of the law have taken place and whether citizens shall be arrested and charged with particular criminal offenses. Moreover, the police department, as an organization, adapts itself to meeting the demands of citizens for them to provide a variety of services, some unrelated to their law-enforcement role. They do so because they are the major emergency arm of the community in times of personal and public crisis.

MAINTAINING THE LEGITIMACY OF POLICE AUTHORITY IN ENCOUNTERS

At law, the police in modern democratic societies such as the United States possess a virtual monopoly of the *legitimate* use of force over civilians.[1] Their legitimate right to intervene in the

Reprinted from *The Police and the Public* (1971), by permission of Yale University Press.

affairs of citizens, to enforce the law and keep the peace, also is unquestioned, provided it is done in legal ways. This monopoly and right to intervention in the affairs of citizens create a number of problems for the society. The principal problems involve maintaining the political neutrality of the police, the use of legal means in police behavior toward citizens, and the assurance that the police will use universal criteria in their discretion to apply the law.

The capacity of the police to maintain legality in their relations with citizens depends to an important degree upon their ability to establish and maintain the legitimacy of their legal authority. This is particularly difficult in a country like the United States where strong institutionalized norms support both aggression and violence on the part of citizens as well as suspicion or hostility toward police intervention.

The legitimacy of police intervention rests in constitutional law and in substantive and procedural law. In recent times much of the controversy over the legitimacy of police intervention has rested in the legality of means as defined in procedural law. Restrictions on search and seizure, interrogation, and privacy, for example, define what constitutes the legitimate use of police authority. Such definitions affect the organization of work within police departments.

A police organization also is confronted with public definitions of the legitimacy of intervention, some of which contravene the organization's legal rights. Illustrations of this disparity between legal and public definitions are evident in the 1960s in such areas as the enforcement of traffic laws and the handling of civil disorders. For example, although they are legal, many Americans object to unmarked police cars and traffic arrests by officers out of uniform. Similarly, command decisions to use plainclothesmen as well as uniformed police to make arrests in situations of public disorder are open to public debate. This practice was challenged when the New York City Police Department used plainclothes detectives to police student disorders on the Columbia University campus.

Nowhere in law enforcement is the problem of establishing legitimacy of authority more difficult, however, than in the day-to-day work of line officers in patrol. An examination of the work role of the patrol officer makes this abundantly clear.

The Work of Patrol

Patrol work usually begins when a patrolman moves onto a social stage with an unknown cast of characters. The settings, members of the cast, and the plot are never quite the same from one time to the next. Yet the patrolman must be prepared to act in all of them.

No other professional operates in a comparable setting. The bureaucratization and professionalization of work ordinarily eliminates this necessity by bringing clients to an office, a clinic, a hospital, or other bureaucratic setting where the client is "not at home." The physician's house call is almost a thing of the past. Now, the patient is usually processed by semi-professionals, clerks, and technicians before the physician sees him. Even social workers have made considerable strides toward bringing clients into offices. So much so, that today the most progressive social-work programs are billed as "detached worker" programs, or "reaching out to the unreachables," where the social worker goes out to the client. Thus, it comes as no surprise that the newer poverty and economic opportunity programs, staffed largely by local community persons, soon succumb to the tenets of bureaucratization and professionalism. The clients are moved to neighborhood or community centers for processing. Even the police, in extending services through community relations programs, end up by opening a neighborhood office for clients. A "walk-in" service, however, usually begins with clients accepting the legitimacy of the enterprise and its personnel. Indeed, the service is designed to serve only those who do.

Patrolmen in a modernized police department are organized around a centralized command where men in cars are dispatched in response to citizen complaints received by telephone. This type of organization sharply contrasts with the traditional department where the foot patrolman (beat officer) moved in a limited territory on foot, knew his turf, and recognized the resident company of actors. Modern patrolmen must move continually from "stage" to "stage" in response to commands from general dispatchers, simply stating: "family trouble," "prowler," "disturbance," "boys in the street," or a "B & E" (breaking and entering). The scenery, the plot, and the actors may change dramatically in the course of a tour of duty.

The central command assigns patrolmen to a precinct commander who in turn assigns them to work in a particular territory or beat. To respond to central commands, each officer assumes the identity of his precinct and beat. He becomes, for instance, a 6–3 or a 9–4. Nominally, the officers on a particular beat are responsible for preventing crimes on their beat and responding to all calls for service within it. In practice, patrolmen are dispatched across the beats of a precinct, and if the beat is located at the perimeter of the precinct, they may be dispatched to another as well. The boundaries of a centralized command and communications system are governed by "who is available for dispatch," not who knows what about an area. The local precinct command tends also to downgrade specific knowledge in assigning patrol in modern departments. Responsive to an almost daily short roster because of furloughs, sick leaves, assignment to special duty, or less than a full complement, precinct captains resort to doubling of beats and reassignment based on prescriptions about generalists rather than specialists. More recently, the implementation of policies for the racial integration of cars on beat patrol has led to frequent rotation of at least some men, particularly those white officers most willing to serve with black officers.

The extent to which men are shifted from beat to beat and from partner to partner is apparent from the assignment of officers in the eight high-crime-rate precincts in Boston, Chicago, and Washington, D.C. Almost daily or weekly rotation of beat assignment was reported by 32 percent of all white and 29 percent of all Negro officers. An additional 14 percent of all white and 16 percent of all Negro officers had spent less than six months on the beat to which they were assigned. The older institution of partners who work closely together on a beat or assignment also appears to be passing; 51 percent of the white and 46 percent of the Negro officers were not assigned regularly with a partner in these precincts, owing partly, in Chicago and Washington, to the racial integration of scout cars. Another 15 percent of the white and 17 percent of the Negro officers had spent less than a month with the partner they had at the time of the observation study. Two-thirds of all the officers, then, were in unstable partner relationships. Knowledge of specific territory and a working partner relationship, while part of the ethos of police work, are hardly operating principles in high-crime-rate precincts.

Even when officers are engaged in preventive patrol responding to their own radar, their sensing devices are generally geared to automobiles; license numbers (hot cars), trouble spots, and suspicious persons or situations. At most, the patrol officer has specific knowledge of places he has been, trouble spots, a few known persons, the best places to pick up "movers" (moving traffic violations), and where the action is in ghetto areas (where the syndicate operates or where one can get most anything). Experience, which cannot be taught in police academies, serves as a guide to situations, plots, and actors. The patrolman comes to know when he is in potential danger even though in practice he may often ignore the signals. He learns to recognize—although, not without error—when a situation demands a quick response, when it is routine, and when, if he is slow to respond, the situation may resolve itself without police intervention.

The order of priority officers gave to dispatched mobilizations was examined in our observational studies of citizen mobilizations of the patrol. Of 4,371 dispatched encounters, the police evaluated 18 percent as requiring an urgent response. They drove rapidly to the scene of the dispatch, often using the flasher or siren to indicate the extreme urgency with which they regarded the dispatch for assistance. However, they treated 73 percent of all dispatches as clearly routine, observing all traffic rules and laws on the way to the scene, even, looking for a reasonable parking space. Six percent of all dispatches were considered so unimportant that police deliberately wasted time in approaching the scene of the dispatch: "It'll probably turn out to be nothing"; "no need to rush"; "we'll never catch him"; "if we go slow, that'll be over before we get there." What is more, in another 2 percent of all dispatches, they treated the matter as lower in priority than some other matter. Half of these higher priorities were purely personal; stopping to buy a pack of cigarettes or pick up dry cleaning, or even selling tickets to the policeman's benefit. For one dispatch in Detroit one evening, we drove to an officer's home more than four miles out of our way to pick up a dog the officer wanted to take to the veterinarian to be "put to sleep so the kids wouldn't know." During the next dispatch we drove more than six miles out of the way to leave the dog with the veterinarian. On the other hand, in about 50 percent of situations, higher priority was given to other police business, such as writing a traffic ticket for a moving violation (usually to fill one's ticket quota) or stopping to respond to the mobilization request of a citizen. In few such cases, of course, does the officer notify the central command that he has shifted priorities.

The social settings or stages where officers will work vary, of course, according to the social composition of the beat. Though the sizes of precincts and beats change with time as does the structure of communities, an officer's operating territory is generally quite variable. He moves across the class structure to a surprising degree, and from commercial to residential, or from "quiet" to "fast" action. A day's work for an officer does not necessarily provide diversity in action, but the weeks and months do. What is a crisis for the citizen and diversion for the outsider, becomes routine for the patrolmen. As already noted, in almost three-fourths of all dispatches, the patrolman moves to the scene in a routine fashion.

The settings in which encounters between the police and citizens takes place are as varied as the locations in any community. Clearly some settings are more common than others for particular types of offenses. To cite the obvious, most traffic violations occur on public streets, particularly moving violations, even though some standing violations occur on private property. As Stinchcombe shows, patterns of offenses known to the police are generally related to institutions of privacy in American society—the degree to which police can penetrate private places.[2] Citizen initiative in calling the police—the complaint—is the major legitimate avenue of the police to private places.

Unfortunately no official statistics are kept for the mobilization of the police to locations for all types of complaints or for offenses known to the police. The information in Table 1 for selected offenses in Seattle, Washington shows the most common setting is the private dwelling (37 percent of all locations), followed by open places (29 percent), and commercial houses (24 percent). Relative to all Seattle locations, commercial houses are overrepresented in these mobilizations of the police.

While the type of crime varies considerably by location, a quick examination of locations to which officers are mobilized will also show that, for any given location such as a street, a business, or a dwelling unit, there is an extremely high probability that an officer, upon arrival, will be confronted by such *routine* matters as offenses against property; larceny, burglary, or destruction of property. In officers' language, such crimes are "cold." The burglary is not in progress; all the patrolman can do is take a report and turn it over to the detectives for investigation. If arrests are eventually to be made, they will be made by the investigating detectives, or the patrolman may later pick up the offender in some other crime situation.

Table 1 Percentage Distributions for Offenses Reported to the Police by Type of Location for Offense: Selected Offenses for Seattle, Washington, 1965

Location of incident	Homicide	Rape and attempt to rape	Robbery	Aggravated assault	Simple assault	Theft from person	Other larcenies	Burglary	Arson	Destruction of property	Total percentage	Total number
Percentage of offenses reported for each type of location												
Open places (streets, etc.)	*	*	4	2	6	2	69	—	*	17	100	6,495
Offices	—	—	2	*	2	—	26	61	—	9	100	675
Commercial houses	*	*	2	1	3	1	54	31	*	8	100	5,311
Public buildings	*	*	1	1	7	1	79	4	*	6	99	776
Semipublic buildings	*	—	*	*	2	*	50	26	1	19	98	876
Dwelling units	*	1	1	2	9	*	43	31	1	12	100	8,134
Total percentage	*	*	2	2	6	1	54	21	*	13	99	—
Total number	24	85	473	374	1,395	231	12,031	4,755	96	2,803	—	22,267
Percentage of locations for each type of offense reported												
Open places (streets, etc.)	12	22	53	29	30	55	37	—	16	39	29	
Offices	—	—	2	*	1	—	1	9	—	2	3	
Commercial houses	17	13	28	16	12	24	24	33	9	15	24	
Public buildings	8	2	2	2	4	5	5	*	2	2	3	
Semipublic buildings	4	—	*	1	1	1	4	5	10	6	4	
Dwelling units	59	63	15	52	52	15	29	53	63	36	37	
Total percentage	100	100	100	100	100	100	100	100	100	100	100	

*Less than 0.5 percent

Similarly, for offenses against the person, information is often general rather than specific. An officer only has cues to work by, such as "disturbance at," "family trouble," or "see a woman at." Even given specific information such as "man with a gun" or "robbery in progress," the scene is far from complete. The basic problem here is that the processing of information depends on relatively limited forms of communication. A citizen telephones the department and an officer must determine whether the situation warrants his making a discretionary decision to dispatch a car. However, the quantity and quality of the information obtained depends on many factors: the skill of the officer in seeking and obtaining information, the amount of time he can spend getting the information, the emotional state of the citizen and his linguistic skills in providing information. In other words, the information an officer must act upon may not only be sketchy, but also misleading.

Our observational studies of police activity in high-crime-rate areas of three cities show that 87 percent of all patrol mobilizations were initiated by citizens. Officers initiated (both in the field and on view) only 13 percent. Thus, it becomes apparent that citizens exercise considerable control over police patrol work through their discretionary decisions to call the police. This is very important in terms of the legitimacy of police authority. When police enter a social setting, it is usually based on the assumption that at least one citizen believes the police have both a legitimate right and an obligation to enter that situation. This does not mean that the citizen mobilizer is always present in the situation to which the officer is called, but it does mean that almost nine out of ten times, the patrol officer enters a situation on citizen initiative.

The telephone is the principal means of communication whereby citizens mobilize the police; it is readily available to most citizens and is the fastest way of exchanging information. Of the 87 percent of police mobilizations initiated by citizens, 87 percent originated with a telephone call, 6 percent through citizen contact with the police at work in the field (e.g., flagging down a scout car), and 7 percent with walk-ins at precinct stations or headquarters. We examined all calls (some 4,000) received at the central communications center of the Chicago Police Department on June 20, 1965, in an effort to determine the content of the information system that originates with a citizen telephone call to the communications center of modern police departments. Table 2 shows the results based on calls to the Town Hall and Fillmore precincts. The information summarized is that which was available to the dispatcher and was usually communicated to the patrolmen in the scout car dispatched to the location of the incident.

The dispatcher possesses somewhat more information about location than he communicates. For example, he knows that some dispatches to a residential unit in Table 2 are to a complainant's own residence while others are not. Nineteen percent of all calls concerned the caller's own dwelling units or premises, but 7 percent were complaints about some other unit within his building and 1 percent was for some other dwelling unit. These calls, 27 percent of all calls, were usually simply dispatches to a residential address so far as the patrolman was concerned. Often, the patrolman does not even know whether the complainant will be present when he arrives. The modal call for June 20 reported an incident in a street or block near the caller, a type of incident common during the summer season. However, in some of these situations, the transactions ultimately transpired within a dwelling unit, since the action moved there before, at the time of, or following the arrival of the scout car. Another 17 percent of calls originated from businesses or quasi-public places such as schools, 4 percent from medical settings, and 8 percent in special street locations such as those of automobile accidents. In 7 percent of all calls, the dispatcher only secured an address, thereby leaving the officer with the minimum amount of information. To be sure, even when the dispatcher possesses information on the type of location, he may not communicate it to patrol. That often lies within his discretion and a dispatch stating the general nature of an incident and the address is considered sufficient.

Table 2 Citizen Calls to Communications Center of Chicago Police Department on June 20, 1965, by Mobilization Location: Town Hall and Fillmore Precincts

Mobilization location designated by citizen's call	Town Hall	Fillmore	Total
Callers dwelling or premises	19	20	19
Caller building but not his dwelling	7	7	7
Dwelling unit of person other than caller	1	1	1
Street or block near caller	38	48	44
Commercial or quasi-public place near caller	18	16	17
Medical setting	6	2	4
Public places at distance from caller, e.g., while driving past	11	6	8
Total percentage	100	100	100
Total number	262	366	628

A communications center screens calls, so that dispatches will not be sent out in all instances. For all dispatches the center operates on the presumption that the information is, in all probability, valid. However, experience indicates that this is not always the case. The Chicago Police Department has found that a substantial proportion of anonymous calls turn out to be fruitless; yet the payoff on many anonymous tips or calls is sufficient in official judgment to warrant investigation. Other reasons why calls may not actually be investigated include matters ranging from errors in communication to situations that change before the police arrive.

Of the dispatches to mobile patrol where one of our observers was present, 30 percent of the citizen initiated incidents led to no police-citizen interaction whatsoever. In many such dispatches it was as difficult for our observers to understand why this was so as it was for the police. Most of these, however, were not criminal incidents, at least as defined by the original dispatch. They included situations in which it was unlikely that a citizen would be present: ringing burglar alarms, parking violations, abandoned cars, and suspicious situations (a car parked with the motor running).

Other cases in which the citizens who made the complaint as well as the citizens reported as offending could not be expected to be present when the police arrived include suspicious persons, or rowdy boys in the street and other noise disturbances in all of which the caller may have already scared off the offenders by threatening to call the police. Still other calls may hinge on unfounded presumptions: calls about prowlers (who may never have been there), or shootings that may not have occurred, or a suspected fire.

For many such cases, when the police arrive and see no one, they may only take a quick look around and leave. When police officers are dispatched to situations where there are no citizens to offer guidelines for action, they do very little. For 1 in 5 such incidents, they do almost nothing, even though our observers thought some investigation could have been undertaken. The officers could have gotten out of the car and looked around, for example, but they did not.

To understand this, one must bear in mind that, for policemen, police work is, after all, work. Much that police officers do not do on their routine tour of duty can be easily explained by simple platitude. Like all jobs, police work includes restriction of output and avoidance of work that cannot be easily assessed or observed. Police, not unlike factory workers, as Collins, Dalton, and Roy, among others, have consistently noted,[3] avoid work as well as do work.

A sizeable proportion of citizen mobilizations of the police are to public places, such as streets, and to quasi-public places, such as businesses and schools (as the data in Tables 1 and 2 show). However, our observations of citizen initiated encounters in eight high-crime-rate areas of Boston, Chicago, and Washington, D.C., indicate that a much higher proportion of calls investigated occur in private places, where citizens are more likely to be present, than in public or semipublic places:

Specific Setting of Encounter	Percentage of All Encounters
Enclosed private place: within dwelling	36
Open private place: porch, yard, premises	34
Semiprivate place: within business	7
Semiprivate place: all other	5
Open public place	18

Indeed, 70 percent of citizen initiated encounters, where a citizen was present when the police arrived, occurred within or about a private place.[4]

One reason for this is that in citizen calls about public places, complainants, or other citizens are less likely to be around when the police arrive than they are in calls about private places. But, there is also a difference in the nature of calls for service in high-crime-rate areas. Despite the high rate of crimes against persons in public places and against businesses in these areas, such crimes comprise less than one-third of all police business in ghetto areas. Citizens in high-crime-rate areas mobilize the police for a large variety of services—sick calls, domestic crises, and disputes of all kinds. The police will not treat most of these calls as criminal matters.

As Table 3 shows, within high-crime-rate areas, a majority of all incidents, other than traffic, took place within or near private places. And, no more than about one-fifth of any type of encounter, other than those involving complaints, took place in an open public setting. Not unexpectedly, however, noncriminal disputes, more than any other type of incident, were mediated or arbitrated in private rather than public places. Even felonies and misdemeanors were primarily breaches of private order. Quite clearly, in the lowest socio-economic areas, citizens get in touch with and have contact with the police primarily about problems that arise within or near their households. Police dealings with lower socio-economic groups involve, for the most part, preserving the integrity of private order.

Police officers must be prepared to deal with varying numbers of people in these different social settings. There may be large numbers in picket lines, sit-ins, unruly crowds or mob, drivers in traffic, or audiences at mass events. Though superficially their role is to preserve the peace by coping with any individuals in the large aggregation who violate laws, they must be prepared to restore order as well. The major work emphasis in such settings is on team work, and, in restoring or maintaining public order, their work is generally paramilitary.

Most of the time, however, officers in patrol work are in two-man teams or alone. They must be prepared to work primarily with more than one individual, particularly in high-crime-rate areas of our larger cities. In only one-fourth of police patrol encounters in Table 4 were the police dealing with a single citizen. The modal police encounter includes more citizens than officers. Assuming, typically, one or two officers in a police encounter with citizens, 54 percent of the observed encounters included three or more citizens and 27 percent, five or more.

Comparing police encounters in high-crime-rate Negro areas with those in white areas, encounters with white citizens were more likely to include a smaller number of citizens. While

Table 3 Percentage of Citizen Initiated Encounters According to the General Type of Incident, by Specific Setting of Encounter

Specific setting of encounter	General type of incident									
	Felony	Misdemeanor	Traffic violation	Juvenile trouble	Suspicious person or situation	Noncriminal dispute	Service	Unfounded	Other	All incidents
Enclosed private place: within dwelling	43	35	6	16	38	55	37	27	47	36
Open private place: porch, yard, etc.	27	33	37	53	37	31	35	34	23	34
Semipublic place: within business	8	10	1	6	7	7	3	14	9	7
Semipublic place: other	5	4	4	3	1	*	10	3	2	5
Open public place	17	18	52	22	16	7	14	21	19	18
Total percentage	100	100	100	100	99	100	99	99	100	100
Total number	(554)	(637)	(154)	(346)	(73)	(467)	(553)	(157)	(47)	(2,988)

*0.5 percent or less

Table 4   Percentage Distribution by Number of Citizens Present in Encounters with the Police, by Race of Citizen and Types of Mobilization of the Police

Race of citizen*	Type of mobilization	Total number of encounters	Total percentage	Number of citizens in encounter (as percentage of total)				
				1	2	3	4	5 or more
White and Negro†	Dispatch	3,010	100	22	22	16	12	28
	On-view	614	100	38	20	14	7	21
	Citizen-in-field	202	100	27	22	20	9	22
	All mobilizations	3,826	100	25	21	16	1	27
White	Dispatch	1,351	100	27	24	16	11	22
	On-view	262	100	44	22	12	7	15
	Citizen-in field	104	100	32	25	19	6	18
	All-white	1,717	100	30	24	15	10	21
Negro	Dispatch	1,540	100	20	22	16	13	29
	On-view	315	100	39	17	16	6	22
	Citizen-in-field	89	100	20	20	19	16	25
	All-Negro	1,944	100	23	21	16	12	28

*Race data are lacking for 165 encounters.
†Excluded are 43 encounters where both white and Negro citizens were present as participants (excluding by-standers).

30 percent of all encounters with whites were with a lone citizen, a lone Negro citizen was encountered in only 23 percent of patrol mobilizations. Five or more Negro citizens were present in 28 percent of police encounters with Negroes as compared with 21 percent of those for whites. Officers in predominantly Negro areas then are faced with potentially greater problems of control solely by reason of larger number of citizens.

Police officers must deal not only with the actors on stage, but often with an audience as well. This audience may be comprised of members of a family, strangers in the street, or a mob. The officers must assess the audience as well as the actors, since the audience may have an important effect on police work. Are the members cooperative or hostile? Can they supply information? How can they be utilized in the situation? The police must be concerned with the audience's acceptance of them as well as with their own judgment and control of that audience.

For our studies, we have chosen five major types of citizen roles that participate in police situations. The principal actors are generally complainants, suspects, and offenders. Minor roles may be played by informants about the central participants, the action, or the situation, or by observer-by-standers, who can shift to more active participatory roles as situations change. For dispatched encounters, citizens stand as the major complainants; in on-view encounters, officers fulfill this role. Many dispatches include only complainants, as when the police are called about crimes that have already occurred. When a situation is in progress at the time the officers arrive, it is fairly likely it will include complainants and suspects or offenders. Of the 72 percent of all encounters that included citizens, offenders or suspects were present in 39 percent.

This characterization of the social stages, the participants, and even of the action for all police work in an area fails to capture the shifts that may occur for a policeman in his tour of duty. No tour of duty is typical except in the sense that *the modal tour of duty does not involve an arrest* of any person, and traffic citations may be written on many such tours depending upon whether or not the department has a quota system of ticket citations for patrol. This is not to say that arrests could not have been made on many tours of duty, but often they are not because the officer exercises his discretion not to make such arrests.

NOTES

1. David J. Bordua and Albert J. Reiss, Jr., "Command, Control, and Charisma: Reflections on Police Bureaucracy," *The American Journal of Sociology* 72 (July 1966): 68–70; Albert J. Reiss, Jr., and David J. Bordua, "Organization and Environment; a Perspective on the Police," in David J. Bordua, ed., *The Police: Six Sociological Essays* (New York: John Wiley, 1967), pp. 28–40.

2. Arthur Stinchcombe, "Institutions of Privacy in the Determination of Police Administrative Practice," *the American Journal of Sociology* 69 (September 1963): 150–60.

3. Orville Collins, Melville Dalton, and Donald Roy, "Restriction of Output and Social Cleavage in Industry," *Applied Anthropoligy* 5 (Summer 1946): 1–14.

4. See Donald J. Black, "Police Encounters and Social Organization: An Observation Study" (Ph.D. diss., University of Michigan, 1968), chaps. 2 and 3.

14

The Kansas City Preventive Patrol Experiment: A Summary Report

by George L. Kelling, Tony Pate, Duane Dieckman, and Charles E. Brown

"It makes about as much sense to have police patrol routinely in cars to fight crime as it does to have firemen patrol routinely in fire trucks to fight fire."

—Carl Klockars,
(1983, p. 130)

Ever since the creation of a patrolling force in thirteenth-century Hangchow, preventive patrol by uniformed personnel has been a primary function of policing. In twentieth-century America, about $2 billion is spent each year for the maintenance and operation of uniformed and often superbly equipped patrol forces. Police themselves, the general public, and elected officials have always believed that the presence or potential presence of police officers on patrol severely inhibits criminal activity.

One of the principal police spokesmen for this view was the late O. W. Wilson, former chief of the Chicago Police Department and a prominent academic theorist on police issues. As Wilson once put it, "Patrol is an indispensable service that plays a leading role in the accomplishment of the police purpose. It is the only form of police service that directly attempts to eliminate opportunity for misconduct." Wilson believed that by creating the impression of police omnipresence, patrol convinced most potential offenders that opportunities for successful misconduct did not exist.

From *The Kansas City Preventive Patrol Experiment* (pp. 20-45) by G. L. Kelling, et al., 1974, Washington, DC: Police Foundation.

To the present day, Wilson's has been the prevailing view. While modern technology, through the creation of new methods of transportation, surveillance, and communications, has added vastly to the tools of patrol, and while there have been refinements in patrol strategies based upon advanced probability formulas and other computerized methods, the general principle has remained the same. Today's police recruits, like virtually all those before them, learn from both teacher and textbook that patrol is the "backbone" of police work.

No less than the police themselves, the general public has been convinced that routine preventive patrol is an essential element of effective policing. As the International City Management Association has pointed out, "For the greatest number of persons, deterrence through ever-present police patrol, coupled with the prospect of speedy police action once a report is received, appears important to crime control." Thus, in the face of spiraling crime rates, the most common answer urged by public officials and citizens alike has been to increase patrol forces and get more police officers "on the street." The assumption is that increased displays of police presence are vitally necessary in the face of increased criminal activity. Recently, citizens in troubled neighborhoods have themselves resorted to civilian versions of patrol.

It was in this context that the Kansas City, Missouri, Police Department, under a grant from the Police Foundation, undertook in 1972 the most comprehensive experiment ever conducted to analyze the effectiveness of routine preventive patrol.

DESCRIPTION OF THE PREVENTIVE PATROL EXPERIMENT

The impetus for an experiment in preventive patrol came from within the Kansas City Police Department in 1971. While this may be surprising to some, the fact is that by that year the Kansas City department had already experienced more than a decade of innovation and improvement in its operations and working climate and had pined for a reputation as one of the nation's more progressive police departments.

Within the South Patrol Division's 24-beat area, nine beats were eliminated from consideration for the experiment as unrepresentative of the city's socioeconomic composition. The remaining 15-beat, 32-square mile experimental area encompassed a commercial-residential mixture, with a 1970 resident population of 148,395 persons and a density of 4,542 persons per square mile (significantly greater than that for Kansas City as a whole, which in 1970 with only 1,604 persons per square mile was 45th in the nation). Racially, the beats within this area ranged from 78 percent black to 99 percent white. Median family income of residents ranged from a low of $7,320 for one beat to a high of $15,964 for another. On the average, residents of the experimental area tended to have been in their homes from 6.6 to 10.9 years.

Police officers assigned to the experimental area were those who had been patrolling it prior to the experiment and tended to be white, relatively young, and somewhat new to the police department. In a sample of 101 officers in the experimental area taken across all three shifts, 9.9 percent of the officers were black, the average age of the officers was 27 years, and average time on the force was 3.2 years.

The 15 beats in the experimental area were computer matched on the basis of crime data, number of calls for service, ethnic composition, median income and transiency of population into five groups of three each. Within each group, one beat was designated reactive, one control, and one proactive. In the five reactive beats, there was no preventive patrol as such. Police vehicles assigned these beats entered them only in response to calls for service. Their non-committed time (when not answering calls) was spent patrolling the boundaries of the reactive beats or patrolling in adjacent proactive beats. While police availability was closely maintained, police visibility was, in effect, withdrawn (except when police vehicles were seen while answering calls for service).

In the five control beats, the usual level of patrol was maintained at one car per beat. In the five proactive beats, the department increased police patrol visibility by two to three times its usual level both by the assignment of marked police vehicles to these beats and the presence of units from adjacent reactive beats.

Other than the restrictions placed upon officers in reactive beats (respond only to calls for service and patrol only the perimeter of the beat or in an adjacent proactive beat), no special instructions were given to police officers in the experimental area. Officers in control and proactive beats were to conduct preventive patrol as they normally would.

EXPERIMENTAL FINDINGS

The essential finding of the preventive patrol experiment is that decreasing or increasing routine preventive patrol within the range tested in this experiment had no effect on crime, citizen fear of crime, community attitudes toward the police on the delivery of police service, police response time, or traffic accidents.

EFFECTS ON CRIME, REPORTING, AND ARRESTS

Finding 1: Victimization

The Victimization Study found no statistically significant differences in crime in any of the 69 comparisons made between reactive, control, and proactive beats.

This finding would be expected for such categories as rape, homicide, and common or aggravated assault. For one thing, these are typically impulsive crimes, usually taking place between persons known to each other. Furthermore, they most often take place inside a building, out of sight of an officer on routine preventive patrol. The spontaneity and lack of high visibility of these crimes, therefore, make it unlikely that they would be much affected by variations in the level of preventive patrol.

Given traditional beliefs about patrol, however, it is surprising that statistically significant differences did not occur in such crimes as commercial burglaries, auto theft, and robberies.

Nonetheless, as measured by the victimization survey, these crimes were not significantly affected by changes in the level of routine preventive patrol.

Finding 2: Departmental Reported Crime

Departmental reported crimes showed only one statistically significant difference among 51 comparisons drawn between reactive, control, and proactive beats.

Statistical significance occurred only in the category of "other sex crimes." This category, separate from "rape," includes such offenses as molestation and exhibitionism. Since this category is not traditionally considered to be responsive to routine preventive patrol, however, it appears likely that this instance of significance was a statistically random occurrence.

Finding 3: Rates of Reporting Crime

Crimes that citizens and businessmen said they reported to the police showed statistical significant differences between reactive, control, and proactive beats in only five of 48 comparisons, and these differences showed no consistent pattern.

Of the five instances of statistical significance, three involved vandalism and two residence burglary. But where statistical significance was found, no consistent pattern emerged. On two occasions, the change was greater in the control beats, on two occasions greater in the proactive beats, and once it was greater in the reactive beats. Given the low number of statistically significant findings combined with a lack of consistent direction, the conclusion is that rates of reporting crimes by businessmen and citizens were unaffected by the experimental changes in levels of patrol.

Finding 4: Arrest Patterns

Police arrests showed no statistically significant differences in the 27 comparisons made between reactive, control, and proactive beats.

While arrest totals for 16 categories of crime were determined, it will be noted that in seven categories—common assault, larceny-purse snatch, homicide, nonresidence burglary, auto theft, larceny-auto accessory, and larceny-bicycle—either the number of arrests was too small to allow for statistical analysis or the preexperimental pattern of arrests was so distorted that statistical significance could not be determined. On the basis of the comparisons that could be made, however, the conclusion is that arrest rates were not significantly affected by changes in the level of patrol.

EFFECTS ON COMMUNITY ATTITUDES

Citizen Fear of Crime

The experiment measured community attitudes toward many aspects of crime and police performance to determine whether varying levels of routine preventive patrol—reactive, control, proactive—had any significant effect upon these attitudes. Previous investigators have shown that citizens can recognize, or at least sense, changes in levels of service or innovations in policing.

Thus, through the Community and Commercial Surveys which provided the victimization information used in the previous section of this summary, citizen attitudes toward crime and police were also measured before and after the experiment.

The first attitude measured was citizen fear of crime, determined by (1) a series of questions in the Community Survey designed to probe levels of fear; (2) a series of questions in the protective and security measures taken by citizens; and (3) questions in the Commercial Survey about protective and security measures used by businessmen at their place of business.

Finding 5: Citizen Fear of Crime

Citizen fear of crime was not significantly affected by changes in the level of routine preventive patrol.

In the Community Survey, citizen estimates of neighborhood safety and perceptions of violent crimes were obtained. Citizens were then asked what they thought the probability was that they might be involved in various types of crime, including robbery, assault, rape, burglary, and auto theft.

Of the 60 comparisons made between experimental areas, statistical significance was found in only five cases. Three involved the probability of being raped, one the probability of being robbed, and one the probability of being assaulted. The change in the level of fear was greater in reactive beats four times and greater in proactive beats once.

Yet when statistical significance is found, the patterns are inconsistent. For example, all cases in which the changes in the reactive beats are significantly higher than in other beats are found in the repeated sample. These findings are not confirmed by the nonrepeated sample, however. The one area in which control registered the higher change occurs in the nonrepeated sample, but this is not confirmed by the repeated sample.

The findings thus lead to the conclusion that citizen fear is not affected by differences in the level of routine preventive patrol.

Finding 6: Protective Measures (Citizens)

Protective and security measures taken by citizens against the possibility of being involved in crime were not significantly affected by variations in the level of routine preventive patrol.

The questions asked of citizens in the Community Survey on this subject dealt with the installation of such devices as bars, alarms, locks and lighting, the keeping of various types of weapons or dogs for protection, and the taking of certain actions, such as staying inside, as preventive measures.

Here, 84 comparisons were made between experimental areas, with statistical significance occurring 11 times. The significance occurred most often (six times) in those beats where preventive patrol had not changed, that is, in control beats. The change in the reactive beats showed significance three times, and in the proactive beats twice. There is no apparent explanation for the fact that the use of protective measures supposedly increased in the control beat relative to the other two conditions. For the most part, the findings are inconsistent and occur either in the nonrepeated sample or the repeated sample but never uniformly in both.

Thus, as measured by the use of protective and security measures, experimental preventive patrol conditions did not significantly affect citizen fear of crime.

Finding 7: Protective Measures (Businesses)

Protective and security measures taken by businesses in the experimental area to protect offices or other places of business did not show significant differences due to changes in the level of routine preventive patrol.

In the Commercial Survey, businessmen were asked such questions as whether they had installed alarm systems or reinforcing devices such as bars over windows, whether they had hired guards, or whether they kept watchdogs or firearms in their places of business.

All told, 21 comparisons were made and statistical significance was found once, where the change in the control beats was the greater as compared with the reactive beats.

Because this was a telephone survey, however, some problems with the findings were evident. Briefly, some businessmen were reluctant to talk about protective measures over the phone to persons unknown to them. This is discussed more fully in the technical report.

The conclusion remains, however, that preventive patrol variations seem to have little effect on fear of crime as indicated by protective measures taken by commercial establishments.

Citizen Attitudes Towards Police

In addition to investigating citizen fear of crime and criminals, the preventive patrol experiment delved into citizen attitudes toward the police. Residents in the experimental area were asked, for instance, about the need for more police officers, about variations in patrol, police officer reputations and effectiveness, police treatment of citizens, and about their satisfaction with police service.

The attitudes of businessmen toward police were studied in the course of the preventive patrol experiment for a variety of reasons. One was simply that businessmen's attitudes have seldom been studied in the past, although these people are often affected by crime in ways more crucial to their survival than are citizens in general. It is not only the businessman's personal comfort and safety that may be involved, but also the ability to remain in business that may be affected by crime. At the same time, businessmen are often influential in their communities. For these reasons, assessing their attitudes is often crucial to the development of new policing programs. Therefore, businessmen were asked similar questions about police effectiveness, treatment of citizens, and so forth.

While the study of such attitudes is valuable in obtaining the impressions of a significant cross section of the community, most of the citizens and businessmen interviewed were unlikely to have experienced recent actual contact with the police. Thus, another part of the preventive patrol experiment focused on determining citizen responses to actual encounters with police officers. To determine such responses, citizens themselves, the police with whom they came in contact, and trained observers were all asked to complete reports on the encounter. Citizens were interviewed as soon as possible after the incident. Separate questionnaires were used, depending on whether the encounter was initiated by an officer or by a citizen.

Finally, a fourth measure was used to determine citizen attitudes. Here, in what has been given the title Police-Citizen Transactions, the trained observers focused on the outcome of police-citizen interactions in terms of the patrol assignment of the officer involved, that is, reactive, control, or proactive.

The next findings deal with citizen attitudes toward police, businessmen's attitudes toward police, police-citizen encounters initiated either by citizens (calls for service) or police (traffic arrests, suspect apprehension, etc.), and finally police-citizen transactions.

Finding 8: Citizen Attitudes Toward Police

Citizen attitudes toward police were not significantly affected by alterations in the level of preventive patrol.

A large number of questions in the Community Survey were designed to measure citizen attitudes toward the police. As a result, more comparisons were made here than in other cases and more instances of statistical significance were found. Altogether, 111 comparisons were made and statistical significance occurred 16 times. Items with significant differences included the need for more police officers in the city, the reputation of police officers, citizens' respect for police, police effectiveness, harassment, and change in neighborhood police officers.

Of the 16 instances of significance, the change in reactive beats was greater five times, in control beats ten times, and in proactive beats once, demonstrating no consistent pattern of statistical significance. The indication is that there was little correlation between level of patrol and citizen attitudes.

Finding 9: Businessmen's Attitudes Toward Police

Businessmen's attitudes toward police officers were not significantly affected by changes in the level of routine preventive patrol.

Like citizens in the Community Survey, businessmen in the Commercial Survey were asked about their attitudes toward police. Some of the questions in the Commercial Survey were similar to those in the Community Survey and some specially selected with regard to businessmen's interests.

In all, 48 comparisons were made to measure differences in businessmen's attitudes, but no statistically significant differences were found or even approached. The clear indication here is that variations in the level of preventive patrol have no effect on businessmen's attitudes.

Finding 10: Police-Citizen Encounters

Citizen attitudes toward police officers encountered through the initiative of either the citizen or the officer were not significantly affected by changes in patrol level.

Citizen attitudes were measured by both questions asked of citizens themselves and observations of trained observers. Citizens and observers alike were asked about such items as response time, characteristics of the encounter, the attitude and demeanor of officers in the encounter, and citizen satisfaction. Observers in officer-initiated encounters also recorded things not likely to be noted by citizens, including the number of officers and police vehicles present.

Including both citizen-initiated and officer-initiated encounters, a total of 63 comparisons were made and no statistically significant differences were found.

Finding 11: Police-Citizen Transactions

The behavior of police officers toward citizens was not significantly affected by the officers' assignment to a reactive, control, or proactive beat.

The finding is distinct from the previous finding in that the focus here is upon the police-citizen interaction in terms of the beat assignment of the officer rather than on the location of the contact. (Many police contacts with citizens take place outside of the officer's beat.) Data were recorded by participant observers riding with the officers. In all, 18 comparisons were made between experimental areas, and no statistically significant differences were found.

OTHER EFFECTS

Experimental Findings in Regard to Police Response Time

The time it takes police officers to respond to a citizen call for assistance is usually considered an important measure of patrol effectiveness. The general principle is that the lower the response time, the more efficiently the police are doing their job.

Response time was studied to see if experimental conditions would have any effect on the amount of time taken by police in answering citizen calls for service. Before the experiment began, the hypothesis was that experimental conditions would affect response time, particularly in the proactive beats. It was believed that since more officers were assigned to proactive beats, response time would be significantly reduced in those beats.

Finding 12: Response Time

The amount of time taken by police in answering calls for service was not significantly affected by variations in the level of routine preventive patrol.

To obtain this finding, data were gathered on such matters as distance from police car to scene of incident, mean time from receipt of calls to start of call, mean time from receipt of call to arrival at scene, and observer's estimate of patrol car speed. Citizen estimates of time and satisfaction were also measured.

In the area of response time, a total of 42 comparisons were made between patrol conditions. Statistical significance occurred only once: in the number of officers present at the scene of incidents in the reactive beats. The reason for this is unclear, but it can be theorized that police officers were exhibiting their concern for the safety of fellow officers and citizens in reactive beats.

While variations in the level of patrol did not significantly affect police response time, the Kansas City findings suggest that more research is necessary. It appears that response time is not only the result of rate of speed and distance, but also reflects the attitude of the officers involved and possibly other variables not investigated in this study.

CONCLUSIONS

The initial impetus behind the Kansas City preventive patrol experiment was the issue of time and staff resources. When the South Patrol Task Force began its deliberations, the concern was that any serious attempt to deal with priority problems would be confounded by the need to maintain established levels of routine patrol. Thus, in addition to testing the effect of various patrol strategies on such factors as crime, citizen fear and satisfaction, and response time, the experiment equally addressed the question of whether adequate time can be channeled to the development testing and evaluation of new approaches to patrol.

From the beginning phases of this experiment, the evaluators formed hypotheses based upon certain assumptions. One primary assumption was that the police, as an institutionalized mechanism of social control, are seriously limited in their ability to both prevent crime and apprehend offenders once crimes have been committed. The reasons for these limitations are many and complex. But they include the very nature of the crime problem itself, the limits a democratic society places upon its police, the limited amount of resources available for crime prevention, and complexities within the entire criminal justice system. As a result of these limitations, many have rightly suggested that we must now begin revising our expectations as to the police role in society.

15

The LAPD is Treated to a Business Analysis and It Comes Up Short

by Jeff Bailey

"As a group they're (the police) the most reluctanat to change I've ever seen."

—Art Maddox,
from *The LAPD is Treated to a Business
Analaysis and It Comes Up Short,*
By Jeff Bailey
(1996)

LOS ANGELES—Glorified in television dramas of years ago, the Los Angeles Police Department has more recently been reviled for the videotaped beating of Rodney King and ridiculed for its handling of evidence in the O.J. Simpson case.

Now, city leaders are looking at the LAPD in a new light: as if it were a business. A swarm of management consultants has been set loose on the $1 billion-a-year department in recent months, picking it apart the way they would a major service or manufacturing company. Their findings suggest the LAPD is far from a return to glory.

Officers who literally couldn't shoot straight, known internally as the "chronic 31," repeatedly failed firing-range tests yet were deployed as patrol officers. Some police-academy graduates aren't any good at using a radio because, the LAPD being short of radios, they were taught by pretending with wooden blocks. Some routine tasks—exchanging shotguns between shifts, scheduling the patrol force—are done in such outdated ways that, added together, they squander the services of hundreds of officers at a time when the crime-weary city is desperate to put more policing power on the streets.

Source: Wall Street Journal, June 11, 1996, pp. A1 and A8. Reprinted by permission of *The Wall Street Journal,* © 1996 Dow Jones & Company, Inc. All rights reserved worldwide.

CALL WAITING

"We were amazed at the lack of discipline and analysis," said Blue Marble Partners, one of the consulting firms called in to assess the LAPD, in its report.

Trying to figure out why the answering of 911 calls is so slow that nearly a quarter of callers hang up, LAPD officials couldn't even tell Blue Marble for sure how many people work in the operation. Says Gregory A. Zikos, a partner at the Torrance, Calif., consulting firm, "They have shortcomings in all of the areas of critical importance."

The LAPD says its training isn't deficient. It says the "chronic 31" have now all passed their shooting tests and that it is working on radio weaknesses.

The consultants' findings are adding to the turmoil at the nation's third-largest police force, after New York and Chicago. An unhappy Mayor Richard J. Riordan wants to get rid of Police Chief Willie Williams. The city council wants to slow down a four-year, 3,000-officer expansion program that is the centerpiece of the Republican mayor's 1977 reelection plan. And veteran police brass beneath Chief Williams, already shellshocked from five years of criticism following the King beating, the 1992 riots and the Simpson trial, seem at times frozen by all the conflicting advice and orders they are getting.

'RELUCTANT TO CHANGE'

"It's a lot of studies and a lot of process," Deputy Chief David J. Gascon says. "A lot of it is probably helpful, but at some point outsiders have to get out of the way and let us try to manage."

Can they? "As a group, they're the most reluctant to change I've ever seen," says Art Mattox, a Xerox Corp. executive who serves on the civilian Police Commission that oversees the department.

The police here long operated as a bureaucratic fortress under a series of chiefs who were all but immune to criticism because they couldn't be fired. A 1981 city audit found some of the same LAPD management weaknesses turning up today. Then-chief Daryl F. Gates responded by hurling a copy of the audit to the floor and stomping on it, calling it "harassment." It was the last city audit.

Then came the King videotape. A year later, a poor early response to the riots further undermined public confidence in the department. Mr. Gates quit under pressure. Sweeping examinations of police violence and racism began, and brutality complaints declined sharply.

CALLING THE CONSULTANTS

But once the scrutiny got started, it spread to nearly every aspect of the LAPD. Eager to better understand and oversee their police, elected officials hired more than a dozen consulting firms. The result has been a rare top-to-bottom evaluation of a major law-enforcement agency's labor productivity and management methods.

As consultants' reports piled up, exposing many inefficiencies, the LAPD's own statistics began to suggest a state of disarray. For instance, Mayor Riordan's expansion—raising the number of police officers to about 11,000 by 1997 from about 8,000 in 1993—was meant to put more officers on the street; but by last October, only 24 more cops were on patrol, while the ranks of detectives—already flush, according to critics—had swelled by 152.

The mayor became incensed, and since then most of the new officers have gone to patrol. But in March, LAPD figures showed that two key measures of effectiveness, the numbers of arrests and of traffic citations, had fallen. Arrests for the June 30, 1995, fiscal year were off 35% from a 1991 peak, and citations were down 38%.

With the police expansion forcing painful budget cuts elsewhere, the mayor was further angered. "We've given them the tools to succeed," he says. "The public has a right to an explanation."

Chief Williams's spokesman, Commander Tim McBride; says arrests fell because crime rates were lower and that ticket-writing fell because traffic cops were shifted to other duties. But he acknowledges a widespread belief within the department: The 1993 jailing of two officers involved in the King beating sapped some officers' enthusiasm for their job.

"There's not less crime," says Bill Hall, a lieutenant in robbery and homicide. "There's less *reported* crime." Patrol officers, he says, "are just driving around." Says Commander McBride: "There may be some of that occurring."

Assessing a police department isn't a straightforward matter. There isn't any widely agreed-upon management model to follow. Private-sector yardsticks can't be mechanically applied to a public-sector function such as policing.

But up close, when the work is broken down into discrete tasks, many LAPD functions don't seem so unique, and ways to improve performance become clearer.

PRESENTING ARMS

For instance, at every change of shift, LAPD patrol officers go through an elaborate sign-out procedure for shotguns, radios and other equipment. It eats up about 30 minutes per shift for each officer, Blue Marble consultants calculated, or the equivalent of 236 full-time cops. The time of 51 additional officers is required to manage the equipment exchange.

Blue Marble suggested this: Buy enough equipment so sharing isn't required. Cost: $5 million at most, producing more than $20 million a year in labor savings, equal to 287 cops.

While some consultants looked at long-term improvements that would cost hundreds of millions of dollars, Blue Marble looked for productivity gains in mundane LAPD tasks.

It found that scheduling and payroll timekeeping are handled in an exquisitely laborious process. Every four weeks, patrol cops spend about three hours each in the station—a combined loss equivalent to 51 fulltime cops—deciding on and requesting in writing their desired days off.

The paperwork is gathered, and on the Thursday of the third week of each deployment period (every four weeks), typically a watch commander, captain, adjutant and timekeeper gather to draw up the deployment plan. It is reviewed and reworked, posted, manually transcribed into the brown time book, sent to division timekeeping and transcribed into the blue book, then onto the green sheets and finally into the city payroll system.

Underpayment and overpayment are common, Blue Marble found. And overtime payments run six weeks behind.

An automated timekeeping system could be had for $650,000 tops, Blue Marble says, producing labor savings among payroll workers of about $1.5 million a year.

Every arrest must be approved by the watch commander. So, two officers drive back to the station, locate the watch commander and get his approval. Often, they stop to shoot the breeze and have a cup of coffee, and then drive the suspect to jail. (Some stations have their own jail.) Since approval is rarely denied, the consultants recommend the policy be scrapped.

Arrest and booking forms require the entry of a juvenile drunken-driving suspect's name 70 separate times. And the forms, filled out manually, end up filed in half a dozen or more separate locations. Mayor Riordan brought a business friend in to see this, Kaufman & Broad Home Corp.'s chief executive officer, Bruce Karatz, and it reminded Mr. Karatz of something: selling a house.

"It's about as many forms as arresting someone," Mr. Karatz says, and that is why Kaufman's sales offices are highly computerized. He helped raise $15 million in private donations to buy personal computer networks for LAPD stations. And even though the department simply loaded 14 duplicative forms into the network—rather than consolidating them, as outsiders suggest—the time saved by reducing paperwork could raise patrol-officer and detective productivity by 10% to 15%, LAPD officials and others estimate.

Taken together, all of these proposed changes could free up the time of hundreds of officers and, by reducing their paperwork and other hassles, perhaps make their jobs a little less aggravating. That in turn could enable the city to improve the LAPD's training, buy some more real radios or perhaps slow the costly hiring program.

BAR CODES

The LAPD is studying the equipment-exchange problem and now plans to buy a timekeeping system. It says watch-commander approval is an important quality-control step in arrests that perhaps could be made less time-consuming.

But unlike productivity-minded companies, the department and its overseers don't try to quantify labor savings from equipment or computer-system purchases in order to make informed choices between more bodies and more machines. "The city council thinks all we need to do is hire more cops and buy more cars. That's a Third World approach," says Joseph Bonino, a civilian LAPD manager who has long argued unsuccessfully for more investment in automation.

Bar-coding systems used in retailing, for instance, would let the department better track the thousands of guns, millions of dollars in cash and mounds of drugs it seizes as evidence each year.

And in detective work, the police could learn something from the financial community, which mines consumers' credit histories to develop lists of sales prospects for credit cards, insurance and the like. If the LAPD's many separate computer systems—which don't communicate with one another—could be connected, parolees' criminal histories and addresses for instance, could be matched against local crime patterns. The department is looking into both of these possibilities.

CHIEF'S ROLE

Reshaping the rigid LAPD bureaucracy, of course, would require tremendously strong leadership, and the department seems lacking in that. Chief Williams, though very popular with the public, has never gained the confidence of the troops since being hired from Philadelphia to replace Mr. Gates in 1992. Assistant Chief Bayan Lewis, head of operations, says "selling the chief to the troops" is one of his duties. "It's not an easy job," he says. "He's viewed as a carpetbagger without qualifications." Mr. Lewis doesn't share that view, he adds.

Chief Williams also isn't hands-on enough as a manager to suit the mayor—a former entrepreneur—Mr. Lewis notes. "Riordan wants a guy down there pressing buttons."

The city charter was amended after Mr. Gates left and gives the chief a maximum of two five-year terms. Chief Williams's first term ends next year, and he says he wants and expects a second one. He says the department was far worse off than anyone realized when he arrived and that his management and policies are turning it around. Police Commission members who will decide whether to keep him won't comment.

Whoever is in charge will face more tough choices. A culture that is transfer- and promotion-oriented has caused instability in some crucial areas.

The much-criticized crime lab, Blue Marble consultants note, has outdated equipment, too few clerks (so that professionals must do what they regard as scut work), and offices that are cramped and scattered over several buildings. Fingerprint examiners are short of cars, so they often keep patrol officers and detectives waiting at crime scenes. And because prints, photographs and other crime-scene materials are handled by three different staffs, detectives at times must make three separate calls for help.

The lab has had 13 commanders in 18 years. Blue Marble notes that "a commander who initiated a bad decision wasn't historically around to suffer the consequences."

DIRECTING TRAFFIC

At the rank of commander, says Art Lopez, "I've averaged about one job a year." Currently he oversees traffic, including motorcycle-riding officers and collision investigators.

So how big is the traffic operation? "Somewhere between 350 and 400 collision investigators," he says, "and 250 to 300 motor officers." He pauses. "Make it 400 [collision investigators] and 260 motor officers." A subordinate says it is closer to 322 and 300.

How many accidents do they investigate? "I'm not quite certain where [that figure] is," Commander Lopez says.

It can be gleaned from the LAPD's statistical digest: They handled 55,114 accidents in 1994, the latest figures available or about 171 per investigator. That is fewer than one per work day.

Productivity isn't helped by deploying collision investigators two to a car. The larger Chicago police force gets by with just 40 crash investigators.

Productivity is tough to assess because the LAPD's statistics are often out-of-date or unreliable. George Callandrillo, a civilian in the traffic division, says he used to contact 22 separate sources to tally by hand how many citations each station issued. Information dribbled in. "It got too sketchy," he says. "I just said [forget] it."

More broadly, department employees don't trust the information, says Philip Friedman, an LAPD senior systems analyst, because "the people who put it in could care less."

16

The Crime Fighter: Putting America's Bad Guys Out of Business

by Jack Maple with Chris Mitchell

"(Jack Maple) is a hero. With the exception of Mayor Rudolph Giuliani, Jack Maple did more than any other person in the last decade to pull New York back from the decline of the 1980's and early 1990's"

—Bernard B. Kerik
NY City's 40th Police Commissioner.
(Kerik, 2001, p. 217)

It Ain't Over Till the Fat Man's Thin

The guy in the suit couldn't have seen what was coming. He was slumped against a wall at the top of a subway staircase at 47th and Broadway, his eyes closed, his tie and collar open, a cardboard party hat fixed with an elastic at the top of his forehead and a gold medallion of some kind draped outside his shirt.

The noise of the crowd that night could have lulled any drunken head into a stupor, and that's what looked like had happened here: This George McFly type wasn't hearing the party horns or the noisemakers anymore, the clap-clapping of hoofs on pavement as mounted patrolled the barriers, or even the icy splash of another champagne bottle or wine cooler shattering on the street. He had been swallowed whole by one of the world's most notorious celebrations and was about to be awakened, minutes before the big ball dropped, by a sudden sting at the back of his neck.

I started moving toward him—invisible, but with my eyes locked on another man. This one had been eyeing the drunk for several minutes, and he was suddenly surging toward his mark

Reprinted from *The Crime Fighter: How You Can Make Your Community Crime-Free* (2001), by permission of Doubleday, a division of Random House, Inc.

with one hand out and the other hidden underneath his coat. That hidden hand was the reason for alarm, but it kept quiet when the free hand shot out and grabbed the chain, so I waited until the chain's new owner turned and came a couple steps across the sidewalk before I threw my open fist at the spot where the hidden hand had been and hit the thief broadside with my right shoulder.

He was built more like a fullback than I'd expected, but I kept driving with my legs the way the high school coaches had taught me, and he fell to the curb under me just as my fingers concluded that only a layer or two of clothing separated them from a familiar casting of steel.

"Gun!" I yelled.

The shouts of the crowd now turned to screaming as the crook and I rolled around in horse-shit and confetti underneath their churning feet. A second crook was already on top of me, and my own pistol was starting to slide up out my waistband into his grasp when Carol Sciannameo jumped onto the pile and pinned my gun against me.

The rest of my crew converged from all sides—Vertel Martin, Richie Doran, Julie Ewbanks, Billy Carter, Joe Quirke, Jeff Aiello, Liz Sheridan, Ronnie Pellechia; Jimmy Nuciforo dropped a party horn to pull another lookout down into the manure. In an instant, all three crooks lay prone in the gutter, and the storm of hoofs bearing in on us came from a world moving at a slower speed.

"Put away your guns," I told my guys. "Get out your badges and your colors."

The spit of the horses sprayed us as their bridles spun them backward in front of us, their riders trying to blink disbelief out of their eyes. We didn't look, I'm sure, like most of the cops they knew.

My gray sable hat had come off in the tussle, so as I got to my feet, I felt for the first time the night's cold breath on my almost barren scalp. There was straw stuck in the tangle of my three-inch beard and clinging to my black zip-front sweater, which wrapped a wreath of white Playboy bunny heads just above my waist. Among those who appreciated crookwear, that sweater was the bomb, and I had the matching Playboy bunny shoes to go with it. In our crew, only Officer Jerry Lyons had clearly outdressed me that night, and he had played the role of the drunk vic in the suit, the party hat, and the gold chain.

Our merry band vanished as quickly as we had materialized, leading the three prisoners downstairs through a locked gate into an empty subway station and then down to the district for processing. The Mole People had made a good catch, but if we had paused a moment to take a last look around at the scene we'd left up on the street, we might have realized that our profession was being handed another humiliating defeat.

It was minutes before midnight, exactly fifteen years before the end of the "American Century," and Times Square, the scene of so many great victory parties across those hundred years, belonged to New York's crooks. Our team had cut short the night of one wolf pack, but there were scores more still snaking through the crowds in their sheepskin coats and Elmer Fudd hats, many of them wearing rings, medallions, and other trophies from crimes past, and some so bold that they couldn't be bothered to hide their foremost thought. "Snatch gold, snatch gold," they'd be hissing. When the ball fell at Times Square, it was like the starter's gun going off. How many pockets would be dug, how many bags snatched, how many windpipes throttled by a well-placed forearm before we all came back in a year to start the count all over again?

Over those next twelve months, the U.S. casualties of crime would come in faster than in any of the years when the news ticker at One Times Square was darkening the streets below with grim reports from the war in Vietnam. Nationwide, murders would leap 10 percent that year to 19,250. More than 500,000 robberies would be committed and almost 800,000 aggravated assaults. Seventy-eight cops would be killed in the line of duty.

And that was only 1986. Crime in America would get far worse before it ever got better.

If you were to return to the corner of 47th and Broadway in 1999, you might be stunned by the change in atmosphere. A gargantuan bas-relief of a Coke bottle still looms directly overhead, but that ad is now affixed to the Renaissance Hotel, one of a half-dozen family-friendly lodging places built at the "Crossroads of the World" in the years since. At one corner of the intersection, mitten-clad theatergoers push the Disney musical Beauty and the Beast—now in its sixth smash season!—to new box office records every night. At another, young tourists sip Starbucks coffee behind a plate-glass window while stock prices sprint past overhead on the towering headquarters of one of the world's largest financial services companies. Twenty paces away, a Planet Hollywood Hotel is rising out of the ground next to a billboard with a giant message paid for by John Lennon's widow. "War is over" read its big black letters.

If people didn't know Yoko Ono better, they might think she was adding her dog-whistle soprano to a national chorus of voices claiming the transformation of Times Square as evidence of a sweeping national victory over crime.

The cops in New York deserve all the accolades they get, and more. In 1993, 1,946 men, women, and children were murdered in New York City; in 1998, the toll stopped at 629. That same year there were about 280,000 fewer victims of serious crimes in the city than there had been five years earlier. While the rest of the country experienced a 23 percent decline in murder over that period, New York's results were three times as good.

But America is like the 600-pound man who's lost 200 pounds. If you've only known him five years, he looks great. If you haven't seen him since 1961, you're amazed at what a fat slob he's become. Today, violent crime—murder, rape, robbery, and aggravated assault—is still being committed at a rate three and a half times higher than it was the year John F. Kennedy was sworn in. Nearly 10,000 more people are murdered in the United States each year than in 1961, and that's despite almost four decades of advances in emergency room medical care. New York City, meanwhile, can't afford to snicker. After five years of intense dieting, its violent crime rate is still double the bloated national figure.

Some of the citizens of this country, unfortunately, take the brunt of the violence. Among black males ages eighteen to twenty-four, the murder victimization rate is about 20 times the national rate, and about nine times that among white males in the same age group. If the sons of senators, congressmen, judges, criminologists, and journalists were dying at that rate, we wouldn't be celebrating any victories over crime just yet. We'd be talking about mandatory conscription for the war raging in our streets.

The truth is, we as a nation have only turned back the clock on violent crime to 1985, the year that ended for me with a roll in the horse manure with two crooks and a couple of loaded guns.

I know we can do better. If the cops of America are given a plan—and worthy leaders—they can make even 1961 look like the bad old days.

It's time to go for the win.

17

Broken Windows: The Police and Neighborhood Safety

by James Q. Wilson and George L. Kelling

"Routine preventive patrol in marked police cars has little value in preventing crime or making citizens feel safe."

—Chief Joseph MacNamara,
Kansas City Police, 1974, after
the infamous patrol study.
(Cole, Gertz, and Bunger, 2002, p. 158)

In the mid-1970s The State of New Jersey announced a "Safe and Clean Neighborhoods Program," designed to improve the quality of community life in twenty-eight cities. As part of that program, the state provided money to help cities take police officers out of their patrol cars and assign them to walking beats. The governor and other state officials were enthusiastic about using foot patrol as a way of cutting crime, but many police chiefs were skeptical. Foot patrol, in their eyes, had been pretty much discredited. It reduced the mobility of the police, who thus had difficulty responding to citizen calls for service, and it weakened headquarters control over patrol officers.

Many police officers also disliked foot patrol, but for different reasons: it was hard work, it kept them outside on cold, rainy nights, and it reduced their chances for making a "good pinch." In some departments, assigning officers to foot patrol had been used as a form of punishment. And academic experts on policing doubted that foot patrol would have any impact on crime rates; it was, in the opinion of most, little more than a sop to public opinion. But since the state was paying for it, the local authorities were willing to go along.

Five years after the program started, the Police Foundation, in Washington, D.C., published an evaluation of the foot-patrol project. Based on its analysis of a carefully controlled experiment carried out chiefly in Newark, the foundation concluded, to the surprise of hardly anyone, that foot patrol had not reduced crime rates. But residents of the foot-patrolled neighborhoods seemed to feel more secure than persons in other areas, tended to believe that crime had been reduced, and seemed to take fewer steps to protect themselves from crime (staying at home with the doors locked, for example). Moreover, citizens in the foot-patrol areas had a more favorable opinion of the police than did those living elsewhere. And officers walking beats had higher morale, greater job satisfaction, and a more favorable attitude toward citizens in their neighborhoods than did officers assigned to patrol cars.

These findings may be taken as evidence that the skeptics were right—foot patrol has no effect on crime; it merely fools the citizens into thinking that they are safer. But in our view, and in the view of the authors of the Police Foundation study (of whom Kelling was one), the citizens of Newark were not fooled at all. They knew what the foot-patrol officers were doing, they knew it was different from what motorized officers do, and they knew that having officers walk beats did in fact make their neighborhoods safer.

But how can a neighborhood be "safer" when the crime rate has not gone down—in fact, may have gone up? Finding the answer requires first that we understand what most often frightens people in public places. Many citizens, of course, are primarily frightened by crime, especially crime involving a sudden, violent attack by a stranger. This risk is very real, in Newark as in many large cities. But we tend to overlook another source of fear—the fear of being bothered by disorderly people. Not violent people, nor, necessarily, criminals, but disreputable or obstreperous or unpredictable people: panhandlers, drunks, addicts, rowdy teenagers, prostitutes, loiterers, the mentally disturbed.

What foot-patrol officers did was to elevate, to the extent they could, the level of public order in these neighborhoods. Though the neighborhoods were predominantly black and the foot patrolmen were mostly white, this "order-maintenance" function of the police was performed to the general satisfaction of both parties.

One of us (Kelling) spent many hours walking with Newark foot-patrol officers to see how they defined "order" and what they did to maintain it. One beat was typical: a busy but dilapidated area in the heart of Newark, with many abandoned buildings, marginal shops (several of which prominently displayed knives and straight-edged razors in their windows), one large department store, and, most important, a train station and several major bus stops. Though the area was run-down, its streets were filled with people, because it was a major transportation center. The good order of this area was important not only to those who lived and worked there but also to many others, who had to move through it on their way home, to supermarkets, or to factories.

The people on the street were primarily black; the officer who walked the street was white. The people were made up of "regulars" and "strangers." Regulars included both "decent folk" and some drunks and derelicts who were always there but who "knew their place." Strangers were, well, strangers, and viewed suspiciously, sometimes apprehensively. The officer—call him Kelly—knew who the regulars were, and they knew him. As he saw his job, he was to keep an eye on strangers, and make certain that the disreputable regulars observed some informal but widely understood rules. Drunks and addicts could sit on the stoops, but could not lie down. People could drink on side streets, but not at the main intersection. Bottles had to be in paper bags. Talking to, bothering, or begging from people waiting at the bus stop was strictly forbidden. If a dispute erupted between a businessman and a customer, the businessman was assumed to be right, especially if the customer was a stranger. If a stranger loitered, Kelly would ask him if he had any means of support and what his business was; if he gave unsatisfactory answers, he was sent on his way. Persons who broke the informal rules, especially those who bothered people waiting at bus stops, were arrested for vagrancy. Noisy teenagers were told to keep quiet.

These rules were defined and enforced in collaboration with the "regulars" on the street. Another neighborhood might have different rules, but these, everybody understood, were the rules for *this* neighborhood. If someone violated them, the regulars not only turned to Kelly for help but also ridiculed the violator. Sometimes what Kelly did could be described as "enforcing the law," but just as often it involved taking informal or extralegal steps to help protect what the neighborhood had decided was the appropriate level of public order. Some of the things he did probably would not withstand a legal challenge.

A determined skeptic might acknowledge that a skilled foot-patrol officer can maintain order but still insist that this sort of "order" has little to do with the real sources of community fear—that is, with violent crime. To a degree, that is true. But two things must be borne in mind. First, outside observers should not assume that they know how much of the anxiety now endemic in many big-city neighborhoods stems from a fear of "real" crime and how much from a sense that the street is disorderly, a source of distasteful, worrisome encounters. The people of Newark, to judge from their behavior and their remarks to interviewers, apparently assign a high value to public order, and feel relieved and reassured when the police help them maintain that order.

Second, at the community level, disorder and crime are usually inextricably linked, in a kind of developmental sequence. Social psychologists and police officers tend to agree that if a window in a building is broken and is left unrepaired, all the rest of the windows will soon be broken. This is as true in nice neighborhoods as in rundown ones. Window-breaking does not necessarily occur on a large scale because some areas are inhabited by determined window-breakers whereas others are populated by window-lovers; rather, one unrepaired broken window is a signal that no one cares, and so breaking more windows costs nothing. (It has always been fun.)

Philip Zimbardo, a Stanford psychologist, reported in 1969 on some experiments testing the broken-window theory. He arranged to have an automobile without license plates parked with its hood up on a street in the Bronx and a comparable automobile on a street in Palo Alto, California. The car in the Bronx was attacked by "vandals" within ten minutes of its "abandonment." The first to arrive were a family—father, mother, and young son—who removed the radiator and battery. Within twenty-four hours, virtually everything of value had been removed. Then random destruction began—windows were smashed, parts torn off, upholstery ripped. Children began to use the car as a playground. Most of the adult "vandals" were well-dressed, apparently clean-cut whites. The car in Palo Alto sat untouched for more than a week. Then Zimbardo smashed part of it with a sledgehammer. Soon, passersby were joining in. Within a few hours, the car had been turned upside down and utterly destroyed. Again, the "vandals" appeared to be primarily respectable whites.

Untended property becomes fair game for people out for fun or plunder and even for people who ordinarily would not dream of doing such things and who probably consider themselves law-abiding. Because of the nature of community life in the Bronx—its anonymity, the frequency with which cars are abandoned and things are stolen or broken, the past experience of "no one caring"—vandalism begins much more quickly than it does in staid Palo Alto, where people have come to believe that private possessions are cared for, and that mischievous behavior is costly. But vandalism can occur anywhere once communal barriers—the sense of mutual regard and the obligations of civility—are lowered by actions that seem to signal that "no one cares."

We suggest that "untended" behavior also leads to the breakdown of community controls. A stable neighborhood of families who care for their homes, mind each other's children, and confidently frown on unwanted intruders can change, in a few years or even a few months, to an inhospitable and frightening jungle. A piece of property is abandoned, weeds grow up, a window is smashed. Adults stop scolding rowdy children; the children, emboldened, become more rowdy. Families move out, unattached adults move in. Teenagers gather in front of the corner store. The merchant asks them to move; they refuse. Fights occur. Litter accumulates. People start drinking in front of the grocery; in time, an inebriate slumps to the sidewalk and is allowed to sleep it off. Pedestrians are approached by panhandlers.

At this point it is not inevitable that serious crime will flourish or violent attacks on strangers will occur. But many residents will think that crime, especially violent crime, is on the rise, and they will modify their behavior accordingly. They will use the streets less often, and when on the streets will stay apart from their fellows, moving with averted eyes, silent lips, and hurried steps. "Don't get involved." For some residents, this growing atomization will matter little, because the neighborhood is not their "home" but "the place where they live." Their interests are elsewhere; they are cosmopolitans. But it will matter greatly to other people, whose lives derive meaning and satisfaction from local attachments rather than worldly involvement; for them, the neighborhood will cease to exist except for a few reliable friends whom they arrange to meet.

Such an area is vulnerable to criminal invasion. Though it is not inevitable, it is more likely that here, rather than in places where people are confident they can regulate public behavior by informal controls, drugs will change hands, prostitutes will solicit, and cars will be stripped. That the drunks will be robbed by boys who do it as a lark, and the prostitutes' customers will be robbed by men who do it purposefully and perhaps violently. That muggings will occur.

Among those who often find it difficult to move away from this are the elderly. Surveys of citizens suggest that the elderly are much less likely to be the victims of crime than younger persons, and some have inferred from this that the well-known fear of crime voiced by the elderly is an exaggeration: perhaps we ought not to design special programs to protect older persons; perhaps we should even try to talk them out of their mistaken fears. This argument misses the point. The prospect of a confrontation with an obstreperous teenager or a drunken panhandler can be as fear-inducing for defenseless persons as the prospect of meeting an actual robber; indeed, to a defenseless person, the two kinds of confrontation are often indistinguishable. Moreover, the lower rate at which the elderly are victimized is a measure of the steps they have already taken—chiefly, staying behind locked doors—to minimize the risks they face. Young men are more frequently attacked than older women, not because they are easier or more lucrative targets but because they are on the streets more.

Nor is the connection between disorderliness and fear made only by the elderly. Susan Estrich, of the Harvard Law School, has recently gathered together a number of surveys on the sources of public fear. One, done in Portland, Oregon, indicated that three fourths of the adults interviewed cross to the other side of a street when they see a gang of teenagers; another survey, in Baltimore, discovered that nearly half would cross the street to avoid even a single strange youth. When an interviewer asked people in a housing project where the most dangerous spot was, they mentioned a place where young persons gathered to drink and play music, despite the fact that not a single crime had occurred there. In Boston public housing projects, the greatest fear was expressed by persons living in the buildings where disorderliness and incivility, not crime, were the greatest. Knowing this helps one understand the significance of such otherwise harmless displays as subway graffiti. As Nathan Glazer has written, the proliferation of graffiti, even when not obscene, confronts the subway rider with the inescapable knowledge that the environment he must endure for an hour or more a day is uncontrolled and uncontrollable, and that anyone can invade it to do whatever damage and mischief the mind suggests."

In response to fear people avoid one another, weakening controls. Sometimes they call the police. Patrol cars arrive, an occasional arrest occurs but crime continues and disorder is not abated. Citizens complain to the police chief, but he explains that his department is low on personnel and that the courts do not punish petty or first-time offenders. To the residents, the police who arrive in squad cars are either ineffective or uncaring: to the police, the residents are animals who deserve each other. The citizens may soon stop calling the police, because "they can't do anything."

The process we call urban decay has occurred for centuries in every city. But what is happening today is different in at least two important respects. First, in the period before, say, World War II, city dwellers—because of money costs, transportation difficulties, familial and church connections—could rarely move away from neighborhood problems. When movement did occur, it tended to be along public-transit routes. Now mobility has become exceptionally easy for all but the poorest or those who are blocked by racial prejudice. Earlier crime waves had a kind of built-in self-correcting mechanism: the determination of a neighborhood or community to reassert control over its turf. Areas in Chicago, New York, and Boston would experience crime and gang wars, and then normalcy would return, as the families for whom no alternative residences were possible reclaimed their authority over the streets.

Second, the police in this earlier period assisted in that reassertion of authority by acting, sometimes violently, on behalf of the community. Young toughs were roughed up, people were arrested "on suspicion" or for vagrancy, and prostitutes and petty thieves were routed. "Rights" were something enjoyed by decent folk, and perhaps also by the serious professional criminal, who avoided violence and could afford a lawyer.

This pattern of policing was not an aberration or the result of occasional excess. From the earliest days of the nation, the police function was seen primarily as that of a night watchman: to maintain order against the chief threats to order—fire, wild animals, and disreputable behavior. Solving crimes was viewed not as a police responsibility but as a private one. In the March, 1969, *Atlantic,* one of us (Wilson) wrote a brief account of how the police role had slowly changed from maintaining order to fighting crimes. The change began with the creation of private detectives (often ex-criminals), who worked on a contingency-fee basis for individuals who had suffered losses. In time, the detectives were absorbed in municipal agencies and paid a regular salary simultaneously, the responsibility for prosecuting thieves was shifted from the aggrieved private citizen to the professional prosecutor. This process was not complete in most places until the twentieth century.

In the 1960s, when urban riots were a major problem, social scientists began to explore carefully the order maintenance function of the police, and to suggest ways of improving it—not to make streets safer (its original function) but to reduce the incidence of mass violence. Order maintenance became, to a degree, coterminous with "community relations." But, as the crime wave that began in the early 1960s continued without abatement throughout the decade and into the 1970s, attention shifted to the role of the police as crime-fighters. Studies of police behavior ceased, by and large, to be accounts of the order-maintenance function and became, instead, efforts to propose and test ways whereby the police could solve more crimes, make more arrests, and gather better evidence. If these things could be done, social scientists assumed, citizens would be less fearful.

A great deal was accomplished during this transition, as both police chiefs and outside experts emphasized the crime-fighting function in their plans, in the allocation of resources, and in deployment of personnel. The police may well have become better crime-fighters as a result. And doubtless they remained aware of their responsibility for order. But the link between order-maintenance and crime-prevention, so obvious to earlier generations, was forgotten.

That link is similar to the process whereby one broken window becomes many. The citizen who fears the ill-smelling drunk, the rowdy teenager, or the importuning beggar is not merely expressing his distaste for unseemly behavior; he is also giving voice to a bit of folk wisdom that happens to be a correct generalization—namely, that serious street crime flourishes in areas in which disorderly behavior goes unchecked. The unchecked panhandler is, in effect, the first broken window. Muggers and robbers, whether opportunistic or professional, believe they reduce their chances of being caught or even identified if they operate on streets where potential victims are already intimidated by prevailing conditions. If the neighborhood cannot keep a bothersome panhandler from annoying passersby, the thief may reason, it is even less likely to call the police to identify a potential mugger or to interfere if the mugging actually takes place.

Some police administrators concede that this process occurs, but argue that motorized-patrol officers can deal with it as effectively as foot patrol officers. We are not so sure. In theory, an officer in a squad car can observe as much as an officer on foot; in theory, the former can talk to as many people as the latter. But the reality of police-citizen encounters is powerfully altered by the automobile. An officer on foot cannot separate himself from the street people; if he is approached, only his uniform and his personality can help him manage whatever is about to happen. And he can never be certain what that will be—a request for directions, a plea for help, an angry denunciation, a teasing remark, a confused babble, a threatening gesture.

In a car, an officer is more likely to deal with street people by rolling down the window and looking at them. The door and the window exclude the approaching citizen; they are a barrier. Some officers take advantage of this barrier, perhaps unconsciously, by acting differently if in the car than they would on foot. We have seen this countless times. The police car pulls up to a corner where teenagers are gathered. The window is rolled down. The officer stares at the youths. They stare back. The officer says to one, "C'mere." He saunters over, conveying to his friends by his elaborately casual style the idea that he is not intimidated by authority. What's your name?" "Chuck." "Chuck who?" "Chuck Jones." "What'ya doing, Chuck?" "Nothin'." "Got a P.O. [parole officer]?" "Nah." "Sure?" "Yeah." "Stay out of trouble, Chuckie." Meanwhile, the other boys laugh and exchange comments among themselves, probably at the officer's expense. The officer stares harder. He cannot be certain what is being said, nor can he join in and, by displaying his own skill at street banter, prove that he cannot be "put down." In the process, the officer has learned almost nothing, and the boys have decided the officer is an alien force who can safely be disregarded, even mocked.

Our experience is that most citizens like to talk to a police officer. Such exchanges give them a sense of importance, provide them with the basis for gossip, and allow them to explain to the authorities what is worrying them (whereby they gain a modest but significant sense of having "done something" about the problem). You approach a person on foot more easily, and talk to him more readily, than you do a person in a car. Moreover, you can more easily retain some anonymity if you draw an officer aside for a private chat. Suppose you want to pass on a tip about who is stealing handbags, or who offered to sell you a stolen TV. In the inner city, the culprit, in all likelihood, lives nearby. To walk up to a marked patrol car and lean in the window is to convey a visible signal that you are a "fink."

The essence of the police role in maintaining order is to reinforce the informal control mechanisms of the community itself. The police cannot, without committing extraordinary resources, provide a substitute for that informal control. On the other hand, to reinforce those natural forces the police must accommodate them. And therein lies the problem.

Should police activity on the street be shaped, in important ways, by the standards of the neighborhood rather than by the rules of the state? Over the past two decades, the shift of police from order-maintenance to law enforcement has brought them increasingly under the influence of legal restrictions, provoked by media complaints and enforced by court decisions and departmental orders. As a consequence, the order maintenance functions of the police are now governed by rules developed to control police relations with suspected criminals. This is, we think, an entirely new development. For centuries, the role of the police as watchmen was judged primarily not in terms of its compliance with appropriate procedures but rather in terms of its attaining a desired objective. The objective was order, an inherently ambiguous term but a condition that people in a given community recognized when they saw it. The means were the same as those the community itself would employ, if its members were sufficiently determined, courageous, and authoritative. Detecting and apprehending criminals, by contrast, was a means to an end, not an end in itself; a judicial determination of guilt or innocence was the hoped-for result of the law-enforcement mode. From the first, the police were expected to follow rules defining that process, though states differed in how stringent the rules should be. The criminal-apprehension process was always understood to involve individual rights, the violation of which was unacceptable because it meant that the violating officer would be acting as a judge and jury—and that was not his job. Guilt or innocence was to be determined by universal standards under special procedures.

Ordinarily, no judge or jury ever sees the persons caught up in a dispute over the appropriate level of neighborhood order. That is true not only because most cases are handled informally on the street but also because no universal standards are available to settle arguments over disorder, and thus a judge may not be any wiser or more effective than a police officer. Until quite recently in many states, and even today in some places, the police made arrests on such charges as "suspicious person" or "vagrancy" or "public drunkenness"—charges with scarcely any legal meaning. These charges exist not because society wants judges to punish vagrants or drunks but because it wants an officer to have the legal tools to remove undesirable persons from a neighborhood when informal efforts to preserve order in the streets have failed.

Once we begin to think of all aspects of police work as involving the application of universal rules under special procedures, we inevitably ask what constitutes an "undesirable person" and why we should "criminalize" vagrancy or drunkenness. A strong and commendable desire to see that people are treated fairly makes us worry about allowing the police to rout persons who are undesirable by some vague or parochial standard. A growing and not-so-commendable utilitarianism leads us to doubt that any behavior that does not "hurt" another person should be made illegal. And thus many of us who watch over the police are reluctant to allow them to perform, in the only way they can, a function that every neighborhood desperately wants them to perform.

This wish to "decriminalize" disreputable behavior that "harms no one"—and thus remove the ultimate sanction the police can employ to maintain neighborhood order—is, we think, a mistake. Arresting a single drunk or a single vagrant who has harmed no identifiable person seems unjust, and in a sense it is. But failing to do anything about a score of drunks or a hundred vagrants may destroy an entire community. A particular rule that seems to make sense in the individual case makes no sense when it is made a universal rule and applied to all cases. It makes no sense because it fails to take into account the connection between one broken window left untended and a thousand broken windows. Of course, agencies other than the police could attend to the problems posed by drunks or the mentally ill, but in most communities especially where the "deinstitutionalization" movement has been strong—they do not.

The concern about equity is more serious. We might agree that certain behavior makes one person more undesirable than another but how do we ensure that age or skin color or national origin or harmless mannerisms will not also become the basis for distinguishing the undesirable from the desirable? How do we ensure, in short, that the police do not become the agents of neighborhood bigotry?

We can offer no wholly satisfactory answer to this important question. We are not confident that there is a satisfactory answer except to hope that by their selection, training, and supervision, the police will be inculcated with a clear sense of the outer limit of their discretionary authority. That limit, roughly, is this—the police exist to help regulate behavior, not to maintain the racial or ethnic purity of a neighborhood.

Consider the case of the Robert Taylor Homes in Chicago, one of the largest public-housing projects in the country. It is home for nearly 20,000 people, all black, and extends over ninety-two acres along South State Street. It was named after a distinguished black who had been, during the 1940s, chairman of the Chicago Housing Authority. Not long after it opened, in 1962, relations between project residents and the police deteriorated badly. The citizens felt that the police were insensitive or brutal; the police, in turn, complained of unprovoked attacks on them. Some Chicago officers tell of times when they were afraid to enter the Homes. Crime rates soared.

Today, the atmosphere has changed. Police-citizen relations have improved—apparently, both sides learned something from the earlier experience. Recently, a boy stole a purse and ran off. Several young persons who saw the theft voluntarily passed along to the police information on the identity and residence of the thief, and they did this publicly, with friends and neighbors looking on. But problems persist, chief among them the presence of youth gangs that terrorize residents and recruit members in the project. The people expect the police to "do something" about this, and the police are determined to do just that.

But do what? Though the police can obviously make arrests whenever a gang member breaks the law, a gang can form, recruit, and congregate without breaking the law. And only a tiny fraction of gang-related crimes can be solved by an arrest; thus, if an arrest is the only recourse for the police, the residents' fears will go unassuaged. The police will soon feel helpless, and the residents will again believe that the police "do nothing." What the police in fact do is to chase known gang members out of the project. In the words of one officer, "We kick ass." Project residents both know and approve of this. The tacit police-citizen alliance in the project is reinforced by the police view that the cops and the gangs are the two rival sources of power in the area, and that the gangs are not going to win.

None of this is easily reconciled with any conception of due process or fair treatment. Since both residents and gang members are black, race is not a factor. But it could be. Suppose a white project confronted a black gang, or vice versa. We would be apprehensive about the police taking sides. But the substantive problem remains the same: how can the police strengthen the informal social-control mechanisms of natural communities in order to minimize fear in public places? Law enforcement, per se, is no answer: a gang can weaken or destroy a community by standing about in a menacing fashion and speaking rudely to passersby without breaking the law.

We have difficulty thinking about such matters, not simply because the ethical and legal issues are so complex but because we have become accustomed to thinking of the law in essentially individualistic terms. The law defines *my* rights, punishes *his* behavior and is applied by *that* officer because of *this* harm. We assume, in thinking this way, that what is good for the individual will be good for the community and what doesn't matter when it happens to one person won't matter if it happens to many. Ordinarily, those are plausible assumptions. But in cases where behavior that is tolerable to one person is intolerable to many others, the reactions of the others—fear, withdrawal, flight—may ultimately make matters worse for everyone, including the individual who first professed his indifference.

It may be their greater sensitivity to communal as opposed to individual needs that helps explain why the residents of small communities are more satisfied with their police than are the residents of similar neighborhoods in big cities. Elinor Ostrom and her co-workers at Indiana University compared the perception of police services in two poor, all-black Illinois towns—Phoenix and East Chicago Heights with those of three comparable all-black neighborhoods in Chicago. The level of criminal victimization and the quality of police-community relations appeared to be about the same in the towns and the Chicago neighborhoods. But the citizens living in their own villages were much more likely than those living in the Chicago neighborhoods to say that they do not stay at home for fear of crime, to agree that the local police have "the right to take any action necessary" to deal with problems, and to agree that the police "look out for the needs of the average citizen." It is possible that the residents and the police of the small towns saw themselves as engaged in a collaborative effort to maintain a certain standard of communal life, whereas those of the big city felt themselves to be simply requesting and supplying particular services on an individual basis.

If this is true, how should a wise police chief deploy his meager forces? The first answer is that nobody knows for certain, and the most prudent course of action would be to try further variations on the Newark experiment, to see more precisely what works in what kinds of neighborhoods. The second answer is also a hedge—many aspects of order maintenance in neighborhoods can probably best be handled in ways that involve the police minimally if at all. A busy bustling shopping center and a quiet, well-tended suburb may need almost no visible police presence. In both cases, the ratio of respectable to disreputable people is ordinarily so high as to make informal social control effective.

Even in areas that are in jeopardy from disorderly elements, citizen action without substantial police involvement may be sufficient. Meetings between teenagers who like to hang out on a particular corner and adults who want to use that corner might well lead to an amicable agreement on a set of rules about how many people can be allowed to congregate, where, and when.

Where no understanding is possible—or if possible, not observed—citizen patrols may be a sufficient response. There are two traditions of communal involvement in maintaining order: One, that of the "community watchmen," is as old as the first settlement of the New World. Until well into the nineteenth century, volunteer watchmen, not policemen, patrolled their communities to keep order. They did so, by and large, without taking the law into their own hands—without, that is, punishing persons or using force. Their presence deterred disorder or alerted the community to disorder that could not be deterred. There are hundreds of such efforts today in communities all across the nation. Perhaps the best known is that of the Guardian Angels, a group of unarmed young persons in distinctive berets and T-shirts, who first came to public attention when they began patrolling the New York City subways but who claim now to have chapters in more than thirty American cities. Unfortunately, we have little information about the effect of these groups on crime. It is possible, however, that whatever their effect on crime, citizens find their presence reassuring, and that they thus contribute to maintaining a sense of order and civility.

The second tradition is that of the "vigilante." Rarely a feature of the settled communities of the East, it was primarily to be found in those frontier towns that grew up in advance of the reach of government. More than 350 vigilante groups are known to have existed; their distinctive feature was that their members did take the law into their own hands, by acting as judge, jury, and often executioner as well as policeman. Today, the vigilante movement is conspicuous by its rarity, despite the great fear expressed by citizens that the older cities are becoming "urban frontiers." But some community-watchmen groups have skirted the line, and others may cross it in the future. An ambiguous case, reported in *The Wall Street Journal* involved a citizens' patrol in the Silver Lake area of Belleville, New Jersey. A leader told the reporter, "We look for outsiders." If a few teenagers from outside the neighborhood enter it, "we ask them their business," he said. "If they say they're going down the street to see Mrs. Jones, fine, we let them pass. But then we follow them down the block to make sure they're really going to see Mrs. Jones."

Though citizens can do a great deal, the police are plainly the key to order maintenance. For one thing, many communities, such as the Robert Taylor Homes, cannot do the job by themselves. For another, no citizen in a neighborhood, even an organized one, is likely to feel the sense of responsibility that wearing a badge confers. Psychologists have done many studies on why people fail to go to the aid of persons being attacked or seeking help, and they have learned that the cause is not "apathy" or "selfishness" but the absence of some plausible grounds for feeling that one must personally accept responsibility. Ironically, avoiding responsibility is easier when a lot of people are standing about. On streets and in public places, where order is so important, many people are likely to be "around," a fact that reduces the chance of any one person acting as the agent of the community. The police officer's uniform singles him out as a person who must accept responsibility if asked. In addition, officers, more easily than their fellow citizens, can be expected to distinguish between what is necessary to protect the safety of the street and what merely protects its ethnic purity.

But the police forces of America are losing, not gaining, members. Some cities have suffered substantial cuts in the number of officers available for duty. These cuts are not likely to be reversed in the near future. Therefore, each department must assign its existing officers with great care. Some neighborhoods are so demoralized and crime-ridden as to make foot patrol useless; the best the police can do with limited resources is respond to the enormous number of calls for service. Other neighborhoods are so stable and serene as to make foot patrol unnecessary. The key is to identify neighborhoods at the tipping point—where the public order is deteriorating but not unreclaimable, where the streets are used frequently but by apprehensive people, where a window is likely to be broken at any time, and must quickly be fixed if all are not to be shattered.

Most police departments do not have ways of systematically identifying such areas and assigning officers to them. Officers are assigned on the basis of crime rates (meaning that marginally threatened areas are often stripped so that police can investigate crimes in areas where the situation is hopeless) or on the basis of calls for service (despite the fact that most citizens do not call the police when they are merely frightened or annoyed). To allocate patrol wisely, the department must look at the neighborhoods and decide, from first-hand evidence, where an additional officer will make the greatest difference in promoting a sense of safety.

One way to stretch limited police resources is being tried in some public housing projects. Tenant organizations hire off-duty police officers for patrol work in their buildings. The costs are not high (at least not per resident), the officer likes the additional income, and the residents feel safer. Such arrangements are probably more successful than hiring private watchmen, and the Newark experiment helps us understand why. A private security guard may deter crime or misconduct by his presence, and he may go to the aid of persons needing help, but he may well not intervene—that is, control or drive away—someone challenging community standards.

Being a sworn officer—a "real cop"—seems to give one the confidence, the sense of duty, and the aura of authority necessary to perform this difficult task.

Patrol officers might be encouraged to go to and from duty stations on public transportation and, while on the bus or subway car, enforce rules about smoking, drinking, disorderly conduct, and the like. The enforcement need involve nothing more than ejecting the offender (the offense, after all, is not one with which a booking officer or a judge wishes to be bothered). Perhaps the random but relentless maintenance of standards on buses would lead to conditions on buses that approximate the level of civility we now take for granted on airplanes.

But the most important requirement is to think that to maintain order in precarious situations is a vital job. The police know this is one of their functions, and they also believe, correctly, that it cannot be done to the exclusion of criminal investigation and responding to calls. We may have encouraged them to suppose, however, on the basis of our oft-repeated concerns about serious, violent crime, that they will be judged exclusively on their capacity as crime-fighters. To the extent that this is the case, police administrators will continue to concentrate police personnel in the highest-crime areas (though not necessarily in the areas most vulnerable to criminal invasion), emphasize their training in the law and criminal apprehension (and not their training in managing street life), and join too quickly in campaigns to decriminalize "harmless" behavior (though public drunkenness, street prostitution, and pornographic displays can destroy a community more quickly than any team of professional burglars).

Above all, we must return to our long-abandoned view that the police ought to protect communities as well as individuals. Our crime statistics and victimization surveys measure individual losses, but they do not measure communal losses. Just as physicians now recognize the importance of fostering health rather than simply treating illness, so the police—and the rest of us—ought to recognize the importance of maintaining, intact, communities without broken windows.

18

The Turnaround: How America's Top Cop Reversed the Crime Epidemic

by William Bratton with Peter Knobler

"The leader must lead from the front—exposing him or herself to the same dangers and hardships as the cops in the field while monitoring whether the department's tactics and strategies are being carried out and whether or not they're working"

—Jack Maple,
(Maple, 1999, p. 244)

DAY ONE

Don't stick your neck out. It's the first principle in running a police organization. Never say your goals out loud; you'll only look bad when you don't achieve them.

That's not me.

New York's newly elected mayor, Rudolph W. Giuliani, had chosen me to be police commissioner of the City of New York—the number one police job in America—and it was time to stick my neck out. The city was a mess. People were afraid of being mugged, they were afraid of having their cars stolen, they were afraid of the everyday assault on common decency and good conduct that had become standard New York behavior. Surveys showed that more than half the people who had recently left the city did so to improve the quality of their lives. And chief among the reasons they couldn't do that in the city was crime.

Although I was born and raised and had worked almost all my life in Boston, I knew New York. My two years as chief of the New York City Transit Police in the early 1990s had given me a full immersion in the way the city handled itself—a view from the underground up. Nothing changes fast in the city. There is the sense that this is the way it is, this is the way it's always been, and this is the way it always will be. New Yorkers respect strength and admire spirit, they pride themselves on their toughness—it's tough enough just to get by—but when I got there they had just about given up.

New Yorkers wanted a way out of the danger and lawlessness they saw around them. They couldn't walk from their apartments to the subway without getting aggressively panhandled or threatened or worse—"Hey, hey, hey, mister, gimme a quarter. That the best you got?" They couldn't walk to work without seeing men and women using the streets and sidewalks as out-door toilets. They couldn't stop their car at a traffic light without some guy smearing their wind-shield with a filthy rag and demanding a dollar for his efforts. Squeegee men, these fellows were called, and to many people it seemed they just about ruled the city. I had joked frequently that they should replace the torch in the Statue of Liberty's hand with a squeegee—it was a more fitting symbol of the welcome many people received when they got here.

New York City felt it was under siege, and there was the widespread sense that no one was doing anything about it. In 1990, shortly after he was elected, Mayor David Dinkins and his entire administration took a major hit when, in response to a particularly bloody week in the city, the *New York Post* ran this tabloid headline in huge type on its front page:

"DAVE, DO SOMETHING"

Mirroring the local perspective, the story went national shortly thereafter. *Time* magazine had a cover story in September featuring "The Rotting of the Big Apple." In response to this challenge, Dinkins was able to pass "Safe Streets" legislation that increased the size of the city's three police departments by over six thousand officers.

But by 1994, even this ongoing infusion of personnel hadn't seemed to help. There was a sense of doom on the streets. The police department seemed dysfunctional. Several genera-tions of corruption scandals had left it seemingly without the will to fight crime. The cops on the beat wanted to do their jobs, but the brass didn't trust them to do it. Corruption on a com-mander's watch can kill his career, so rather than aggressively attack the places where most crime occurred, particularly drug-related crime, police officers had been ordered by their supe-riors to stay out of them; the feeling behind many desks was that it was better for cops to stay away from criminals and steer clear of temptation than to chase them down and put them away.

Mayor Giuliani was a former federal prosecutor. He liked putting criminals in jail; it was what he had done for a living. Giuliani was elected mayor in 1993 largely on the quality-of-life and crime issues, and, impressed with my earlier record as transit chief, he brought me in to help clean up the rest of the city. I brought to New York a lifetime career in law enforcement and had led the turnaround of four major police departments, including the New York City Transit Police and the Boston Police Department. Like most American police departments, for the last twenty-five years the NYPD had been content to focus on reacting to crime while accepting no responsibility for reducing, let alone preventing it. Crime, the theory went, was caused by soci-etal problems that were impervious to police intervention. That was the unchallenged con-ventional wisdom espoused by academics, sociologists, and criminologists. I intended to prove them wrong. Crime, and as important, attitudes about crime, could be turned around. Using law enforcement expertise, leadership and management skills, and an inspired workforce, I intended to create an organization whose goal and mission was to control and prevent crime—not just respond to it. By turning around the NYPD, and reducing crime and fear, we would turn around the city. And, who knows, maybe even the country.

I believed that police could, in fact, be counted upon to have a significant effect on crime. With effective leadership and management we could control behavior in the street, and by con-trolling behavior we could change behavior. If we could change behavior we could control crime.

When I interviewed with Giuliani for the police commissioner's position, I told him we could reduce crime by 40 percent in three years.

On December 2, 1993, at the announcement of my appointment as the city's new police commissioner, a little more than a month before I took office, I stood beside the mayor and made this promise: "We will fight for every house in this city. We will fight for every street. We will fight for every borough. And we will win."

The turnaround had begun. Like Babe Ruth pointing his bat to the bleachers indicating where his next home run would land, I was confidently predicting the future. I was a leader who had spent my whole professional life seeking out and turning around low-performing, dysfunctional police departments. Now I had been given the challenge of a lifetime—the NYPD. One of my predecessors, Commissioner Lee Brown, when he led the department, likened the experience to trying to "turn an aircraft carrier around in a bathtub." I intended to turn it around with the speed of a destroyer.

I spent the next five weeks putting my team together. I interviewed men and women at all levels of the NYPD and matched people to positions; you can seriously undermine an organization by putting the right person in the wrong job. My team and I planned our strategies and prepared to hit the ground running.

On Sunday, January 9, 1994, the day before I was scheduled to be sworn in as commissioner, several members of my new team were to meet at the apartment of John Miller, who was going to be my deputy commissioner of public information (DCPI), to go over what we were calling the rollout, our first major changes. Miller, a television-news reporter for the local NBC affiliate, was best known for sidling up to organized-crime don John Gotti and getting him to talk. In his $2,000 suits, John looked fearless on the tube; in real life, he is a guy who loves being on the scene. Aggressively single, John was an excellent reporter with great contacts; he knew just about everybody in town, and the cops loved him. He was taking a $500,000 pay cut to become my DCPI because it was the job he had always wanted. As a reporter, he'd had a front-row seat to the New York circus; now, he was in the center ring.

Peter LaPorte, my new chief of staff, was there. So were consultant John Linder, chief of department and soon-to-be first deputy commissioner Dave Scott, and newly appointed deputy commissioner for crime-control strategies Jack Maple, whom I had brought with me from my years in transit. Maple is a barrel-chested Queens native who favors homburgs, double-breasted blazers, bow ties, and two-toned spectator shoes. He is a character out of *Guys and Dolls,* with a brilliant police mind.

My term as commissioner was to begin officially at midnight, and I was taking the five o'clock shuttle out of Logan Airport in Boston. After an early dinner in New York with friends, I was to join the gang at Miller's apartment before heading up to the 103rd Precinct in Queens for my first official act: attending roll call and addressing the officers as they began their shift.

Late in the afternoon, the phone rang at Miller's east-side apartment. Apparently, a situation was developing around a mosque in Harlem that looked like it could be potentially troublesome. Maple said to Miller, "I'm going to meet the Commish out at the airport. Why don't you go up and get a handle on this mosque thing?" Miller called down to police headquarters at One Police Plaza. The night sergeant gave him the rundown.

There had been a gun run; a phone call had come in on the emergency number, 911, saying there was an armed robbery in progress, two men with guns. Police had responded, and the location turned out to be the Nation of Islam Mosque Number 7, Louis Farrakhan's operation, at Fifth Avenue and 125th Street, on the third floor. The first officers to arrive, a male-female team, were met by Muslim security, which is usually very tight. Police officers are particularly focused when there is the possibility of a firearm involved at a scene, and New York City's Nation of

Islam members are very sensitive about police issues. The Muslims didn't want the police entering their place of worship carrying weapons. When the officers evidently tried to brush by, a fight ensued, with some people rolling down a flight of stairs. The cops were overpowered, one of their guns and their radio were taken, and they were literally thrown out into the street.

It was snowing and blustery, the streets were icy, and the temperature had fallen to around fifteen degrees. Snow from the previous week was now rock hard. The fight in the street became one of those cartoon battles, except serious; you swung at somebody and ended up falling on your butt on the ice, which is how bones get broken.

A crowd started to gather. The cops called for backup, and so did the Muslims. Finally, there was a standoff, the cops controlling the outer perimeter and the Muslims controlling the inner. It was shaping up to be one of those New York confrontations, greater than the sum of its parts.

I wasn't even police commissioner yet—I was a civilian until midnight. My predecessor, Ray Kelly, had already resigned and was on a plane to Europe. John Pritchard, the first deputy, had also resigned. Dave Scott, who as chief of department was the number-three man, was up there running the show. That was fine. Scott had a foot in each administration; I had asked him to be my first deputy commissioner, and he was going to be the senior ranking uniformed officer on both sides of midnight. Miller ran up there with him.

Maple briefed me when I got off the plane. Welcome to New York. Without official authority until midnight, I didn't feel it would be appropriate for me to be on the scene, so we went to a restaurant and kept in constant contact by telephone. Our cellular phones didn't work inside, so Jack and I kept shuffling out to the car to talk to Miller and Scott and the mayor.

Early reports from the scene seemed to indicate that the cops had done nothing intentionally wrong. A report of a firearm is very serious, and the officers had every right—indeed, the duty—to investigate thoroughly. When you think of a mosque, perhaps you get the image of the splendor of Mecca or the Muslim equivalent of Saint Patrick's Cathedral. Mosque Number 7, however, sat in a commercial building, next door to a supermarket. Far from assaulting an imposing place of worship, the officers thought they were entering a commercial property. They never got near the third-floor mosque itself.

The mayor believed that where there is room for benefit of the doubt, that benefit should go to the police. I agreed completely. The first thing we asked was "Were our officers right?" When the answer came back affirmative, we were in the position to support our men and women. Our early comments to the press said just that.

This came as a surprise to the press and to the cops. For years, the brass had backed away in times like these, adopting a wait-and-see attitude that allowed the media to shout any damn thing they wanted without strong pro-police input from City Hall and One Police Plaza. When the bosses don't back you up, the attacks in the papers and on the air get very shrill and ugly. Cops had come to expect such softness from their superiors, and they resented it. That had to stop. The newly elected mayor believed that, and so did I.

Chief Joe Leake was borough commander of Manhattan North. Leake, himself black, was on the scene, trying to broker a deal in which the police would search the mosque to obtain the gun and radio in exchange for letting the people who were inside leave. Everyone in the mosque was a potential suspect, and they were going nowhere without being identified. The Muslims were refusing to give anything up or anyone over.

Of course, the mayor was involved. He had been sworn in ten days earlier as a law-and-order mayor, and he had made it clear during the campaign that he was not going to give special treatment to any group—black, white, Asian, Hispanic. And race was an issue. African Americans in particular feared that his administration would be insensitive to them. For twenty-five years, they and other groups in the city had been treated gingerly by City Hall. Now Giuliani had come in and said, Everybody's going to be treated the same. In addition, the black community felt injured by the fact that they had lost David Dinkins, an African American, as mayor. For several years, New York had had a black mayor and a black police commissioner, Lee Brown. Now they had a white police commissioner from Boston and a white mayor whom they really did not trust.

Furthermore, much of the overwhelmingly white constituency that had elected Giuliani felt that the black community in particular had gotten away with too much already. The black community knew this and resented it. Farrakhan's Muslims had gone out of their way to depict Islam as "the black man's religion," and this current situation, cops in a mosque, had the potential to become a community rallying point. Add this to Giuliani's impulse to support cops when they were doing the right thing and you could understand why the tension was high.

I don't know that the incident would have been treated very differently if it had happened at a Catholic church. Giuliani felt previous administrations had backpedaled too much in dealing with many special-interest groups around the city, and he was going to put a stop to it. Giuliani saw this as purely a police-and-order issue, and he was determined to put his stamp on the city right away.

All this was in play on this bitterly cold, windy, snowy Sunday night, with the leadership of the police department still in the hands of men who for twenty years had been taught and had learned through bitter experience to respond in a very low-key, sympathetic manner to many of the city's special-interest groups—in a nutshell, never to stick their neck out.

Giuliani was not happy with the standoff. His position, basically, was: You've got criminals in there. Go in and get them.

Relying on Scott and Leake and my own sensitivities to this issue, I felt that would exacerbate the situation. No one in New York law enforcement was unaware that in the 1970s a police officer had been shot during a standoff at a city mosque, and we didn't want another seventies-style situation on our hands. I had worked for two years as transit police chief and was mindful that sometimes negotiations are appropriate.

This wasn't sitting well with the mayor. He kept calling me and Scott and Leake. "You have police officers injured," he said. "You have stolen police property. Why aren't you going in?" It was a legitimate question, but it was asked continually. The command post was in a supermarket next to the mosque, and Leake kept getting pulled out of negotiations to talk to someone from City Hall. He told them essentially, with grace and tact, "Nothing has changed because every time we go to negotiate, we get pulled back into the supermarket to talk to you."

The Muslims, meanwhile, had none of these problems; they weren't answering to Farrakhan every five minutes. They had a chain of command and were making decisions. We had a level-three mobilization of cops and they had a level-four mobilization of Muslims. We were being outflanked.

"There ought to be arrests tonight," the mayor insisted. "No one is to be D.A.T.'d." (A D.A.T. is a desk appearance ticket, known to cops as a "disappearance ticket" because most people who get them don't show up in court.) "I want arrests!"

Giuliani seized upon this incident to draw his line in the sand; here's how he was going to be different from Dinkins. He was going to be aggressive, hands-on. Giuliani would have preferred to keep everybody locked inside the building until they surrendered the people who assaulted the officers and stole the radio. However, Scott and Leake were handling the situation masterfully. They had been field commanders for many years in the department and knew the community— were of that community—and felt that the tensions were so high that to make the point that we, the police, were in charge would have raised the potential for bloody consequences.

Leake had two jobs that night; one was to catch the guys who assaulted the cops, and the other was to prevent a riot. His view was, "Let's prevent the riot first, and then we'll get down to getting these mugs. We have a description, we know where they come from. Detectives have caught a lot of people on a lot less than that. We'll get them." I concurred.

I used the weather conditions to bring the point home to the mayor. "It's a very tenuous situation up there," I told him. "We have a lot of police, and if we attempt to, if you will, assault the place—to go in using force—there is the potential to have this escalate. We ought to step back and allow the negotiation process to work."

Ultimately, a deal was worked out in which Scott and an aide went into the mosque, searched the premises, and retrieved the radio and the gun. Then there was a walk-by; although many people involved in the incident had left the scene, the individuals who remained in the building were brought out in a long line so the officers who had been assaulted could make identifications and arrests. A promise was obtained from the Muslims that the next day they would surrender the people they knew to be involved in the assault and theft. The Muslims agreed, Scott and Leake agreed, I agreed, and finally, so did the mayor.

I still wasn't commissioner.

Eight officers had been hurt, and the mayor and I went to the hospital to visit the most seriously injured. The cops were very glad to see us and to hear the mayor's early comments supporting their actions. We could use the incident to get out dual messages. To the cops: I'll support you with the benefit of the doubt. To the city: There's a new sheriff in town, and we're not going to tolerate disrespect for the police.

Leaving the hospital, Miller, Maple, and I headed up to the 103rd Precinct in Jamaica, Queens, for roll call. (In the peculiarity of New York police jargon, the 103rd Precinct is not pronounced the "one hundred and third," it is the "One-oh-three." This is for radio purposes; the "Three-oh," the "Three-three," and the "One-one-three" are more likely to be understood and less likely to cause confusion over static-filled airwaves than the "thirtieth," the "thirty-third," and the "hundred-and-thirteenth." By now, it's just the way cops talk.)

The 103 was a microcosm of the city: Multiethnic and multiracial, it had good neighborhoods, bad neighborhoods, and some in-between. It was Governor Mario Cuomo's home precinct, but it had all kinds of crime problems. John Miller was very conscious of New York history and symbolism and had suggested we go to the 103 because it was an example of the city being out of control. The 103 was the precinct where Eddie Byrne had been killed.

In February 1988, Police Officer Ed Byrne was sitting in his patrol car, guarding the home of a man who had informed on a drug dealer, when he was shot to death by drug dealers. It was a vicious and cold-blooded murder, and they did it to send a message: This was their turf, their world, they had the power. But massive police response to that homicide had changed that perception of the 103. We now intended to change it for the rest of the city.

I might not have told the 103 I was coming. Tradition held that before a police commissioner visited a precinct a call would be put in saying he was coming. It was a not-very-subtle message that if the commanding officer was working, he'd better be there; that if he wasn't working, he might think about working; that if he still wasn't working, then the executive officer better be there; that the broom better be taken to the place; that the girlie pictures go down and the color photos of the brass get straightened. Three parking spaces were to be cleared in front for the commissioner's car, his advance car, and his backup car. It was expected to be expected.

I preferred it another way. I was a cop going to visit a police station, no advance notice. All my advance guy would do was make sure there wasn't total pandemonium.

I walked in before the midnight shift.

It's funny about the world of police; there are the cops of the day and the cops of the night. Cops of the night are a different breed. Their uniforms tend to be a little less neat, they're a little more unkempt. They look like people who belong in the dark. As I entered the muster room of the beat-up old station, twenty-odd pairs of eyes turned to size up their new leader.

"This is my first official act as police commissioner," I told them. "I came a long way to get here. I know you're thinking: Who's this guy who talks funny, this guy from Boston who's the new commissioner.

"It's odd that this is a department I've dreamed of my whole life. I don't know why a kid from Dorchester was dreaming of being a New York City cop, but I do remember a picture book I kept checking out of the library that had illustrations of all the units and divisions of this department, and I know how I used to feel about the traditions of the NYPD. I want you all to feel the same way that I do.

"I said when I took this job that we would take this city back for the good people who live here, neighborhood by neighborhood, block by block, house by house. But I'm going to need your help in doing that. I'm going to need all of you in the game.

"I want my cops to be cops. I want them to be assertive. I don't want them walking by or looking the other way when they see something. No matter what the old rules were, I expect you to see something and take proper police action.

"I expect you to be honest. I expect you to uphold the oath that you took on the first day. If you get into problems doing your job, and you're doing it right, I'll back you up. If you're wrong, I'll get you retrained and back to work. If you're dirty or brutal, I'll see to it that you're arrested, you're fired, and you're put in jail.

"I like cops. I've been with cops most of my adult life. I want to bring three things to this department: Pride, Commitment, and Respect. I want you to be proud of your city, of your department, and of yourselves. Proud that you're cops in the greatest police department in the world. I also want you to take pride in your appearance, in your uniforms, and in how you wear them."

I looked out at these guys. The 103 was a good place to start in terms of improving appearances. They as much as said, You couldn't have given us an hour's notice? We could have gotten a haircut or something.

"I want you to have commitment," I told them. "Commitment to do the job. Oh, yes, we are in for some rough times here. We've seen what the Mollen Commission found"—the Mollen Commission was investigating corruption in the NYPD—"and I'll tell you now there's more to come. It's not enough just for you to uphold your oath. When that man or woman next to you is brutal or corrupt or stealing, it is part of your oath that you just can't stand by, that's not enough.

"You all have families back home, wives and kids who depend on you. Mothers and fathers who love you." There were two generations of officers in front of me; some were kids who went home and lived with mommy and daddy, others were men in their forties who went home to kids. "When some cop that you work with is robbing drug dealers or beating people, that puts you all in danger. Because then we're asking the criminals to be able to tell, is that the good police coming through the door or the bad police?

"What happens when a cop gets shot because some drug dealer thought that cops weren't coming to arrest him but to beat him and rob him?"

The 103 stared at me.

"I want you all to know right now, I know what I'm asking of you, and I'll tell you what I intend to give you in return.

"If you do your jobs, I will back you to the hilt. We had an incident tonight which we're looking into. And if I find the officers acted properly—and it appears they did—then I will back them up publicly. We will be sailing in harm's way as we take back this city together."

Miller was watching the cops. He remembers, "A third of the cops were saying, 'This guy's too good to be true.' Another third were saying, 'Uh oh, this guy's going to be trouble.' And a third were wondering which way to go." Cops had heard the brass say they were going to get tough on cops before, but they had never heard a commissioner come in and say he was going to back them up. The old brass had come through a long police culture in which the assumption was that if there was an "incident," the officer must be guilty, and even if he wasn't guilty, it was easier to hang him out to dry than to fight the public and the press. So the cops were listening to me and figuring, "Break our balls and back us up, that might not be a bad deal; we'll take that."

I also talked to them about respect, both for themselves and for the public they serve. "We're going to work very hard to take this city back, but all our good work can be undone by one cop who treats a citizen disrespectfully," I told them. "We have to keep the public's respect for us. If we do our job brutally, if we do it criminally, if we do it thoughtlessly, then we're going to lose the public's respect and all the good work you do will be overshadowed by the sense that we're a brutal corrupt force. Pride, Commitment, Respect."

Leaving the roll call, Maple, Miller, and I crammed into the back of my department-issued four-door Mercury. In the front sat my security detail, Detective Al Powlett and Detective Jimmy Motto, who was driving. There's no sight in the world quite like the New York skyline all lit up, if you stop and pay attention to it. We were in the center lane, cruising over the Triborough Bridge from Queens into Manhattan, when the digital clock on the dashboard hit 12:00. "It's midnight, Commissioner," said Detective Motto. "Raise your right hands," I said to Maple and Miller. We all laughed. "Okay, we're onboard now." It had been a long day and a longer night, and as we passed through the toll booth, I was finally commissioner. Life was going to change and I was ready.

While I could be completely happy sitting in my room and reading, I definitely liked getting attention. I was in my glory in sixth grade when they made me school crossing guard and gave me a white strap to wear across my chest (I always kept it spotless) and a shiny silver badge. My post was the corner of East Street and Adams, and I would stand there with my book bag and my metal lunch box—Hopalong Cassidy, Wild Bill Hickok, Zorro, Davy Crockett, whoever was the latest craze—and I would stop traffic and cross the kids from one side of the street to the other. Everybody stayed between the white lines while I was on duty.

Maybe I took it a little too seriously; a gang of girls used to chase me home at the end of the day.

That year, I really started to shine. If there was a center stage, I sought it. When I brought my clay figures into school and talked about my hobbies, the teacher was so impressed she sent me to see the principal, who assigned me to be master of ceremonies for our celebration of Flag Day. I stood in the auditorium in front of the whole school in my Boy Scout shirt (we didn't have enough money to buy the pants) and my good school trousers, which always seemed to be too short.

I graduated with honors and passed the exams to get into the most prestigious public school in the city, Boston Latin. The best part of Boston Latin was getting there. I walked up Meeting House Hill and then down to Kane Square, and every day I passed the same police officer at the same crossing. His car was always parked in exactly the same spot and was one of the first I'd seen with the new-style rotating gumball-machine light, so that fascinated me. Every morning, this red-faced Irish cop with a cigar in his mouth had the police radio running through his loudspeaker so he could hear his calls while he was on his post. I'd hear the crackle as I crossed the street.

I never talked to him.

Kane Square was a turnaround for the trackless trolley. I got on and rode through Upham's Corner and into Roxbury, the all-black neighborhood of Boston, to Dudley Street station, a big hub of trolleys, trains, and buses. At Dudley Street, I fought a thousand other kids to get onto rickety old Mack buses, the oldest and most dilapidated in the fleet.

Those buses were already riding on their rims and were serving their final days jam-packed, creaking, and chugging up and down hills, shuttling schoolkids to Boston Latin and to English High School. English was for rough-and-tumble types, dead-end kids; Boston Latin was for us smart guys, and those rides were filled with hard rivalries.

You had to study hard at Boston Latin. I was used to getting good grades and not putting in much effort, but that didn't work here. I did okay in most classes, but I found I had absolutely no proficiency with foreign languages, particularly Latin, which was a requirement. I just could not pick up the language, and in eighth grade I flunked out.

It was humiliating. I had been the boy wonder, off to conquer the world, and now I was back at Grover Cleveland Junior High School with the rest of the kids from the corner. The only saving grace was that Boston Latin had been all boys but Grover Cleveland was coed. Having girls in class was a big improvement. Not that I was a great success with the girls. I spent one full school year pining for Camille Grasso. Camille was a pretty girl who lived around the corner, and I passed her house every day. I'd see her and never know what to say. I never got up anywhere near the nerve to ask her out.

In ninth grade, I passed the exams and got into Boston Technical High School. Boston Tech was so named because it was a multiple-career-path school. You could graduate with technical engineering and shop skills, or you could take an academic curriculum with machine shop and engineering on the side. I chose academics.

Boston Tech was in Roxbury, and this was my first significant exposure to black people, or Negroes as we called them in those days. I had seen blacks on my train expeditions with Franny McNulty and out the window on the trolley to Boston Latin, but if a black person walked past our corner in Dorchester, all of us really took note. We didn't see black people often because there were no black residents in the neighborhood and little-to-no work for outsiders.

Boston Tech was about 10 percent black, and while there were tensions and a growing awareness of race conflicts—this was 1962 to 1965, a volatile time in race relations—by and large we all got along pretty well.

Race was never really an issue for me. While I was not one of the white kids who hung out with a black crowd, I had enough black friends to the point that it didn't make a difference. A lot of the people I grew up with didn't have the opportunity to interact with blacks, which sometimes led to unfortunate generalizations and misunderstandings. I didn't think of it at the time, but going to high school in the middle of Roxbury turned out to be a positive influence.

On occasion, I walked home from school, about a mile total. It was a distressed area, and I did feel uncomfortable—even in those days Roxbury was a high-crime neighborhood—but I never had an incident. Mostly, I looked forward to passing the Drake's Devil Dog factory and smelling the sweet little chocolate cakes. From there I'd pass the famous Kasonoff Bakery and breathe in the rye bread. It was a tantalizing walk home.

We were Catholics, but not very observant, my father more involved in religion than my mother. I had a brother who died shortly after birth, and although they never discussed it with me, I always had the feeling his death might have distanced them from the church. We went to church for the holidays, but other than that my mother almost never went, except for weddings. At the post office where my father worked, there was a chapel where a fifteen-minute quickie service was performed each Sunday without a sermon, so he tried to get there. After I made my first communion and got confirmed, my parents left the decision whether to continue to go to Sunday school up to me. I had no interest, and I stopped going.

So one day here comes Father Carney up the front stairs. Father Carney was a young priest, kind of a Bing Crosby type, popular with the kids, the sort who was put in charge of the Little League. I answered the door when he knocked. I hadn't seen him in a while.

"Hello, Billy. I'd like to see your father."

My dad was in the living room, reading. He didn't invite Carney in; he left the good father standing in the hall. Not to invite a priest into your home was unusual in our neighborhood. If we went to Mass, we'd hear buzzing in the pews about that one.

"You son's not been attending our Sunday school courses," Father Carney told him.

"Well, Father," said my dad, "I told him once he got confirmed that it would be his choice to go or not, and I guess he's made it."

"You know, it's your obligation as a Catholic father to make sure your son is all right in the eyes of the Lord. Our courses . . ."

"There's nothing wrong with my son."

They went at it pretty good. My father had made a commitment to me, I was old enough to make my own decisions, and no matter how the priest invoked the Lord and Scriptures, my dad was never one to bend to unreasonable authority. Father Carney never got his foot in our door, and I never set foot in Sunday school again.

Very early one hot and quiet summer Sunday morning when I was about fifteen, my father took me out in the car to teach me to drive. I didn't have a learner's permit, so I guess he was at some risk on his insurance, but he put me behind the wheel and off we went. There was not much traffic in Dorchester on Sundays.

We drove by the corner of Morrissey Boulevard and Freeport Street with the windows rolled down, and there was a cop at a call box, swearing a blue streak. Every other word out of his mouth was f-ing this and f-ing that, so routinely. It rubbed me the wrong way. For some reason, that stuck with me.

After I got my learner's permit, my father and I routinely spent Sunday mornings driving around Codman Square, a business district of Dorchester. One morning, we stopped behind a cop car at a red light. We were the only two cars at the intersection. The light turned green, and the two cops were busy shooting the breeze. They weren't moving. We waited.

"Toot the horn," my dad said finally.

"What?"

"Toot the horn, get 'em going."

So I tooted the horn.

Cops being cops, they pulled out, let us pass, and then pulled us over. Both officers got out of the cruiser and sauntered toward us.

"You honk your horn?"

"The light changed, you weren't moving." My father was immediately on his high horse. "Yeah, we honked at you. How'm I supposed to let you know that it turned green?" They straightaway got into a pissing contest.

I was sweating there with just a learner's permit, fearing that any confrontation would end my driving career. One officer was leaning at the window, an arm cocked on the roof, the other at his gun belt, talking over me to my father on the passenger side. My father never let up. I just kept both hands on the wheel and my eyes on my dad.

Fortunately, it was toward the end of the morning. If they'd met up with us in mid-tour, they probably would have busted my father's chops a little, but these guys had been riding around for eight hours and all they were interested in was getting home. My father couldn't have known that. He was interested in not getting pushed around.

19

Directed Patrol Exponential: the Philadelphia Police & Compstat

by John Hill

"The practice in organizing the work in almost all police departments has been to distribute the patrol force evenly among three 8-hour shifts and to assign the officers to beats of equal area. This method of distribution was evidence either of a lack of knowledge concerning the hourly and geographical fluctuations of the police (work) load or of indifference to the possible increase in efficiency resulting from a distribution of the force on the basis of need throughout the day over the area to be served"

—Nathan F. Iannone,
(Iannone, 1987, p. 358)

Upon leaving New York City, John F. Timoney was appointed as Police Commissioner in the City of Philadelphia, Pennsylvania. Jack Maple went on to address crime problems and consult agencies in compstat strategies in New Orleans, Newark, and other cities struggling to get a handle on crime. Sadly, his life and career were cut short it their apex when he succumbed to cancer in August of 2001 (*American Police Beat,* 2001, October, p. 34).

December 20, 2001: The day begins with Compstat for members of the Philadelphia Police Department. The City is still waking up, as police vehicles arrive in a steady flow at the Pennsylvania Convention Center at 6:45 A.M. The center is located within walking distance from Philadelphia Police Headquarters, known in local parlance as "the Round House" because of its circular architecture. Other than newspaper delivery trucks, the city is pretty much still asleep. An occasional patrol car rumbles past, as does a lone police officer patrolling on bicycle, subtle yet reassuring reminders of a vastly changed police force in the City of Brotherly Love.

It is still dark outside, and briskly cold, less than a week before Christmas. Philadelphia Police Commissioner John F. Timoney is scheduled to leave his position in just two weeks.

Timoney, a career New York City police officer, had reached the status of second in command as the former First Deputy Commissioner for the NYPD. During the administration of NYPD Commissioner Bratton (1994–1996) Timoney was a principal player in New York's miraculous crime-reduction efforts. In probably the greatest New York blunder since the Mets let base-ball pitcher Tom Seaver go, the City of New York lost Timoney to Philadelphia. New York's loss was most assuredly Philadelphia's gain.

Timoney was appointed Philadelphia Police Commissioner on March 9, 1998 (2000a). Having been largely responsible for developing Compstat in New York, Timoney knew firsthand how important a role it had played (and continues to play) in reducing crime in that city (2000b). Upon arrival in Philadelphia, Timoney promptly introduced the Compstat process to that city's police department.

Patrol cars, mostly unmarked, emerge out of the darkness to converge on the convention center, the location of this week's Compstat meeting. Patrol District Commanders emerge from their vehicles—captains mainly, but also special unit commanders from such entities as aviation unit, detectives, narcotics, highway patrol, as well as inspectors—the division commanders above the various districts. Most of these "top brass" arrive in uniform shirts. Once outside their vehicles, most commanders remove a crisp uniform blouse coat from the back seat area of the vehicle, and liberate it from the dry-cleaner's plastic. Compstat is taken very seriously, and looking sharp is part of the equation of professionalism.

The serious nature deferred to Compstat, the priority, is emphasized by the start time of the meeting, 7:30 A.M. And, that means things start at 7:30 sharp, hence the early arrivals. In many places, the police brass are just waking up at 7:30 A.M. to meander in to work by 9:00 A.M. In Philadelphia, the brass arrive before dawn for Compstat. This is the way it should be. Bad guys don't work bankers hours, so neither should cops (Maple, 1999, p. 23). Plus, it shows the street cops, like the officer that rode past on bike patrol, that the administration is up early too, fighting crime.

There is coffee and water available at the entrance to the Compstat room, but hardly anybody stops to partake. This is perhaps because the sense of urgency is palatable, like with ballplayers before a big game. On the far eastern side of the room is a projection map of the city. To the left of that is a long conference table set up for Commissioner Timoney, and his six deputy commissioners. Directly across from them are two rows of long conference tables for division commanders, district commanders, special unit commanders, and executive officers. At the bottom of this horseshoe-shaped arrangement, is a table with civilian employees operating the GIS (Geographic Information System) technology. GIS is a comprehensive mapping/presentation system for both tactical and strategic planning as well as for day-to-day operational needs (ESRI, 2001). Behind that table, are the press and any other invited guests.

On this morning, the 35th District and the 9th District are "presenting"—reporting what the crime situation is in these precincts. Neither of these districts are strangers to crime. District, or precinct, commanders from the respective "houses" and their executive officers are questioned about recent crime activity in their areas. Their "bosses," the division commanders, jump in when necessary. Accountability is thick in the room. Woe be it to the district commander who cannot answer a question about a particular crime, or crime pattern, being displayed on the large computerized projection map. When an incident or pattern is delineated, the area commander is asked, "what are you doing about it?" At times the presentation, or inquiry, becomes a grilling. But, coupled with the "stick" of accountability, is the "carrot" of agency resources. Commanders are frequently offered help by one of the commissioners, "Do you need detectives?, narcotics division?, highway patrol?"

This is Compstat in Philadelphia. Although born in New York City, Compstat matured greatly in Philadelphia. In Philly, Compstat would be taken to much higher levels. In Philly, Compstat would grow exponentially. Compstat would grow from an all-inclusive proactive crime reporting system, to a comprehensive strategic planning and police management information system that also tracks overtime, police vehicle accidents, citizen complaints, and other supervisory issues.

Like a private sector corporation every possible eventuality or possibility is thoroughly gone over with attention to detail. Indeed, what private sector corporation could match the responsibility level of a big city police department responsible for the public safety of millions of people? Compstat assures that, in layman's terms, "no stone goes unturned." After one District presented, a robbery trend was indicated. The District was then grilled about what progress is being made. When the reply was given that a palm print was lifted at one crime scene, that seemed to be the end of the inquiry, until the commissioners pressed even further, asking "Okay, what came out of the palm print?"

Even many robbery victims are discreetly checked for warrants. Especially if they act suspiciously, for example if they don't call police at first but choose to go directly to the hospital. Why were they robbed? Was it drug-related? The science of Criminology tells us that many victims are simply the less fortunate of two perpetrators. The search for crime and its causation is so relentless that even suspects already in jail are repeatedly interviewed by Philadelphia Police.

The Compstat process continuously strives to get to the causes of crime. Questions come in an incessant barrage; What are the ages of these suspects? What are the causes of these shootings? Are these robberies? Are they narcotics related? In the unremitting quest for comprehensiveness, the Philadelphia city police work closely with the area university and college police, the Southeastern Pennsylvania Transit Authority (SEPTA) "Transit" Police, housing police and various federal law enforcement agencies based in the city.

There is a relentless search to uncover trends and patterns. After a few presentations that detailed elderly victims, Commissioner Timoney became expressly concerned. Most cops have a special place in their hearts for elderly persons victimized, as well as young children. Timoney, a cop's cop, is no different as evident by his special concern. Commanders are grilled whether they see a trend or increase in attacks on the elderly. They are urgently informed to make this concern a priority. The top brass get very frank, blunt, and hold the precinct brass highly accountable. An especially terse exchange takes place over the report of an elderly woman who had been stabbed repeatedly in broad daylight on a city trolley. Still, resources are frequently offered to address problems. Unique to this case, was the suggestion by Timoney to even consider crime prevention techniques to educate the elderly on avoiding victimization.

Crime is attacked from every conceivable angle. A City Police Inspector gives a briefing on a particularly thorough and innovative approach to a stolen car problem occurring in his district. Aside from targeting when and where cars are stolen, an "opposite direction" approach takes the form of surveilling areas where these autos are dumped, as well as what type of car is most frequently stolen. A radio car team on patrol could potentially see a certain make and model of car passing by and know, based on Compstat intelligence, that that particular type of car is stolen quite frequently. If nothing else, they could then run a computer check on the license plate.

Similar to the opposite direction approach to stolen cars, reported rapes were put through the same scrutiny. Aside from analyzing where rape victims were confronted and what kind of force/method was used, it is important to note *where* these victims were taken to be assaulted.

The pick-up and forced attack location is no less important than the location where the attack took place, and why the perpetrator selected that location. The GIS mapping is effective for this type of multi-directional approach to combat crime, and as such the system is relied upon heavily in the Compstat process.

Conjoined with accountability is praise, where appropriate. Various commanders and districts were openly congratulated for successes, crime reduction efforts, good arrests, and the like. Compstat, on this day in Philly, concludes with a touch of relevancy and attentiveness as Timoney reminds everyone in attendance that the holiday season is peaking, to particularly watch commercial establishments, holiday shoppers, and not to "drop the ball" so close to the holiday, especially after a solid year of crime control successes. The police professionals in participation all rise upon being dismissed by the police commissioner and hurriedly pour from the Compstat meeting to set about the unrelenting task of making the city safer. There is a sense of "wow, now the work is just beginning" but also a satisfaction in that Compstat has provided the means necessary to successfully complete the daunting task.

SUMMARY

Compstat, although "born" in New York City, spread across the nation to other police departments as the best and brightest NYPD commissioners and chiefs went on to police service in others cities. In Philadelphia, Police Commissioner John Timoney proved that Compstat would work outside of New York. Crime in Philadelphia dropped continuously every year (1998–2001) that Timoney served as Police Commissioner (Philadelphia Police Department, 2000d). Timoney also saw that Geographic Information System-GIS technology was added to the Compstat process. GIS is a comprehensive mapping/presentation system for both tactical and strategic planning as well as for day-to-day operational needs. Timoney continued the relentless assessment, evaluation, and follow-up that is critical to the Compstat process (Philadelphia Police Department, 2000b). In Philadelphia, Timoney, considered a cop's cop, inherited a historically troubled agency and steered it toward respectability (Shuster, 2002).

20

What We've Learned About Policing

by William J. Bratton and William Andrews

"A thin blue line of inexperienced, undertrained, and undersupervised cops doesn't stand a chance against the hit-and-run tactics of the criminals. If they are all spread out and aren't following a game plan, they're nothing but scarecrows—to borrow a metaphor from John Timoney."

—Jack Maple,
Former Deputy Commissioner, NYPD
(Maple, 1999, p. 131*)*

Everyone knows about New York's spectacular crime turnaround, with murder down 68 percent and overall felonies down 50 percent in the five years since 1993. But how we accomplished that turnaround—and what we've learned about how to police New York—isn't widely known or fully understood. It should be, because the New York story adds up to a textbook on how to police any big city.

Our success rested on two major changes. First, we had to remake the NYPD into an effective, focused organization. Second, we had to use this instrument actually to police the city by developing strategies and tactics that would prevent and uproot crime rather than just react to it. In practice, of course, these were parallel, often overlapping efforts. The re-engineering was more challenging than the strategizing; and if we hadn't changed the way the department did business, it wouldn't have mattered what field strategies we chose, because we wouldn't have been able to translate them into practice.

Professors of business administration and organizational management would have caught on to what we were doing right away, since it was no different from the restructuring and re-engineering that had transformed American business in the late 1980s and early 1990s. Like the corporate CEOs of that era, we began with a large, unfocused, inward-looking, bureaucratic organization, poor at internal communication or cooperation and chronically unresponsive to intelligence from the outer world. We reduced layers of management, drove

Reprinted by permission from *City Journal* 9, no. 2 (1999).

responsibility down to the operating units, improved communication and data processing, tightened accountability, and rewarded results. In short order, we had the NYPD's bureaus and divisions competing with criminals, not with one another.

Police work is by nature decentralized and discretionary. The cop in the field, the front-line supervisor, the precinct commander—these are the real decision makers in day-to-day police work. The only way you can control a police department from headquarters is if your aim is to prevent police from doing anything, rather than to have them function effectively—and for many years that was precisely the aim of the NYPD. The organization didn't want high performance; it wanted to stay out of trouble, to avoid corruption scandals and conflicts in the community. For years, therefore, the key to career success in the NYPD, as in many bureaucratic leviathans, was to shun risk and avoid failure. Accordingly, cops became more cautious as they rose in rank, right up to the highest levels.

One anecdote that a deputy chief likes to tell perfectly captures how risk-averse the department had become. One weekend in the late eighties, when he was serving as duty captain in upper Manhattan, he arrived at a crime scene where cops had arrested two drug dealers, one of whom had tried to flee to an apartment. The deputy chief helped the cops secure search warrants for the apartment and a safe they found inside it—which contained drugs, cash, and weapons. The next day, the borough commander—"apoplectic with rage," the deputy chief recalls—called him in to yell at him for seeking a warrant. "It's people like you who cause problems in the department," the commander roared. If something like that happens again, the commander ordered, "you will walk away." Sums up the deputy chief: "I, as a captain, was not supposed to encourage these officers to do police work. My job was to stop them from doing police work." After all, something could go wrong.

As for its management philosophy, the NYPD combined the worst of both worlds: it was a micromanaged organization that was strategically adrift. "Cops felt," as one prosecutor remembers it, "as if the brass were checking up on them, not backing them up." Management consisted of sending sergeants around to make sure that patrolmen were at their assigned posts. Woe to the cop who wasn't there—even for a good reason—when the sergeant came at regular intervals to sign his memo book. The message: just sit there and get your ticket punched.

We had to change the department's methods and mind-set. The first step, when author Bratton became commissioner in 1994, was to draw as many people as possible into the planning process, especially the precinct and unit commanders, who corresponded to a corporation's middle managers, and the sergeants and lieutenants, who were, in effect, the front-line supervisors. "Bratton ran an organization that was open to talent," says Jack Maple, a former NYPD deputy commissioner for crime-control strategies. "It was an organization of inclusion, where people weren't afraid to come up with the wildest ideas." Maple himself was a prime case in point. When only a Transit Police lieutenant, he caught Bratton's attention with an idea-crammed memo on how to control robberies in the subway, and he rose rapidly thereafter.

We brought almost 500 people into the planning process, serving on 12 re-engineering teams that questioned everything in heated debate that sometimes escalated to a free-for-all. "An organization as big and as venerable as the NYPD accumulates a lot of bad habits," points out John Timoney, who was chief of department in 1994 and first deputy commissioner in 1995 and is now Philadelphia's police commissioner. "We did things a certain way because we had always done them that way. We had to banish the phrase, 'We have always' from our vocabularies. We had to start asking, 'How should we do it?' and 'How can we do it better?'"

Ideas and innovations bubbled up. The commissioner didn't originate most of the ideas that ended up transforming the way we did business; instead—and crucially—he created the atmosphere in which paradigm-breaking ideas could flourish. A December 1994 plan of action listed more than 600 recommendations, of which we adopted more than 400. We raised recruiting standards and improved training for the real world of police patrol. We redesigned the uniform with input from the officers who wear it, and, with the advice of the police unions, we revamped the archaic discipline system to make it swifter. We retooled our job-performance evaluation system. We even changed our super-secret internal-affairs process, bringing precinct commanders into internal investigations, which strengthened our capacity to prevent and detect police corruption and abuse. Formerly, only a half-dozen internal-affairs officials attempted to control misconduct in a 38,000-person department.

But the most important reform we made was decentralizing the department, devolving power to the precinct commanders and creating a career path for them to ascend. In the old NYPD, precinct commanders had little genuine authority. They couldn't conduct an anti-prostitution operation or use plainclothes officers in anti-drug operations; they couldn't secure search warrants and conduct searches. These constraints reflected a deep mistrust of the precincts, a fear that something could go terribly wrong out there that would embarrass the command staff. But as Robert Johnson, head of the private First Security Services and a member of Bratton's kitchen cabinet, puts it: "A management team that concentrates on preventing failure usually forecloses success. When you don't trust your basic resource, it's hard to perform your basic business."

The precincts are the primary unit of policing, and the precinct commanders are policing's equivalent of corporate line managers. It was just plain crazy to limit their options. Worse, the precinct commander's job was all downside risk in 1993, just before we arrived; there was no real way to succeed and a dozen ways to fail. An outstanding precinct commander's performance against crime would have gone largely unnoticed—nobody was monitoring that kind of success—but a corruption scandal or a mishandled community incident could set a career back years. No wonder that captains tried to hurry through their precinct commands and move on to less career-threatening assignments in the bureaucracy at 1 Police Plaza.

We gave precinct commanders—typically people with 15 years' experience, a college education, and a sophisticated knowledge of the city and the department—the authority to run what amounted to miniature police departments. John Timoney devised a new career ladder for these commanders, ascending from one of the 35 "C" precinct houses with moderate workloads to one of 31 higher-pressure "B" houses and ultimately to one of the 10 extremely busy "A" houses. As a commander rose through these steps, he could advance from captain to deputy inspector to inspector without ever leaving the precincts. A few battlefield promotions made it clear that precinct command was the place to shine in the NYPD.

The good commanders reveled in their new authority, and their precincts became natural arenas for team building. Their cops were energized. Cops like to do police work: stinging a drug dealer with a buy-and-bust operation, executing a search warrant at the apartment of a gun dealer, even catching someone blasting a car radio with a decibel meter—these are interesting jobs compared with regular patrol. They are also team activities that give the workers a shared sense of purpose and a renewed sense of energy.

Accountability goes hand in hand with decentralization; you can't give all that power away without a means of maintaining strategic oversight. The NYPD does that through its now-famous Compstat process, which uses computerized crime statistics, electronic crime maps, and intensive crime-control management meetings to guide and monitor the department's anti-crime strategies.

From the start, Jack Maple had insisted on timely weekly data about crime in the precincts, an approach completely foreign to the NYPD, where crime data typically lagged events by up to three months. Because we couldn't live with flying blind, not knowing what was actually happening precinct by precinct and week by week, Maple, Chief Louis Anemone, and Anemone's staff developed the basic format for the weekly report that the department has been using ever since. It showed weekly felony crime and arrest data for every precinct, comparing it with the totals for the previous week and the month- and year-to-date totals. Compstat was the computer-file name of this report, a contraction of "comparison statistics." Maple and Anemone began going over the new data at meetings with precinct personnel, quizzing commanders about crime in their precincts and what they were doing about it. Soon they were using pin maps and acetate overlays to display the patterns of criminal activity. They began calling in special unit commanders and narcotics commanders. The Compstat process was off and running.

As Compstat grew more sophisticated, we began computer mapping the crime patterns and displaying the maps on large overhead screens. We could identify local crime increases almost immediately and respond to them rapidly with effective measures before they could add up to a big, citywide crime spike. You could see the clusters of shootings, robberies, burglaries, and car thefts. We mapped arrest and patrol activity and compared crime incidents with police response. If the two didn't match up, you knew you were doing something wrong. We compared our deployment patterns with time-of-day graphs that showed when crime spikes were occurring. Compstat's maps helped make sure that we were putting our resources where the problems were, and when they were happening. We could quickly assess whether new strategies and tactics worked or failed.

Compstat enforced cooperation among the department's many bureaus and units. Every week, a different group of commanders from a particular part of the city stands up at the podium to get grilled about crime and prevention in their precincts, but every other relevant special unit and task force commander for that area of the city is also present and must be prepared to respond. Just having them all in one room instantly cut the bureaucratic Gordian knot. Chief Anemone and Deputy Commissioner Maple could broker solutions to current problems on the spot. Was drug dealing causing an increase in shootings? Narcotics enforcement could be called in swiftly. Were burglaries on the rise in a community? The warrant division could search for wanted burglars in the area. Were auto thieves following a certain route to a nearby highway? Highway units could set up a checkpoint.

Above all, as John Timoney puts it, "Compstat is the greatest accountability tool ever." It's an instrument for holding precinct commanders responsible for crime in their areas, rewarding them if they push crime down and removing them if they don't come up with plans to do so. In addition, it gets the whole department, top brass included, involved in thinking about how to push back crime, and it lets precinct commanders know, on a weekly basis, that their bosses support their efforts. Eventually, we used Compstat to manage everything from civilian complaints to overtime to police auto accidents.

It's not too strong a statement to say that we reinvented police strategy in 1994. Before then, the prevailing criminological wisdom held that the police couldn't do much about crime and that police strategies and tactics didn't really matter. In that spirit, the NYPD and most other police departments spent almost no time thinking about anti-crime strategies. Police brass lurched from emergency to emergency, with no one looking at the overall picture.

Strategy is a way of seeing things whole, of focusing on the entire system of crime and how it operates. Since 1994, the NYPD hasn't just been solving crimes; it has been dismantling criminal enterprises and support systems. It has been taking away the things that criminals need to function: their guns, their fences, their chop shops and auto exporters, their drug-buying and prostitution customers, their buildings and apartments, their cars, and the unpoliced sectors of the city where crime used to thrive.

In early 1994, the department developed strategies on guns, drugs, youth crime, domestic violence, and quality of life. Though much has been made of quality-of-life enforcement as key to the overall New York strategy, it was hardly the whole story. To say that "zero tolerance" policing turned New York around, as if driving away squeegee men and panhandlers could by itself cut the robbery and burglary rates, is a gross oversimplification. To succeed, we had to employ the quality-of-life strategy in concert with a range of strategies targeting felony crime.

But quality-of-life enforcement is important for three reasons. First, most neighborhoods are usually more concerned about prostitution, low-level drug dealing, excessive noise, underage drinking, and other minor offenses than major crimes. Citizens want the police to do something about these highly visible disturbances. Second, as George Kelling has persuasively argued in the pages of *City Journal,* disorderly environments breed both crime and fear. Third, criminals who commit serious crimes frequently commit minor violations as well; quality-of-life enforcement lets cops intervene with this population and sometimes prevent serious crimes before they happen.

In 1994, we took quality-of-life enforcement to the streets. Author Bratton had pioneered this style of policing in Boston in the 1970s. He imported it to New York when he became chief of the Transit Police in 1990, and it had transformed the subway from a place where young thugs thought they could get away with anything into a place where they felt they could get away with nothing, with a steep drop in crime as a result. So, too, with the city as a whole: as Kelling has observed, New York City had "depoliced" its streets in the quarter-century prior to 1994. Police officers were walking by disorderly conditions and letting them fester. They were openly giving freedom of the streets to the drug dealers, the gangs, the prostitutes, the drinkers, and the radio blasters. A sense of fear and anarchy pervaded many neighborhoods. The traditional order-keeping forces, the responsible adults in these communities, played less of a role as their own fear and uncertainty grew. They—along with the wrongdoers—had gotten the message that even the cops didn't care, and they were understandably hesitant to put themselves on the line.

The newly empowered precinct commanders targeted prostitution, public drinking and underage drinking, street drug dealing, and excessive noise. They instructed patrol officers to intervene in street disorder and to try to restore a sense of civility and safety to neighborhoods. "We had always been telling the cops what not to do in street situations," says Michael Julian, formerly chief of personnel and now a private security executive. "They needed training in what they could do."

As part of the quality-of-life initiative, the police checked identification of people stopped for minor offenses. When the checks turned up a wanted person, a parole violator, or a repeat offender, cops arrested and searched him, instead of letting him off with a relatively toothless desk-appearance ticket, as is usual with minor offenders.

This intensified police presence had an almost immediate impact on illegal guns. We flooded shooting hot spots, identified through the Compstat maps, with both uniformed and plain-clothes enforcement teams. People carrying illegal guns quickly realized that they risked gun charges after being arrested for minor crimes. After rising briefly in 1994, gun apprehensions then began to fall; the gunslingers were leaving their weapons at home. With far fewer guns on the street, far fewer people were shot and far fewer were killed. In month-to-month comparisons from

1993 to 1994, homicide was down 32 percent in September 1994, 46 percent in October, 28 percent in November, and 34 percent in December.

At the same time, we brought the department's detectives more forcefully into play. We told them to make shootings a priority and to investigate every one as if it were a murder. "There was no good reason why the detective response to a killing was always so much greater than to a shooting," says John Timoney. "An aggravated-assault victim is just a lucky homicide victim whose assailant missed." To keep on top of the issue, Jack Maple had the operations center beep him every time a shooting occurred. In 1994, he got beeped nearly 4,500 times, day and night.

We enlisted detectives in an anti-gun offensive, instructing them to grill anyone arrested in a shooting or on gun charges about how and where he had acquired his weapon. The murderer who fired on Jewish students in a van on the approach ramp to the Brooklyn Bridge, killing one boy, was in custody within a few days; within a week, so was the gun dealer from whom he had purchased his weapon. By the end of 1994, the NYPD had arrested more than 200 gun dealers and confiscated their supply of weapons. Between 1993 and the end of 1995, handgun homicides declined by 40 percent, and shootings declined by more than 2,000 cases.

We fed information about gun trafficking from the precinct interrogations to the NYPD's joint task force with the federal Bureau of Alcohol, Tobacco, and Firearms, which in turn used this intelligence to make arrests for illegal gun trafficking in the main states that supply weapons to New York City. The task force also began closely scrutinizing applicants for federal firearms-dealing licenses, in the belief that some dealers would use the right to buy guns in quantity to sell them illegally to unlicensed New Yorkers. In the first years of the program, 92 percent of applicants for new licenses and for license renewals either failed to win approval or—once they knew the police were watching them—withdrew their applications.

Precinct detective squads adopted a new intelligence-gathering strategy. They began to question all arrestees not only about crimes that they might have committed themselves but also about any other crimes that they knew anything about. Detectives asked arrestees about open homicides, about robbery and burglary patterns, and about where drugs or firearms were for sale. Some talked in return for a promise of more lenient treatment, but many were willing to talk gratis, swelling the NYPD's supply of criminal intelligence and case leads. A car thief turned in a fence, who turned in a father-and-son gun-dealing team. A gun-crime debriefing in the 46th Precinct in the Bronx led to several arrests in a year-old murder case and to arrests for a recent stabbing and a carjacking in the neighboring 43rd Precinct.

Detectives began using the department's improved intelligence to identify robbery patterns more quickly and to apprehend the robbers on the second or third crime of the pattern rather than the ninth or tenth. Identifying a pattern early, staking out the locale, and catching the guy can prevent 20, 30, or even 50 robberies a year. We also told detectives to pursue all accomplices in any robbery, instead of playing the old detective game of building clearance rates by closing cases with just one arrest. Our goal was preventing crime, not closing cases. Robbery fell by more than 26,000 incidents, or 31 percent, in 1994 and 1995. By 1998, it was down 55 percent from its 1993 level.

The Detective Bureau also placed a new emphasis on warrants and on finding wanted fugitives, since warrant absconders who fail to show up for their court appearances are frequently recidivists who will continue to commit crimes for as long as they are free. We expanded the warrant division and doubled warrant apprehensions between 1993 and 1995. Detective Bureau arrests of all kinds, including warrant apprehensions, are up about 138 percent since 1993.

To control burglaries and thefts of car radios, we went after fences who traffic in stolen goods, another thing that the NYPD had never bothered to do. Early on, police used sting operations to nail two major fences in Brooklyn, recovering enough stolen merchandise to fill a warehouse. Eventually, the fences helped identify a who's who of Brooklyn burglars; one fence even had security videotape showing many of the burglars' faces. Even when it doesn't lead directly to mass burglary arrests, as this operation did, shutting down local fences can have a dramatic impact on neighborhood burglary rates. It may take burglars a while to find another outlet for their stolen goods, and they can't go back to work until they can move the hot merchandise. Burglary was down 25,000 incidents in 1994 and 1995, or 25 percent. By 1998, it was down 53 percent.

When we arrived, New York City, and especially the borough of Queens, looked like the car-theft capital of the world, with more than 112,000 cars, worth about $400 million, stolen in 1993. Organized-crime groups stole an estimated 70 percent of them, for parts and for export. Using the same logic that we had applied to burglary, we went after chop shops and auto exporters. In 1995, we set up more than 30 phony fencing operations to catch car thieves, and we conducted more than 60 operations in which undercover officers offered supposedly stolen parts to dealers. We also used stings to make cases against exporters of stolen cars to Russia, the Dominican Republic, Saudi Arabia, Nigeria, and Colombia. We requested district attorneys in Queens and Brooklyn to prosecute auto thieves routinely and send them to jail. Car theft plummeted by more than 40,000 cases in 1994 and 1995, or 36 percent. By 1998, it was down 61 percent.

We knew, as Michael Julian puts it, that "drugs were causing probably half of the crime and a lot of the fights and gunplay." There was no way to reduce crime without going after narcotics. But the department had long been combating drugs in the wrong way, arresting street dealers and seizing drugs—commodities that were expendable, and almost infinitely renewable, as far the drug gangs were concerned. We believed that we had to concentrate on the local drug gangs and dismantle them. These are the critical middlemen between the street dealers and the international drug importers.

Narcotics Division commander Pat Harnett developed a new strategy in 1995 and 1996: he established turf-based drug units that would concentrate on reclaiming individual neighborhoods, investigating and dismantling the drug gangs operating in an area,however long it took. They made drug buys, infiltrated organizations, cultivated informants, planted wiretaps, investigated bank accounts, and built solid cases against all the participants in a gang or group of gangs. When a case was ready, they would roll up 20 or 30 members of a gang in a single day. The department supplemented these investigations with civil actions and eviction proceedings against drug dealers' buildings and apartments. It also sent out uniformed patrolmen in force, to hold the gains and discourage drug buyers from reentering the neighborhood. Everywhere the drug initiatives have gone, they have driven down murders, shootings, and street crime.

All these strategies—and a host of other ones targeting youth crime or family violence, for example, or using civil lawsuits to hamstring criminal enterprises—send one clear message to the criminal population of New York: "It's not your street," as one cop put it. "This street belongs to the people of New York. We are going to take it back."

Many criminologists, as you'd expect, are sticking to their guns and insisting that nothing we have done had the slightest effect on New York's crime drop. Crime fell not just in New York but nationwide, they say, proving that some impersonal force much bigger than the NYPD has come to bear on all of urban America. In truth, however, in 1994 and 1995, the drop in New York crime accounted for more than half of the crime decline in the entire country: we weren't part of the national trend; we drove the trend.

But what reasons do the experts proffer to explain the drop in crime? The crime-prone youth population shrank, they argue, and employment expanded. In New York, however, the teenage population was stable in the early 1990s, not declining, and the minority teenage population was actually on the rise. Between 1990 and 1994, New York City public high school enrollments were up 12 percent. Throughout the period of steep crime decline, moreover, New York had an unemployment rate of between 8 and 10 percent, just about double the national rate. According to the demographic and economic theories, crime should have been raging out of control instead of falling off the charts.

"The experts will never forgive Bratton and Giuliani for proving them wrong," says Tom Repetto of the Citizens' Crime Commission. "They want to believe that crime can only be reduced by sweeping social change. But they do have a fallback position: if the police did reduce crime, they did it by illegitimate means."

The claim of "illegitimate means" is growing more insistent, accompanied by accusations that the NYPD routinely uses unconstitutional searches and "Gestapo tactics." Policing in New York, critics charge, has been "militarized," as if SWAT teams were roving around the city on search-and-destroy missions. The tragic shooting of Amadou Diallo in February and the outrageous abuse of Abner Louima in 1997 have fanned this talk significantly. Many who claim to speak for minority communities say that they now fear the police more than they fear the criminals.

The fear may be understandable, but the problem has been overdrawn. The NYPD is not a racist or brutal department. It won its gains against crime not by abusing citizens but by strategically managing and focusing its resources. Its problem is a problem of attitude: cops need to be more respectful in their encounters with the public. With crime under control, we have the breathing space to provide much better training in the human side of policing and to build trusting relationships in every neighborhood in the city. The NYPD rose to the challenge of crime in the mid-1990s; it certainly can rise to this challenge now.

Though the department can do much more to win the confidence of minority communities, it has already done the most important thing: today, those communities receive the level of police protection and service they deserve. They aren't written off as unimportant and unpoliceable. The Compstat revolution had the effect of allocating resources to the neighborhoods that needed the help most. "All the dots representing crime on Compstat maps are the same size, whether the victim is Leonardo DiCaprio or Fred Mertz," says Jack Maple. "The resources go where the problems are." As a result, minority neighborhoods like East New York and Washington Heights have seen huge crime drops. Kids can play on the street again; they don't go to bed to the sound of gunfire anymore.

What we learned above all from the New York experience is that police can control and manage virtually every type of crime in virtually every neighborhood. No place is unpoliceable; no crime is immune to better enforcement efforts. Though underachieving in the past, American police departments can take the lead in restoring safety and order to communities all over the country. After a generation of police executives who were convinced that cops couldn't cut crime, a new group of leaders is following the New York example and sending the message that police can make a difference. These leaders are junking the old reactive model, in which police responded to crimes and filed reports, in favor of a new strategic policing that gets criminals on the run and keeps them running. American police departments are beginning to live up to the boast posted by an anonymous officer in the NYPD Command Center in 1995: "We're not report takers," it read. "We're the police."

21

Philadelphia Police Go Online to Fight Crime

by ESRI

"(Patrol allocation) should be apportioned on a more logical basis than emotion, political considerations, or mere guesswork"

—Nathan F. Iannone,
(Iannone, 1994, p. 238)

The Philadelphia Police Department (PPD) handles about three million 911 calls annually—a workload that could prove overwhelming to a limited staff. To help with its management, the PPD relies on a sophisticated geographical database to generate up-to-date maps for use in crime analysis.

September 1997 marked the official launch of the Crime Analysis and Mapping Unit of the PPD. Small though it may be—three civilians and one officer—it serves the needs of 7,000 police officers and 1,000 civilian personnel. Since 1992, the City of Philadelphia has made great strides in developing a GIS infrastructure that today is the largest distributed, integrated municipal GIS in the country.

PUTTING THE MAPS TO WORK

Along with producing maps using ESRI's ArcView GIS Version 3.1, the crime unit provides input on the analysis of patterns in the data with the help of ArcView Spatial Analyst. The PPD holds crime analysis meetings on a rotating weekly schedule with two to three divisions scheduled per week and all nine divisions covered over one month. The maps include sheets for homicide,

For more information contact Robert Cheetham (tel.: 215-686-1198, fax: 215-686-3337, or e-mail: cheetham@pobox.upenn.edu).

aggravated assault, property crimes, vehicle-related crimes, rapes, robberies, and narcotics. The Crime Analysis and Mapping Unit, which is staffed by GIS programmer/analysts Lorlene Hoyt, Robert Cheetham, and Kevin Switala, and officer Joe Blickley, also produces maps for special requests such as gunshot incident density and recent criminal activity for helicopter crews.

Within a few months after the system's implementation, the PPD was seeing a difference. The maps played a part in the PPD's locating and busting vehicle "chop shops," where stolen cars are dismantled and sold for parts. Another benefit came as high crime patterns were identified on the maps; police patrols were realigned to fit the need.

Robert Cheetham and Kevin Switala, both GIS programmer/analysts for the unit, have been working on developing more applications for the crime unit. Switala developed a stolen vehicle tracking application that enables officers to see the location of recovered vehicles in relation to the area in which they were stolen.

The crime analysis unit has begun to use ArcView Spatial Analyst to observe crime densities. This application proved particularly useful in breaking a large drug enforcement case. Street maps showing building footprints and crime densities have enabled the PPD to do more effective planning in the operation. Cheetham says, "They didn't realize how bad crime was in some areas until they saw the patterns on the density maps."

Continuing to develop applications, the crime unit is taking its endeavors several steps further with the objective of automating the map production process and enabling personnel within each of the PPD's districts to map results of ad hoc queries.

Cheetham and Switala were well aware of how their efforts were benefiting the PPD, but they also knew that the sheer volume of events had the potential to slow down the map production process. They envisioned a plan to decentralize the mapping functions to each of the district offices, enabling any officer or detective to generate customized maps.

"What the officers are really interested in is getting more timely maps. We already produce a lot of maps in hard copy that are sent out, but they want to get more—they want to see patterns faster," says Cheetham. "The more information officers have, the better equipped they are to do their job."

Cheetham and Switala decided to work with ESRI's MapObjects Professional, which can be used with common desktop software in each of the district offices, and began constructing incident query forms using Visual Basic applications to integrate into MapObjects Professional.

The generic incident mapping application they designed will enable officers to define a series of parameters on a form, submit the request, and have a map of incidents returned. Identification requests will return multiple incidents and show related arrest information.

Cheetham says, "The decision to go with MapObjects was not just a software choice. The entire component software approach has allowed us to rapidly construct several small, focused applications with customized interfaces and capabilities outside that of ArcView GIS."

Application Distribution

With the applications construction issue dealt with, they were still left with the problem of distribution. Although MapObjects Professional does not require the system and hardware resources necessary to run ArcView GIS, it does require a 32-bit Windows operating system and the PPD is standardized on Windows 3.1. Unless workstations were upgraded to Windows 95 or NT, the MapObjects Professional applications couldn't be installed in the district offices. A Windows NT infrastructure is being phased in, but the crime analysis and mapping group was concerned about the potential systems administration burden when the mapping applications were installed in the district offices.

MapObjects Internet Map Server responded to this concern with its ability to serve dynamic maps and data quickly on a variety of servers. Using the solution, the crime unit will be able to serve multiple applications from a single server to any number of clients. It also centralizes the administration of both data and applications and can easily accommodate expansion of the system as the number of clients rises.

Officers will be able to access several reports including summaries of activity for a user-specified period, lists of incidents occurring at a single address, and charts analyzing day-of-week and time-of-day relationships for aggravated assaults and robberies. Another benefit of the Intranet-based applications will be the team's ability to turn around late-breaking information immediately.

Cheetham and Switala have deployed the general mapping and analysis tools in a pilot program with good results, and they anticipate January 1, 1999, as the City-wide rollout.

22

How to Run a Police Department

by George L. Kelling

"Law enforcement is no longer seen as mere work, involving discretion, boredom, and unpleasantries; it becomes sort of a creed"

—P. Manning
(Bolman & Deal, 1997, p. 220)

From Plato in Athens to Police Commissioner William Bratton in New York, experts on public order have ceaselessly worried over one key problem: how to control the police who maintain that order. Truly, it's a conundrum. The police, unlike almost everyone else in American society, are commissioned to use force, even deadly force. But unlike other groups licensed to use force—prison guards, say, or soldiers—they are not sequestered in prisons or on bases. They don't operate in groups under close command. They are dispersed throughout society. And as they patrol the streets unsupervised, singly or in pairs, their power exposes them to mighty temptations.

Citizens and politicians constantly urge them to "do something, *now*," about drugs, crime, and violence. Hampered by constricting criminal procedures, and at times by the lack of authority or resources, officers feel pressure (even from the administrators of their own departments) to do "what has to be done"—that is, to abuse their authority by settling matters with their own version of street justice. In addition, police become enmeshed with society's most troubled and most needy, as well as with its most vicious and most depraved. Their immersion in the world of vice and misery can breed cynicism and contempt for those around them and can tempt them to commit crimes like accepting payoffs not to enforce the law or even shaking down drug dealers.

Recently, Commissioner Bratton has had more reason than ever to ponder this problem: even as his aggressive anti-crime push has dramatically cut the city's crime rate—with murder down an astonishing 32 percent and robbery down 22 percent—the NYPD's well-publicized instances of lawlessness and corruption in the 30th Precinct, along with officers'

Reprinted by permission from *City Journal* 5, no. 4 (1997).

unwillingness to finger their colleagues who made a drunken shambles out of a Washington police convention, have dramatized just how hard it is even for a successful top cop to keep his troops in line. The solution Bratton brings to that problem is as innovative and promising as his crime-busting strategies.

In fact it is, at bottom, the same strategy. If you can devise ways of reducing crime that work dramatically, most police officers will find success so gratifying that their own self-image, their pride in being part of a winning organization, will serve as an internal bar to misbehavior. If you set up a managerial structure that keeps everyone focused on the department's core crime-reducing mission, that in itself will go far to controlling officers. And if you make sure officers have the legal tools to do the job properly, they won't feel pressure to exceed their authority, and they won't develop the cynicism that comes from trying to do a job whose requirements are in irreconcilable conflict.

But here's the rub: this winning strategy is so far in advance of the conventional wisdom that New York State's legislators and judges don't begin to understand it. In June the State Legislature, pushed by the state's judiciary, blunderingly passed a little-noticed amendment to the budget that inadvertently stripped New York cops of the legal authority they need to police in Bratton's twenty-first-century style. New York City officials are scrambling to undo the Legislature's blunder, which threatens to subvert the city government's biggest success in years. As Bratton told me, "If this is not corrected, it has the potential to undermine the whole effort."

Bratton's solution to the problem of control flies in the face of an orthodoxy that goes at least as far back as the early twentieth century. Since then, the effort to prevent corruption and control officers has shaped virtually every aspect of police organization, administration, and tactics. By mid-century, police and political leaders throughout the United States had established a rigidly hierarchical command structure designed for this purpose, a structure that remains in place today.

Rules and regulations cover every conceivable aspect of organizational life. Extensive training socializes not just recruits but also seasoned personnel. Until recently, departments kept officers in cars to prevent "contamination" by citizen contact, and regulations prohibited cops from making drug arrests, so as to forestall seduction by the mountains of money involved in drug dealing. A central 911 emergency call system screens requests for police service to ensure that individual officers aren't asked to do improper things. A powerful, secretive internal affairs bureau penetrates every nook and cranny to guard against corruption. And police administrators have tried to restrict cops to dealing with only the most serious crimes, since enforcement of laws against minor crimes like panhandling and disorderly conduct plunges patrol officers into ambiguity and requires them to exercise considerable discretionary judgment.

Given all these tools of control and socialization, managers should be able to shape a powerful, unified culture that would dominate their departments and prevent corruption. But no. Instead, police departments—the NYPD included—have two separate cultures: the cop culture and the management culture. The cop culture's most visible manifestation is the blue curtain— the protective allegiance of cops to one another, their in-the-trenches loyalty that places a higher value on solidarity and protecting comrades than on professional standards of conduct. But the cop culture, as researcher Elizabeth Reusslanni has shown, is more than that. Penetrating deep into police departments, it shapes how cops view citizens, public managers, and their work. Line officers believe that managers' only concern is getting ahead, and that they have "sold out" to politicians, the media, civilians, and others who don't understand "real" police work, with its constant ambiguity and relentless pressure to "do something, now." Officers believe they are on their own, forced to do society's dirty work with little understanding from the public and little support from their leaders.

Recent internal surveys in the NYPD confirm the deep-rootedness of this culture: 91 percent of patrol officers believe the public has little understanding of police problems; 75 percent disagree with the statement that the police and the community have a good relationship; 81 percent agree with the statement that the public believes that police use too much force; and 72 percent disagree with the statement that the Internal Affairs Bureau is fair to police officers and exonerates them when they're innocent.

How do such cynical views perpetuate themselves? Why do so many of the idealistic young men and women who enter policing turn against their organizations and citizens and tolerate corruption and brutality?

We can begin to answer these questions by looking more carefully at officers' experiences as they do their jobs. Take a concrete scenario: a police officer sees a cabdriver and a patron in a dispute. It is vehement and might erupt into violence. A good officer will step in and resolve the dispute. That's the end of it. No crime has occurred; no arrests. Officially, nothing has happened. Although the event does not exist officially, it is typical of routine police work: relatively unremarkable events that have the potential for mayhem but that the officer exercising skill and good judgment can resolve without fanfare.

Now change the scenario slightly. Suppose the officer ignores the dispute, and it turns violent. *Then* the officer moves in and makes an arrest or two. Something official has now occurred. According to the traditional law-enforcement view, the officer has achieved a valued outcome by arresting someone—never mind that the officer ignored his responsibility to keep the peace. The officer who does his job well goes unrecognized, because nothing has happened officially, while the negligent officer gets credit for an arrest.

Change the scenario again, and it becomes apparent that the officer's incentives are even more perverse. Suppose the officer intervenes in a potential conflict, and something untoward happens—the officer makes a mistake, or one of the disputants is dead-set to cause trouble. One of the disputants files a complaint against the officer. Then too the event becomes official, at considerable risk to the officer's career. We begin to see the officer's dilemma: not only is the vast majority of his work unofficial, unrecognized, and unrewardable, but the official outcome of much of his work can only be trouble.

The patrol officer's dilemma goes deeper still. Many police believe that managers exploit them by sending double messages. Thus—to use an example well-known in policing—when the message comes down to cops from on high, "Bums are bothering secretaries in the park; don't do anything illegal, but get them outta there," officers nod and smile ruefully. They understand the real message: "Do what you gotta do and cover your ass." Doing "what you gotta do"—whether dealing with vagrants, drug dealers, squeegee men, or whoever—is tacitly understood in policing as an underhanded deal in which police use illegal means to accomplish what may be a desirable goal. This dilemma has progressively deepened since the 1960s, as the courts, under militant pressure from groups like the New York Civil Liberties Union, have outlawed many traditional and appropriate techniques of maintaining order.

More than anything else, the disparities between "official" police work and actual police work are what breed frustration, cynicism, stress, and a wary, isolated culture among officers. When officers say that "citizens don't understand" or "you had to be there to understand," when they view citizens as actual or potential enemies, they are expressing their deep frustration at a system in which success or humiliation can so often be based on random luck, departmental politics, or wildly unpredictable encounters with citizens.

A recent example from New York City illustrates the kind of administrative action that breeds rank-and-file cynicism. In 1989, Robert Kiley, then chairman of the Metropolitan Transportation Authority, asked transit police management to develop plans to deal with the "homeless" problem in the subways. (This was a misnomer: the problem was the illegal disorderly behavior of individuals who mostly were not homeless.) After fussing about what they couldn't do, police managers proposed that maintenance crews should go into subways with high-power hoses to "clean" the areas in which the "homeless" congregated. Police, in support of "cleaning" operations, would eject the "homeless." This, of course, was a transparent ruse designed to evade serious constitutional, moral, and practical concerns. Officers were keenly aware of the duplicity and the risk for them. When things went wrong, the "white shirts," as officers called managers, would either be closeted in their offices or nicely home in bed, while line officers would face the glare of cameras and the wrath of advocates. Officers could hardly look to management for support and protection. Instead, they would do what they had to and pull the blue curtain around their activities. Happily, Kiley rejected the idea.

Police pundits have argued that the self-protective culture of line officers persists because police managers don't carry out their control strategy very well. Managers, for their part, blame police unions—though the blue curtain long predated unionization. But in fact the cop culture is an understandable though troubling response to the simple reality that the management practices that have dominated policing for most of the twentieth century don't work.

As Bratton understands, the control strategy is fundamentally flawed. And for a simple reason: most police activities are not under the control of central administrators at all. To be sure, the command-and-control paradigm of management has an impeccable pedigree. From Adam Smith through Frederick Taylor to General Motors, the principles of task routinization and simplification, the assembly line, and bureaucratic notions such as layers of control, span of control, and extensive rules and regulations were at the forefront of organizational thinking. Yet however well this model once worked in factories, it has never worked well in police departments.

After all, police work cannot be broken into simple tasks. Police deal with extraordinarily complex human interactions. Furthermore, police work cannot be scrutinized by overseers. Most police work is performed either by an officer alone or with a partner. The nature of their work requires officers to make fine judgments, often in dangerous and confusing circumstances, usually by relying on their internalized values, knowledge, and skills rather than on direct oversight.

In ignoring these factors, police leaders have constructed control systems that leave the vast majority of police work uncontrolled. Departmental regulations are the most obvious example. Up to 80 percent of rules cover the internal manners and mores of the organization: issues like wearing uniforms, filling out forms, saluting, and handling property. The rest deal with very important but rare events: use of force, hot pursuit, and processing arrests. When sociologist Egon Bittner asks indignantly, "What has all of this to do with *policing*?" he is only slightly exaggerating, since actual police work consists primarily of helping people manage crises and conflicts. Most police officers, for their part, would give a cynical answer to Bittner's question: "What all these rules and regulations have to do with police work is that they can be used to 'get' officers when they make a mistake or when things go wrong and it gets publicity."

Nonetheless, in the 1960s and 1970s a conventional wisdom developed not only among police managers and policy makers but also within the elites and the press. The reflexive solution to every police problem was more centralization and stronger controls. Even chiefs who wish to move away from the command-and-control paradigm can't, for fear that they'll be labeled "soft" on corruption. In New York City's current public debate about how to deal with corruption, this centralizing impulse goes largely unchallenged. The only question is how to do it: one side of the debate favors strengthening the Internal Affairs Bureau; the other, instituting a system of external review.

We can't solve the problem, however, merely by pointing out that traditional control measures don't work. Somehow, line police must be controlled. Although the forces that corrupt police may change over time—machine politics yesterday, drug money today—they are always powerful. But paradoxically, the only way to control police effectively is not to focus primarily on controlling them. Instead, police departments must concentrate with utter dedication on their principal mission: preventing crime and keeping order. If managers win officers' commitment to that primary goal, cops' own internal values will make them resist corruption as inconsistent with the kind of officer they are dedicated to being.

Evidence is accumulating that Commissioner Bratton's new solutions to the problem, based on this principle, are beginning to work. As Harvard criminologist Mark H. Moore describes it, the trick for any leader trying to change an organization radically—to transform its culture so completely that employees feel a profoundly changed relation to the whole enterprise—is to find methods of change that will shake the organization to its core. Bratton has done this in two ways: by sending a powerful message to his officers about their work, and by devolving authority down so as to encourage creativity, while establishing a process to hold key staff accountable. In important instances, he uses the same technique to achieve both goals.

First, the message. Bratton has made sure that everyone understands the business of the NYPD: to reduce crime—not just a little, a lot. ("Think bold," he said shortly after taking office. "I don't want a 2 to 3 percent reduction in crime this year—I want 15 to 25 percent." And he got it.) Police can reduce crime now, within constraints—they needn't wait for new cars or computers, more cops, bigger budgets, or more overtime. But meanwhile, of course cops should have semiautomatic weapons, because they deserve the best equipment and, with training, they can be trusted to use it properly. Cops deserve smart-looking uniforms—and should wear them smartly—because they represent both the city and the profession. When cops come under criticism for doing their job properly, as they do on occasion, they deserve wholehearted support.

Bratton also sends strong messages about his disgust with corrupt police. When cops are corrupt, the commissioner goes out to arrest and publicly shame them—taking their shields, symbolic of their oaths, from them personally. Reinforcing the message, Deputy Commissioner Jack Maple reminds police over and over: "Do not lie to get an arrest." If an officer inadvertently conducts an illegal search, he should admit it. "Don't start making things worse by inventing stories like: 'The bag of white powder was sitting on the front seat alongside the driver when I made the traffic stop.' Don't ruin your career by escalating a simple mistake into perjury."

Bratton's most powerful message is about the seamless web that connects disorder, fear, serious crime, and urban decay. He makes the Broken Windows argument that James Q. Wilson and I developed: disorder and petty crimes, left untended, signal that no one cares, and lead to fear, serious crime, and urban decay.

Broken Windows flies in the face of the assumption that serious crime is the only proper business of the police, an assumption that unites two utterly opposite ideologies: the traditional law-enforcement view of the police as crime solvers and felon catchers, and the radical individualism of the sixties that tolerated all forms of nonviolent deviance, lawful or not. The Broken Windows theory emphasizes instead that the best way to prevent major crimes and urban decay is to target minor crimes—panhandling, youths taking over parks, prostitution, public drinking, and public urination. Bratton's message goes something like this: People should not urinate publicly (or drink in public, or engage in prostitution, and so on). If they do, cite them. If they do it again, arrest them. If they appear to be carrying a weapon, search them; and, in any case, question them about other neighborhood problems. (Police ask suspects questions like: Do you know where to get a gun? Do you know where to buy drugs?) If information about other problems surfaces, relentlessly pursue it.

For many officers, steeped in the traditional police culture, this is a hard sell. In their minds, they are so busy dealing with "important" problems that they can't be bothered with trivial offenses, regardless of how bothersome they are to citizens. Real policing is arresting felons.

But now the NYPD troops are buying Bratton's message. Anecdotes about how well the policy works abound in the department, passed on from cop to cop with the same enthusiasm that transit police felt five years ago when they started arresting fare-beaters at the orders of their then-boss, Bratton, and discovered that these seemingly inconsequential lawbreakers often turned out to be carrying illegal weapons. In the 9th Precinct, a man arrested for public urination provided information about a neighbor who was handling stolen property, especially guns. Police arrested the man and recovered a stash of weapons.

What makes these experiences in the NYPD so convincing, even in advance of formal research, is that the department itself has called the shots. It publicly declared it would improve the quality of life in New York, and it is doing so—the virtual elimination of the squeegee nuisance is just one example. It said it would take guns off the streets, and preliminary evidence suggests that it is doing so: in August 1995, for instance, the proportion of arrested suspects who were carrying guns was 39 percent lower than two years earlier. The department has said that taking guns off the streets would reduce violent crime, and statistics show that it has. Because its successes are not random, it's hard to attribute them to luck or to anonymous "larger forces," such as demographics.

One place where the NYPD calls its shots is in its published anti-crime strategies. Distributed to everyone in the department from sergeants and up, political leaders, journalists, and interested members of the public, the strategies target specific issues: illegal guns, youth violence, domestic violence, quality-of-life crimes, and police corruption. "Police Strategy No. 5: Reclaiming the Public Spaces of New York" puts forward the underlying premise of New York's anti-crime strategy: "By working systematically and assertively to reduce the level of disorder in the city, the NYPD will act to undercut the ground on which more serious crimes seem possible and even permissible." It then goes on to document particulars: precinct commanders will have the authority to maintain order and will be free to conduct their own operations against prostitution, 'boom box cars," sales of liquor to minors, and other forms of disorder. It's crucial that the department is enhancing individual officers' authority to control such problems, first, by allowing them to arrest persistent offenders; second, by seeking new legal tools, such as antipanhandling ordinances; and third, by training officers in the use of civil procedures, like injunctions and nuisance-abatement laws (for which the thresholds of evidence are different from those of criminal laws), to deal with problems such as crack houses and prostitution.

These published strategies amount to a contract between the NYPD's leadership, its officers, and the citizens of New York. They expose citizens to departmental thinking while communicating directly to patrol officers what the department expects of them and what steps the department will take to achieve its goals—steps that can be monitored by those who will be accountable for success or failure. They commit the department to report publicly on the results of its efforts.

Police officers may be buying Bratton's strategy, but neither the Legislature nor New York's judges seem to have any idea what lies behind the city's amazing drop in crime on Bratton's watch. In the name of cost reduction, they have pulled the rug out from under Bratton's winning methods. Judges persuaded legislators that having the criminal courts deal with minor offenses against public order is costly and inefficient. The courts, they claimed, could save $1 million a year by moving such offenses to administrative rather than criminal jurisdiction. The more likely reason is that judges feel as reluctant to deal with such seemingly trivial dirty work as cops were before Bratton won them over. In any event, legislators bought the argument and made the change, which took effect October 1.

The result: New York's cops have lost their principal tool for order keeping. Until October 1, officers could control public drunkenness or public urination or squeegeeing because they could arrest people who failed to answer summonses for such offenses. They could require people they stopped for such offenses to identify themselves and could then check if they had any warrants outstanding. But with these offenses moved to administrative jurisdiction, cops have lost the authority to make arrests. They can hand out tickets, but if offenders don't answer them, as most don't, police can do . . . nothing. Nor can officers compel offenders to identify themselves. As a practical matter, the Legislature has made the laws against such offenses unenforceable.

New York City officials are desperately trying to repair this incalculable damage. The NYPD's legal staff is scrambling to identify other sources of authority to arrest people for some of these offenses: public urination, for instance, may qualify as a misdemeanor violation of the health code. Officials persuaded the City Council to restore some offenses to criminal jurisdiction by elevating them from administrative offenses to misdemeanors. But the Council refused to recriminalize the most important offenses to the Bratton strategy—such as public urination, drunkenness, and squeegeeing. Officials have asked the Legislature to reconsider the change, and meanwhile they have asked the courts to stay the new arrangement. If nothing is done, the Legislature will have committed its biggest offense against the public interest in many years. "It's obvious," Bratton says, "that judges and legislators haven't gotten the message from citizens that police departments have."

Drawing upon the re-engineering experience of private industry, Bratton has made changes in the department's management structure that aim to do much more than merely cure bureaucratic paralysis and organizational bloat. The crucial goal is to create a unified police culture that both empowers officers to do police work and ensures that they will do if properly—reflexively, out of habit. Bratton's most important move has been to push decision making downward, under the assumption that the closer to the ground the decision makers are, the more likely that they will be focused on and responsive to neighborhood needs. The most natural level of decision making seems to be the precincts, geographical entities with histories and traditions. With 200 to 400 employees, they are small enough that commanders can wrap their minds around them.

Consequently, Bratton has moved aggressively to devolve authority to precincts. Early in his tenure he sent the message that the NYPD's most capable mid-managers would head precincts. The transfer of power from the department's 55 chiefs to these new precinct commanders has been real. Frank Hartmann, director of Harvard's Criminal Justice Program, has conducted focus groups with precinct commanders to help Bratton understand their problems. Hartmann has described to me the heady, almost giddy experience that young and highly motivated commanders are having with their newly acquired power to administer their districts. In response to concerns commanders have voiced in these focus groups—lack of some basic equipment, uncertain authority, staff scheduling problems, lack of support from specialized police units—chiefs, the commanders' superiors, now *guarantee* that legitimate needs will be met in a specified way, by a specified date, and in ways that satisfy the precinct commanders. This idea, picked up from business, is another revolution in police thinking.

How will police leaders ensure that precinct captains' new authority will be used to implement Bratton's strategy to prevent crime and keep cops clean? In the NYPD, a powerful new management tool—crime control strategy meetings—has become the primary means of translating Bratton's vision of policing into action and of holding precinct commanders, as well as other personnel, accountable. These dramatic meetings have not only captured the imagination of the NYPD; they have attracted attention around the world. Mayors, police chiefs, and scholars from San Diego to Singapore to Saudi Arabia have come crowding into the NYPD's meeting room to learn firsthand how this new technique works.

Participation in the three-hour, twice-weekly meetings is mandatory for all 76 precinct commanders, super-chiefs, deputy commissioners, and borough chiefs. In the department's high-tech command and control center, the operational "guts" of the NYPD during riots or other calamities, a lectern beneath a huge projection screen looks out over tables arranged in a U. A placard to the left of the screen lists the "4 Steps to Crime Reduction" in bold print: "Accurate & Timely Intelligence; Rapid Deployment; Effective Tactics; Relentless Follow-Up & Assessment." To the right hangs the slogan, "We're not just report takers; we're the police." Along the sides of the U sit a dozen or so precinct commanders and the detective lieutenants from the borough that will be the focus of this particular meeting. At the end of the U, Chief of Detectives Charles Reuther, Chief of Patrol Louis Anemone, Chief of Narcotics Patrick Harrnett, Chief of Organized Crime Control Martin O'Boyle, and Deputy Commissioner Maple (specially appointed by Bratton and known by everyone to be one of his closest and most loyal sidekicks) face the speaker at the lectern. Around the sides of the room sit or stand representatives of schools, district attorneys' offices, and the parole department, along with heads of NYPD special units and support staff. Outside observers fill out the standing-room-only space. Maple runs the meetings: whether he is sick, hoarse, or simply exhausted from being called out in the middle of the night, the show will go on.

Steaming coffee cups in hand, people flow into the room to typical cop talk: aggressive humor, teasing. Maple calls the meeting to order—on time. The banter stops. The first of the five or so precinct commanders to speak on any given day takes the lectern. On the screen above appears every conceivable bit of information about the commander's precinct: the crime rate over time as reflected by index crimes (murder, rape, robbery, aggravated assault, larceny, and car theft); arrest data; shooting victims and incidents; lists of precinct residents who are on parole or have felony or parole warrants outstanding; and data on summonses for quality-of-life violations like public drinking and public urination. A map of the precinct displays the geographical distribution and clustering of crimes. Meeting participants receive printouts that include data about precinct citizen complaints, overtime, and the proportion of calls for service that prove unfounded (if too large, it's a signal that the precinct commander may be cooking the books to make the crime rate appear lower than it is). A picture of the precinct commander, along with background information about him, appears in the upper-right corner of the printout, making clear who is in charge and has to answer for what's happening in the precinct.

A few minutes into the commander's presentation, Maple begins to probe: "Your commercial robberies are up. How many of the robberies are kids stealing cupcakes? How many are guys walking in with Uzis?" The commander begins to unpack the robberies, describing them in detail. He tries to get back to the formal presentation, but Maple continues to scrutinize the data.

"What about household burglaries? They're down." The commander shoots back: "Yeah, we got wind of about four really active burglars, so we targeted on them." He provides details about how the police recognized the pattern, gathered information, devised a plan, and made arrests. The commander's peers break into applause.

Another commander steps up to the podium. "You had eight rapes this month, four above last year," Maple says. "What's going on?" The commander begins disaggregating: "Four rapes involved friends and family, one was a date rape, and three were stranger rapes. Two of those appear to be the work of one person." Maple turns to the detective lieutenant assigned to the precinct and standing beside the commander. "Tell me about the investigation." The lieutenant moves to the podium and describes the investigation. Maple interrupts and addresses another precinct commander seated at the table: "You had a similar problem a couple of months ago, didn't you? How did you handle it?" Later in the presentation, while discussing auto theft, the commander asks if it's legal to stop tow trucks towing cars (a common method of theft). Several people call out a jumble of opinions. Maple cuts them off. Nodding to the head of the legal department, he guarantees the captain a quick response: "We're not sure. Legal will get back to you with an answer by the end of the day." Finally, after half an hour or so, Maple allows the commander to wrap up his presentation.

Before he steps down, though, the commander recognizes two patrol officers: "I would like to introduce officers Jacques Guillois and John Bakke. Recently we were having particularly vicious robberies in Queens and Brooklyn.

Crime analysis identified that robbery pattern 27 in Queens and 40 in Brooklyn were virtually identical. [The NYPD assigns a number to every robbery pattern—mode of operation, number of offenders, descriptions, and so on.] There were also similar robberies in Nassau County. The violence was worsening with each robbery: it was only a matter of time until someone was killed. We convened a special crime control strategy meeting [of super-chiefs, borough chiefs, precinct commanders, heads of special units, and Nassau police]. We shared information and developed a coordinated response. We alerted units in Brooklyn, Queens, and Nassau County. Officers Guillois and Bakke, while patrolling in an unmarked car, recognized the license number [which had been identified in the robbery patterns], stopped the car, and arrested two persons—the driver for being unlicensed and the passenger for having three bags of marijuana. Guillois and Bakke arranged for a lineup so that a victim could make a positive identification. The pair was identified as the robbers we were looking for by a Burger King employee. Officers Guillois and Bakke, please stand up."

Along with the rest of the participants and the audience, chiefs, *super-chiefs,* rise and applaud—applaud patrol officers. The officers have been assigned to a month of special duty in the detective unit, a career-enhancing honor.

In another case, participants in a meeting were perplexed by a burglary pattern in Washington Heights: burglars were concentrating on cable TV boxes. Maple and Anemone pushed the issue, instructing the commander of the 34th Precinct to find out where the boxes were going and report back at the next meeting. Back in the precinct, the commander assembled a team of officers who put together a plan: youthful officers posing as burglars worked the street trying to sell "hot" cable boxes actually supplied by the cable company. Finally they found someone willing to buy them. They obtained a warrant and searched the buyer's residence, where they found a cache of stolen boxes that he planned to resell. At the next meeting the precinct commander proudly announced that the problem was solved: by arresting the suspect, police had shut down the market for the stolen boxes. He introduced the team of officers, who received a hearty round of applause.

The crime control strategy meetings have captured the imagination of the New York City Police Department and have riveted the attention of everyone in the department on neighborhood problems. Those familiar with contemporary management theory will recognize the meetings as the NYPD's version of what Robert Simons of the Harvard Business School calls an "interactive control system." In an elegant and simple way, the meetings portray the devolution of authority to precinct commanders and the corresponding increase in their accountability. They dramatize the department's new processes for extending services to communities; they give immediacy and urgency to crime control (not "Send your request to legal," but "We'll have an answer for you"); and they reinforce Bratton's vision of policing as central to controlling disorder, fear, and crime in the city's neighborhoods.

These changes will permanently alter the police culture if the Legislature restores the legal authority the department needs. Indeed, the culture is different already. Anyone familiar with policing can feel the re-invigoration of officers. Like the transit police before them, officers throughout the NYPD have had the experience of successfully restoring order and preventing crime. Some have heard their efforts applauded at One Police Plaza; many others have received applause from the citizens they serve. The lesson is overpowering: deal with the little stuff, and the big stuff will follow.

Nothing will change cop culture so fast as adopting a management culture that understands and affirms the true nature of police work. Managers, or "white shirts," are now preoccupied with what is happening on the ground. Woe to the commander whose attention is not riveted on precinct crime and problem patterns. Moreover, woe to the commander who is not scanning the entire city to see if similar patterns are developing elsewhere, and quickly working to coordinate efforts if they are.

As the NYPD devolves authority to precinct commanders and below, how will it prevent corruption? Police leaders are striving to ensure that the new police culture will be a culture of integrity. The message to officers is: management will not subtly ask you to make dirty deals and be duplicitous. If the department doesn't have the authority to deal with a problem, it will not ask you to "do what you have to do." Instead, it will seek legitimate authority—by, for example, proposing new laws to deal with panhandling, as the department is now doing. There's no reason for you to worry if you've made an honest mistake. If the NYPD itself is scrupulously honest, Bratton believes, officers will be less prone to, and tolerant of, corrupt behavior.

Moreover, precinct managers have also been made directly responsible for keeping their personnel clean. Each precinct has an integrity control officer; both he and the commander have the power to launch a corruption investigation. Just as they are learning to scan for neighborhood problems and street crime, managers are now learning to scan complaints against officers for patterns that may indicate corruption.

Bratton's message has inspired officers, and the processes he has established have changed the accountability structure of the NYPD. Even if the Legislature acts responsibly, could these changes be wiped out by a new police administration? Certainly, for Bratton's effort to change the department remains incomplete; the final step will be for precinct leaders to come up with ways of devolving authority to their staffs, especially to patrol officers, to win them over irrevocably to the new culture and the new mission. Yet it is hard to overturn dramatic success. Recall that since Bratton reoriented the transit police in 1990, not only has order been re-established in the subway, but felonies are down 75 percent in four years. This pattern now is repeating itself on the city's streets and in its neighborhoods. Cops truly aren't just report takers—they're the police. And proud of it.

23

Smart Cop: John Timoney's Formula for Success: Modern Science and Common Sense

by Howard Goodman

"Police chiefs have always sweated out the results (of the FBI Uniform Crime Report), but the only tactics they used to bring the numbers down involved crossed fingers or erasers."

—Jack Maple,
Former Deputy Commissioner, NYPD
(Maple, 1999, p. 97)

Eight A.M. The top brass of the Philadelphia Police Department—as well as much of the lesser brass—is seated around two U-shape tables, one ring outside the other, in a half-lit room dominated by computer-generated crime maps of city neighborhoods projected onto a wall-size screen.

In a place of no particular distinction sits Commissioner John F. Timoney, in blue shirt-sleeves, the .38 from his street-cop days hidden in an ankle holster. He's sipping sweetened coffee and getting ready, maybe, to have a commander or two for breakfast.

Alongside him sit his deputy commissioners. Across the way, the heads of special crimes, narcotics, highway patrol, detectives. Elsewhere are perched representatives from SEPTA, the Philadelphia Housing Authority and Amtrak; probation and parole officers; court system guys who chase bench-warrant beaters; visiting police officials from Saginaw, Mich.

They're all watching Capt. Tom Nestel 3rd, third-generation Philadelphia cop, all looking over the crime statistics for his district, the 14th, a relatively peaceful slice of the Northwest that runs from Chestnut Hill to Logan.

Nestel is first up for the grilling called "Compstat," a neologism formed of computers and statistics. Invented by the New York Police Department, Compstat is a marriage of computers

Reprinted from *Philadelphia Inquirer Magazine*, March 14, 1999, by permission of the *Philadelphia Inquirer*.

and common sense to spot and stop crime trends. It's the organizational heart of Timoney's overhaul of the Philadelphia Police Department.

Key statistics look good this week, Week 44 of 1998. Citywide, homicide is down 18 percent from a year ago, auto theft down 16 percent. Narcotics arrests have nearly doubled. Complaints against police, meantime, have fallen by more than a third.

But in other categories—aggravated assault, rape, theft, burglary—numbers are higher, largely because Timoney has insisted that police properly record each reported crime. Amazing! For decades, standard procedure was to classify many offenses as less serious than they really were:

> The less crime reported, the less work detectives would have to do, and the more police officials—and mayors—could boast that Philadelphia was one big city that was safe.

Timoney, the Dublin-born New Yorker hired by Mayor Rendell last March to jump-start a police force increasingly disparaged as hidebound and ineffectual, took a close look at the stats and declared them worthless. Threw them out! Crime would now be counted and mapped promptly and precisely.

And key players in the department . . . ate it up! People who had spent entire careers working under the old system became converts to the new!

Gravel-voiced, scolding, funny, sarcastic, profane, unpredictable Chief Inspector Frank Pryor, head of the Patrol Division, runs Compstat. At the weekly ritual, a rotating series of captains confronts the crime numbers, saying what they're doing to make the citizens safer.

"What's your most serious problem?" Pryor asks Nestel in his standard opener.

"Robbery."

Pryor peppers him: Where did most robberies take place? What time? Gun or strong-arm?

Nestel, a spunky man with a buzz cut and a bandaged left leg—he tore a knee ligament tackling a car thief a couple of weeks earlier—says his information is incomplete: "I looked at all the 48s"—the basic crime report—"and I found out that cops aren't asking enough questions. Forty-six percent of the 48s did not have complete information.

"What's the guy look like? There's no description there. I went back and asked the officer, 'Why didn't you put down his age?' He says, 'The guy [the victim] didn't give it to me.' I said, 'You didn't ask?' How can we look for the guy [the suspect] and stop more robberies if we don't know how old he is?' That's ridiculous."

It's hard to blame the street cops. For generations in Philadelphia, Timoney has said, uniformed cops "were report-takers, and not very good report-takers at that." Their sketchy reports went to detectives to investigate. But under Timoney, street cops are expected to know what's happening on the street.

"What's the supervisor doing while this is going on?" Pryor demands. "I mean, this isn't brain surgery. It's who-what-where-when-how. I want to see supervisors riding on these jobs."

They move on to other crimes. Burglary. Aggravated assault with a gun.

Who would have thought it? Here is the Philadelphia Police Department, gathered in one place, focused on the specifics of crime, with individual divisions talking to one another instead of jealously guarding turf. Less than a year ago, the department was a closed and sullen shop, hobbled by bad habits and outmoded strategies, dispirited, directionless, defensive. But at this Compstat meeting in mid-November, there's an air of alertness, intensity and purpose. An undercurrent of pride.

One man has sparked all this.

With the soul of a street cop, the analytical skills of a professor and the gruff tenacity of—in his words—an "egomaniacal loudmouth," 50-year-old John F. Timoney has awakened the slumbering, self-satisfied 7,000-officer Philadelphia Police Department and introduced it to modern problem-solving.

In less than a year, he has reversed decades of top-down management, giving new authority to district commanders to cope with crime in their neighborhoods as they think best, with the top brass offering advice and resources, then holding the captains accountable for results. He has improved police training. He opened the department's windows wide and invited the media to gaze inside, a glasnost to go with his perestroika. He launched Operation Sunrise, a long-term assault on drugs, violent crime and squalor in the city's most neglected neighborhoods. But he didn't drain other resources to do it; police activity rose in neighborhoods all over the city.

"I can walk and chew gum at the same time," Timoney likes to say. He seems to be walking, chewing gum, juggling bowling pins, playing the harmonica, kicking a can, carrying groceries and checking his wristwatch at the same time.

All the while, he's refocusing the department's eye on a single target: reducing the number of victims in a city accustomed to 100,000 major crimes a year.

"Timoney's a crime-fighter," says Capt. Jack McGinnis, head of the Major Crimes Unit, a 27-year veteran. "I think everybody on this force became a cop to fight crime. And 95 percent of what we were doing was social work.

"He's reenergizing people's original ideas on why they became cops."

Capt. Joseph O'Brien, head of the 35th Police District (Oak Lane, Fern Rock, Olney) is next up for Compstat treatment. A savvy, 27-year veteran with rotund features and jet-black hair, he says the 35th's biggest problem is also robbery.

"We've had 25 Dunkin' Donuts robbed this year," O'Brien reports. No discernible patterns. No standout similarities. Probably a crime of opportunity, O'Brien says, with most of the stick-ups late at night, when Dunkin' Donuts is the only place open and the lone employees are often young women.

"So your strategy," Pryor cracks, "is to encourage us to go and have coffee and doughnuts."

They talk about the month's three homicides. Then Eileen Bonner, captain of the Special Victims Unit, recounts the rapes. When she gets to the 11-year-old girl assaulted by two men at a bus stop, Timoney, who has said little up to now, speaks up.

"What proactive steps are you people taking?" he asks, eyes searching.

Bonner, a little flustered, says her unit is distributing flyers.

Timoney presses her. One man has been arrested. "Have we checked out his associates? Checked out prior arrests, see what we can learn about him?"

She shakes her head.

Timoney now speaks to everyone. "We have to care about every victim," he says with gravity, but we need to take it very, very personally when children or the elderly are involved. We've got to get out there and do whatever it takes."

For a moment, the room is quiet. There is no mistaking the man's seriousness.

The odds were supposed to be against the new guy. He was an outsider, and the Philadelphia Police Department abhors outsiders; only twice before in this century was the top cop picked from outside the organization. Worse, this new guy was also a New Yorker, about as welcome as a Giants fan in the Vet's 700 level.

He would be hampered by a civil service structure that gave him virtually no room to name his own management team. He'd be dogged by the Fraternal Order of Police, a powerful union with a loyal membership. He'd be undermined by an arbitration board that frequently reversed attempts to discipline bad cops.

Or so Philadelphia—city of skeptics—said.

But Timoney—a cop's cop from his pink Irish complexion and mischievous eyes to the mirror-gloss polish of his shoes—quickly won over the troops. Timoney came from big-city policing. Personified it, in fact. In 29 years with the NYPD, starting in the tough South Bronx and on through narcotics, organized crime and internal affairs, he rose through the ranks to become in 1994 the NYPD's youngest-ever four-star chief, in charge at age 44 of the day-to-day crime-fighting operations of more than 25,000 officers. In 1995, Commissioner William Bratton made him first deputy commissioner, the department's second-highest post. Timoney oversaw the NYPD's absorption of the transit and housing police, creating a unified city force of 39,000 officers and 9,000 civilian employees—more than six times the size of Philadelphia's.

Along the way he earned 65 departmental medals, as well as master's degrees in American history and urban planning. He left the department in 1996 in the bitter fallout of Mayor Rudolph Giuliani's jealousy-tinged firing of Bratton.

"He's incredibly smart and he knows everything," says Officer Edward Salamon, an aide to Pryor. "There's nothing he doesn't know something about or hasn't had some experience with. It's amazing. I'm just amazed that this type of individual runs the department.

"And he sounds like a cop—he knows where cops are coming from. As a cop, that makes you feel good."

Timoney let none of the supposed barriers discourage him. "Two phrases he's banished around here," says Bradford Richman, a Timoney adviser. "We've always done it this way. And You'll never get that done."

"I have never seen anyone have such an impact on a city department, with the possible exception of David L. Cohen," James Jordan, the Police Department's integrity and account-ability officer and a former assistant city solicitor, says of the mayor's former chief of staff.

"We can see a palpable change throughout the department since March," Jordan adds. "People are sitting up straighter, dressing neater, keeping their offices cleaner. People are looking like they're busy, not sitting around and staring at the ceiling.

"People are invigorated, and for a lot of them for the first time in their careers they can sense some loosening up of the deep freeze the department was in."

Says Will Gonzalez, executive director of the Police/Barrio Relations Project, a watchdog on police misconduct issues: "I don't want to sound like a cheerleader—there are so many challenges that still have to be met, and he is not omnipotent—but he is taking serious steps to change the culture of this department."

Even police union head Richard Costello, who tends to be a harsh critic of any commissioner, says, "Timoney seems to be an uncharacteristic excellent pick."

But Costello adds, "A lot of his ideas don't seem to be getting down to the rank and file." Too many commanders "are the same old gang," not transmitting the commissioner's message. And Costello worries that Rendell will prove less committed to Timoney's revolution than he has promised.

"One cop said the other night, 'Timoney's like a Winston Cup driver sitting in a Monte Carlo with four flat tires,'" Costello said recently. "He seems to have all the abilities to run a race, but in the wrong vehicle."

About the harshest criticism of the commissioner comes from J. Whyatt Mondesire, president of the NAACP of Philadelphia, who was a staunch defender of the former commissioner,

Richard Neal. Mondesire gives Timoney's performance so far a B-minus. "I don't think he has reached out to different groups in the activist community on a personal level," Mondesire says.

Bradford Richman, a lawyer who works as a Timoney assistant, thinks he understands Timoney's approach to crime-fighting. It came to him one night when he triumphed over a household mouse.

Night after night, this mouse was scampering through Richman's kitchen, unimpressed by many mousetraps. One night Richman hung around to watch the rodent. Learned his route.

"I put the traps in his path. And I caught him!" Richman says.

"That's what this proactive policing is all about. It's using our brains to attack the problem. "It's getting in front of the mouse."

That can't happen in a police department without making lots of behind-the-scene changes. For starters, Timoney placed key crime-fighting decisions in the hands of commanders. For decades, captains like Nestel and O'Brien had to check with police headquarters, Eighth and Race Streets, before risking anything close to an original action.

"Our organization was always top-down. Captains weren't allowed to be freethinkers," Nestel says. "In a Timoney organization, you're not successful unless you are a freethinker."

Before Timoney came along, a captain was empowered to put only two of his hundreds of officers in plainclothes. To add more, he would need permission from the upper ranks. Dressing officers in plainclothes is a key tactic against drug dealing, but it also increases opportunities for corruption. So headquarters tended to say no.

Timoney, however, says: "There's always going to be corruption in a police department. It's a fact of life. The answer is good supervision. And when it happens, you take care of it. You discipline. But you don't fold up your tent because a few officers are breaking the law."

Now captains have the ability to deploy their troops however and wherever crime patterns warrant. In the busiest districts, they have their own narcotics teams. The catch is, Timoney puts performance under a microscope.

"Timoney came here with this really bizarre idea," Nestel says, "the idea that the police should be doing police work. And he's encouraging us to do that. We weren't doing police work before.

We were radio responders."

After the 911 emergency number came into being in the early 1970s, American policing went wild for the "three R's"—rapid response, random patrols and reactive investigation. The thinking was: Answer calls fast enough to catch crooks red-handed or at least while the trail is still warm.

That made officers reluctant to leave their patrol cars, lest they miss a radio call and face potential discipline.

"We never got out of that mode," says Lt. Martin Taylor, who came on the force in 1970.

In the 1980s, attention shifted to the Police Department's legacy of brutality and its tensions with black Philadelphia. To build bridges with an estranged population, Commissioner Kevin M. Tucker ushered in "community policing." The police dotted the city with ministations, ran Boys Club-style mentor programs, "dialogued" with neighborhood groups, went through sensitivity training. Under Tucker's successors, Willie Williams and Richard Neal, community policing remained central to the department's mission.

At the same time, the city's finances were nose-diving. From a high of 8,500 officers in 1979, the force fell to 6,300 in 1989. Stung by misconduct scandals, the depleted department became increasingly timid, disbanding district-level drug enforcement, for example, because it escaped central oversight. Drug arrests fell from 11,300 in 1991 to 7,800 in 1996, according to police data.

Arrests for the "quality of life" crimes of vandalism, prostitution, drunkenness, disorderly conduct, vagrancy and minor disturbances plunged from 17,000 in 1991 to 11,000 in 1996.

Arrests for major crimes (homicide, rape, robbery, aggravated assault, burglary, theft and auto theft) went from 30,000 in 1991 to 25,000 in 1996.

The department's fortunes fell so low that police needed private funds to buy bullet-proof vests.

Ninety miles north, meantime, the New York Police Department was shaking off its lethargy. In 27 months under Bratton, who became commissioner in 1994, serious crime in the supposedly least-manageable of cities fell by 33 percent and the murder rate was cut in half.

By the spring of 1997, a growing chorus of Philadelphia community leaders, City Council members and state legislators was clamoring for the Philadelphia Police Department to get off its duff and do something about open-air drug corners, do something about the unyielding murder rate. The critics were not mollified by Rendell's assurances that Philadelphia was among the safest of American big cities.

Richard Neal, who got the top job in 1992, proved an ineffective spokesman for the department—on those few occasions when he spoke. A solid, gentlemanly, taciturn cop, he had little feel for being a CEO. He delegated very little. His office was piled high with paperwork that he would often haul home in the carts that flight attendants use. He insisted on making every decision—then didn't decide. When Timoney took over, he found 500 disciplinary cases awaiting action stuffed in a box in the commissioner's office, according to Timoney deputies.

As criticism of the department mounted, Neal "developed a siege mentality," Costello says. "He didn't trust anyone, and for a year the department was essentially paralyzed. People who worked up on the third floor said he'd come in in the morning and shut the door, and they wouldn't see him until it was time to go home." Neal has refused comment.

Neal resigned in early 1998 to take a consultant's job with Drexel University, a face-saving career change that Rendell insists he played no role in. Trumping his critics, who had demanded a New York City-style attack on crime, Rendell promptly announced his new police commissioner—Bratton's top deputy, John Timoney.

"Rendell offered the job with no strings attached," Timoney says. "He said, 'Come down here, look the place over, make all the changes you want, there'll be no interference from City Hall.'"

Timoney, at the time a long-shot candidate for top cop in Chicago and Washington as well, thought "it would be fun to work for Rendell." His $113,000 salary was $10,000 more than Neal got, but $17,000 less than he made as Bratton's deputy.

In philosophy, Timoney represents a turn away from community policing—or, in his derisive description, "sitting around the trees, holding hands and singing 'Kumbaya.'" He views Philadelphia's 22 police mini-stations and 12 mobile mini-stations—standout achievements of previous commissioners—as a fraud upon the public. "They call it community policing, and I call them hangouts for cops. It's an insane system. I don't want cops hanging out. I want to get them out on the street, in uniform, where people can see them." Timoney hopes to phase them out—slowly, in light of their popularity.

Cops throughout the city seem more attentive to citizens' tips and complaints. "You feel you're going to get somewhere," says C.B. Kimmins, a veteran activist who heads Mantua Against Drugs. "You don't hear the old, 'Well, OK, we'll see what we can do,' or, 'There's a shortage of manpower.'"

Stefan Presser, legal director of the American Civil Liberties Union of Pennsylvania, says that, despite hundreds of arrests in Operation Sunrise, "essentially we heard only one or two complaints. . . . And this is a department that was never able to undertake a major operation without trampling on the Constitution and the Bill of Rights.

"I'm forced to believe that his message—'We're not going to tolerate the breaking of the law to enforce the law'—must have gone out, and must have been heard for the first time."

Three days after the Compstat where the Dunkin' Donuts robberies came up, a task force of uniformed officers, plainclothes officers and detectives stakes out a doughnut shop on North Broad Street and catches a man in the act. The guy admits to 13 robberies known to the 35th District.

Some days later, more good news: A couple of police officers and court officials, working from a sketch, spot the second suspect in the rape of the 11-year-old walking down a street and arrest him.

When the North Division reappears at Compstat in December, the arresting officers stand up and take a bow.

Right off the bat, he made the right moves. At his swearing-in, he spoke—in Spanish!—to the Latino community, saying that everyone could expect a fair shake from the cops. "No one had ever done that before," Gonzalez, of the Police/Barrio Relations Project, says. "And he's following through."

First morning on the job, Timoney trekked to the city's bleakest station house—the 24th/25th District, Front and Westmoreland Streets—to meet cops at roll call. He said, in a brogue-Bronx mix: "You're going to work harder [hahd-a], and we're going to work smarter [smaht-a], and I'm going to give you the education and training and resources [resauces] that you need." They hadn't seen even a deputy commissioner out there in ages.

"He didn't meet with us, the commanders, for weeks," Nestel says. First Timoney went to roll calls at all 23 police districts, three shifts a day. At one roll call he gave a commendation to an officer—unheard of! The paperwork had been stalled for months. Timoney asked the cop where he wanted to work—highway patrol—and transferred him that night.

"That spread like wildfire," Nestel says. "People saw that good work was going to be rewarded."

In his first wave of promotions, 55 men and women were made sergeant. Timoney sent nearly every one of them to the Patrol Division. Unprecedented! Instantly, gritty old neighborhood police work got new respect. It was the first round of promotions in memory in which the cops with connections didn't get cushy office jobs.

Timoney stripped two district captains of their command for downgrading crime reports.

Suddenly, crime numbers shot up across the city, commanders now careful to report each incident correctly.

When a teenager was released on DNA evidence after spending a year in jail on a rape accusation, Timoney said police had made mistakes in the case and that he wasn't satisfied with explanations he'd heard. Before, "you never saw the chief of police acknowledge wrongdoing," says Richman, his assistant.

When an underling made a mistake—distributing as policy a proposal still in the discussion stages—Timoney took full responsibility, though he had been taken by surprise. "I really admired that," says Costello, the FOP president.

In his first weeks, Timoney took a close look at the department's organizational chart. Judged it a mess. "It was organized incorrectly to fight crime in any serious fashion," he says. Various detective units reported to three different bureaus. There were four internal affairs units, "none of them talking to each other," he says, nor reporting directly to the commissioner. Five hundred police officers were unaccounted for, squirreled away in long-forgotten task forces or specialized units.

Timoney told top commanders to play "this little game: Let's Find the Officers." They did. At one point, Deputy Commissioner Sylvester Johnson, then head of narcotics, discovered a puzzling 13-officer outpost called the Commissioner's Complaint Unit. "You go back there and tell them I have no complaints," Timoney told Johnson, "and feel free to disband that unit and get them involved in fighting crime."

Timoney consolidated, streamlined, untangled the chain of command.

When cops were acccused of brutality—notably in a melee at last summer's Greek Picnic and in the Oct. 1 shooting of an unarmed black man, 19-year-old Donta Dawson—Timoney withheld snap judgments. Yet once the District Attorney's Office charged Officer Christopher DiPasquale with manslaughter in the Dawson shooting, Timoney did not hesitate to suspend the officer with intent to fire.

His actions sometimes annoyed the FOP, sometimes the NAACP. Not that he cares.

"I am not going to succumb to any group pressure," Timoney told a TV interviewer. In controversial cases, "I will make a determination based on my own objectivity, as much as humanly possible. I'm sure that no matter what I decide, some people are not going to be happy."

Timoney was appalled by the department's methods of making promotions and transfers and of disciplining officers. In Philadelphia, cops believed, the only way to get ahead was to know the right person. "Ring-kissing," Costello calls it.

"The way to deal with that," Timoney says, "is create career paths that are transparent, that are in writing, where everyone can see how he or she gets ahead in the organization."

"Music to my ears," Costello replies.

So Timoney ordered up new policies. What came back from aides was less intelligible than Internal Revenue Service regulations. He ordered a rewrite. But the second effort "was more obtuse and longer than the first try," Costello says.

And so the new approach to discipline and transfers remained stymied weeks after Timoney had hoped to implement it.

"He's got this great idea," Costello said last month, "but he hasn't been able to get it off the ground."

Timoney keeps long hours, starting at 6:15 or 6:30 a.m. with a six- to 10-mile run. His workday starts around 8 and stretches into the evening with community meetings, charity receptions, and surprise visits to police districts.

His door swings open all day. "I run a very informal setup," he says. "There's nothing worse than formal setups. What they do is discourage people from coming in with bad news."

Shortly after noon, Gordon Wasserman, his chief of staff and a recognized expert in police technologies, comes in with a checklist of the day's chores.

"The Brit!" Timoney greets Wasserman. A former Rhodes scholar from Quebec, Wasserman, 60, worked nearly 20 years in London for the British government. The two of them grin like kids getting off from school. As if nothing could possibly be more fun than running a big-city police department.

"What's doin', kiddo?" Timoney's voice rings.

Wasserman hands Timoney a piece of paper. Timoney pretends to tear it up. "More of your . . . memos," Timoney mock-snarls.

"I'm only here because of him," Wasserman says later. They met when Wasserman was doing consulting work for the NYPD. "His education, the breadth of his interests, his willingness to do things in new ways, it's just remarkable," Wasserman continues. "The combination of high culture and street smarts, I've never seen anything like it."

Timoney leans toward Russian novels, James Joyce's The Dubliners, Malcolm Lowry's Under the Volcano and the works of Tom Wolfe, a friend who attended Timoney's Philadelphia swearing-in ("It's nice to see nice guys finish first," said the white-suited author).

Timoney loves theater—"serious drama, the more depressing the better." Musical tastes run from Sinatra to Van Morrison to Blood, Sweat and Tears to the latest program at the Curtis Institute.

He has run in 14 marathons. One year, he did the New York and Dublin marathons in the insane span of a single week. Since moving to Philadelphia, he has taken up rowing.

He says he is not terribly introspective. But now and then, on a long run, he'll think back over his life. "It is a bit of an amazing story," he says, "an immigrant coming in, the youngest four-star chief in New York history. You know, there are certain milestones that I've accomplished."

He thinks he knows what drove him. "If you're an immigrant you bring with you an inferiority complex," he says. "You want to show you're up to what the Yanks are."

"Dublin was a dreary, dreary town," he recalls—wet and cold and jobless.

His father followed a brother to America in 1960. Finding work as a doorman, he summoned the rest of the family in 1961. Timoney was 13 when he sailed into New York Harbor with his mother and younger brother and sister. His father was waiting at the 56th Street pier, "about 112 pounds and half a neck, it was awful." He had been diagnosed with throat cancer since they had seen him last.

It was a hot July day and the cab ride was terrifying. Timoney and his brother, Ciaran, had expected the America of Elvis Presley, swimming pools, the movies. Instead, the cab came to a halt at a walk-up in Washington Heights. The neighbor boys were out front playing a game, setting fire to water bugs with lighter fluid, then whacking them with sticks.

Timoney remembers his mother's dismay: "Oh, my God! We've left Ireland for this?"

Timoney's father died on a vacation trip to Ireland in 1966. Then his mother moved back with their daughter. But John, 19, and Ciaran, 16, kept the apartment, finishing high school, John earning money by washing dishes at a hospital.

"He felt obligated to be the man of the family," says Noreen Timoney, who has been married to John for 28 years. "There is this sense of honor."

He never aspired to be a cop. Didn't even like them. "Cops broke our chops when we were kids," he says. But during his senior year at Cardinal Hayes High School, he took the police exam as a lark, along with some friends. They all joined the force. Put in your 20 years and retire with a pension, the thinking went.

But as soon as Timoney put on the uniform in 1967, he loved it. "It was, 'Oh man, this is cool,'" he says. At 19, too young to be a sworn officer, he started as a clerk-typist in the 17th Precinct on the tony East Side. His academy training was fleeting; a recruit then spent most of his time erecting barricades at antiwar demonstrations.

He says he was a "bit of a rebel" and a "bit of a wise guy," his hair inching over his ears. But he impressed his bosses with hard work in the tough South Bronx. He wooed Noreen, a cop's daughter from upper Manhattan, by teaching her to drive a stick shift. She says: "I saw somebody who was committed and energetic, maybe driven. A little rough around the edges, but you got past that and saw some genuine caring qualities."

Nights and weekends, he went to college. Four times a week, he played touch-tackle football.

At the same time, he says, "I was locking up the world."

In 1976, while working nights as a cop, he was teaching American history by day. He seriously considered switching careers when suburban Tarrytown High School offered him a job. "But the thought of working 7 to 3, Mondays through Fridays, summers off—I couldn't do it," he says. "It was just too regular."

Instead, he transferred to the narcotics division, where he was nearly shot in a gunfight.

Amid New York's fiscal crisis, Timoney was not promoted to sergeant until 1980. But then he shot up the ladder. "Everybody knew Sean would go places," says Bronx Lt. Brian Nicholson, one of Timoney's old crowd, using Timoney's childhood name. "We just didn't know it would be that fast."

Noreen also advanced at ABC-TV, where she worked 17 years in finance, planning and management. She now runs a small consulting business.

There were, however, troubles at home. The couple's son, now 18, has endured Lyme disease and a serious knee injury. Their daughter, 20, has struggled with heroin addiction for at least four years, plunging the family into a maelstrom of dependency, rehab, fractured hopes. The Timoneys, protective of their children's privacy, will not discuss details.

On the job, Timoney says, "You think in segments. You keep stuff like that away. It probably isn't good, but how else can you survive?"

Loosen civil service's grip on promotions, widen the range of police recruiting, fight for limits on gun sales, take on those arbitrators who saddle the police force with bad cops, civilianize 500 police positions to get more cops on the street. . . . So much still to do, so little time.

Rendell leaves office in January, and that's the end of Timoney's guarantee of employment as Philadelphia police commissioner. Timoney says he would love to stay, but the offer will have to come from Rendell's successor.

Costello, of the FOP, says, "I think he deserves a minimum of four years." It's impossible to effect permanent change in two years."

"I don't want this to be our Camelot," he says. "With Timoney gone, then we're back to the usual collection of politically connected incompetent morons."

Speculation abounds that Timoney will dash to New York City when Giuliani's mayoralty ends. "Not true," says Timoney.

Still, a man can daydream. The other day Timoney recalled a comment that Jack Maple, the New York policing genius who invented Compstat, made to Giuliani. Maple told him that if he really wanted to straighten out the troubled city school system, he should name Timoney chancellor.

"I was sitting there," Timoney says, "and they kind of took it as a joke. But Jack was quite serious. And Jack was right.

"I would have shook the . . . out of that place! They wouldn't know which way we were coming! No more excuses! I would have loved that challenge."

Timoney, a man with a police department just learning how to count crime correctly, smiles.

"But I have a challenge down here, and I'm very happy with it, thank you very much."

24

Crime Control by the Numbers: Compstat Yields New Lessons for the Police and the Replication of a Good Idea

by David C. Anderson

"Proportionate need can be established with some accuracy by the development of a simple formula which has been found useful by many enforcement agencies in distributing and deploying personnel chronologically and geographically"

—Nathan F. Iannone,
(Iannone, 1994, p. 261)

Officer John Spence steers his patrol car through the streets of Philadelphia's 18th police district, pointing out certain landmarks: Here are corners where rival groups of drug dealers engage in shootouts; there is a notorious crack house—bullet holes pierce the rear window of a car parked out front. Down this street, an abandoned vehicle recently yielded up the body of a man bound in duct tape and shot through the head; down another, that very day, Spence and his partner had confiscated an assault pistol and stash of crack from occupants of a car they chased down after it fled when they approached.

A few hours earlier, some miles away, police executives gathered in a gymnasium of the city's police academy had pondered another rendering of events in the 18th district projected onto a giant screen. Here were homicides and shootouts, drug arrests, robberies, rapes and burglaries reduced to dots on a street map grid, shifting and blinking as chiefs asked questions and a computer technician clicked on her mouse.

Reprinted by permission from *Ford Foundation Report* (2001).

However removed from each other the two scenes might seem, they are connected intimately as part of a rapidly spreading approach to police management known as Compstat. Street cops' reports of crimes and other events feed powerful data bases that information specialists shape into electronic documents for rapid distribution departmentwide. The flood of timely information gives chiefs a way to hold district commanders accountable for responses to crime and forces police at all levels to communicate and coordinate their efforts more efficiently than ever before.

Compstat, short for either "computer statistics" or "comparative statistics" depending on whom you ask, began in New York City in the early 1990's and won an Innovations in American Government Award in 1995. Today it is credited with transforming law enforcement in New Orleans, Philadelphia, Newark, Minneapolis, Baltimore and dozens of other cities, large and small, across America. In a few places, urban managers have even begun adapting its principles for broader use.

Last fall, Compstat gained legitimacy of another sort as scriptwriters for "The District," a television drama about a fictional police commissioner in Washington D.C., gave it a central role in his efforts to revitalize the police force and fight crime. "That says a lot about the dissemination of an idea," observes Rosann Greenspan, a senior research associate of the Police Foundation currently at work on a national study of Compstat programs.

Beyond crime control, therefore, Compstat also raises the issue of replication: How has it succeeded so handsomely at "going to scale" when so many other attempts at innovation in government or social service never get beyond the demonstration phase or can't survive the departure of leaders who inspired them? In Compstat's case, the story of replication involves plenty of happenstance, but it also yields useful insights.

William Bratton, who served as New York City's police commissioner from 1994 to 1996, developed Compstat with the help of a deputy commissioner, Jack Maple, in order to get control of the city's huge police force. Both men are fond of military analogies, and their explanations of Compstat often begin with a reference to the Battle of Britain. The German Luftwaffe had more bombers and pilots than England's Royal Air Force, Maple writes, "but Britain had been quick to appreciate the value of radar." Precise knowledge of when and where German planes were approaching allowed English Spitfire pilots to focus their efforts where they would do the most good, greatly enhancing their ability to hold off air attacks.

In that spirit, Maple and Bratton elaborated the four conceptual pillars of Compstat:

- Accurate, timely intelligence
- Rapid deployment
- Effective tactics
- Relentless follow-up and assessment

While these concepts are hardly original, taking them seriously required radical change in both the operations and institutional culture of police departments used to leisurely collection and analysis of crime statistics and to reactive crime fighting based on response to 911 calls. Implementing Compstat began with demands that New York precincts update crime statistics on a weekly or daily basis rather than monthly or quarterly. Computers helped. New mapping software makes it possible to plot clusters of crimes on the map of a neighborhood, correlating them with drug sale sites, addresses of people previously arrested or released from prison, areas of gang activity, schools, shopping centers, public housing projects and other relevant locations. Huge amounts of data can be configured in a variety of formats and transmitted departmentwide in a matter of seconds, rather than days or weeks.

Data in hand, Bratton and Maple began convening formal meetings where they projected the crime mapping and other data on a huge screen and challenged precinct captains to explain how they planned to address crime problems the data revealed.

A typical exchange: "Captain, I see that there are a lot of armed robberies occurring on the corner of 4th Avenue and Third Street on Saturday nights."

"Well chief, we're thinly staffed on Saturday nights, with people off for the weekend. . . ."

"Captain, the crooks don't seem to be on your schedule. They are working on the weekends. What's your plan for dealing with them?"

Those who came up with good answers and followed through to produce results won praise and promotions; those who did not were demoted. Determined in their belief that crime could be addressed only if it was truthfully assessed, Bratton and Maple reserved greatest scorn for those they suspected of lying. In one incident well known in police circles, Maple projected a computer image of Pinocchio, his nose growing longer and longer, behind a hapless commander as he gave his report. Though the deputy commissioner later apologized, the message quickly filtered down through the ranks: Fudging of statistics and covering up lapses would no longer be tolerated. The department added review procedures to guard against manipulation of crime reporting to effect statistical readouts. Bratton and Maple emphasized that they would not be upset by figures showing increases in crime so much as by a captain who either tried to deny them or did not have a serious plan to address them.

In addition to the basic data mapping and accountability meetings, Bratton and Maple ordered new tactics designed to keep fresh sources of information flowing. Responding to the mayor's concern about low-level "quality of life" offenses like panhandling and drinking or urinating in public, they dispatched cops on sweeps to confront violators; instead of simply handing out tickets, however, they took offenders into custody, checked to see if they had outstanding arrest warrants, then questioned them about recent crimes in their neighborhoods. These activities generated a constant flow of new data going into the computers and enriching the Compstat maps.

All this coincided with a dramatic decline in crime rates in New York City. While skeptics pointed out that crime was simultaneously dropping all over the country, and in places that had never heard of Compstat, the New Yorkers could argue that their declines were greater. A conclusive answer awaits further research, but many objective observers came to believe that rigorous analysis coupled with efforts to hold precinct commanders accountable had sharply increased the effectiveness of police on the streets. The national news media took an interest, producing favorable stories, and soon New York was receiving visitors from other departments seeking to learn more.

Bratton, an entrepreneurial police executive who deeply understood the importance of favorable publicity, realized that he and his staff were onto something important. They were glad to push the idea and welcomed the media attention, admitting reporters to Compstat meetings some chiefs might reflexively have kept closed.

The first big test of Compstat's greater viability came when the commissioner, who had fallen out of favor with Mayor Rudolph Giuliani, decided to resign in 1996. Maple soon followed. Could Compstat survive the departure of the people who invented it? Was the new willingness of police to fight crime really the result of maps and meetings, or had it depended more on a commissioner's personality and leadership style? The answer was apparent soon enough. Bratton's successor, Howard Safir, kept a much lower profile within the department and in public, but he continued Compstat, and it still worked: Data collection and mapping proceeded; meetings focused on problems and sought solutions; captains remained accountable; crime rates kept going down.

Meanwhile, New York's Compstat veterans began sharing their experience directly with other departments. Maple and John Linder, a consultant who had worked closely with Bratton, formed a company that contracted with New Orleans, Baltimore, Newark, Philadelphia and other cities to help set up Compstat. In 1998 John Timoney, who had served as Bratton's chief of department, was hired to be Philadelphia's police commissioner, and in 2000, Edward Norris, who had stayed on after Bratton's departure and helped to run Compstat meetings for Howard Safir, took over as police commissioner in Baltimore.

At the same time, other cities, large and small, began setting up versions of Compstat on their own. Minneapolis called its program CODEFOR (Computer Optimized Deployment-Focus On Results), basing it on the four principles of Compstat. Lowell, Massachusetts, a city of 120,000, created a Compstat program tailored to a smaller department, with meetings every two weeks. Overall, about a third of the nation's larger police departments (those with more than 100 sworn officers) now say they have implemented some form of Compstat, and another quarter say they are planning to do so, according to Greenspan, who has been studying the phenomenon with David Weisburd and Stephen Mastrofski.

Not all are necessarily as rigorous as the original New York model. In his book The Crime Fighter, Maple laments the "knock-off versions of Compstat" where police "just sit in a circle and chat about the intelligence." And police administrators who set up more faithful imitations tend to be leery of the original model's reputation for humiliating mid-level commanders in front of the top brass. "We're probably a little less adversarial than they are in New York," says Lieutenant Michael Martin of Minneapolis. "Rather than just catching people not acting properly, we'd rather have them come in prepared to explain what they did and see if we can learn from them." New York officials, however, insist that the program there now also functions in a similar way.

Practitioners and students of Compstat say at least four elements have contributed to its successful replication.

1. Seeds of the idea fell on fertile soil. The public, politicians and police themselves recognize that all has not been right with urban law enforcement in the United States for many years. Invasions of crack and guns caused a spike in cities' violent crime rates in the mid-1980's that confounded the whole criminal justice system. One result was a big buildup in the prison population that cost taxpayers a fortune and raised moral issues. News of a sensible-sounding response at the front end of the system easily won support from political leaders and the public.

In some cases, chiefs and mayors have presented Compstat to their cities as a way to acknowledge a history of failure and turn around a demoralized police department. Faced with a soaring murder rate along with police corruption and brutality scandals, New Orleans' Chief Richard Pennington hired Maple and Linder in 1996 to set up Compstat as part of a general reorganization. Before John Timoney took over in Philadelphia, "the general sense was that we were not an effective police department," says Bradford Richman, a special assistant to the commissioner. "We were still working with old theories, old equipment, old mentalities."

Compstat also coincided with advances in computer technology. The use of mapping software became widespread during the 1990's among urban planners and environmentalists; some police departments had already begun to experiment with it and had it in place when the chief decided to set up Compstat. "Nothing guarantees a successful replication," Greenspan says, "but a good rapid data system is essential. Before the PC, Compstat would have had a different model."

2. It isn't political, and it isn't rocket science. All too often, discussions of criminal justice policy deteriorate into shouting matches between conservatives demanding harsher penalties and liberals pleading for attention to poverty, racism and other "root causes of crime." Both sides can support a strategy based on practical management rather than ideology. And if the four Compstat principles strike some people as obvious, that may be an important part of their appeal. Precinct commanders may object to being called to account, but they can't claim to misunderstand the process or its goals.

"It's a very intimidating thing to be sitting on one side of a table with the entire command staff across from you," says Captain Frank Gramlich of Philadelphia. "You are sitting there with your robberies up all over the map, and they say, 'Frank, what do we have going here?' I'd be sitting there, my palms soaking with sweat."

The word easily reaches officers on the street as well. "There's a lot more accountability among the commanders, and that transfers over to patrol," says Officer Spence. "I like it. The captain knows a lot more about what's going on in the district, and that increases the police officers' awareness of what's going on. Everybody's more informed."

"Simplicity is really the key to it," declares Michael Enright, Baltimore's first deputy mayor. "The four principles-that appeals to us just on a very fundamental management level."

3. It doesn't cost much. A police department may already possess most of what it needs to set up a Compstat program: computers, projection equipment, a large meeting room. Off-the-shelf mapping software works well. A few people need to be hired or diverted from other duty and trained to do the computer work. To create the CODEFOR program in Minneapolis, says Lieutenant Martin, "we got by pretty inexpensively. We already had the computer infrastructure in place. Everybody had desktops in their offices and in the precincts. It was just a matter of buying the software."

In Lowell, Massachusetts, Chief Edward Davis says that "the cost is mainly people." He used state and federal grants for the $100,000 it took to hire four additional employees for the first year. The city then picked up the cost.

4. It appears to work. Crime rates continue to fall in Compstat cities, and whatever research may eventually show, police administrators give the maps and meetings plenty of credit. In 1994 there were 421 murders in New Orleans; by 1999 the number had declined 55 percent to 162, and police say Compstat played a major role. Minneapolis credits CODEFOR with double digit decreases in homicides, aggravated assaults, robberies, burglaries and auto thefts from 1998 to 1999. In 2000 Baltimore saw the number of homicides drop below 300 for the first time in 10 years. In Philadelphia, homicides declined in the two years after introduction of Compstat and Commissioner Timoney firmly believes in a direct connection. Social conditions in the city haven't changed radically in the two years, and "we have the same police department, the same number of officers," he says. "Nothing has changed but how we deploy them and utilize them."

Other benefits of the program are quickly apparent, often in ways that impress the police even more than the public. "The biggest difference I see with Compstat is the way the commanders communicate with one another now," Gramlich observes. "If I had a violent crime problem, a lot of shootings going on, and we sensed that they were drug related, I'd call [the head of the special narcotics unit]—'What intelligence do you have? Can you help me out? Let's flood an area.' That never would have happened before."

Linda MacLachlin, captain of Philadelphia's 18th district, points out that before Compstat, district captains rarely had access to the department's high command. "Compstat allows us . . . to sit down and share information and get all of these commanders whose time is so limited to give you insight."

Compstat also offers some possibility of reward at the patrol level. "If you get a lot of really good arrests, the captain will take you to Compstat and you can stand up and explain exactly what you did," Spence says. "It's a big deal to hear the commissioner telling you it's a job well done; that means a lot."

Urban administrators are so intrigued with Compstat that they are beginning to find uses for it beyond police departments. New York City's Correction Department credits its TEAMS (Total Efficiency Accountability Management System) program, based on timely statistical reporting and greater accountability, for a dramatic reduction in violence among inmates. Stabbings and slashings dropped from a total of 1,093 in 1995 to only 70 in 1999. Jail managers then expanded its scope, pushing wardens to focus on staff use of overtime and sick time, maintenance issues, health care, compliance with food service regulations and other issues. (New York's correction officials were so proud of TEAMS that they submitted it for an Innovations in American Government Award in 2000; it was a finalist.)

"A lot of police and corrections agencies create their strategies based on negative trends in quarterly, biannual, or annual reports," observes New York's Police Commissioner Bernard Kerik, who started TEAMS when he was Correction Commissioner. "If you wait three months to six months before you start creating initiatives, you've wasted three months to six months of time."

The city of Seattle, meanwhile, has obtained a grant from the National Institute of Justice for a Compstat-like process to improve law enforcement, but involving many city agencies, not just the police department. COMPASS (Community Mapping, Planning and Analysis for Safety Strategies) will use mapping software to plot social as well as law enforcement factors: use of mental health, drug and alcohol services; school data; demographic data; health related data; transportation routes—"a whole array of social indicators that you wouldn't typically think of in terms of criminal justice processes," explains Sid Sidorowitz, director of the project.

As an example, he describes a part of the city overtaken by homeless youths who engage in prostitution, alcohol and drug abuse, and who camp out in a park. "The standard law enforcement response might be to increase the frequency of police intervention in the area, visit the park more at night, lock down the bathrooms, force the youth to move on," Sidorowitz says. COMPASS will ask, "Where are these kids coming from? What kind of services do they need? What kind of broader strategies might work?"

The most aggressive expansion of Compstat may already be in place in Baltimore, where Mayor Martin O'Malley, impressed with police use of the idea, decided to create CitiStat for the whole city. "Mayor O'Malley is convinced that this same process can be used not only for crime but for every City agency from Public Works to Health," reads a description of CitiStat on Baltimore's Web site. "In short, CitiStat is how the Mayor runs the city."

In meetings that take place every two weeks in a conference room outfitted with computers, all city agency or bureau heads face questioning from the Mayor and his high command.

During its trial phase last year CitiStat meetings produced a 25 percent reduction in overtime in the Water and Waste Water Division of the Department of Public Works and cut unscheduled leave by more than one third.

Such matters used to come to light only in annual budget meetings, notes First Deputy Mayor Enright. "You'd say, 'Your overtime is out of control. Do something about it. See you next year.' I now tell people that [CitiStat] is the way municipal services are going to be delivered in the future."

References

American Police Beat (2001, October). The Best and the Brightest: Jack Maple. *Copy Editor, 8, 8,* p. 34.

Anderson, D. C. (2001). *Crime Control by the Numbers: Compstat Yields New Lessons for the Police—and the Replication of a Good Idea.* New York, NY: Ford Foundation Report.

Bailey, J. (1996). The LAPD is Treated to a Business Analysis, and it Comes Up Short. *The Wall Street Journal* (06/11/96, pp. A1 and A8). New York, NY: Dow Jones & Company Inc.

Bolman, L. G., & Deal, T. E. (1997). *Reframing Organizations: Artistry, Choice, and Leadership* (2nd Ed.). San Francisco, CA: Jossey-Bass.

Bratton, W. J., & Knobler, P. (1998). *Turnaround: How America's Top Cop Reversed the Crime Epidemic.* New York, NY: Random House.

Bratton, W. J., & Andrews, W. (1999). Crime and Punishment: What We've Learned About Policing. *City Journal, 9, 2.* New York, NY: The Manhattan Institute for Policy Research.

Cole, G. F., Gertz, M. G., Bunger, A. (2002). *The Criminal Justice System: Politics and Policies* (8th Ed.). Belmont, CA: Wadsworth/Thompson Learning.

Conlon, E. (2004). *Blue Blood.* New York, NY: Riverhead Publishers.

Environmental Systems Research Institute-ESRI (2001). *Philadelphia Police Go Online to Fight Crime.* Redlands, CA: ESRI. Retrieved December 18, 2001 from the world wide web: http://www.esri.com/industries/lawenforce/05-philapolice.html

Goodman, H. (1999, March 14) Smart Cop: John Timoney's Formula for Success: Modern Science and Common Sense. *Philadelphia Inquirer Magazine.*

Harper, J. (2000, June) Cop, Killer: A Real-Life Dirty Harry. *Gear.* New York, NY.

Hill, J. (2004). *Exploring the Police: A Book of Readings.* Boston, MA: Pearson Publishing.

Hogan, J. I. (2005). *Turnpike Trooper: Racial Profiling and the New Jersey State Police.* Philadelphia, PA: Xlibris Corporation.

Iannone, N. F. (1987). *Supervision of Police Personnel* (4th Ed.). Englewood Cliffs, NJ: Prentice Hall.

Iannone, N. F. (1994). *Supervision of Police Personnel* (5th Ed.). Englewood Cliffs, NJ: Prentice Hall.

Johnson, H. A., & Wolfe, N. T. (2003). *History of Criminal Justice* (3rd Ed.). Cincinnati, OH: Anderson Publishing.

Jurgensen, R., & Cea, R. (2006). *Circle of Six: The True Story of New York's Most Notorious Cop-Killer and the Cop Who Risked Everything to Catch Him.* New York, NY: The Disinformation Company Ltd.

Kelling, G. L., Pate, T., Dieckman, D., & Brown, C.E. (1974). *The Kansas City Preventive Patrol Experiment: A Summary Report.* Washington, DC: The Police Foundation.

Kelling, G. L., & Wilson, J. Q. (1982). Broken Windows: The Police and Neighborhood Safety. *Atlantic Monthly, 249.*

Kelling, G. L. (1999). How to Run a Police Department. Broken Windows: *City Journal, 5, 4.* New York, NY: The Manhattan Institute for Policy Research.

Kerik, B. B. (2001). *The Lost Son: A Life in Pursuit of Justice.* New York, NY: Regan Books/Harper Collins.

Kirkham, G. L. (1974, March). A Professor's Street Lessons. *FBI Law Enforcement Bulletin.* Quantico, VA: Federal Bureau of Investigation.

Kirkham, G. L. (1976). Signal Zero: *The True Story of the Professor Who Became a Street Cop.* Philadelphia, PA; J. B. Lippincott and Company.

Klockars, C. Ed., (1983). *Thinking About Police.* New York, NY: McGraw-Hill.

Laffey, M. (2002). Cop Diary. In C. Willis (Ed.) *NYPD: Stories of Survival from the World's Toughest Beat* (pp. 30–51). New York, NY: Adrenaline Books/ Thunder's Mouth Press. (Marcus Laffey is a pseudonym for Edward Conlon (see above reference, Blue Blood).

Maple, J. (1999). *The Crime Fighter: Putting the Bad Guys Out of Business.* New York, NY: Doubleday and Company.

McDonald, C. P. (1991). *Blue Truth: Walking the Thin Blue Line - One Cop's Story of Life in the Streets. Donald I.* Fine Publishing. New York, NY: Penguin Group.

Milland, C. (1986, April). Why Cops Hate you: If you Have to Ask, Get Out of the Way. *Gallery.*

Philadelphia Police Department (2000a). *Biography: Commissioner John F. Timoney.* Retrieved October 23, 2001 from the World Wide Web: http://www.ppdonline.org/ppd_pcbiography.htm

Philadelphia Police Department (2000b). *The Philadelphia COMPSTAT meetings.* Retrieved October 23, 2001 from the World Wide Web: http://www.ppdonline.org/ppd_compstat2.htm

Philadelphia Police Department (2000b). *The COMPSTAT process.* Retrieved October 23, 2001 from the World Wide Web: http://www.ppdonline.org/ppd_compstat.htm

Reiss Jr., A. J. (1971). *The Police and the Public.* New Haven, CT: Yale University Press.

Sheppard, A., & Schmetterer, J. (2006). *E-Man: Life in the NYPD Emergency Services Unit.* Lincoln, NE: iUniverse, Inc. Publishing.

Sheppard, A., & Schmetterer, J. (2007). *E-Man: Life in the NYPD Emergency Services Unit* (Revised Edition). Bloomington, IN: Rooftop Publishing.

Sherman, L. (1982, Winter/Spring). Learning Police Ethics. *Criminal Justice Ethics.* New York, NY: John Jay College of Criminal Justice—CUNY.

Schmalleger, F. (2003). *Criminal Justice Today* (7th Ed.). Upper Saddle River, NJ: Prentice Hall.

Shuster, B. (2002, September 20). *Finalists Offer Distinctly Different Pluses for Hahn.* Los Angeles, CA: Los Angeles Times.

Skolnick, J. (1966). The Police Officer's "Working Personality". *Justice Without Trial: Law Enforcement in a Democratic Society.* New York, NY: John Wiley & Sons.

Wagner, J., & Picciarelli, P. (2002). *My Life in the NYPD: Jimmy the Wags.* New York, NY: ONYX/ Penguin Putnam, Inc.

Wilson, J. Q., & Kelling, G. L. (1982, March). Broken Windows: The Police and Neighborhood Safety. *Atlantic Monthly.*

Author's Note:
About the Author

A third-generation street cop, Dr. John Hill (*Ed.D., 2007; and D.C.J., 2001*) served 20 years as a municipal Police Officer, and as a Sheriff's Officer, in the State of New Jersey. During this time he earned 18 police valor medals, five police service medals, and some 30 other awards and written commendations. He is proud to have spent nearly his entire career on the "front lines"—street patrol working rotating shifts. Dr. Hill's father and grandfather both served as police officers, then as detectives, with the City of Newark Police (NJ).

Retired from his police career in 2000, Dr. Hill presently serves as a (tenured) Associate Professor of Criminal Justice at *Salt Lake Community College.* Additionally, as an Adjunct Professor of Criminal Justice at a number of colleges and universities, on an as-needed basis. Previous Adjunct assignments include *Hudson County Community College* (NJ), *Harrisburg Area Community College* (PA), *Weber State University* (UT), and the *University of Phoenix* (Utah Campus).

Dr. Hill has earned; a *Doctor of Education Degree (Ed.D.) in Higher Education,* with a *Criminal Justice* specialization, a second doctorate, the *Doctor of Criminal Justice Degree,* a *Master's Degree in Criminal Justice,* and a second *Master's Degree in Psychology.* His undergraduate studies include a *Bachelors Degree in Human Services,* an *Associate Degree in Criminal Justice,* a second *Associate Degree in Public Administration,* and two *Certificates in Highland Bagpiping.*

Dr. Hill has published over 25 articles in various criminal justice publications, including the *FBI Law Enforcement Bulletin* and the *Law Enforcement News* of *John Jay College of Criminal Justice—CUNY.* He has also published papers on crime, directed police patrol and service-driven policing, police heroism on 9/11, police racial profiling, and municipal government corruption in the 2002, 2003, 2004, 2005, 2006, and 2007 annual peer-reviewed editions of the *Journal of the Utah Academy of Sciences, Arts, & Letters* (ISSN-0083-4823). In 2003, Hill was awarded Outstanding Paper Award in the Division of Social Sciences by the *Utah Academy of Sciences, Arts, & Letters.*

Additionally, Dr. Hill authored the textbooks *Directed Police Patrol: and Other Service-Driven Police Strategies* (Pearson Publishing, 2004, ISBN-0536704457), and *Exploring the Police: a Book of Readings* (Pearson Publishing, 2004, ISBN-0536758824).

Dr. Hill divides his time between Salt Lake City, Utah, and Lancaster County (Amish Country), Pennsylvania. Some eighteen years ago (about halfway through his police career), he established a home in Pennsylvania's Amish Country, as an escape from the stressors of police work in urban northern New Jersey.

He can be reached at *ProfessorJohnHill@yahoo.com*

Afterword

Readers of the preceding chapters often express a desire for more on the subject. I hasten to remind them that, in most cases, the chapters presented herein represent only a minor portion of the author's complete composition. The (aforementioned) References section and the Recommended Reading lists (below) shall provide guidance for those individuals with an inclination for expanded subject matter.

THE DYNAMICS OF STREET COPS

The Author's *Recommended Reading* List:

1. *Danger, Duty, and Disillusion: The Worldview of Los Angeles Police Officers,* by Joan C. Barker, 2002, Waveland Press.

2. *Signal Zero: The True Story of the Professor Who Became a Street Cop,* by George L. Kirkham, 1976, J. B. Lippincott Company.

3. *Blue Truth: Walking the Thin Blue Line - One Cop's Story of Life in the Streets,* by Cherokee Paul McDonald, 1991, Donald I. Fine Publishing.

4. *Blue Blood* by Edward Conlon, 2004, Riverhead Publishers.

5. *My Life in the NYPD: Jimmy the Wags,* by James Wagner and Patrick Picciarelli, 2002, ONYX/Penguin Putnam, Inc.

6. *E-Man: Life in the NYPD Emergency Services Unit* (Revised Edition), 2007, by Al Sheppard and Jerry Schmetterer, Rooftop Publishing.

SERVICE-DRIVEN POLICING

The Author's *Recommended Reading* List:

1. *Turnaround: How America's top cop reversed the crime epidemic,* by William J. Bratton, with Peter Knobler, 1998, Random House, Inc.

2. *The Crime Fighter: Putting the Bad Guys Out of Business,* by Jack Maple, with Chris Mitchell, 1999, Doubleday and Company

3. *The Police and the Public,* by Albert J. Reiss, Jr., PhD, 1971, Yale University Press.

4. *Managing Patrol Operations,* published in 1977 by the National Institute of Justice, Bureau of Justice Programs.

5. *Managing Police Operations: Implementing the New York Crime Control Model—Compstat,* by Phyllis Parshall McDonald, 2002, Wadsworth Group.

6. *Leadership,* by Rudolph Giuliani (with Ken Kurson), 2002, Miramax Publishing.